MORAL MEASURES

Moral Measures: An Introduction to Ethics West and East is a clear, introductory, yet critical study of Western and Eastern ethics that carefully introduces the difficult issues surrounding cross-cultural ethics and moral thought. By examining Western and Eastern moral traditions, Jim Tiles explores the basis for determining ethical measures of conduct across different cultures. This much-needed book discusses three kinds of moral measures: measures of right, of virtue and of the good. Drawing on a rich array of ethical thinkers, including Aristotle, Kant and Confucius, Jim Tiles argues that there are ethical problems shared by apparently opposed moral traditions and there is much to be learned by comparing them.

Moral Measures: An Introduction to Ethics West and East is one of the first books to explore properly the relationships between Western and Eastern ethical thought. The book assumes no prior knowledge of philosophy or religion and is ideal for anyone coming to Western and Eastern ethical traditions for the first time.

Jim Tiles is a Professor of Philosophy at the University of Hawai'i at Mānoa. He is the author of *Dewey* (1988), also published by Routledge, and the co-author of *An Introduction to Historical Epistemology* (1992).

MORAL MEASURES

An Introduction to Ethics West and East

J.E. Tiles

Routledge
Taylor & Francis Group
LONDON AND NEW YORK

First published 2000
by Routledge
2 Park Square, Milton Park, Abingdon, Oxon, OX14 4RN

Simultaneously published in the USA and Canada
by Routledge
711 Third Ave, New York NY 10017

Routledge is an imprint of the Taylor & Francis Group

Transferred to Digital Printing 2007

Typeset in Times by Florence Production Ltd, Stoodleigh,
Devon

British Library Cataloguing in Publication Data
A catalogue record for this book is available from the British
Library

Library of Congress Cataloging in Publication Data
Tiles, J.E.
Moral Measures: an introduction to ethics West and East / J.E. Tiles
p. cm.
Includes bibliographical references and index.
1. Ethics I. Title
BJ1012.T55 2000   99–053170
170–dc21

ISBN 0–415–22495–0 (hbk)
ISBN 0–415–22496–9 (pbk)

CONTENTS

Preface   ix
Acknowledgements   xii

1   The field of ethics – a preliminary survey   1

Approaching the subject: Something old,
    something peculiar   2
Creatures of habit: Habit, custom and culture   5
Impulses to approve or to condemn: Harmless
    ritual and ritual cannibalism   10
Conflicting responses: Foot-binding, genital
    mutilation and abortion   15

2   Concrete moralities   24

Conventions, laws and climates of attitude:
    The revenge ethic and the spirit of capitalism   25
Psychological foundations and mechanisms of
    reproduction: Guilt and shame, ritual and myth   30
Manners and morals: Etiquette, diet and fashion
    as moral phenomena   37
Law and morality: Rough music and rough handling   41

3   Sources of validity   50

Tradition and charisma: Spartans, Socrates and
    their nomoi   51
Nature: Ritual purity, karma *and incest   56*
God's will: The impatience of Job and the
    submission of al-Ashʿarī   61
Reason: The lex talionis *and reason's aesthetic   66*

4   Conflict and the search for standards   73

*Conflict: The anguish of Arjuna and the arrogance
    of Euthyphro   74
Standards: Straight thinking and right-angled
    conduct   79
Rational authority: Two ways to straighten the
    use of words   86
Reason and reality: Seductive and authoritative
    objects   92*

5   Man as the measure   101

*Relativism: Protagoras, conventionalism
    and tolerance   102
Anarchism: Intuitions, optimism and the* tao
    *of Chuang Tzu   107
Skepticism: From peace of mind to 'queer' entities   112
Non-cognitivism: Emotivism, prescriptivism
    and distant views   117*

6   Law as measure   126

The lawful and the just: Lex *and* ius   127
Procedures, rules and particulars: Oracles and
    kadis, *precedents and statutes   133
Equity and casuistry: A mute divinity, the Lesbian
    rule and the tyranny of principles   139
The diversity of justice: Equality, self-determination
    and collective responsibility   145*

7   The measure of law   153

*Persons, rights and roles: God, slaves
    and corporations   154
Natural slaves and natural law: Contours
    of nature and the flow of rhetoric   160
Kant's canon: Reason and its imperatives   167
Taking legal measures: Respect for persons
    and the limits of coercion   174*

CONTENTS

8   The qualities of exemplary persons   183

*Duties of virtue: Perfection of self and duties
    of beneficence*   184
*Classical virtues and the rule of ritual: Elite and
    demotic virtues, setting a good example*   191
*Where the standard resides: Rituals, laws
    and sage kings*   197
*The analysis of virtue: Choice, the mean,
    reason and practical wisdom*   202

9   The end as a standard   213

*The role of reason: Teleology, deontology and
    deliberative rationality*   214
*The appeal to human nature: For the standard
    of what it is to live well*   220
Eudaimonia *and the ethical excellences:
    Contemplation and public service*   227
A Confucian take on eudaimonia: *Blending
    reason and ritual*   234

10   Pleasure as the measure   243

*The protean standard of hedonism: Whose
    pleasures? Which assessment of risk?*   244
*Private pleasures and public responsibilities: Selves,
    friends and fellow citizens*   251
*The universal standpoint: Concern for everyone,
    general happiness*   257
*The golden rule and the expanding circle: Respect for
    sentience and the throne of pleasure and pain*   264

11   The self as a problem   273

*Asceticism and salvation: Dependencies, holy
    virginity and soteriology*   274
*Suffering as the problem: Four noble truths and
    an eight-fold noble path*   279
*Apathy (*apatheia) *and non-attachment (*anupādisesa):
    The pathology of the passions   285
*In the world but not of it: Hermits, monks and
    early capitalists*   292

12   Conclusion: Measures that fall short?   301

*Challenging the sovereignty of reason: Slaves
versus managers of the passions*   302
Social animals: Associates, friends, communities   307
*Concern for everyone: Charity, compassion and
contracting circles*   311

Character table   316
References   317
Index   327

PREFACE

This book began as a collection of materials used to supplement textbooks for an introductory course on ethics. One objective I had was to make clear to students the extent to which ethics as a normative theoretical activity is prompted by and is addressed to social phenomena. A second objective arose from the emphasis placed on including non-Western traditions in the study of philosophy by the department where I have taught for the past ten years. In order to encourage this ecumenical spirit in my students at the beginning of their experience of philosophy, I assembled accounts of what I thought were instructive contributions to the subject drawn from a variety of non-Western sources. As my efforts to explain this material inevitably drew on what I knew of ethical traditions in the West, and as I found that my appreciation of what had been for me familiar traditions was undergoing some radical changes, the material grew into a series of comparative essays that functioned as the primary text for my course.

In the course of this development, the image of a standard or measure appeared frequently in the material on which I was drawing, and that image provided an organizational principle, so that the essays acquired the structure, and suggested the argument, of a book. The result is offered to readers as a general introduction to ethics based on the cross-cultural theme of ethical standards ('moral measures'). It includes a discussion of moral attitudes as sociological phenomena and their relationship to the phenomena of etiquette and fashion and to the institutions of law (Chapter 2). It considers in detail three common approaches to ethical standards: (1) laws and rights, or 'practical deontology' (Chapters 6 and 7); (2) human exemplars and their qualities, or the virtuous and their virtues (Chapter 8); and (3) teleological or consequentialist ethics based on an idea of human good (Chapters 9 and 10). Connected to the last of these is a survey of what might be called 'the bad for man' – 'soteriological ethics,' or ethical traditions that proceed from one or another form of the assumption that we need salvation of some kind (Chapter 11). As a preamble to the detailed treatment of the three kinds of standard, there is a discussion of the reasons commonly given for thinking that there can be no rational or objective standards (Chapter 5) for our moral attitudes.

I have drawn throughout on non-Western as well as Western traditions and practices, and on both historical and contemporary sources. The treatment is organized conceptually, not chronologically or geographically. There are lists of further reading at the end of all but the final chapter for readers who wish to see detailed treatments of the practices and traditions, philosophers and schools, on which I draw to illustrate the conceptual material presented here. Part of my aim has been to show that the systematic study of ethics is a highly suitable vehicle for broadening the cultural horizons of students and to contribute what I can to the momentum toward less cultural parochialism in education generally and in philosophy in particular.

Another part of my aim has been to work for a broader perspective on the nature of moral phenomena and the responsibility we have to invest critical thought in examining our attitudes toward conduct. I have adopted a position with respect to standards that might be termed 'methodological pluralism,' have argued for a form of 'naturalism' – that a conception of our own nature as a species provides the basis for measures of all three kinds – and have suggested in conclusion reasons for thinking that such a basis cannot by itself support certain common attitudes toward ethical principles without an extension of that basis in ways that bring it closer to doctrines found in a number of religious traditions. I hope that professional scholars and teachers of ethics will not only find some of the information assembled here useful but will also find some of the arguments and conclusions fruitfully provocative. The argument of the book is given in brief in the synopsis that follows. Readers who wish to see a more detailed synopsis of the argument will find at the beginning of each chapter a recapitulation of the previous chapter and a prospectus of the chapter to follow.

Brief synopsis

What distinguishes the actual ('concrete') morality of a group of people from a mere fashion or mere matter of etiquette is their belief that the attitudes expressed in what they condone and condemn have some basis beyond the fact that as a group they hold these attitudes (Chapter 2). This belief is what gives rise to the widespread feeling that in cases of uncertainty or conflict there ought to be measures or standards by which to determine what should be condoned and what should be condemned (Chapter 4). This image has been put to use even by some who reject the very idea that there can be an objective basis on which to determine what it is we should approve or condemn (Chapter 5). A fundamental question that the systematic study of ethics has to address is what basis, if any, there is for our impulses to approve or condemn (Chapter 1) and hence what basis, if any, there is for any standard or measure that might be used to resolve conflicts and uncertainties.

Three identifiable kinds of measure or standard are found in a variety of moral traditions, which, as societies develop and become more complex, replace the three ('pure') sources of authority identified by Max Weber: tradition, charisma and reason (Chapter 3). Tradition works to stabilize itself in forms (often general imperatives or rules) that give rise to the institutions of law and the 'measure of right' (Chapters 6 and 7). Efforts are made to demystify charisma by identifying the characteristics (excellences or virtues) that make individuals genuinely worthy of admiration and of being treated as patterns to be followed, and these give rise to the 'measure of virtue' (Chapter 8). Although the process by which an exemplary or virtuous individual resolves uncertainties and conflicts must be responsive to the particulars of the problematic situation, there is need for the guidance of a general conception of what humans should try to achieve or preserve in their lives as a whole; this gives rise to the 'measure of the good' (Chapters 9–10). (This last, it should be observed, gives a role to practical reason that appears to be quite unlike the institutional rationality that Weber had in mind as a source of authority (Section 4.3).)

The image of measuring devices to aid practice should not encourage the expectation that just one of these three measures will be sufficient to provide the guidance needed to resolve uncertainties and conflicts (Section 4.4). As successive chapters explore how measures of these three kinds serve to guide judgment, support emerges for the claim that all three kinds have a role to play wherever thought is invested in the moral life.

A wide variety of measures of all three kinds may be offered as candidates for adoption. Different rules can be formulated, different kinds of people can be admired and used as examples to be followed, and different ways of living can be aimed at as best suited to human beings. The question 'what basis, if any, have we for approving or condemning attitudes and patterns of conduct?' becomes 'what basis, if any, have we for selecting any of these measures?' A device for 'calibrating' measures of right offered by Immanuel Kant (Section 7.3) points to an objective basis for assessing attitudes toward conduct in the difference between persons and things. The distinguishing feature of persons lies in their discursive capacities and the special kind of freedom this gives them. This feature, moreover, if its social foundations are adequately understood, can be seen to provide a basis for measures of virtue and of the good that were first advanced by Aristotle. The final chapter, 12, assesses to what extent this basis can answer questions about human relationships and support the ideas of human fulfillment and salvation that are canvassed in the previous two chapters, 10 and 11. The conclusion is that some common, if not universally embraced, ethical principles would need an additional basis, perhaps in something akin to religious belief.

ACKNOWLEDGEMENTS

I was fortunate to have a sabbatical semester in the spring of 1996 (the first in what was by then a twenty-one-year teaching career), during which time I was able to give this material the shape of a book. I am grateful for the tolerance and patience of approximately one hundred students in four different sections of an introductory ethics course whose primary text consisted of one of three very differently organized and progressively refined versions of this material. I am particularly grateful for useful feedback from Bernice Pantell and Richard Otley and for an excellent suggestion from Paula Henderson regarding the overall structure of the material. At various stages in developing this I received valuable help, suggestions and reassurance from permanent and visiting colleagues who specialize in the various traditions on which this book draws – Roger Ames, Arindam Chakrabarti, Eliot Deutsch, Lenn Goodman, David Kalupahana, Ken Kipnis and Donald Swearer – and I have learned much from graduate students whose interest in comparative philosophy brought them to Hawai'i, Donna-Marie Anderson, Steve Bein, Menaha Ganesthasan, Peter Herschock, Li-Hsing Lee, Sang-im Lee, Viren Murthy and Sor-hoon Tan. I am also grateful to Roger Ames and Daniel Cole for help with preparing the character table which appears in this book. Reports from referees for Routledge prompted a further substantial reworking of the text over the summer of 1999; I hope I have responded with sufficient imagination to their guidance. Finally, I wish to acknowledge with gratitude what I have learned over a lifetime from my father, Paul R. Tiles, about the refining of instruments of measurement and their use in both instrumental reasoning and constructive activities.

1

THE FIELD OF ETHICS – A PRELIMINARY SURVEY

[In ancient times] east of the state of Yüeh there was the tribe of K'ai-shu. Among them the first-born son was dismembered and devoured after birth and this was said to be propitious for his younger brothers. When the father died, the mother was carried away and abandoned, and the reason was that one should not live with the wife of a ghost. This was regarded by the officials as a government regulation and it was accepted by the people as commonplace. They practised it continually and followed it without discrimination. Was it then the good and the right way? No, it was only because habit affords convenience and custom carries approval.

(Mo Tzu (fifth century BCE); Mei 1929: 133)

Prospectus: Ethics as a distinctive field of study was first conceived to be about the good and bad habits that people acquire in response to what pleases and pains them. A more recent common approach is to conceive ethics as concerned with the process of deliberating about a particularly compelling kind of obligation, 'moral obligation.' In order to expose clearly the dimension in which ethical life lies outside the individual and mark out a framework, which will enable us to relate ethical traditions and theories found in different parts of the world at different times in history, it is more useful to begin by exploring the phenomena of habituation than that of obligation. People's habits co-ordinate to form customs, and their customs provide the material of their culture, one important aspect of which constitutes the primary phenomena of ethics. In particular, people are prone to approve and condemn the practices of other people, both those found in other cultures and those engaged in by some members of their own society. This widespread tendency influences the behavior of people in a society and helps to solidify a common culture. The central question to be addressed in the systematic study of ethics is, 'what basis, if any, do people have for approving or condemning the practices of other people?'

1

1.1 Approaching the subject

Something old, something peculiar

The earliest surviving books to bear the title 'ethics' are works by Aristotle, who lived in the fourth century BCE. He left materials from a connected set of lectures, which were compiled and edited by his associates into two somewhat different versions (the 'Nicomachean' and the 'Eudemian') under the general title 'Ethics.' These lectures were on concepts and questions that Aristotle regarded as important preliminaries to the study of politics. He considered, for example, such questions as what sort of life is worthwhile or fulfilling for a human being? What acquired characteristics make people especially worthy of admiration? What is pleasure and what role should it have in human life?

When Aristotle began his consideration of traits that make humans especially worthy of admiration, he singled out those 'excellences' (*aretai*) to which the adjective 'ethical' (*ēthikē*) could be applied, explaining that these are acquired by habituation and suggesting that this word derives from *ethos*, custom, usage, manners, or habit (1103a19).[1] The phrase *ēthikai aretai* is also frequently translated into English as 'moral virtues.' This derives from the way this phrase was translated into Latin. Aristotle's word *ēthikē* was translated as '*moralis*,' a word derived from *mos* (*moris*), which also meant both habit and custom. This is the source of our word 'moral.' For most everyday purposes, 'ethical' and 'moral', 'ethics' and 'morals' are synonymous. 'Virtue,' as a translation of *aretē*, derives from a Latin word for exceptional strength or courage (of a man – from *vir*, male human being) and is now so closely associated with moral appraisal that 'moral virtue' is almost a pleonasm. The older sense of 'excellence in general,' however, survives in the English term (imported from Italian) 'virtuoso,' usually applied to a person from whom people have come to expect outstanding performances (especially of music).

Aristotle contrasts two ways in which more mature and experienced people educate those who are less mature and experienced. If they are trying to pass on information or understanding, they will 'instruct' their pupils; if they are trying to develop excellences, including 'ethical excellences,' they will 'train' their pupils, rather than instruct them, by getting them to follow good examples and by correcting inadequate performances until certain habits have developed (1103a14–25). This is also the way a music teacher or an athletics coach proceeds, and this is not surprising as Aristotle regards excellences – ethical, musical, athletic, etc. – all as the sort of state or condition of a person which he calls a *hexis* (plural *hexeis*). This is another word that could be translated 'habit' – in fact it was translated into Latin as *habitus*, which is the source of our word 'habit.' A person with what Aristotle calls a *hexis* will respond (easily, predictably) one way rather than another in a certain class of circumstances, e.g. a pianist will use fingering that either helps or hinders the smooth playing of difficult passages; a hurdler will adopt a stride that either helps or hinders stepping smoothly over the hurdles.

What, then, distinguishes the excellence of a musician or an athlete from what Aristotle would call an 'ethical excellence?' Aristotle provides both a long and a short answer to this question. The long answer involves a very precise definition of 'ethical excellence,' which we will examine in Section 8.4. For now, the short answer will do. What makes a *hexis* fall within the concern of ethics is that it is a certain way of responding to (or to the prospect of) pleasure and pain (1104b27–8). As Aristotle puts it, 'the whole concern both of [ethical] excellence and political science is with pleasures and pains; for the man who uses these well will be good and he who uses them badly [will be] bad' (1105a10–13). So we can say roughly that ethics as a systematic study began by considering the good and bad habits *of* response that people acquire *in* response to what pleases and pains them.

That was over twenty-three centuries ago, and although this way of conceiving ethics is still influential, the systematic study known as ethics has come since then to be conceived in a variety of other ways. The currently most influential alternative approach arises from narrowing the focus of concern to one important aspect of what Aristotle identified as an ethical excellence. As we will see in Section 8.4, an important part of every ethical excellence is responding in a way characteristic of a person who is able to deliberate well. Deliberation is the thought process that addresses questions of the form 'what should be done in these circumstances?' and concludes by endorsing some courses of action as preferable to others. Aristotle's word for this thought process (*bouleusis*) suggests a collaborative activity; it and its cognates invoke the process of 'taking counsel' along with others. The most common approaches today, however, not only consider how deliberation should proceed without reference to the character of the person deliberating but they also frequently assume that in the typical situation people deliberate by themselves, so that cultural influences that might be shaping the process are left out of the picture along with the character of the deliberator.

Narrowing the focus of ethical inquiry to the process of deliberation, abstracted from the culture and character of the person who is deliberating, requires answering a question similar to that about what makes an excellence 'ethical.' After all, people can deliberate about a great many things, such as when to take their paid vacations, what food to serve their guests, whether to buy a new or used car. What deliberations constitute the subject matter of the systematic study of ethics? The answer appears to be 'when the deliberation is governed by *moral* reasons and the conclusion is a determination that a person has (or does not have) a *moral* obligation.' (If the conclusion is that there is no moral obligation to follow a particular course of action then one *may* in a *moral* sense of permissibility adopt a different course of action.)

There is, according to Bernard Williams (1985: chapter 10), a 'range of ethical outlooks' embraced by this notion of *moral obligation*, which together constitute what he calls 'the peculiar institution' of morality. Some of the features that characterize the notion of moral obligation are that it must be given highest deliberative priority (184) and is 'inescapable' (177). People may be bound (*obligare* is Latin meaning to bind, tie or fasten) whether they want to be or not: 'there is nowhere outside the system' (178). The 'must do' that a moral obligation attaches to a prospective course of action is 'a "must" that is unconditional and *goes all the way down*' (188). Only another stronger and conflicting moral obligation can release one from a moral obligation (180); thus, although one cannot escape the system, one can escape particular obligations – obligations do not and 'cannot conflict, ultimately, really, or at the end of the line' (176). Part of the philosophical project of morality is to determine how obligations are to be systematically reconciled. Those who do not live up to their obligations are subject to blame and should feel self-reproach or guilt. Although it is not a necessary feature, there is a tendency in 'the morality system' to make everything into obligations and to eliminate the class of morally indifferent actions (180–1).

In Williams' view, the eighteenth-century German philosopher Immanuel Kant provides the 'purest, deepest and most thorough representation of morality' (174, but see Sections 7.4 and 8.1 of this book). The overriding imperative in Kant's ethics is to do one's duty (whatever one is under an obligation to do) for no other reason than that it is one's duty. But theorists opposed to Kant share the same outlook – many utilitarians (see Sections 10.1 and 10.3–4 of this book) work for the good of humanity because they 'think this is what they ought to do and feel guilty if they do not live up to their own standards' (178). Ethical thought that survives from the ancient Greeks, most of whom operated within a framework of questions about what sort of life we should lead, does not share this outlook – an outlook that is, Williams contends, a development of modern Western culture (6).

Williams' personal view (174) is that we would be better off without this outlook. His sentiments are echoed by Charles Taylor (1989: 85, 88), who looks askance at 'this vogue of theories of obligatory action.' We do not, however, need to evaluate the 'morality system' at this stage. It is enough to identify it so that we do not assume inadvertently that it constitutes the framework of all the phenomena that are of interest to the systematic study of ethics.

Apart from the incoherence that Williams claims to find in this 'peculiar institution,' there are important aspects of ethical phenomena which it obscures:

[An] agent's conclusions will not usually be solitary or unsup-
ported, because they are part of an ethical life that is to an important
degree shared with others. In this respect, the morality system
itself, with its emphasis on the 'purely moral' and personal sentiments of guilt and self-reproach, actually conceals the dimension
in which ethical life lies outside the individual.

(Williams 1985: 191)

There is the even more serious danger that if we assume that ethical
phenomena have the features of this 'peculiar institution,' we will be unable
either to recognize ethical phenomena or to understand attempts in other
cultures to think systematically about it. If for example we assume that
obligations 'cannot conflict, ultimately, really, or at the end of the line,' we
will be unable to understand the ethical culture of Japan, where the obligations to the emperor (in earlier times to the shogun) (*chu*), to one's parents
(*ko*) and to personal honor (*giri* to one's name) can in some circumstances
be reconciled only in suicide (Benedict 1946: chapter 10). To assume that
the morality system structures ethical phenomena the world over would be
like assuming that religion had to be monotheistic, so that we could not recognize the existence of religion that was not Christian, Jewish or Islamic.

While it is not the aim of this introduction to provide a comprehensive
survey of ethical traditions, it is intended to show how traditions found
both in the West and beyond address common phenomena and how both
the similarities and differences found in the variety of the traditions that
deal with these phenomena can illuminate them for us. In the remainder
of this chapter (as well as in the two chapters that follow it), the purpose
will be to explore 'the dimension in which ethical life lies outside the
individual' and to bring systematicity to the social phenomena that constitute the proper object of the systematic study of ethics. We will begin by
distinguishing questions about these phenomena that are proper to that
systematic study, and to do this we will return to Aristotle's starting point,
the role that habit plays in human life.

1.2 Creatures of habit

Habit, custom and culture

This fact that people acquire habits is extremely important. If typing on
a keyboard, finding one's way home from work or obtaining the help or
co-operation of other people did not become habitual, we could never turn
our attention to new things. Everything we did in our lives would remain
as time-consuming and thought-provoking as when we first took it up. If
people did not acquire habits, we could not anticipate them enough to co-
operate with them. And as pleasure and pain are involved in the most

fundamental of the motives that prompt people to act, it is clear that the habits that we acquire of responding to pleasure and pain are potentially the most disruptive of our interactions with one another.

Habits not only allow us to profit from experience and from other people, they also help to stabilize the social environment. In a psychology text-book written over a century ago, William James explained 'the ethical implications of the law of habit' in these terms:

> Habit is thus the enormous fly-wheel of society, its most precious conservative agent. It alone is what keeps us all within the bounds of ordinance, and saves the children of fortune from the envious uprisings of the poor. It alone prevents the hardest and most repulsive walks of life from being deserted by those brought up to tread therein. It keeps the fisherman and the deck-hand at sea through the winter; it holds the miner in his darkness, and nails the countryman to his log-cabin and his lonely farm through all the months of snow; it protects us from invasion by the natives of the desert and the frozen zone. It dooms us all to fight out the battle of life upon the lines of our nurture or our early choice, and to make the best of a pursuit that disagrees, because there is no other for which we are fitted, and it is too late to begin again. It keeps different social strata from mixing. Already at the age of twenty-five you see the professional mannerism settling down on the young commercial traveller, on the young doctor, on the young minister, on the young counsellor-at-law. You see the little lines of cleavage running through the character, the tricks of thought, the prejudices, the ways of the 'shop' in a word, from which the man can by-and-by no more escape than his coat-sleeve can suddenly fall into a new set of folds. On the whole, it is best he should not escape. It is well for the world that in most of us, by the age of thirty, the character has set like plaster, and will never soften again.
>
> (James 1890: Vol. I, 120–2)

A fly-wheel is a heavy wheel that once made to turn is so difficult to stop that it will drive a machine long after its engine is cut off. Habit keeps society moving; it ensures that people will perform their roles; it preserves distinctions between occupations and social classes; it creates barriers that prevent people changing their station in life. It is because people know what to expect from one another that they can live with one another, compete with one another, frustrate one another, exploit one another. However people live with one another – in happiness or in misery, to benefit or to oppress, sharing prosperity or enduring hardship – habits constitute the fabric of human association.

Human association requires not merely that people have habits but that they share habits. Habits that people share are called customs. Customs may be uniform patterns of behavior to which everyone conforms, such as taking off one's shoes before entering a house. But customs may require different patterns of behavior from different people, as in the different roles assigned to different people in rituals such as getting married, celebrating mass, introducing strangers to one another, eating in a restaurant.

A complex of customs shared by people who interact with each other on a regular basis may constitute what is recognized as a culture. Often society is sufficiently complex that groups within it share enough special customs not followed outside those groups for this group to possess a subculture. People who engage in certain occupations, as James observes, behave in distinct and recognizable ways. Everyone who moves into a new culture (or even subculture) has important adjustments to make. Our understanding of the people around us depends on our ability to anticipate what they will do. Individuals who live comfortably in one culture frequently find it difficult to move into another, even when they have been informed in advance of how customs will differ. When large-scale migrations bring different cultures into contact there is ample scope for mutual misunderstanding; commonly, tensions build up between the two groups; sometimes hostilities break out. But frequently it is only the experience of another culture that makes us aware of how deeply and pervasively our lives are structured by the habits we share with the people around us.

To emphasize this depth and pervasiveness, it may help to stress the special uses being given to three words here: 'habit,' 'custom' and 'culture.' We often think of habits as patterns of behavior, which we fall into and find difficult to change even when there is no narcotic involved (as in the smoking habit). People who have the habit of brushing their teeth after they eat feel uncomfortable until they have brushed them. But habits, as James stressed, are also empowering: as a result of 'being in the habit' we find it easy to do certain things that other people find that they do only awkwardly, such as conduct business over the telephone or find misprints in a letter. As we mature we come to do so many things with ease, without thought, that we have no conception of the depth of the sediment of our habits. Our habits shape not only what we do but also what we perceive – for noticing (a pattern or other visual cue) often takes practice. Habits shape not only what we perceive but also what we want – for it also takes practice for an activity or experience to become easy enough to be enjoyable and thus something we are eager to do again.

The word 'custom' makes one think of easily imitated patterns of behavior such as the Japanese custom of *kodomatsu* – placing bamboo and evergreen sprigs at the entrance to one's house at the start of the new year. However, customs are frequently very unobvious until they have been flouted. The penalty for failing to observe a custom may be clear signs of disapproval from other people, but one may also simply be ignored, left on the outside. What may seem perfectly natural to people in one group may be something that is 'simply not done' in another. What one group of people pays a great deal of attention to, another group may ignore altogether. What one group of people regards as highly desirable another group may regard as silly or trivial or repulsive.

'Culture' is sometimes applied to especially refined activities and their enjoyment (opera, ballet, poetry). The complex of customs that constitute the culture of a group of people need not be especially refined activities. Paul Willis explains the sense of the word 'culture' that we need here:

> Culture is not artifice and manners, the preserve of Sunday best, rainy afternoons, and concert halls. It is the very material of our daily lives, the bricks and mortar of our most commonplace understandings, feelings, and responses. We rely on cultural patterns and symbols for the minute and unconscious, social reflexes that make us social and collective beings: we are therefore most *deeply* embedded in our culture when we are at our most natural and spontaneous: if you like, at our most work-a-day. As soon as we think, as soon as we see life as parts in a play, we are in a very important sense, already, one step away from our real and living culture.
>
> Clearly this is a special use of the concept of culture. In part it can be thought of as an anthropological use of the term, where not only the special, heightened, and separate forms of experience, but *all* experiences, and especially as they lie around central life struggles and activities, are taken as the proper focus of a cultural analysis.
>
> (1979: 185)

Ethics, as we will see, not only needs a number of concepts used by social anthropology but is also concerned with some of the same phenomena that interest social anthropologists. But the questions it asks about these phenomena are very different.

Information about other cultures, both historical and contemporary, has long been gathered and discussed, but systematic efforts to understand that involve investigators placing their own culture on the same footing as those being investigated are a recent development. Ethics as a systematic study is much older. It was prompted by the dissatisfactions that people experience with the way others behave both within their own societies and in other societies with which they have come into contact. Ethics as a systematic study came in two general forms, depending on which of two common assumptions were made. These assumptions can be explained in terms of the traits that render individuals admirable in the way that Aristotle marks with his word *ēthikē*.

8

One assumption is that people naturally want to respond well rather than badly to the experiences that afford them pleasure and pain, but that it is not always easy for them to figure out what is the best response, what it is they should do. In other words, people in general can easily bring themselves to do what should be done when they know what it is; those with ethical excellence simply have a superior ability to discern what should be done. The other assumption is that clear guidance is available to everyone as to what should be done; the problem is to act as one should, for the prospects of pleasure and pain frequently exert strong pressures that lead people to do the very opposite of what they should. People with ethical excellence have no better ability to discern what should be done than does anyone else, but they have more strength than ordinary people to resist pressures and to do what should be done.

These assumptions are not incompatible. To be the sort of person who responds to pleasures and pains in a way that merits admiration might well require both exceptional discernment and exceptional strength of will. But there has been a marked tendency to think in terms of one or the other. Aristotle, for example, did not assume that people in general wanted to respond well rather than badly, but he did assume that members of his audience were mature and not the sort 'to pursue each successive object as passion directs . . . but desired and acted in accordance with discursive thought (*logos*)' (1094b28–1095a17). Thus Aristotle could conceive his role as offering to people like this help in understanding better the principles that should govern their discursive thought.

Doctrines associated with Aristotle's intellectual predecessor, Socrates, involved the more radical (and self-consciously paradoxical) claim that everyone always wants what is best and only does what is wrong out of ignorance.[2] This makes notions of 'strength' and 'weakness' inapplicable and reduces moral excellence to the ability to discern what should be done in some area of human activity. Cowards lack, what the courageous have, an ability to discern when they should face danger; adulterers lack, what the honorable and faithful possess, a grasp of when they should avoid an affair; thieves lack, what the honest have, an appreciation of when they may not appropriate something. Kant, on the other hand, conceived virtue as a matter of strength (*fortitudo*; see Kant 1797: 380).[3] He took it that there was a way to figure out what should be done that was accessible to everyone, and that what wrong-doers lack is the strength to resist their natural inclinations to avoid danger, to engage in sex or to appropriate things that seem to them advantageous to possess.

The problems that arise in the course of seeking to motivate people or of trying to shape their characters are commonly left to priests and parsons, educators and counselors. The only motivational questions that arise in the systematic study of ethics have to do with considerations that should motivate an ideally rational or reasonable person – questions similar in form to those that come up in logic about what an ideally rational or reasonable person should accept as true, given other beliefs that this person has. The systematic study of ethics has taken upon itself the responsibility for investigating what, if any, intellectually sound guidance can be given to people performing in these roles – guidance to help them to clarify their goals and the criteria they use to assess people and situations. For example, did Kant really identify a way to figure out what should be done that is accessible to everyone? (On this see Section 7.3.) Are there ever good reasons to try to overcome one's natural fears? What obligations and rightful claims are generated by the institutions of marriage and of property?

Before the rise of the systematic study of cultures and societies in the nineteenth century, knowledge that people in other parts of the world had different institutions of marriage or expected different degrees of self-control from people experiencing fear, pain or discomfort, prompted from people the same kind of response as would deviant behavior in their own society. They either condemned what they heard and defended their own customs or treated what they heard as more enlightened and used the information to criticize their own customs. Once it became common to look upon one's own culture as a possible subject of anthropological investigation, the project of ethics did not end, but it became possible to subsume many of its concerns under more comprehensive questions: what, if any, basis might there be for recommending one practice or way of life over another? What, if any, grounds might there be for condemning or approving a habit or custom?

1.3 Impulses to approve or to condemn

Harmless ritual and ritual cannibalism

Social anthropology gathers information about human social formations and tries to explain what has been observed. Ethics concerns itself with judgments about what should or should not be done – including judgments about what customs should be changed, even suppressed – judgments that many social scientists regard as not properly a part of their concerns. Judgments of this sort are made from time to time by members of a society about their own or another culture. It may be a fact that certain segments of a society disapprove of the habits or customs of some other segment of their own society or of a neighboring society and believe that these customs should be abandoned. This would itself be one of the phenomena that social anthropology might report and try to explain. But social scientists normally regard it as improper for their practitioners (when they are speaking as social scientists) to express their own judgments about whether what they observe should be permitted and even encouraged, or should be discouraged and (if possible) suppressed.

To clarify further what ethics is about, let us look at two reports generated by social scientists about cultures that are not their own and identify some of the impulses that generate phenomena proper to ethics (that is, impulses which lead to judgments about what should be permitted and encouraged and what should be discouraged and suppressed). When reading these examples, consider not only your own reaction to them but also the way members of your own culture are likely to respond to them.

The first example is a report of a contemporary practice of the indigenous popular religion in China known as Taoism, an initiation ceremony of a future great master of a local Taoist guild.

> The ordinee, who has been standing in the lower part of the ritual area dressed simply in the Taoists' black gown and wearing cloth shoes, his hair unbound, now receives the robes of Great Master. First his shoes are replaced by thick-soled boots – a sort of buskin – embroidered with cloud patterns. The formula accompanying this gesture goes as follows:
>
> > Shoes that soar through the clouds as flying geese,
> > With you I shall climb the nine steps of the altar of Mysteries;
> > My exalted wish is to roam in the Three Worlds,
> > To ride the winds all over the sky
> > Today I vow that with these shoes
> > I shall proceed to the audience before the Golden Countenance.
>
> Afterwards his hair is gathered and knotted in a bun on top of his head. The knot is covered with a crown – variously called *golden crown*, *golden lotus*, or *crown of stars*.
>
> (Schipper 1992: 70–1)

The report goes on to give the words that accompany this gesture, then it describes how the ordinee is given an embroidered apron and a robe and the words that accompany this stage of the ceremony. Next the ordinee is given ritual instruments, and finally the 'Initiating Master takes a flame-shaped pin which he sticks onto the top of the ordinand's crown' conveying the flame, the energy which he is now 'able to recognize and externalize ... to make his body shine and to create his own universe, a place of order and peace, a sanctuary in which all beings passing through will be transformed' (*ibid.*).

This report probably generates no impulses to judge favorably or unfavorably. The report may only make one think of similar ceremonies in our own culture, for example the conferring of degrees, ordination of priests, etc. Members of our (North Atlantic) culture will almost certainly not take seriously the significance that participants find in this ceremony, because they will not share the beliefs that are woven into and sustain it, but few will feel there is anything described here that should be discouraged or forcefully suppressed. People with strong religious convictions might condemn the ceremony as an expression of false or unenlightened beliefs, but this is not to find fault with the ceremony as such. However, it appears that the general reaction to other ritual practices would be very different.

In 1529, a few years after Cortés had conquered the Aztec empire in Mexico, a missionary, Father Bernardino de Sahagún, arrived in Mexico. After learning the Aztec language, he obtained the help of native informants and native scribes and produced a substantial record of ritual practices prior to the conquest. The following extract is a mixture of summary and quotation from de Sahagún's *General History of the Things of New Spain*:

> On the first day of the second month, the Aztec celebrated a feast in honor of the god called Totec or Xipe at which time they slew and flayed many slaves and captives. On this feast day all who had been taken captive died – men, women, and children. After the hearts, the 'precious eagle-cactus fruit,' were sacrificed to the sun god – to 'nourish' him – each body was rolled down the side of the pyramid and taken to the house of the captor to be eaten. At the house of the captor they portioned the body out:
>
>> They cut him to pieces; they distributed him. First of all, they made an offering of one of his thighs to Moctezuma. They set forth to take it to him.
>>
>> And as for the captor, they there applied the down of birds to his head and gave him gifts. And he gathered together his blood relatives; the captor assembled them in order to go to eat at his home.
>>
>> There they made each one an offering of a bowl of stew of dried maize, called *tlacatlaolli*. They gave it to each one. On each went a piece of the captive.
>>
>> (Sanday 1986: 172–3)

The reactions of someone from our culture to this description are likely to range from horror to disgust. Whatever one might say against a *conquistador* such as Cortés, that he is regarded as having put a stop to such practices would be counted a mark in his favor by a large body of opinion. Colonialism is widely condemned nowadays for its oppression and exploitation of indigenous peoples, and along with this is condemned the lack of respect that colonial authorities showed to the beliefs and practices of indigenous cultures, but it is hard to include in that general indictment the attempts by colonial authorities to stamp out practices of cannibalism and ritual murder (in the relatively few places where it is thought they were practised).

Under prevailing conceptions of what a social science should do, it is not the business of social anthropology to approve or condemn the customs found in other societies. All an anthropologist or social theorist may do is try to piece together an account of a culture's system of beliefs and practices that may help us to understand how such customs – abhorrent to us – might seem perfectly reasonable to the people who follow them. This is what Peggy Sanday tries to do in the book from which the above description of Aztec ritual was taken.

It is a cultural fact that people (in most cultures, not just in ours) respond favorably or adversely to some practices found in their own and in other cultures. Even if the account of Aztec rituals given above is not actually true, it remains true that the belief, that ritual murder and cannibalism were practised by the Aztecs before the conquest, has currency in our culture. Anthropologists such as Sanday take Sahagún's account as data to be explained; other anthropologists, such as William Arens (1979), raise doubts that cannibalism has ever existed as a cultural practice (as opposed to isolated pathological behavior) and offer instead to explain why we have these beliefs (and why our ancestors had such beliefs, for people have been attributing cannibalism to remote tribes since they started to write history). Perhaps these 'myths' about other people serve to make us feel superior to them. Exaggerated accounts of the barbarity of a people may also serve to justify their conquest or colonization.

Some social anthropologists may seek thus to explain what they may take to be false beliefs that people hold (together with the very negative judgments that are made on the basis of those beliefs). But, as we have already noted, under a widely held view of what a social scientist is supposed to do, anthropologists are not, in their role as social scientists, supposed to make (favorable or adverse) judgments about those beliefs or even about the practices represented in those beliefs. The thought of ritual murder and cannibalism may appall them as much as anyone else (whether or not they believe it has ever taken place), but social scientists do not regard it as part of their task as social scientists to sanction the negative response of horror and revulsion. That is thought to be the task of ethics.

This does not mean that it is the primary concern of ethics to endorse or condemn any set of customs in our own or in some other cultural system. Rather, it is the responsibility of ethics to determine what, if any, authority or validity such judgments (expressing negative or positive attitudes) may claim. The notion of authority or validity here is not that involved in questions of historical fact – for example, have we adequate (authoritative) reason to believe that a given culture actually engaged in ritual murder and cannibalism? The notion of validity here applies to the revulsion that commonly accompanies the thought of anyone engaging in these practices. We can divide responsibilities for the different questions as follows: it is the task of history and archaeology to determine *the strength of the reasons we have for believing that* a given culture ever engaged in ritual murder and cannibalism. It is the task of social anthropology to explain *why a culture might have done so* if it did, or *why other cultures might be prone to believe that it did* if in fact it did not. It is the task of ethics to consider *what, if any, basis there is for condemning a practice* such as ritual murder.

If what is involved in this last responsibility still seems unclear, consider the two descriptions quoted above. The priest of (what is to us) an exotic religion is installed with a ritual that from the description appears innocuous. The gods of (what is to us) an exotic religion are propitiated by a ritual that from the description appears abhorrent. It is a fact about us that we are likely to be much more tolerant of what is described in the first example than in the second example. Can we say not only that we (in general) *have* these responses but also that they are the *right* responses? *On what basis* could we say they were the right responses?

We might begin to defend our responses by saying that obviously the second case involves taking the lives of human beings who have done nothing more to deserve their fate than to have been taken captive in war or to have been bought in a slave market for the purpose of being sacrificed. Is that not the basis of the difference? Our Aztecs (the Aztecs as described), however, believe that taking the lives of captives and slaves in this way is perfectly acceptable. We can imagine trying to persuade them that they are doing something horribly wrong and finding that they would point to our own culture and observe that we daily slaughter and eat animals. We would probably reply that we draw a firm line, which precludes human animals from that practice, but our Aztecs might ask why the line should be drawn where we draw it rather than in a way that permits some humans to be treated as we treat sheep, pigs and cattle. (Indeed, some people in our culture, 'animal rights activists,' would urge that we should abhor this treatment of sheep, pigs and cattle as much as we would abhor this treatment of human beings.)

At this point, some members of our society might appeal to the principle that human life is sacred; but unless there are religious beliefs behind the use of the word 'sacred,' to use the word is merely to reiterate what has already been said, namely that we feel strongly that humans should not be slaughtered like animals. So unless and until our Aztecs share the framework structured by the required religious beliefs, this appeal is not likely to carry much weight with them. This is not to say that the appeal should not carry weight but merely to observe what our Aztecs may lack so that they fail to see what is wrong with their practice. If this *is* all they lack and this *is* all that could justify our negative responses to ritual murder and cannibalism, then the basis that ethics seeks lies (at least in this instance) in religion.

Many members of our culture, who have a more secular orientation, might argue, on the other hand, that every human being is born with a right to life, and the ritual taking of human life (except perhaps of victims who have been properly convicted of some sufficiently serious crime) violates that right. To appeal to a right is not necessarily to seek a basis for our revulsion in religion. Although some of those who seek in that direction might insist that this right is 'God given,' it could be treated as having another basis by the non-religious. Both of these appeals (to the sanctity of human life and to the secular notion of a right of human beings to life) clearly need further development (see Chapter 7) and might well produce quite different ethical theories. They illustrate how it is possible for people who agree in condemning some practice to disagree over the correct basis for a condemnation. As we shall see, not all ethical disagreements begin from this sort of agreement; people disagree not only over the basis for condoning or condemning practices, they also often violently disagree over what practices should be condoned or condemned

1.4 Conflicting responses

Foot binding, genital mutilation and abortion

The examples we have considered in order to clarify what ethics is about have been rather remote from us, and doubt has been cast on the historical authenticity of the more unsavory of them. This should not be allowed to encourage the thought that ethics is not a very important concern. There are many well-documented customs – some still widely practised (such as the torture of political prisoners), others that have only recently been abandoned or suppressed (the practices associated with the institution of slavery; see Sections 7.1 and 2) – that elicit condemnation from members of the very culture in which they are found, as well as from outsiders. A number of examples are related to the status that women have (or have had in the past) in the culture concerned.

In some places in India, for example, it was the custom for widows to commit suicide by throwing themselves on the funeral pyres of their husbands. This custom of *sati* was outlawed by the British colonial authorities and is still forbidden by law in India. Nevertheless, there continue to be sporadic reports in Indian newspapers of this taking place – over forty reported cases since 1947, with one as recent as 1987 (Oldenburg 1994: 101). Where there is reason to suspect that the widow was pressured by her husband's relatives to follow this custom, the custom appears close to that of ritual murder, and the response of many people to it is not unlike that of their response to purported descriptions of Aztec ritual.

If this custom merits condemnation – if revulsion has a firm (ethical) basis – does that basis extend to the condemnation of other customs? In

China until relatively recently, it was the custom in certain social classes to bind the feet of girls in order to produce adult women with dainty feet. This was for the girls who endured it a long, painful and ultimately crippling process. It can hardly be said that the girls who were subjected to this always underwent it willingly:

> Although largely filtered through male voices during the period when foot-binding was under attack, testimonies of foot-bound women attempted to find words for the kind of pain experienced in binding – burning, throbbing feet swallowing the body in fire – from severe traumas that created months, even years of oozing sores, bandages stiff with dried pus and blood, and sloughed off gobs of flesh. These accounts tell of girls losing appetites and sleep, running away, hiding, surreptitiously attempting to loosen their bandages, and enduring beatings while trying to comply with their mother's demands.
>
> (Blake 1994: 682)

What basis, if any, would there be for condemning attempts to reintroduce this practice?

In several regions in Africa, for example Sudan, young girls are forcibly subjected to forms of genital mutilation that vary from removing the tip of the prepuce of the clitoris to complete removal of the clitoris, labia minor and labia majora. The effects and recent history of this practice are described by a Sudanese physician who herself endured the operation at age eleven.

> The operation is usually performed when a child is four to eight years old but sometimes as early as seven days old. The result almost invariably causes immediate and long term medical complications, especially at childbirth. Consummation of marriage is always a difficult experience for both partners, and marital problems often result. Psychological disturbances in girls due to circumcision are not uncommon.
>
> Female circumcision in the Sudan was first seen as a social problem in the late 1930s, when it was widely discussed by the British administration and enlightened Sudanese. The majority of educated Sudanese felt that it was the duty of their generation to abolish this custom. In 1946, the Legislative Assembly passed a law making Pharonic [the more extensive] circumcision an offence punishable by fine and imprisonment. (The sunna circumcision [less extensive] was considered to be legal). This measure, however, proved to be a failure.
>
> (El Dareer 1982: iii–iv)

El Dareer reports (*ibid.*: 1) that in 1980 in large regions of Sudan more than 98 percent of women had undergone circumcision, more than 80 percent the extreme 'Pharonic' version, even though this procedure was illegal. The tension in Sudanese culture between those described above as 'enlightened' and those who might be described as 'traditionalist' had not been resolved.

Not everyone from our own (North Atlantic) culture feels it appropriate to condemn this practice out of hand. The French anthropologist Louis Dumont viewed a campaign launched in his own country 'against the "sexual mutilations" inflicted by certain societies upon "millions of young and adolescent girls"' with some hesitancy. His response went beyond the reluctance to condemn the practices of another society that one would expect of an anthropologist speaking as a member of his profession. Along with his sympathy for the 'modern values underlying the protest' he confessed to a disquiet over what 'would amount to authorizing interference in the collective life of a population' (Dumont 1982: 208–9, n.5). Moreover, Sudanese traditionalists familiar with our ways might remind us of the practice common in our country of surgically modifying children who are born with 'ambiguous genitalia,' estimated at one in 2,000 (Kipnis and Diamond 1998: 401a). Does the widespread feeling in the USA that something needs to be done to all these children, Sudanese traditionalists might ask, have any better foundation than the widespread feeling found in Africa that something needs to be done to all girl children?

Considering purported cases of *satī* where the widow appears willing (so that it does not appear to be anything like murder), many people from our culture would still forcefully condemn the practice – suicide is regarded by them as nearly as abhorrent as murder. But a significant number would not be so quick to condemn in this case – whether to die or to go on living, they believe, is a choice that should be left up to the individual who has to do the living or dying. (This is one difference of judgment that is correlated strongly with whether the people making the judgment believe ethics has a religious basis or a secular basis.) These opposing views have recently generated a clash over whether it should be illegal to assist someone to commit suicide. Tensions of this sort, in other words, are not confined to 'non-Western' cultures which have segments of their populations that have acquired a 'Western' perspective on their own cultural practices.

Indeed, in the United States the conflict over assisted suicide has been nothing like as violent as that over abortion. To one body of opinion, abortion is tantamount to the murder of an innocent human being. Those who hold this view respond to the practice – an estimated 1.5 million abortions in the USA in 1988, which is slightly more than one-fourth of all pregnancies (Luker 1996: 165) – as they would to reports of the practice of ritual infanticide in another culture. Another body of opinion in our society does not regard the human embryo – at least during the early stages of pregnancy – as a human being. Although those who hold this latter view often insist that the decision to terminate a pregnancy should not be taken lightly, they do not regard ending the life of a very undeveloped embryo as anything like murder.

It might seem that this bitter conflict is over a narrowly focused difference of opinion about what level of development is required for a human organism to count as a human being. The conflict, however, is not one that might be settled by clarifying the facts of human development, since none of these facts is in dispute. Those who tolerate abortion (known as 'pro-choice') do not deny that human beings begin to exist as living organisms at conception. Those who condemn abortion (known as 'pro-life') do not deny that in the early stages of its development the human embryo is distinguished from fairly primitive life forms only by the potential it has to grow into a human being. The parties simply draw the line that determines what is to count as a human being in quite different places.

Behind this narrowly focused dispute, however, are differences of outlook that are both deep and far-reaching. A study of activists who campaign on behalf of one or the other side has shown that views of the two parties on a wide range of subjects are diametrically opposed to one another. The following paragraphs summarize observations made by Kristen Luker (1984) in a chapter that documents the observations using statements taken in interviews with activists.

> Pro-life activists believe that men and women are intrinsically different, and as a result of these intrinsic differences, have different roles to play: men are best suited to the competitive world of work, and women are best suited to managing the home in such a way as to create a nurturing environment in which to rear children and care for husbands (159–160). Because the demands of work and homemaking are emotionally so different, they regard women who work full time outside the home as risking damage to themselves as well as to members of their families (161). If this became the norm it would result in a deep loss; for tenderness, morality, caring, emotionality, and self-sacrifice are the exclusive province of women; and if women cease to fulfill this traditional role, 'who will do the caring, who will offer the tenderness?' (163).
>
> Pro-life people consider sex to be sacred because it has the capacity to bring human life into existence and believe sexual activity should not be engaged in where that capacity is routinely interfered with by contraception (let alone abortion). They are disturbed by the values which support the idea of 'recreational' sex – 'Values that define sexuality as a wholesome physical activity,

as healthy as volleyball but somewhat more fun, call into question everything that pro-life people believe in' (165).

Pro-life people treat parenthood as a 'natural' rather than a social role (168). They feel that sexually active people should be married, that all married people should be (or be willing to be) parents, that parents should welcome a child whenever it arrives, however inopportune the time may be, and that women who become parents should be prepared to place their roles as wife and mother ahead of their careers in the public world of work (169). Pro-life people regard it as wrong and foolish for men and women to control their fertility in order to achieve or maintain material prosperity. They claim to detect an anti-child sentiment in our culture and resent what they perceive as a prejudice against families with more than two children. 'Since one out of every five pro-life activists in this study had six or more children, it is easy to see how these values can seem threatening' (170). It follows from the norms (that marriage is for having children and that sexual activity should be confined to marriage) that pro-life people will regard premarital sex – which is not normally engaged in by people who are 'open to the gift of a new life' and who are frequently too young to be emotionally or financially prepared to become parents – as morally and socially wrong (171). They oppose policies that allow teenagers to have treatment for vene-real disease and contraceptives (let alone abortions) without parental knowledge or consent (173).

Pro-choice activists believe that men and women are substan-tially similar, and as a result see women's reproductive and family roles not as 'natural' but as cultural roles which, because of their traditional low status and poor economic reward, present poten-tial barriers to the social and economic equality of men and women. From the pro-choice point of view, women's control over their own fertility is essential for them to realize their full potential as human beings. They agree that raising children is an important and rewarding part of life, but also that there is danger in being too dependent on one's husband for economic support and thus women need marketable skills.

Pro-choice people, moreover, regard as absurd the idea that sexual activity is only valuable – indeed sacred – because of its capacity to bring new life into existence. They not only value 'recre-ational' sex, they 'argue that belief in the basically procreative nature of sex leads to an oppressive degree of *social regulation of sexual behavior, particularly the behavior of women*, who must be protected (in their viewpoint, repressed)' (176–7). Commonly, seeing the primary moral value in sexuality as its potential for creating intimacy, pro-choice people have no objection to pre-marital sex – indeed, many believe that people need to practise those skills, perhaps with more than one person, before making a long-term commitment to someone. They consequently have no objection to contraception, or to making it freely available to teenagers (183). Many, however, oppose the use of abortion as a routine method of birth control. This is because, although they do not regard the embryo as a full person, they do view it as a poten-tial person which acquires more of the rights of a full person as it develops (179–80).

The pro-choice view of the responsibilities of parents extends beyond bringing children into the world and providing a nurturing home environment. Parents also have duties to prepare their chil-dren materially, emotionally, and socially for their futures as adults – duties that demand financial resources. Parents should not come under pressure to the point where they resent their children, as this will interfere with their ability to provide them with a nurturing environment in which they will feel loved and will develop self-esteem. Control of the timing of the arrival of their children is thus needed by prospective parents who take their responsibilities seriously (181). While not feeling that abortion should be under-taken lightly, pro-choice people feel that its availability contributes to the scope for enhancing the quality of parenting by making it optional (rather than a mandatory consequence of sexual activity) and thus see themselves as on the side of children when they advocate it (182).

A lesson that might be drawn from this conflict is that wherever people are intensely divided – as they are over abortion – there may well be more at stake than the issue that is at the focus of the dispute. Behind the prac-tice, which some condemn (and wish to see made illegal once again) and others condone (and wish to be continued as an option), are different views of the roles of men and women in society, different attitudes to sexual activity and different conceptions of parents' responsibilities to children. Taken together, this dossier of differences might well characterize two distinct cultures. As a matter of fact, the two groups of activists do not inhabit different regions of the world – they were all residents of California – although given differences in religious affiliation and socio-economic status, these complexes of attitudes might be taken to constitute two distinct subcultures.

It will be found (see the references cited) that behind the other instances mentioned in this section – *sati*, foot binding, and genital mutilation – there are similar cultural complexes and that those who insist on maintaining the practice in question often fear that the whole of a cultural complex that gives their lives meaning and orientation will unravel if the practice is abandoned. Blake's thesis about foot binding illustrates this point, for he argues that the custom of foot binding interlocked with other features of the culture of neo-Confucian China (the period from the tenth to the end of the nineteenth century CE).

> Foot-binding cannot be fully explained without reference to the historical system of material production in which the sexual, repro- ductive, and economic products of women's labored bodies were systematically appropriated to make possible a Neo-Confucian way of being civilized. The remarkable fact about foot binding is that while the modern world has relegated it to a historical curiosity, it exchanged untold amounts of human energy on a daily basis without direct force of law – even in violation of imperial edicts – and it lasted for a thousand years across generations, centuries, and dynasties.
>
> (Blake 1994: 698–9)

Through the imposition of the practice, Chinese women taught their daugh- ters a discipline of the body that prepared them for the traumas of marriage and childbirth and for the kinds of social self-discipline and self-sacrifice which that society expected of women. The custom helped to create a role in a gender hierarchy in which women had no voice in public affairs and functioned principally as vehicles for the perpetration of a male line of descent. It also contributed to an image of 'women's labor as worth- less in view of the obvious, if indeed artificial, disability of their bodies.' This served to 'mask' the contribution that women made to families in a society that valorized males. 'Foot binding was the way women in China supported, participated in, and reflected on the Neo-Confucian way of being civilized' (708).

What is at stake in the conflicts that practices such as these generate is thus commonly more than isolated patterns of behavior. This observation is meant neither to defend these practices nor to condemn any culture that includes them. It is to suggest what we must bear in mind if we are to address the questions of ethics fruitfully. Ethics inquires into the basis that people might have for the responses of approval and disapproval with which they view habits and customs in their own and other societies. To understand what this sort of inquiry is about requires an appreciation of what is often (felt to be) at stake when these responses are made – which is nothing less than extensive portions of the whole of a way of life that is shared by a group of people.

To insist that ethical inquiry cannot ignore the social dimensions of its field of inquiry is not to deny that individuals may come to their own (possibly idiosyncratic) views about what is to be approved, tolerated or condemned. If ethics must recognize that its primary field of interest is constituted by social phenomena, it is not thereby precluded from recognizing that individuals' judgments and decisions also constitute part of this field. What is being maintained, however, is that if we insist on undertaking ethical inquiry by considering individual judgments and decisions in isolation from their social context and asking what basis individuals might have for their habits of approval and disapproval, we will reach only impoverished and distorted answers to our questions.

Before taking up the questions proper to ethics, we need to look more closely at the relevant social phenomena as social scientists might look at them and ask whether it is possible to identify precisely the phenomena that give rise to ethical inquiry. Some idea of what appear to be 'the nature of the facts' will help to clarify what basis we may have for the attitudes we take toward them.

Further reading

Williams' main discussion of the 'morality system' is found in chapter 10 of his *Ethics and the Limits of Philosophy* (1985). He devotes some of this chapter to examining the developments in the theory of obligation found in Ross (1930). Charles Taylor devotes chapter 3 of his *Sources of the Self* (1989) to showing historically 'how heavily overdetermined is this vogue of theories of obligatory action.' For an approach to social theory that emphasizes the importance of habit, and uses the medieval word *habitus* as a key technical term, see Bourdieu (1980). On *satī*, see Hawley (1994), especially the editor's 'afterword.' On foot binding, besides Blake (1994), see Jackson (1997). In addition to El Dareer (1982), there have recently been numerous newspaper articles on efforts to change attitudes to female genital mutilation in Africa. An example is an interview with Waris Dirie, 'the United Nations special ambassador on female genital mutilation' (Finnerty 1999). On the practice in the West of modifying the genitalia of 'intersexed' babies, see Kipnis and Diamond (1998). For differing views on the history of attitudes to abortion, see Luker (1984) and Noonan (1970).

Notes

1   Page references to Aristotle's writing are usually given by the line number of the Greek edition of Immanuel Bekker, 1831. The Greek where Aristotle makes this etymological connection of *ēthikē aretē* to *ethos* will be found in line 19 of the first (or 'a') column of page 1103 of Bekker's edition. Almost all English translations of Aristotle provide numbers in the margins to indicate what page and (commonly) what column and line of Bekker's edition is being translated, so these references are easy to follow regardless of what translation is being used.

2   Socrates died about fifteen years before Aristotle was born, but these 'Socratic para-
    doxes' are found in early dialogues written by Plato, who had been associated with
    Socrates during his early twenties. Aristotle studied at, and later taught in, Plato's
    academy and addressed some of the implications of these doctrines (as they are found
    in Plato's *Protagoras* 345e) at 1145b21ff. References to the works of Plato, like those
    of Aristotle, will be given here by their location in a standard Greek edition; in Plato's
    case, this is the edition published by Henri Estienne (Henricus Stephanus) in 1578.

3   Kant frequently supplies Latin equivalents for his key German terms in this work.
    References to Kant will be given here by indicating the page number in the German
    edition of Kant's works published by the Berlin Academy *circa* 1902. These are found
    in the margins of the translations used here.

2

CONCRETE MORALITIES

> Impulses have the same basic content as duties and virtues,
> but in impulses this content still belongs to the immediate
> will and to instinctive feeling; it has not been developed to
> the point of becoming ethical. Consequently, impulses have
> in common with the content of duties and virtues only the
> abstract object on which they are directed, an object inde-
> terminate in itself, and so devoid of anything to discriminate
> them [sc. impulses] as good or evil. ... But when individ-
> uals are simply identified with the actual order, ethical life
> (*das Sittliche*) appears as their general mode of conduct, i.e.
> as custom (*Sitte*), while the habitual practice of ethical living
> appears as a second nature which, put in place of the initial,
> purely natural will, is the soul of custom permeating it
> through and through.
>
> (G.W. Hegel 1821: §§150–1)

Recapitulation: We noted in the previous chapter that ethics and
social sciences such as anthropology are interested in some of the
same social phenomena but raise very different questions about
them. Where ethics asks what, if any, basis there is for the widespread human impulse to approve or condemn certain forms of
conduct, social science is taken to be concerned only with determining facts (e.g. whether people have ever practiced ritual
cannibalism) and with explaining facts that are taken to be well
established. Among the facts that might interest social scientists
are the patterns of approval and disapproval that characterize a
given society. But although social scientists may describe and even
offer to explain why such patterns obtain, they will not consider
whether the attitudes in question are ultimately justified.

Prospectus: This chapter proceeds from the premise that any
consideration of questions proper to ethics will be helped by at
least a brief look from the standpoint of the social sciences at
the phenomena that give rise to ethical inquiry. It will locate the
phenomena that interest ethics within more general classes
of phenomena, consider how these phenomena arise and are
sustained over time, determine to what extent they can be

distinguished from such phenomena as fashion and etiquette, and examine how they are related to the institutions of law.

2.1 Conventions, laws and climates of attitude

The revenge ethic and the spirit of capitalism

The social theorist Max Weber (1864–1920) applied the term 'usage' (*Brauch*) to regularities in human conduct. Some conduct is regular because people derive advantages from the regularity, e.g. a fisherman who returns to a spot where the fish often bite or a salesman who calls on customers at regular intervals. Some regularities are sustained because they simplify the organization of life: they cut down the time spent making decisions, help to co-ordinate activities with other people, and generate the satisfactions of conformity. A regularity (e.g. in matters of dress) that is known to have arisen recently and is followed partly for its novelty is a 'fashion' (*Mode*). A long-standing regularity is a custom (*Sitte*) (Weber 1978: 29).

Some customs can be broken without other people giving this more than passing notice. Other customs, if broken, lead people to communicate their disapproval and may bring sanctions that range from boycotting or ostracizing offenders to expressions of intense hostility. If these expressions of disapproval arise from a general belief that the custom in question has something that Weber called 'validity' (*Geltung*) or 'legitimacy' (*Legitimität*), then he called the custom a 'convention' (*Konvention*). If in addition a group of people could be identified whose special responsibility it is to enforce conformity to the custom, then it had, for Weber, the status of 'law' (*Recht*) (34).

The concepts that are marked out by Weber's definitions are important even if the English words 'convention' and 'law' are not commonly used in this way. 'Convention,' for example, often means a regularity that people have agreed to follow (or at least could agree to change). Breaking a 'convention' does not always entail risk of disapproval, but the concept of a custom that does entail this risk – as does 'convention' in Weber's sense – will be useful for our purposes. It is also clearly important to observe where institutionalized means for enforcing conformity to customs exist. It may be disputed whether the existence of such institutions is either necessary or sufficient for the application of the English word 'law,' but Weber's word, *Recht*, may also be translated 'right' and 'justice.' (There is a different German word, *Gesetz*, for what legislators produce.) What Weber intends to mark with the word *Recht* is the domain where coercion is thought to be appropriate. Kant had used the same term to mark out the same domain more than a century before (Kant 1797: 231).

Central to both convention and law in Weber's senses is the belief (*Vorstellung*) that the custom in question possesses 'validity.' Since 'validity,' along with 'legitimacy,' are words that naturally come to mind if one tries to unpack the meaning of the question about the 'basis' that people have for approving or condemning a practice, ethics will clearly be interested in conventions and laws in the senses Weber uses. What the words 'validity' and 'legitimacy' point to is that people will not only feel approval or disapproval of some form of conduct but they will also regard the way they feel as correct or appropriate, as conforming to some notion they possess of how (objectively) they should or ought to feel. It is not, however, easy to make this notion more precise.

The question whether people in a given society will feel and express disapproval when one of their customs is broken (so that the custom is a 'convention' in Weber's sense) is the sort of factual question that social scientists regard as proper for them to address, and such questions can often be settled by observation. The question whether a custom is regarded as having validity is also a factual question, but it is often more difficult to settle by observation, especially where people are motivated in some way not to observe the custom rigorously when no one else is watching or not to make evident their feeling that the custom should be observed by others. Bad faith and weakness of resolve complicate social reality. Habitual adulterers do not necessarily reject the validity of marital fidelity. Corruption may be widespread enough to reduce those who do not profit from it to intimidated silence, while the nudges and winks of those who do profit constitute back-handed acknowledgement of the validity of what they flout.

The validity of laws (customs that some group of people is taken to have authority to enforce) may also in some circumstances be difficult to determine, particularly in societies where laws are not written – difficult even for those responsible for enforcement. In societies with written legal codes and well-developed constitutional traditions, on the other hand, it is in most cases straightforward for citizens as well as outside observers to determine which customs are in fact laws or 'have legal validity.' But the 'validity' in this case is a very different kind of notion (about which more will be said in Section 2.4); conformity to a legally valid statute may be regarded by most people as a matter of indifference and attempts to enforce it as anything from unnecessary inconvenience to tyrannical oppression.

Because it is for the most part straightforward to determine whether breaking a custom will arouse disapproval but more difficult to determine what (moral) validity, if any, people attribute to that custom, let us begin by describing the social phenomena that are of interest to ethics in terms which avoid the concept of validity and take up that concept in subsequent sections of this chapter. We can proceed by advancing the following two-part claim (using a slightly elaborated version of Weber's notion of convention in order to highlight features that have so far been left in the shadows). In every society we find that:

26

1   members approve or condemn certain practices (found in their own
    or in other cultures); and
2   these practices are reinforced or discouraged as a consequence of this
    climate of approval or disapproval.

This is a (very plausible) generalization about human society. Attitudes of
this sort – together with the patterns of motivation that they generate –
exist and are important constituents (although by no means the only
constituents) of a culture.

Could we say that whenever a group of people share enough attitudes
of this sort, they have a common 'ethic' or a common 'morality?' The
concept we are trying to capture at this point is sometimes referred to as
a 'concrete ethic' or 'concrete morality.' Stress on the importance of this
concept is associated with the name of Hegel (see the quotation at the
head of this chapter).

> The set of obligations which we have to further and sustain a
> society founded on the Idea is what Hegel calls '*Sittlichkeit*'. This
> has been variously translated in English as 'ethical life', 'objec-
> tive ethics', 'concrete ethics' . . . '*Sittlichkeit*' is the usual German
> term for 'ethics', with the same kind of etymological origin [as
> the words 'ethics' and 'morals'], in the term '*Sitten*' which we
> might translate 'customs'. . . . These obligations are based on estab-
> lished norms and uses and that is why the etymological root in
> '*Sitten*' is important for Hegel's use.
>
> (Taylor 1975: 376)

This notion can be usefully studied and applied in isolation from the rest
of Hegel's theoretical apparatus and does not have to be treated as consisting
exclusively of a set of obligations.

The adjective 'concrete' serves to distinguish the social phenomenon
that we are considering from 'abstract or ideal ethics (morality),'
which is generated by reformers or theorists who have worked out some
idea of how people should conduct their lives (or perhaps merely
have some idea of how eventually to discover how people should conduct
their lives). A concrete morality is an aspect of a living culture or way of
life; it is what people actually live by and may not necessarily be something that is held up as an ideal and may not even be something to which
people pay lip service. (Normally, however, people believe that what they
live by is compatible with their professed ideals and they will speak in
its defense.)

Concrete moralities found in different historical contexts often have
enough features in common to constitute generic types. For example, many
cultures in which there are no other institutions for maintaining public

27

security rely on a commitment to a concrete morality known as the revenge ethic. A group of people, typically an extended family, may feel with considerable justification that if it does not maintain a credible threat to exact vengeance for injuries to any of its members, it will find its property and the lives of all of its members in jeopardy. Maintaining its credibility may well extend to inflicting physical punishment for symbolic injuries and affronts (to 'the family honor'). Carrying out revenge may require the physical strength of the men of the family, but sustaining the attitude that the imperative to seek vengeance should override everything else is commonly shared by all members of the family. Vilhelm Grönbech, who draws on literature to illustrate the revenge ethic in medieval Scandinavia, gives this example from the *Laxdoela Saga*:

> Gudrun was up at sundawn, says the saga, and woke her brothers. 'Such mettle as you are, you should have been *daughters* of so-and-so the peasant – of the sort that serve neither for good nor ill. After all the shame Kjartan has put upon you, you sleep never the worse for that he rides past the place with a man or so ...' The brothers dress and arm themselves.
>
> (1931: 57)

Claire Longrigg cites evidence of the same attitudes today among women of Mafia families in Southern Italy: 'Women are responsible for keeping the flame of vendetta alight, and reminding successive generations of their duty toward the dead, with theatrical displays of grief, keening over the body and swearing vendetta over open wounds' (1997: 81).

The obligation to seek revenge is one of the concrete phenomena reflected in an abstract form in 'the morality system' (Section 1.1). What is not reflected in this system is the sense of honor that is at stake where there is a debt to be repaid, a sense that may tie together phenomena we are inclined to think of as distinct:

> The Japanese do not have a separate term for what I call here 'giri to one's name.' ... The fact that Western languages separate [an obligation to return kindnesses and offenses] into categories as opposite as gratitude and revenge does not impress the Japanese. Why should one virtue not cover a man's behavior when he reacts to another's benevolence and when he reacts to his scorn or malevolence?
>
> (Benedict 1946: 145–6)

The same grouping together of repayments for favors and gifts with those for insults and injuries is reported among the Kabyle of North Africa by Bourdieu (1980: 190–2) and includes in their case an imperative to reacquire any ancestral lands that have been sold because of economic hardship.

Max Weber's name is perhaps most commonly associated with the thesis that a secular ethic, which he called 'the spirit of capitalism,' was a product of an ethic that first developed among Protestant sects in Northern Europe in the sixteenth and seventeenth centuries. The uniqueness of the phenomena and significance of the connection that Weber claimed to have found have both been intensely disputed, but the existence of certain widely shared attitudes is not in dispute. Weber found his paradigm of the spirit of capitalism in Benjamin Franklin, whose moral attitudes were carefully weighed against their effects on his ability to prosper materially. 'Honesty is useful, because it assures credit; so are punctuality, industry, frugality, and that is the reason they are virtues.' According to Weber:

> the *summum bonum* of this ethic [is] the earning of more and more money, combined with the strict avoidance of all spontaneous enjoyment of life ... [and this] is thought of so purely as an end in itself, that from the point of view of the happiness of, or utility to, the single individual, it appears entirely transcendental and absolutely irrational.
>
> (1930: 52–3)

Like the revenge ethic, this set of attitudes toward what is good and how and why to behave has been shared by neighbors and family members in significant segments of societies in a variety of places.

What Weber claimed to be the historical root of this ethic – having similar features but with significant religious elements – appears among early modern Protestants, who believed that God could call men to all manner of mundane occupations and that economic prosperity was a sign of being in a state of grace. Maintaining that state, however, required that one not allow business to acquire overriding importance in one's life: Reformation culture emphasized the biblical parable of the nobleman who, having left money with his servants, rewarded those who had multiplied their deposits by trading and reprimanded the one who had managed only to keep his deposit secure.[1] This was interpreted to mean that all people should see their roles as productive stewards, neither attached to nor enjoying what God had placed in their trust. Weber quotes from a seventeenth-century Puritan, Richard Baxter:

> If God shows you a way in which you may lawfully get more than in another way (without wrong to your soul or to any other), if you refuse this, and choose the less gainful way, you cross one of the ends of your calling, and you refuse to be God's steward and to

accept His gifts and use them for Him when he requireth it: you
may labour to be rich for God, though not for the flesh and sin.

(ibid.: 162)

What God gives in trust is, however, not to be used for oneself, above all
not for spontaneous enjoyment. Wealth is to be increased but not used to
live a care-free life. Sports, entertainments, amusements, idle conversation, earthly vanities are to be eschewed as distracting and unproductive.
Under such constraints, material gain could only, once the means of life
and necessary operating expenditures had been met, be devoted to generating more gain, consumed only in further investment. This concrete
morality, which Weber contends would have struck earlier cultures as
bizarre, developed first among small tradesmen, who amassed only modest
fortunes. It nevertheless served as a cultural environment in which the
spirit of capitalism could flourish and, when the technology became available, provided – this is the disputed part of Weber's claim – a *sine qua
non* of the Industrial Revolution.

These examples are enough to illustrate the idea we are trying to capture
with the term 'concrete morality.' The account given above identifies crucial
features of what morality as a social phenomenon involves. Until we take
up some problem cases (see Section 2.3) and consider what role the concept
of validity needs to play, let us refer to phenomena with these features as
'climates of attitude.' The phrase 'climate of attitude' may be regarded as
short for 'causally efficacious climate of attitudes of approval and disapproval.' 'Causally efficacious' means that individuals' awareness of what
people around them will approve, tolerate or condemn has some effect on
their conduct. Although the usual effect is to encourage conduct that is
approved and discourage what is condemned, these effects are not necessary. Knowledge of other people's attitudes may simply encourage
individuals to exaggerate their claims to be doing what is approved and
to take steps to avoid being observed doing what is condemned.

2.2 Psychological foundations and mechanisms of reproduction

Guilt and shame, ritual and myth

It is not difficult to appreciate why people should be sensitive (and find
it important to respond in some appropriate way) to what they perceive
to be the climate of attitude around them. People's attitudes serve as guidance to successful social interactions as well as warning signs. Approval
of one's actions makes one welcome and more likely to receive help; disapproval may be followed by unwelcome consequences, ranging from
withholding co-operation to physical violence. People who disapprove of

certain conduct will, even if they do not persecute offenders themselves, tend to approve when sanctions are applied to prevent or punish that sort of behavior. Apart from the fact that other people can make life physically uncomfortable for individuals who do what is condemned and fail to do what is expected, human beings have deep-seated needs to feel that they are accepted and approved by at least some of their fellow human beings. Even where doing what is disapproved of entails no physical discomforts, most people will avoid doing (or being seen to do) such things simply because it is uncomfortable to feel that other people disapprove.

The desire to be accepted (the more warmly accepted the better) and to avoid being shunned or driven away from the society of other people is very powerful. Individuals' sense of their own worth depends in important ways on how they believe other people regard them. People who are confident of the association, respect, admiration and (on occasion) praise of other people will have a sense of their worth that is sometimes called '(high) self-esteem.' Praise and other signs of respect and admiration will generate feelings of pride. Experiences that tend to undermine self-esteem – being treated with contempt, shunned, ridiculed, reviled – are commonly accompanied by feelings of shame. Expectations that people will respond either with ridicule or contempt are attached to various ways of acting, and the feelings of shame that are generated by these responses are often felt by people when they are acting in this way, even though no one is present to witness them. They may even experience the feeling of shame from no more than contemplating action of a sort they know will be greeted with contempt.

Contempt is not the only form of rejection that people may experience. The feeling that one has done something that if discovered would earn the reproach, hostility or anger of others is known as guilt (self-reproach). Anger normally involves the desire to see its object suffer in some way that goes beyond being made to feel small or ridiculous. Hostility will likewise give rise to efforts to inflict suffering, if only in order to drive the object of this attitude away. Reproach, rebuke and blame serve to warn people that their actions are tending to elicit hostility or anger, that they deserve (or are close to deserving) being made to suffer for their conduct. Guilt, like shame, may be felt by people whose misdeeds are not known to other people.

Individuals who are in this way sensitive to other people's attitudes toward conduct, whose anticipations of either contempt or reproach bring about conformity, are said to have internalized those attitudes. A sign that people treat a custom as having validity is that they have internalized the attitudes of reproach and contempt and feel either guilt or shame. Otherwise, their anticipations of rebuke or ridicule from others will elicit indifference, resentful fear, or defiance.

Blame and guilt (or self-reproach) are, according to Williams (see Section 1.1) the characteristic reactions of the morality system – the responses to failures to fulfill one's obligations. One aspect of the ethical life that the morality system tends to overlook is the importance of contempt and shame – responses to failures to live up to expectations. Weber (1978: 31) held that customs had validity or legitimacy to the extent that people accepted them as obligatory (*verbindlich*) or exemplary (*vorbildlich*). To accept something as obligatory is to believe that one is bound or tied by that thing. To accept something as exemplary is to treat it as something one should try to approximate, imitate or emulate. Someone whose efforts to follow what is exemplary are pathetic will be held in contempt; people who hold themselves to higher than minimal standards – who want to excel – may feel shame even when no one else is inclined to hold them in contempt.

The ethical life, moreover, is by no means entirely a matter of living so as to avoid the external sanctions of contempt and reproach and the internal sanctions of shame and guilt. Exemplars offer people something to live up to and afford them both the satisfaction of achievement and the means of assessing their efforts. Obligations may bind, but they also indicate to people, who want, more often than not, to do their part and give what is due from them. Thus the vocabulary of duty interlocks with and reinforces that of obligation.

There is a positive side to internalizing a climate of attitude that needs to be stressed. The central Sanskrit ethical term, *dharma*, which in many contexts is translated 'duty', has no corresponding etymology that suggests something is 'owed.' The root verb, *dhṛ*, means to hold on to or to carry, and the noun may be applied to anything concrete or abstract that is capable of being carried – but not necessarily in the sense of a burden. One may carry a thing for guidance, for comfort, for reassurance. Another meaning of *dharma* is doctrine or teaching, what one is given by a teacher to be held on to. In Buddhism, the Buddha's teaching, the *dharma*, affords a refuge – the Sanskrit root of the word for 'refuge' suggests a source of help, preservation or a safe place in which to reside (Saddhatissa 1970: 35, 42–3). A concrete morality is more often a source of comfort and guidance than an imposition or a burden – something that is held on to by people as much as it holds them.

How individuals acquire a sense of the climate of attitude around them is not as easy to understand as one might at first expect. People do from time to time openly express their approval and disapproval either directly to individuals behaving in the manner in question or indirectly to third parties by way of commentary, and people learn about the prevailing climate of attitude from seeing how others are regarded as well as from experiencing the approval and disapproval of others. But this appears not to happen often enough to account for the full complexity of the sense that people have of this climate – just as direct and indirect correction of children's speech patterns, although common, is hardly enough to account for their evident mastery of the grammatical complexities of their native language or dialect.

A great deal of the mastery of the climate of attitude in one's social environment must rely on assuming that what people are observed to do meets with general approval, just as what they are heard to say conforms to how they regard it as proper to speak. How individuals internalize knowledge of the principles of the climate of attitude around them, as distinct from internalizing the attitudes themselves, is an aspect of a general problem encountered elsewhere, that of understanding how people extract general concepts, rules or principles from their experience of particulars.

The two, internalization of knowledge and internalization of attitude, however, do not commonly occur separately; if a person knows a climate of attitude but does not share it, it is because the attitudes of others conflict with attitudes which that person acquired from somewhere else. This happens, for example, when young people who have been brought up in a distinct subculture, say of immigrants or religious dissenters, are exposed to the wider culture around them.

Since climates of attitude are shared forms of habitual or customary response and hence are aspects of a culture or subculture (Section 1.2), the process by which attitudes are recognized and internalized is an aspect of the phenomenon known as cultural reproduction. Cultures change over time, some radically, some hardly at all, but where there are similarities in the cultures of a biologically continuous population at different times, a transmission from the older to the younger generation is assumed to have taken place. The population has reproduced itself culturally as well as biologically.

Apart from pointing again to the fact that human beings have a strong tendency to acquire the habits of behavior and attitude of those around them, not much can be said to clarify the process of cultural reproduction, except to point out some of the less obvious features of the cultural environment that embody the principles that younger members of a population must internalize for cultural reproduction to take place. We have already noted some of the obvious features: expressions of approval and disapproval directed at individuals or at third parties in the course of casual conversation or gossip. Students of social phenomena also stress the extent to which information about cultural attitudes is found encoded in rituals and in oral and written narratives such as myths. A Sri Lankan scholar offers this personal testimony to the importance of both of these: 'We participated in Buddhist rituals and ceremonies . . . and listened to many, many Buddhist stories. That is how we learned to be Buddhists' (Obeyesekere 1991: x).

Myths and other narratives often identify certain characters who are worthy of admiration and imitation, while other characters represent traits that are disapproved of or condemned. Where the guidance embodied in a story is this obvious, it constitutes an extension of the phenomenon of gossiping about third parties, an extension that is less constrained by reality and hence more readily admits elements of the magical and fantastic. A character held up to Hindus as the ideal of womanhood is Sita, the wife of Rama:

> From earliest childhood, a Hindu has heard Sita's legend recounted on any number of sacral and secular occasions; seen the central episodes enacted in folk plays like the *Ram Lila*; heard her qualities extolled in devotional songs; and absorbed the ideal feminine identity she incorporates through the many everyday metaphors and similes that are associated with her name. Thus, 'She is as pure as Sita' denotes chastity in a woman, and 'She is a second Sita,' the appreciation of a woman's uncomplaining self-sacrifice. If, as Jerome Bruner remarks, 'In the mythologically instructed community there is a corpus of images and models that provide the pattern to which the individual may aspire, a range of metaphoric identity,' then this range, in the case of a Hindu woman, is condensed in one model. And she is Sita.
>
> (Kakar 1978: 64)[2]

Sita endures not only an ordeal by fire to prove her innocence and purity following a kidnapping episode but also repeated bouts of mistrust and jealousy from a husband who, although a god-like hero, is prone to take gossip seriously and to conform readily 'both to his parents' wishes and to social opinion. These expectations, too, an Indian girl incorporates gradually into her inner world' (*ibid.*: 66).

Myths, however, do not always encode information in a straightforward way. Folklore gathered from around the world, as well as from ancient traditions, commonly tells stories of gratuitous violence and brutality (not infrequently involving rape and sodomy, incest and the cannibalism of close relatives), where any apparent 'moral to the story' is not likely to strike members of our culture as particularly edifying. But, as Robert Darnton explains, comparative folklorists 'do not expect to find direct social comment or metaphysical allegories so much as a tone of discourse or a cultural style, which communicates a particular ethos and a world view' (1985: 23).[3]

Darnton applies his own knowledge of French social history to the folklore collected from seventeenth- and eighteenth-century Europe and offers some generalizations about the 'characteristics, overarching themes, and pervasive elements of style and tone' (26) of French folk tales, whose 'elements stand out as distinctly as the garlic and mustard in a French salad dressing' (24).

Without preaching or drawing morals, French folktales demonstrate that the world is harsh and dangerous ... They show that
generosity, honesty, and courage win rewards. But they do not
inspire much confidence in the effectiveness of loving enemies
and turning the other cheek. Instead, they demonstrate that laud-
able as it may be to share your bread with beggars, you cannot
trust everyone you meet along the road.

(59)

As no discernible morality governs the world in general, good
behavior does not determine success in the village or on the road,
at least not in the French tales, where cunning takes the place of
the pietism in the German.

(60)

The trickster heroes stand out against a negative ideal, the numb-
skull. In the English tales, Simple Simon provides a good deal of
innocent amusement. In the German Hans Dumm is a likeable
lout, who comes out on top by good-natured bumbling and help
from magic auxiliaries. The French tales show no sympathy for
village idiots or for stupidity in any form, including that of the
wolves and ogres who fail to eat their victims on the spot.

(62)

Drawing conclusions about a climate of attitude from a body of narratives
that represents a culture is sometimes a far from straightforward matter.

This is perhaps even more true of ritual or ceremonial practices. Many
activities that humans engage in (alone or together) involve significant
portions that are structured sequentially in advance like a narrative. (In
stories, one thing is told after another, even when the episodes are not
told in the same order they have in the plot; in ritualized ceremonies, the
actions of some individuals take place simultaneously, but there is a recognized place in a sequential order for each constituent action.) The function
of ritual, according to one student of religious practices, is 'first and fore-
most, a mode of paying attention ... A ritual object or action becomes
sacred by having attention focused on it in a highly marked way.'[4]

Donald Swearer offers an important type of Buddhist ritual, consecrating
an image of the Buddha, as an illustration of this claim. The all-night
ceremonies in northern Thailand that Swearer studied not only serve to concentrate attention on a material object, thereby effecting its transition to
a living representation of the historical figure who serves as the supreme
moral exemplar in this culture, but also offer an occasion to rehearse important narratives as the image is instructed ('trained') in the life of the person
it is to represent. 'Coincidentally, of course, the assembled congregants have

also been "trained" ' (Swearer 1995: 275). In the course of the ceremony, some participants rehearse roles they are expected to perform every day in rural Thai society. Monks 'renowned for their attainment of extraordinary power associated with trance states' are invited to meditate (274); 'sweetened rice is cooked in the early morning hours over a wood fire stirred by young, prepubescent girls and then divided into forty-nine bowls symbolizing the seven days the Buddha spent at each of seven sites after his enlightenment' (275–6).

The attitudes embodied in venerating a man who achieved perfect detachment from the world provide a striking contrast to the exemplars of ruthless cunning that Darnton finds in French folklore. Whereas 'good behavior does not determine success in the village or on the road, at least not in the French tales,' a significant portion of the narratives recited in the consecration ceremony are devoted to the Buddha's defeat of the forces of Māra, who, in the text Swearer translates, confront the Buddha in a 'procession eighty-five miles in length and breadth and sixty-three miles in height':

> Then by their magical powers Māra's army assumed awesome forms that aroused great fear. They carried spears and swords, bows and arrows, and raised a deafening cry. They surrounded the Great Being and then launched their attack, but no harm came to the Blessed One due to his great merit.
>
> (276–7)

Northern Thai customs thus offer (280) an illustration from a different, albeit Theravādan, Buddhist culture to that of Obeyesekere's testimony above, to the 'immediacy, concreteness and ethical saliency' that ritual and story give to 'the abstractions of Buddhist doctrine.'

But where aspects of a climate of attitude may be gleaned from literary and ritual traditions that highlight and focus attention on ideals and exemplars, as well as from observing explicit expressions of approval and disapproval, there are aspects of such climates that are conveyed in other fashions. Laughter accompanies some of the mechanisms of cultural reproduction across the whole spectrum from explicit to implicit. Derisive laughter and ridicule are direct ways of expressing disapproval; jokes and humorous anecdotes are part of folklore that embody a range of attitudes toward actual and potential ways of behaving. Ribald humor (and forms that are sometimes labeled 'sick') serve to both communicate attitudes and vent anxieties.

Some matters, 'taboo subjects,'[5] are shrouded in silence – either never openly discussed or spoken of with evident discomfort or embarrassment. This too communicates an attitude; it may indeed focus attention, particularly on matters that people otherwise have reason not to overlook, in a way that is every bit as powerful as ritual. It is important to appreciate how attitudes toward something are shaped when the matter cannot be discussed in 'polite society,' is greeted with embarrassment within the family circle and is the subject of 'off-color' jokes within circles of gender peers. One effect is to sustain interest in matters that (although not everyone may realize it) serve to encode symbolically anxieties or obsessions.

Apart from intensifying anxieties and obsessions, another likely consequence is confusion. An illustration of how a code of silence can foster false assumptions about what attitudes actually constitute a prevailing climate appears in Kristen Luker's discussion of why the US Supreme Court decision legalizing abortion (Roe vs Wade 1973) came as a shock to many Catholics, who had regarded abortion as abhorrent. They assumed that everyone felt about abortion as they did:

> In particular, they interpreted the relative social invisibility of abortion prior to the 1960s as proof that their opinion was the common one. And in a way, their assumption was plausible. If people didn't talk about abortion very much (or talked about it only in hushed tones in back rooms), wasn't that because most people believed it was the taking of an innocent life, hence morally repugnant? What these early pro-life activists did not understand was that for many people abortion was 'unspeakable' not because it represented the death of a child but because it represented 'getting caught' in the consequences of sexuality. Sex, not abortion, was what people didn't talk about.
>
> (Luker 1984: 128–9)

To point out the consequences of a climate in which there is disapproval of talking about something is not necessarily to approve of speaking openly. There are also consequences of discussing matters openly, not all of which may be salutary. The important point here is that information about what a climate of attitude is may be contained in a variety of forms, ranging from explicit to implicit. The latter, however, entail risks of misunderstanding as well as the failure to reproduce a climate of attitude, because one set of attitudes may under the cover of silence simply replace another without anyone noticing.

2.3   Manners and morals

Etiquette, diet and fashion as moral phenomena

We have approached the notion of a concrete morality, what people live by rather than norms and ideals to which they merely pay lip service, via a version of Weber's notion of 'convention' – a version that leaves the notion of validity to one side and focuses on 'causally efficacious climates of attitudes of approval and disapproval.' A quick survey of what counts as a climate of attitude will reveal instances that people might hesitate to count as having anything to do with morality, particularly if they are accustomed to thinking within the framework provided by the 'morality system' (see Section 1.1). These instances fall into the categories of fashion (ways of dressing), etiquette (ways of interacting with people), diet (what is eaten), taste (what one enjoys), and even ways of speaking and writing.

There are groups of people where a preoccupation with fashion leads to approval or condemnation of certain ways of dressing, and as a consequence of these attitudes being recognized, some ways of dressing are reinforced and others discouraged. The same applies to the observance of some social rituals, for example those associated with dining. Poor table manners are frowned on, and the effect is to discourage some forms of behavior and reinforce others. Neither of these phenomena seems to fit comfortably under the notion of a 'concrete morality.' It is not that people do not live, or at least allow their conduct to be influenced, by these attitudes; it is rather that such matters do not appear to fall within the sphere of what is thought of as 'moral concerns.'

What people eat as well as how they eat is subject to climates of attitude that encourage individuals to eat or be seen eating what is known to be approved, attitudes that often last longer than mere fashion. That something is not eaten – even where there is a palpable climate of disgust at the thought of eating such a thing – may be nothing more than a cultural prejudice. Westerners recoil at reports that people in the Far East eat dog meat. The British find the thought of eating horse meat distasteful, and the attitude is one more difference that separates them culturally from the French, who raise horses for meat. At the same time, we recognize that some dietary taboos (pig meat for Jews and Muslims) unquestionably belong to their concrete moralities.

If we accept that a concrete morality may include food taboos, a little reflection will reveal that how one dresses is not entirely outside the sphere of what we regard as morality. Breaking the custom of keeping certain parts of the body covered in public will result not only in very severe disapproval but also likely interference from those charged with 'maintaining public decency.' Questions of where a hemline should fall or how much cleavage to display provoke from time to time conflicts with evident moral overtones. There are societies with notions of decency in dress more restrictive than ours (e.g. for women in many Islamic countries); others have been far less restrictive (e.g. the tolerance of male nudity when exercising in ancient Greece, which scandalized neighboring peoples – see Plato's *Republic*: 452c). These customs (both conventions and laws in Weber's sense) clearly fall under that part of a culture that constitutes its concrete morality.

Not knowing which fork to use may not be a moral failing, but manners at the table and elsewhere are ways of expressing consideration (or lack of it) for other people present. Someone whose lack of consideration for others manifests itself in extreme ill manners may come under what is clearly a species of moral condemnation. In some societies, notably those with a strong Confucian tradition, a great deal of social interaction is structured by ritual forms (governing etiquette, dress and a great deal more), forms that are treated with such respect that not to observe them is regarded as a serious moral failing. Confucians treat as morals what strike others as matters of mere etiquette. Strict Muslims insist that women keep their heads (and in some countries their faces) covered and allow a man up to four wives; North Atlantic societies forbid polygamy and regard head coverings as strictly a matter of fashion. Hindus regard the cow as sacred and will not injure it, let alone eat it; Americans treat ground beef as a commodity to be marketed around the world with something close to missionary zeal.

If concern with dress, diet and etiquette appeared initially to be distinct from moral concerns, further thought has revealed that they sometimes overlap, even in our own culture. What marks the difference? What is it that distinguishes a moral from a non-moral attitude? When does a concern with something count as a moral concern? It may well be that nothing useful can be said in response to these questions. Max Weber was of the opinion that sociology could not generalize about this matter:

> From a sociological point of view an 'ethical' standard is one to which men attribute a certain type of value and which by virtue of this belief, they treat as a valid norm governing their action. ... Whether a belief in the validity of an order as such, which is current in a social group, is to be regarded as belonging to the realm of 'ethics' or is a mere convention or a mere legal norm, cannot, for sociological purposes, be decided in general terms. It must be treated as relative to the conception of what values are treated as 'ethical' in the social group in question. What these are is, in the relevant respect, not subject to generalization.
>
> (1978: 36)

Weber seems to assume that even if he cannot say in advance what it is that constitutes a value as 'ethical,' he can nevertheless recognize one when he encounters it. Can we say nothing in general about the type of value that gives validity to a custom of dress or diet, even if what is accorded this value varies from culture to culture?

The reluctance of a Western gentile to partake of a plate of stir-fried dog meat and that of an observant Jew faced with a plate of stir-fried pig meat clearly do not have the same significance. The first is the product of a distaste that arises from unfamiliarity and differs little from the distaste that children commonly have for unfamiliar food. It has nothing one might be tempted to call 'validity'; there is no sense in which eating the dog meat would be a mistake. The second reluctance persists, even if the plate seems appetizing, as it would be a mistake for an observant Jew to partake. The observant Jew accords a validity to this reluctance that is tied to Jewish cultural identity and is underwritten by what is believed to be the will of God.

It is possible to make mistakes about fashion and etiquette – advice can be sought and experts relied upon for guidance – but the validity of the advice extends no further than the fact that this is what people will accept or reject, approve or condemn. People may follow the customs because this way of dressing is 'in fashion' or this way of behaving is 'good manners,' but they are 'in fashion' or 'good manners' for no other reason than that people follow them. By contrast, the Confucian's attention to ritual detail in matters of dress and conduct is underwritten by authoritative texts set down long ago by individuals who are believed to have been exceptionally wise. The validity that raises a convention to the level of the ethical life seems to need a source beyond the mere thought that 'this is what people around me expect.' At the very least, there has to be some possible reason for assigning importance to doing what people around one expect. This may arise from no more than an inability to think outside the framework constituted by what is expected of one – a failure in effect to grasp or apply the concept of a mere fashion or mere matter of etiquette. But it commonly involves the thought that the reason for conforming lies in a source – nature, God, exceptionally wise human beings – that cannot be challenged.

There are thus, embedded in various cultural traditions, answers, both implicit and explicit, to the question, 'what basis is there for approving or condemning the conduct of other people?' In the next chapter, we will survey and catalogue some of these answers, but something further needs to be said in this section about the type of value that gives ethical validity to a custom. Even where one might reject the basis of their practice offered by participants in a concrete morality, because one conceives nature differently or does not accept the religious faith invoked or rejects the authority of the founders of its tradition, one can nevertheless recognize the function performed by the climate of attitudes that constitutes it as a concrete morality. For certain customs structure a society in ways that, if taken away, threaten to leave its members feeling lost, disoriented and unable to find their way around their social environment.[6]

An individual's social environment is structured by the attitudes and expectations of other people – individuals who do not recognize and render what is due from them as 'their part' in the constitution of that environment are marginalized and find themselves subjected to discomforts ranging from neglect to physical abuse. Here we find concrete instances of the abstract obligations to which the 'morality system' (see Section 1.1) reduces the ethical life. But we also find the sources of people's goals and aspirations, their sense of what it is for them or others to do well or badly, as well as the well-springs of their admiration and contempt for various individuals around them.

Accepting the expectations that tie one into a social network gives an individual a place in the social environment and allows other people to identify who a person is. Shared sets of expectations of this kind constitute the social roles that shape interactions between individuals who stand in lifelong relations (male to female, parent to child, sibling to sibling), or in transitory relations (buyer and seller, team-mates, fellow jurors) as well as relations that may vary in length (superior and inferior, business partners, friends). Roles are key components of the structure of the social environment, and each is circumscribed by behavior that is customary for that role.

Females may not only have to dress and conduct themselves in certain ways to distinguish them from males but they may also be expected to use distinctive forms of speech, or be assigned a different diet. Social class, status or caste is also marked by forms of speech, diet, dress and etiquette – the caste system in India is sustained by a bewildering complexity of all of these kinds of custom. If how one speaks and what one eats or wears does not set one above or below others, it can still set one apart – as does the diet and head covering of the observant Jew and the speech and dress of the Amish – and serve to mark one's identity as a member of a subculture.

The intensity with which people insist on a custom being observed is a measure of the centrality of the distinctions and relations that these serve to mark. A woman who is offered no way of assessing herself as a woman except by the size of her feet will ensure the place of her daughter in society by restricting the development of the girl's feet. A person who measures social standing by some possession or privilege may display intense hostility toward any move that might result in the loss of these and the resulting shame associated with loss of standing. People who rely on one another to perform some service or to keep a trust will be critical of those on whom they feel they cannot rely to perform in the required roles, whether the roles be permanently assigned or temporarily adopted. The more that is at stake, the more likely it is that the pattern of behavior assigned to a role will qualify as part of the concrete morality of a group of people. How much is at stake in the observance of any custom varies from society to society.

2.4   Law and morality

Rough music and rough handling

Recall that for Weber customs that count as 'conventions' are regarded as possessing 'validity' and are reinforced by expressions of approval (for keeping them) and disapproval (for breaking them). Expressions of dis-approval may involve spontaneous violence. In the south of India until the mid-nineteenth century, untouchables (men and women alike) were forbidden to wear clothes above the waist, and well into this century an untouchable man risked a beating for wearing a jacket (O'Malley 1932: 149). Unless the enforcement of these customs rests in the hands of some recognized group of people, however, these are still in Weber's terms matters of convention rather than law. All over India, on the other hand, there are caste councils that see to the enforcement of customs within castes and that may penalize or excommunicate offenders (*ibid.*: chapter II; Hutton 1963: chapter VI), and this qualifies a caste's own customs as law in Weber's sense. But these councils are largely autonomous, and if members of one caste (Rajputs) spontaneously (even if violently) prevent members of another caste (Chamars) doing what their own (Chamar) customs do not forbid, but which the former see as their privilege (wearing gold ornaments; *ibid.*: 85–6), the privilege is not a matter of law in Weber's terms.

Even an informal power structure that organizes or carries out measures, either violent or non-violent, to enforce a custom is enough to qualify the custom in Weber's terms as a 'law' (*Recht*). Until the nineteenth century in European societies, neighbors took it upon themselves to enforce domestic peace on households where disharmony reached the point that quarrels came to public notice. In colonial New England, 'Quarreling couples were subject to gossip, and, when this did not bring peace to the household, they were visited with ritual shaming in the form of the chari-vari, which in the Anglo-American world was known variously as "rough music," "shivaree," or "skimmingtons"' (Gillis 1996: 142). It was not uncommon for village elders to arrange for 'rough music' – a parade in front of the offending household, including beating on pans and blowing horns, effigies and crude parodies – and leave it to the young people to carry it out (Gillis 1985: 76–81). Behavioral expectations enforced by groups whose recognized role is to authorize and orchestrate sanctions, whether of shame or violence, count as matters of law in Weber's sense.[7]

The unfamiliarity of the notion of 'law' that appears here was noted in Section 2.1, as well as the special connection of the German word that it translates to the application of coercion. To count as law in Weber's sense, there do not have to be written statutes or ways of settling disputes based on recorded precedent or even much in the way of recognized forms of procedure. There have been and still are societies without written laws but which nevertheless had recognized authorities to whom individuals or households could appeal if their neighbors were treating them badly or encroaching on what they regarded as properly their own. The appeal would commonly be to a shared sense of what is fair and proper but, because custom provides the shape to what a society will think of as fair or proper, the appeal could simultaneously be to the customary ways of the society.

In ancient Greece, improper behavior was said to be contrary to *nomos* (custom; plural, *nomoi*), and allegations of such behavior were subject to scrutiny in public hearings and, if substantiated, the behavior subject to publicly organized sanctions. In time, what constituted an offence against the *nomoi* was fixed by codification and recorded precedent, and as a result the word *nomos* is usually translated 'law.' But there are earlier contexts where to think in terms of the institutions we associate with the word 'law' would be very misleading. In one of Plato's dialogues (set in the late fifth century BCE), a character named Pausanias claims that *nomos* approves the otherwise unseemly behavior of a lovesick older man camped out on the doorstep of an attractive boy (*Symposium*: 183ab). Even if this claim about the social tolerance of an erotic subculture is exaggerated (Dover 1974: 215), to translate this as 'law' rather than 'custom' (as an indication of public approval) risks prompting the bizarre image of the Athenian assembly passing an ordinance expressing approval of the erotic pursuit of boys by older men. In any case, there is hardly any written law and very little deliberate law making at this stage in Athenian history.

Although Weber's concept requires little that is found in modern institutions of law, his distinction between convention and law is important because it marks out two importantly different questions about someone's conduct. It is one thing to disapprove of a pattern of behavior and another to adopt institutionalized means (or to approve of adopting such means) to try to modify that behavior. Normally, a group of people who recognize their mutual disapproval of something will, if individuals in their midst persist in defiance, resort to organizing coercive measures. But as the institutions for organizing and applying coercion come to be placed in the hands of specialists, and recognized procedures are adopted for determining what is to count as an occasion for the application of coercion, the distance between the questions 'do we disapprove of this?' and 'is anything to be done about it?' becomes more perceptible.

In analysing what constitutes 'law' in the sense of judicial institutions such as we have, H.L.A. Hart has argued (1961: 6–7, 77) that an apparatus for enforcement is not essential. What is essential is an operative distinction between two kinds of rule, the first governing how people are to conduct themselves, the other governing the determination of law, 'law finding', in two senses. One sense involves determining what are the rules of the first kind, including when 'law making' or legislation has been properly carried out; the other is determining when the laws of the first kind have been broken and when prescribed punishments are properly visited on wrongdoers. Hart denies that enforcement is essential to the concept of 'law' that he is defining, because some laws provide individuals with facilities (create legal rights and powers) rather than impose duties (27).

But no rights or powers have legal effect unless coercive force can be applied against attempts to deny the rights or thwart the powers. Even in societies without public institutions of enforcement (e.g. Northern Europe in the early Middle Ages) the judgment of a law court in favor of plaintiffs was an authorization for the plaintiffs to resort to 'self-help,' i.e. for them to try to enforce the decision on their own behalf.

Hart's concept of law is not easily applied to illiterate societies or to societies that do not have self-conscious constitutional traditions (written or otherwise), but it does identify important central components of developed legal systems and makes clear how there can be customs that are legally valid but that have no ethical validity, and *vice versa*. For Hart's rules of the second kind (roughly, the rules explicit or implicit that make up the constitutional tradition of the society) may determine that a rule of the first kind is valid. But what makes it valid – being, for example, a statute passed by two houses of a legislature and 'signed into law' by the chief executive officer – may bypass altogether the consensus of public opinion. Legislators frequently enact laws for the sake of expediency (often for even less worthy motives), which few ordinary people regard as having any validity, although the same people will accept that it is valid to enforce it.

As a result, people may not accord statutes the same degree of validity that they are prepared to recognize in a convention that no one troubles to enforce. Occasionally, even those who enforce the law do so with the feeling that the law they are enforcing lacks that non-legal kind of validity that is sometimes spoken of as 'moral' or 'ethical.' Thus a judge carrying out what is prescribed by law may sentence a doctor who has helped a terminally ill patient to commit suicide, while personally feeling that this should not be a criminal offence; and police may seize commodities that are illegal, but which they personally feel people should be entitled to buy and sell (e.g. 'soft' drugs or pornography). However, law and the prevailing concrete morality do frequently coincide. There may be a degree of popular sympathy in our society for felons convicted of tax evasion, but there is widespread loathing of people convicted in the courts of child abuse.

Indeed, historically the institutions and procedures that embody law and legality are responses that have grown out of attempts to make prevailing climates of attitude more determinate, more salient and more difficult to resist. Even where people recognize that legal and moral validity may drift apart, the assumption is commonly made that the two should coincide or be made to coincide, because some people rely on the law as a guide and others rely on it to reinforce attitudes and conduct they think should prevail. Arguments in favor of making something illegal include the claim that doing so 'will send a clear signal that society does not approve' of it. Resistance to legalizing divorce or abortion in a Catholic country like Ireland or the smoking of marijuana in the United States comes from the fear that doing so will undermine the attitude that these should not be condoned.

Nevertheless, it is common to insist that law and morality are, and ought not to be regarded as anything other than, distinct.[8] The point of insisting on this becomes clear once it has been appreciated to what extent the interpretation and application of the law is not cut and dried – even within legal institutions with as much written statute and recorded precedent as ours. Problematic cases arise where it is not clear whether the accused has disobeyed the law or violated someone's rights; sometimes applying existing statute and precedent to a case generates an outcome that would appear to be a travesty of justice. In these circumstances, it might be tempting for judge and jury to convict or acquit on the basis of their sense of prevailing concrete morality. In less complex and record-bound legal systems, after all, decisions of the judicial authorities are accepted because they are taken to represent the best available indication of a shared sense of justice and propriety.

Those who for one reason or another harbor doubts about whether a shared sense of justice and propriety exists, is sufficiently coherent or can be made determinate insist that judges and juries should not allow any sense of morality (their own or what they take to be prevailing in the society around them) to influence their decisions. If the law appears to be generating a miscarriage of justice, then so be it; if the law is unclear and a decision has to be made, it should be acknowledged that the decision was freely made, not constrained either by law or by anyone's moral sense. There are clear advantages to being governed by procedures that exclude the distorting influence of people's sympathies and antipathies. To allow our legal system to respond to these feelings is to defeat its purpose.[9]

It is plausible to argue that to make a complex society possible, institutions have to be established upon rules that regularize procedures, standardize decisions and keep out the influence of idiosyncratic responses. Our legal system includes a hierarchy of courts to hear appeals, as well as recourse to legislative reform if existing laws generate results that enough people feel to be improper. Those whose task it is to make the institution work should allow the institution to handle their misgivings and should not 'take the law into their own hands.' But it is implausible to treat our institutions of law, Ronald Dworkin (1967) argues, as consisting exclusively of rules. There are aspects of our legal institutions that are properly governed by something less precise, which he calls 'principles,' distinguishable from rules, which embody moral values and which judges at the appropriate levels in the legal hierarchy may apply in clarifying what the law is.

Whether one is inclined to side with Hart or with Dworkin on this issue will depend on how one answers the question about the basis that people have for their responses of approval or disapproval, acceptance or condemnation, of the behavior of people around them. Belief in a basis for the validity of at least some of a society's shared attitudes about what behavior should or should not be sanctioned will leave one comfortable with the idea of treating these attitudes as implicit parts of our legal institutions. Doubts about there being any basis (beyond that of a mere fashion) will incline one to insist that moral attitudes be kept out of law altogether.

The second view, however, faces this problem: when judicial decisions clarify or settle indeterminate law by setting binding precedents to be followed, this will have to treated as law making rather than law finding – as there is acknowledged to be no law (embodied in what Dworkin calls principles) to be found. If someone is convicted in a criminal action or ordered to pay damages in a civil action, the law will have been made, *ex post facto*, after the fact of the offence (*ibid.*: 64). Applying sanctions under laws made *ex post facto* is forbidden under Section 9 of Article I of the US Constitution (an example of the second of Hart's two kinds of rule); where there is no clear law, it seems to follow, there can be no conviction or settlement of a civil action by a court.

Even if moral attitudes are kept from having operative influence on, and are treated as belonging outside, our legal institutions, there remain questions about how these attitudes may influence or be reflected in legislation. People, it was noted above, expect law to be at least not badly out of harmony with their moral attitudes, but it was also noted that the questions of whether there is a basis for a climate of attitude toward some conduct and whether there is a basis for the attitude that publicly organized sanctions should be applied to that conduct are distinct. Section 7.4 will look at what basis there may be for the attitude that coercion should be applied to discourage certain kinds of behavior. Here, in light of the phenomena surveyed so far, it will be useful to conclude with a look at the claims advanced by the British law lord Patrick Devlin at the time that Britain was contemplating decriminalizing homosexual acts committed in private between consenting adults.

Lord Devlin replied to the argument that private morality – or as he preferred to describe it, 'private behaviour in matters of morals' (1965: 9) – should not be the concern of the criminal law by insisting on a number of points similar to ones made in this chapter. There is, he claimed, such a thing as public morality, 'ideas a society has about the way its members should behave and govern their lives' (*ibid.*), and this public morality helps to constitute the identity of that society. Some of these attitudes, like some institutions, 'are built into the house in which we live and could not be removed without bringing it down' (*ibid.*). When people perceive a threat to the fabric of the society in which they live, they will not only take steps (resorting to legal coercion, if need be) to preserve that fabric, but they are, Devlin argued, right to do so.

Most of Devlin's claims have been echoed in this chapter, specifically those about the existence of public morality, the centrality of at least some of its features to the cohesiveness of social groups, and the intensity with which people are likely to try to preserve what they perceive as central to their social identities. But whether people might be right to take any given measure to preserve their way of life has been left open, for it cannot be addressed independently of the question we are here taking as central to ethical inquiry: what basis, if any, is there for the attitudes these people share? To say that the basis lies in the fact that these attitudes constitute the unity of these people as a society does not yet explain why no other attitudes might perform this function equally well.

Even if we accept centrality to cohesiveness as an adequate basis for applying coercive measures, there would remain the question of whether these particular attitudes had been correctly identified as indispensable bonds that hold the community together. The question 'What will happen to this society if it gives up this long-held practice, e.g. genital mutilation, which many of its members feel is integral to their life as a people?' is not easy to answer. Reactions to the proposal to give up the practice may suggest that most members of the society feel deep disquiet at the prospect, but they could be wrong about either the centrality of the attitude or practice or about the value of a way of life that relies on that attitude or practice. Their children might look back at the history of their culture and thank their parents or grandparents for giving up the practice – as many Chinese women today are grateful to have been born after the practice of foot binding ended.

Devlin's test for the centrality of an attitude was to consider the strength of feeling of typical members of the society. Expecting that most Britons of his time regarded homosexuality as 'a vice so abominable that its mere presence is an offence' (*ibid.*: 17), he concluded that it would be a mistake to decriminalize the activity (even carried out in private between consenting adults). But intense feelings are not always reliable indicators of the centrality of a practice to the social cohesiveness of a people. It is reasonable that the laws of a nation reflect the values of its people, but laws channel coercive forces, and whatever valid basis there may be for disapproving of something may not be grounds for using coercion to discourage it.

Further reading

Although it dates from the beginning of this century, Westermarck (1906: chapters XIV–XLVI), is still a usefully comprehensive catalogue of disparate moral attitudes and practices. Studies of particular societies and regions have been conducted from a variety of perspectives: Brandt (1954) and Ladd (1957) are studies in the manner of field anthropologists of Native American peoples, Hopi and Navajo, respectively, by Americans of European descent whose profession is philosophy. The team that produced the source book on Hawaiian culture (Pukui *et al.* 1972) included one native Hawaiian as both informant and as a contributing scholar of considerable stature. Danquah (1968: 78–103) and Ackah (1988) are studies of the Akan people of Ghana by European-educated native Africans. Mbiti (1990) is a survey by a similarly educated native African of African traditional concepts and practices in regions where the influence of Islam and Christianity has not been extensive. Hibino (1904) was written as a piece of inspirational literature for Japanese youth, while Benedict (1946) is a by-product of an American academic anthropologist's efforts to make an understanding of Japanese culture available to US military intelligence. Three Indian scholars offer differing perspectives on ethical phenomena in the history and culture of their subcontinent: Sharma (1965) has chapters on component traditions – Jainism, Buddhism, Samkhya, yoga, etc. – as well as modern trends; Maitra (1925) is organized according to Western analytical categories, with chapters on duties, volition, conscience, motives, etc.; Aiyar (1935) considers the development of institutions such as caste, slavery, law, etc. over time. Dover (1974) offers a view of classical Greece which, like that of the medieval Scandinavians in Grönbech (1931), relies on evidence found in the literary remains of the culture. Whatever the validity of the thesis of Weber (1930), it affords a compelling portrait of the ethical phenomena it seeks to explain. Weber (1978) is assembled from several previously published partial translations of his *Wirtschaft und Gesellschaft* (1921). The portion (pp. 29–36, 212–55) used in this and the next chapter is also available in Weber (1964). Taylor (1985) offers detailed philosophical treatment of the concepts of guilt and shame. Hart (1958, 1961), Devlin (1965) and Dworkin (1967) contain more on the issues discussed in Section 2.4.

Notes

1   Luke, Chapter 19: 16. 'Then came the first, saying Lord, thy pound hath gained ten pounds. 17. And he said unto him, Well [done], thou good servant; because thou hast been faithful in a very little, have authority over ten cities. . . . 20. And another came, saying, Lord, behold, *here is* thy pound, which I have kept laid up in a napkin. . . . 24. And he said unto them that stood by, Take from him the pound and *give it* to him that hath ten pounds. . . . 26. For I say unto you, That unto every one which hath shall be given; and from him that hath not, even that he hath shall be taken away from him.' (Wherever there is occasion here to quote the Bible, it will be in the King James version.)

2   The citation of Bruner is from 'Myths and Identity,' *Daedalus*, spring 1959: 357.

3   For 'rape, sodomy, incest and cannibalism', see p. 22. Darnton begins his essay (pp. 17–18) with a common eighteenth-century version of Little Red Riding Hood in which the wolf serves Red Riding Hood a meal consisting of the flesh and blood of her grandmother then orders her to perform a striptease before getting into bed with him, whereupon he eats her. Darnton comments: 'She had done nothing to deserve such a fate; for in the peasant tales, unlike those of Perrault and the Grimms, she did not disobey her mother or fail to read the signs of an implicit moral order written in the world around her. She

simply walked into the jaws of death. It is the inscrutable, inexorable character of the calamity that makes the tales so moving, not the happy endings that they frequently acquired after the eighteenth century' (*ibid*.: p. 60).

4   The thesis about ritual is cited from Jonathan Z. Smith, *To Take Place, Toward Theory in Ritual*, Chicago: University of Chicago Press, 1987: 104–5 in Swearer (1995: 264–5).

5   'Taboo' subjects are any that it is felt improper to discuss. Europeans who first encountered the various Polynesian peoples found elaborate customs that marked the special and sacred nature of numerous things by forbidding certain classes of people to make use of, or even to come into contact with, these things. The phenomenon was so striking that Europeans borrowed the Tongan word *tabu* and have applied it since then wherever they encountered something that a group of people felt strongly should not be done. (Maoris, Samoans and Tahitians use the phonetically related word *tapu* and Hawaiians the word *kapu*). Sexual relations between siblings or between parents and their children are almost universally regarded as abhorrent, and this has become known as the 'incest taboo'. The word 'adult' applied in our society to sexually explicit literature or films is an indirect way of saying that these are taboo to children.

6   The use of the word 'anomy,' or 'anomie,' as a technical term for this phenomenon was established in Durkheim (1897) – from Greek 'a' (lacking) + '*nomos*' (custom/law). For further on *nomos* see the discussion near the beginning of Section 2.4.

7   For a further example that illustrates the temporal and geographical extent of the phenomena as well as the level of violence and kinds of customs that were enforced, see Rossiaud (1985) on the situation in French towns such as Dijon, Arles and Lyon in the period 1440–1490.

8   See, for example, Hart (1958).

9   The issue here will be explored further in Section 6.3.

3

SOURCES OF VALIDITY

> [Xerxes:] For grant your Greeks to be five thousand, we should then outnumber them more than a thousand to one. For, were they under the rule of an emperor according to our ways, they might from fear of him show a valor greater than natural, and under compulsion of the lash might encounter such odds in the field; but neither of these would they do so long as they were free.
>
> [Demaratus:] Free they are, yet not wholly free; for *nomos* is their master, whom they fear much more than your men fear you. Whatever this one [*nomos* = master] commands them, that they do; and the command is always the same, that they must never flee from battle, whatever the odds, but must stay in formation, to conquer or die.
>
> (Herodotus (fifth century BCE); Godely
> 1922: VII 104, 105)

Recapitulation: In the previous chapter, 'climates of attitude' were defined as causally efficacious shared habits of approval and disapproval. We concluded that if a climate of attitude forms (at least some part of) the 'concrete morality' that people live by (participate in), it helps them to constitute their social identities, know what is expected of them in their central social roles and find their places in society. However, we noted that the validity of a concrete morality involves (at least in the minds of those who participate in it) something beyond the thought that 'this is what is (or is not) to be done because people around me approve (or disapprove) of doing it.' Those who participate in a climate of attitude believing that it has no basis other than this are participating in something tantamount to (mere) fashion or (mere) etiquette. The question of what, if any, further basis people might have for approving or disapproving (condoning or condemning) is a question, we have noted, that is proper to ethical inquiry.

Prospectus: The task of this chapter is to survey the sorts of bases that people commonly believe their attitudes, values and norms to have. One way to find out what people take to be the sources of the validity of what they live by is to see what kinds of appeals can be made by those whose authority on how to behave is accepted and followed without threats or coercion. For socio-logical purposes, Weber identified three pure types of authority (*legitime Herrschaft*), the ability to command or direct because the command or direction is accepted as valid (1978: 215): charis-matic, traditional and rational. We will begin by considering the first two of these and will find that these pure types of human authority interact in complex ways with each other, as well as with beliefs about the natural world, to bestow validity on appro-bations, permissions and prohibitions. Weber's thoughts about the third type were tied closely to complex legal and bureaucratic institutions, but a more comprehensive understanding of 'rational' will be used here, and the exploration of this third kind of authority will extend into the next chapter.

3.1 Tradition and charisma

Spartans, Socrates and their nomoi

A custom with a history that spans some period, typically several gener-ations, is known as a tradition, a word that derives from a Latin verb meaning to hand over or convey. If in justifying (saying why one should retain) a practice or attitude, an appeal is made to the fact that it is a tradition, a long-standing custom, this will sound like a claim to little more than the sort of validity that a fashion or a rule of etiquette possesses: this is to be welcomed because people welcome it, or carried out because people carry it out. The appeal to tradition, however, may be seen to have more force than this. That people tend to accord more validity to a custom the longer they believe that custom to have been in force (handed down from their forebears) cannot be dismissed as a benighted response. What has been in effect for a long time is clearly something that people can live with, and it can to some extent be relied upon not to have untoward consequences.

Appeals to tradition may serve to determine forms of rituals to be observed, the procedures and precedents that are to be followed in settling disputes, what powers various individuals or subgroups may exercise and what duties they must perform. A society that looks mainly to what it believes about its past to settle questions about how currently to conduct its affairs, as well as to what to condone or condemn, is known as a 'tradi-tional' society. Traditional societies may constantly draw upon and defer to past practice without placing much stress on the importance of doing so, but those who do (individuals or societies as a whole) are known as 'traditionalists.' Just as not all traditional societies make enough noise about the importance of tradition to qualify as 'traditionalist,' not all traditionalists have the fortune to live in traditional societies. The shrillest traditionalist voices are sometimes heard in societies that have turned their backs on tradition. (Jaroslav Pelikan offered this epigrammatic contrast: 'whereas tradition is the living faith of the dead, traditionalism is the dead faith of the living.'[1])

A traditional society that lacks any form of writing (a purely oral culture) must rely on the memories of its members for its knowledge of what its traditions are. Older members, by virtue of their experience, and those whose role it is to memorize ('oral literature') and memorialize (ritualized celebrations) those traditions, exercise authority based on their special standing as a source of tradition. In societies with only a few literate individuals (primarily oral cultures), the mere fact of being able to read whatever written records there are confers some claim to authority, although ultimately it is custom that determines what records are treated as authoritative sources of tradition and who is qualified to interpret them.

Authority based on tradition occasionally has to compete with authority based on charisma. Charisma is a quality that sets certain individuals apart and enables them to exercise power or leadership over other, more ordinary, people. Usually, charismatic figures have exceptional talents, which enable them to impress their followers by appearing to influence events in miraculous ways. The term may be applied to the effects on people of shamans, healers, prophets, heroes, generals, judges, statesmen or wise men. Viewed from outside a culture, from a 'behaviorist perspective,' charisma may appear to be nothing more than a mysterious charm exerted on people. From this standpoint, we speak of pop stars and political leaders as 'charismatic' while recognizing that their talents may be limited to the ability to entertain or to persuade people to vote for them. By virtue of being able to fascinate or beguile, such individuals acquire trust and devotion.

But charisma, as a technical term for a source of authority in Weber's vocabulary, does not consist simply of possessing a psychological hold over one's followers. It rests rather on the belief that marvelous talents or miraculous feats are signs that a person is somehow especially favored by the powers that govern the world at large. This is reflected in the etymology of the word 'charisma', which is derived from a Greek word meaning 'grace,' 'favor,' 'a free gift'; the term is found in the vocabulary of early Christianity, 'the gift of grace.'[2] Its use by Weber was intended to mark the belief that the marvels witnessed and the charm felt are taken as signs that people are called upon by higher powers (and 'have a duty') to follow the person who performs the marvels or exerts the charm. It thus excludes pop stars unless their cult acquires some form of religious or mystical dimension, and it excludes political leaders unless their policies are believed to be direct expressions of the will of God.

52

Charismatic individuals offer their followers a window through which to glimpse the direction that should be taken to achieve fulfillment, either material or spiritual. Followers believe that by following a charismatic person, they will obtain what they want (health, wealth, success in the hunt, victory in battle) or possibly will understand more clearly what, from the standpoint of the universe at large, they should want, what they should be striving for. A charismatic leader may bring about radical changes in what a group of people approves and condemns as a result of convincing them that their attitudes and practices have hitherto not been properly adjusted to the way the world around them is ordered.

Charismatic figures can thus disrupt tradition and as a result come into conflict with individuals whose authority rests on the belief that, because of their age or special training, they speak for tradition. Charisma and tradition can also complement one another. The latter operates to stabilize the reproduction of a culture; the former introduces variation and allows for flexibility in response to unusual stresses (war, famine, internal strife, etc.). A change in a way of life initiated by charismatic authority will, if it allows a society to cope successfully (win a war, re-establish material prosperity, heal internal divisions), often be made routine in some way and handed on by means of the exercise of traditional authority.

Indeed, tradition often contains elements of charisma that have been either made matters of routine (ceremonies of consulting oracles) or ritualized in some way (ceremonies that confer or transmit charisma, for example by anointing). Institutionalized taboos may serve to create or reinforce the charismatic authority of a leader or of a small ruling class. In pre-contact Hawaiian society, commoners and members of the lesser aristocracy believed that the shadow of a high-ranking chief was taboo – should it fall on them, it would harm them – and correspondingly it was taboo for them to let their shadows touch such a 'sacred' person (Pukui *et al.* 1972, Vol. I: 10). Incest was taboo to all except the highest-ranking families, where it was something of an obligation, as no one of lesser rank could be a suitable mate (*ibid.*, Vol. II: 86). Custom also institutionalized a form of charismatic authority for high-ranking chiefs by granting them the power to create taboos by their own edicts (*ibid.*, Vol. I: 41).

The symbolic transmission of personal charisma to the descendants or chosen successors of a great leader may thus create a position in society that confers despotic authority regardless of whether its occupant has any personal charisma. The passage from Herodotus at the head of this chapter epitomizes a conflict between a society based on the institutionalized charisma of a despotic emperor and a culture that believed that the authority of its traditions was above any living human embodiment. Herodotus records what purports to be a conversation between a deposed king of Sparta, Demaratus, and the Persian king, Xerxes, who having given asylum to Demaratus asks whether the Greeks will resist his plans to conquer them, given that they are vastly outnumbered. Demaratus replies that Greeks serve a master, their *nomoi*, their customs and laws, whom they fear more than a despot such as Xerxes.

Greeks of the classical period (fifth and fourth centuries BCE) applied the word *nomos* (plural *nomoi*) to customs that people strongly disapproved of violating and had (in Weber's sense; see Section 2.4) the force of law – city officials could enforce the observance of such customs. Many Greeks of this period saw themselves as unconditionally bound by the *nomoi* of their cities, and they took pride in their fidelity to their customs. For the most part, these customs were not written down. Athens established a public written record of a core part of its *nomoi*, and insisted that legal proceedings be brought under it, only at the end of the fifth century.

When Demaratus spoke of *nomos* as a master, he was, as a Spartan, no doubt thinking of the rigorous military discipline that dominated the culture of Sparta. At the age of eight, boys[3] were placed in barracks under the supervision of older boys, where they lived an austere existence (long marches, minimum food, beds of rushes) under severe discipline. They became eligible for military service, citizenship and marriage at the age of twenty but continued to live in barracks until the age of thirty; even after that age, when they could live in their own homes, they were required to eat in a common mess with other male citizens.

This regime fostered intense group loyalty, which together with constant drill gave Sparta a formidable infantry for more than three centuries and made many Greeks think first of Sparta when they spoke of living under good customary laws (*eunomia*), i.e. in a well-ordered commonwealth. (The basic features of this concrete morality are found today in many elite military training establishments.) Other Greek city-states left the education of children to their natural parents, but the identity of a city-state was closely tied to its own *nomoi*, and loyalty to one's city was thus intimately bound up with loyalty to its *nomoi*. The *nomoi* of all Greek cities placed its citizens under an obligation to defend the interests of their cities in battle.

It is noteworthy that Demaratus does not use a vocabulary that translates directly into the notion of obligation, although he might well have said that it was *deon* (needful, proper, from a verb meaning 'to bind') to stand and fight. Instead, he uses the image of fearing a master for what was literally an intense reluctance to face being put to shame before one's comrades for breaking the custom that Spartans *never* break ranks. 'Master' (*despotēs*) in Greek is a word that applies to the male head of a household, a patriarch possessing autocratic authority over wife, children and servants.

The *nomoi* of another Greek city, Athens, appear in a similar image in one of the shorter dialogues of Plato, the *Crito* (50a–54e), where Socrates is facing an imposition even more severe than merely being required to fight in defense of his city. He has been tried by his fellow citizens under the *nomoi* of his city and unjustly condemned to death. In discussing whether he should try to escape and evade his sentence, Socrates imagines what the personified *nomoi* of his city would say about his trying to evade even an unjust sentence of death.

If a private citizen can choose to annul a decision reached by the courts, the *nomoi* argue, this 'will destroy us.' To the suggestion that the city has wronged Socrates by condemning him unjustly to death, the *nomoi* reply that Socrates is their creation: his parents were married under the *nomoi*, he was born, nurtured and educated under the *nomoi*; he is (as his ancestors were) the offspring and servant of the *nomoi*.

> And if this is so, do you think that what is right [or 'just', *to dikaion*] as between us rests on a basis of equality, so that whatever we undertake to do to you it is right for you to retaliate? There was no such equality of right between you and your father or your master, if you had one, so that whatever treatment you received you might return it, answering them back if you were reviled, or striking back if you were struck . . . and do you think that it will be proper for you to act in this way toward your fatherland and the *nomoi*, so that if we undertake to destroy you, in the belief that it is right, you will undertake to destroy us, the *nomoi* and your fatherland, so far as you are able, and will say that in doing this you are doing the right thing?
>
> (based on Fowler 1914: 50e–51a)

The personified *nomoi* also appeal to the fact that by remaining in Athens all his life, apart from a period of military service, Socrates has voluntarily undertaken to accept what is imposed on him in accordance with the *nomoi*.

Their most potent argument, however, is that their authority is akin to that of a parent or of the master of a household. If a child is immature, it might be argued that parental authority in such cases has a validity based in nature; for as children are not capable of fully informed independent action, it is right for them to accept direction from their parents. But the notion that grown children should continue to accept the authority of their parents in all matters – or that some people are assigned permanently to the class of slaves and must always accept the authority of their masters – is a matter of custom (and by no means in *all* societies). Such customs may claim to be underwritten by tradition, but not in such a way as to give tradition any independent basis for its authority. It is evidently circular to argue that traditional customs are like parents, and as it is traditional to accept the absolute authority of one's parents it follows that one must accept the authority of tradition.

The *nomoi* of the various Greek city-states were attributed (by tradition) to one or another law giver, e.g. those of Athens to Solon, those of Sparta to Lycurgus. The special wisdom that these law givers were supposed to have – one not sufficiently common in latter days for ordinary mortals to presume to make changes in the *nomoi* – constituted a tradition that in effect assigned charismatic authority to them. Such authority, as we have seen, depends on the belief that it is possible for extraordinary individuals to be in tune with the powers and principles that govern the world and to reveal to the rest of mankind a basis for its attitudes and conduct – a basis that lies in a correct understanding of how the world around us has been ordained and currently operates. Ultimately, the legitimacy of charismatic authority rests on beliefs about nature.

3.2   Nature

Ritual purity, karma *and incest*

'Nature' is a name for the concept that we apply to what we are given in our environment and believe we have to accept and work with, if we are to survive, make our way, achieve our goals. Nature is what we cannot change and hence what we would be foolish to try to change. To the extent that a practice or climate of attitude is in accord with nature, it needs no further justification. Nearly all customs, including those embodying attitudes, values and standards, rest in some measure on beliefs about nature, but none can claim to rest exclusively on what is natural. As it is easy to lose sight of the fact that some of what we take for granted is customary (or 'socially constructed' as it is nowadays fashionable to say), it is correspondingly easy to offer nature as a basis for customs and attitudes even when nature simply cannot provide an adequate basis. To pretend or accept uncritically that a socially constituted arrangement is natural is known as 'naturalizing' that arrangement. Naturalizing is a fallacious way of providing a basis for practices and attitudes and for protecting them from critical scrutiny.

There is a basis in nature – in the nature of what immature humans can and cannot do – for the attitude that small children should obey their parents. The older a child becomes, the less this natural dependency carries any justificatory weight and the more the attitude that offspring should respect or obey their parents requires a different basis if it is to be accorded more than the validity of fashion or etiquette. Aristotle (1254a17–55b39) attempted to naturalize the institution of slavery which prevailed in his society by arguing that some people are by nature incapable of self-government. Even if this were true, there is no basis in nature for an institution whereby those who are capable of self-government should take over the control of those who are not (however one might go about determining the incapacity in question) and use them for their own purposes. (This will be discussed further in Section 7.2.)

Direct experience is by no means the only source of what people believe about the world they live in. A great deal of what they believe rests on the same basis as their customary practices and concrete moralities: they believe something because (1) they have heard it from a person whose words carried conviction (in some cases from an individual with personal or institutionalized charisma); have come to believe it because (2) it was handed down to them from the past (or merely handed over in the form of recent hearsay); or believe it because (3) it is the outcome of a more or less complex thought process that they have gone through known as 'reasoning.'

Beliefs, like practices and attitudes, form more or less systematic cultural complexes – indeed, beliefs, practices and attitudes are more often than not inextricable constituents of a single cultural phenomenon. This is important, because a concrete morality rests in part on beliefs that might conceivably be shown to be false. In other words, it has a basis in (what is believed about) nature, and this basis may prove on closer examination to be totally misconceived. At the same time, the procedures for examining beliefs and possibly loosening the hold that they have on the minds of people are themselves cultural practices. People have to accept the practices of (epistemological) inquiry, which might undermine their beliefs, before these beliefs become vulnerable; if they perceive that such practices of inquiry threaten other practices that structure their lives, they may simply not treat such inquiry seriously.

An important part of the belief system that has long sustained the caste system in India is structured by the familiar concepts of cleaning and cleanliness, and of preventing or removing unwanted contaminants. Many cultures have systems of beliefs about how contamination by dangerous pollutants can be incurred and about the appropriate ways of cleansing the person who becomes polluted in some way. Many of these beliefs and customs do not involve coming into contact with what in 'the modern scientific outlook' are 'natural' substances and do not involve efforts to remove such contaminants by 'natural' processes. As a consequence, these beliefs are commonly spoken of as involving forms of 'ritual pollution,' to be remedied by acts of 'ritual cleansing': the state restored by successful cleansing is known as 'ritual purity.' Concepts of ritual purity cover dietary practices and reproductive phenomena. Some foods are unclean and must never be eaten, e.g. pig meat in the Jewish and Islamic traditions. Menstruating women are regarded as ritually impure in many cultures. Some cultures require ritual purification following sexual intercourse or childbirth.

Hindus who fail to maintain appropriate standards of ritual purity, in particular standards relating to food, are subject to expulsions from their caste – expulsions that in many cases follow formal hearings by a 'caste council.' One can also be 'cast out' for marrying someone of the wrong caste, but it has been suggested by J.H. Hutton that rituals governing not merely what food can be eaten but also how and by whom it may be prepared and served and with whom it may be eaten (commensality) are more central to the caste system than are attitudes toward whom one is permitted to marry (*conubium*):

> It is not uncommon in some parts of India for a man of one caste to keep a concubine of a lower caste, or even a non-Hindu, and he is not outcasted by his caste fellows on that ground, though he may be, and often is, on the ground that he has eaten food cooked or served by her or taken water from her hands.
>
> (1963: 71)[4]

Hutton's point is that being unable to have a woman prepare food for a man because she is of lower caste is by itself a significant barrier to marrying such a woman.

The constraints imposed by what it takes to maintain and restore ritual purity are an integral and long-established aspect of how Hindus conduct their lives. O'Malley cites a case (from 1926) of a student hostel in Allahabad that had to provide thirty-seven kitchens for a hundred students because various higher castes observe 'punctilious exclusiveness' about the preparation of food. He also quotes from an account of brahmin sepoys on active service during the First World War. At meal times, the regiment would spread out over a large area because each man established his own *chauka*, an area marked off for cooking and eating:

> Only in the case of near relatives will two men sit in the same *chauka*. In spite of the cold, one or two of them were naked except for the loin cloth. The others wore vests of wool, which (apart from the loin cloth) is the one and only material that Brahmans may wear at meals. All had first bathed and changed their *dhoti* [loincloth] according to the prescribed rites, and carried water with them to wash off any impurity from their feet when they entered the *chauka*.
>
> (O'Malley 1932: 106–7)[5]

The concrete moralities that are articulated in terms of beliefs about how to maintain or restore purity serve to structure Indian society into a hierarchy of exclusive groups, each intensely conscious of its place in the hierarchy, its traditional roles and privileges and the standing of its members within the group. Observers from outside the culture are no doubt right to imagine that this product of long-standing customs must be experienced by participants as part of the natural world. But the natural world itself is experienced as structured by forms of causality that sustain the social hierarchy, the exclusiveness of its different groups and the importance of a person's place in that hierarchy.

The belief that people's actions can stain them in a way that may take strenuous efforts to remove is integrated with another central belief found in the religious traditions of the Indian subcontinent: Hinduism, Buddhism and Jainism. After death, we are reborn to another life in this world, where our advantages or disadvantages (whether we are reborn rich or poor, male or female, superhuman, human or animal) correspond to merit that we achieved or failed to achieve in previous lives through our deeds (*karma*). This belief system appears to help to sustain the caste system; people born into low-status castes are offered the hope of being assigned to higher castes in their next lives, providing they diligently carry out the role (the caste *dharma*) assigned to their current station in life.

In the *karma* system, the effects of one's deeds appear automatic, as though good and bad were quasi-physical properties of deeds that had cumulative (quasi-)natural effects on where in the world hierarchy the person doing the deed will be reborn. Although Buddhism fostered attitudes that tended to undermine the caste system during the centuries when it was dominant in India, a useful statement representative of the beliefs surrounding *karma* is found in a text (Horner 1959: 248–53) purporting to be an account of a conversation between the Buddha and a young brahmin, who asks: 'What is the reason that lowness and excellence are to be seen among human beings while they are in human form.' The Buddha replies: 'Deeds [*karma*] are one's own, brahman youth, beings are heirs to deeds, deeds are matrix, deeds are kin, deeds are arbiters. Deeds divide beings, that is to say by lowness and excellence.'

Asked to elaborate, the Buddha specifies that those who killed and maimed sentient beings in a previous life are born short-lived; those who inflicted pain are born sickly; the ill-tempered are born ugly; the jealous and vengeful are born to a sorrowful life; the stingy are born poor; the callous and proud are born lowly; those who did not seek to learn from the wise are born weak in wisdom. Each virtue earns a corresponding reward. This cycle of rebirth (*saṃsāra*) is endless, although the Buddha held out the hope that certain exceptional individuals might through special achievements bring about the termination of the cycle of their lives (see below Section 11.2).

The mere idea that our actions may have consequences that cause suffering to us and those around us can hardly be treated as a superstition. Those who pretend that their hangovers have no connection to their drinking bouts the night before, or that certain deformities their children suffer have no connection to their exposure to radiation, hazardous chemicals, drugs, alcohol or disease, are said to have 'gone into denial.'

Well-established causal relations provide an important part of the basis (a part 'in nature') for many practices and attitudes – e.g. that one should not consume more than small amounts of alcohol immediately before driving a car or during pregnancy. What counts as a well-established causal relation, however, varies from culture to culture.

Where we feel we have found a valid basis in nature for an attitude, we are likely to think that people who share our attitude, e.g. the abhorrence of incest, appealed to the same basis. Knowing what we do about the effects of inbreeding – that 'individuals produced by inbreeding are commonly less vigorous and less fertile than their non-inbred fellows,'[6] – the taboo on incestuous marriage has for us a validity based on our causal beliefs. Discovering evidence that brother–sister marriage had been common and accepted for at least two centuries in Roman Egypt led Keith Hopkins to consider whether the effects of inbreeding are readily accessible matters of experience. He concluded: 'In conditions of high mortality . . . the extra deaths caused by inbreeding would probably not have been visible' (1980: 326–7).[7] As long as families did not maintain brother–sister marriage in successive generations (Hopkins estimates that only 40 percent of parents in Roman Egypt had pairs of sons and daughters who survived to marriageable age) the effects would not be noticeable.

The widespread prevalence of a strong incest taboo is thus not adequately explained by experience of its natural consequences, its genetic effects. Indeed, in the light of Hopkins's survey of other common explanations, this socio-psychological phenomenon (the strength and prevalence of the taboo) is something of a mystery. Moreover, it is likely that our own knowledge of these effects does not adequately explain the intense feelings about incest in our culture. There is no comparable taboo against, no comparable disgust felt toward, potential couples whose genetic background suggests that there is a substantial risk of birth defects if they marry and have children.

Beliefs that the effects of what one does may reach a long way, further than would be explained by currently accepted causal mechanisms, are found in traditions outside the *karma* framework of the Indian subcontinent, particularly in those that regard the world as in the power of one or more supernatural persons who take an interest in what we do. The idea that the descendants of transgressors might suffer for the misdeeds of their ancestors appears, for example, in the Old Testament, where Yahweh threatens to visit 'the iniquity of the fathers upon the children unto the third and fourth generation' for the specific sin of idolatry (Numbers 14: 18; Deuteronomy 5: 9). The Augustinian doctrine of original sin holds that the whole of mankind suffers because of the sin of the first man, Adam, through a change (the introduction of a weakness) in human nature. When, however, in the New Testament Christ's disciples inquired about 'a man which was blind from his birth . . . who did sin, this man or his parents, that he was born blind?' (John 9: 1–2), it is not clear that they assumed that God had punished the man with blindness for misdeeds that he or his parents had committed. Perhaps one or more parents were believed (correctly or incorrectly) to have done something prior to the man's birth that had resulted in his blindness through something like natural causes. Christ replied that in this case no one had sinned, but the status of the general principle is left unclear. Birth defects do naturally raise the question 'what went wrong?' often in the form 'what did they do wrong?'

In general, people do not always find it easy to disentangle the attitudes they feel about individuals who are afflicted with disease from those they have toward individuals whose conduct is disapproved of. Incidents of sexually transmitted diseases, such as syphilis and AIDS, that do afflict the children of those who have the diseases are the outcome of conduct that is in some cases widely condemned. Facts of this sort reinforce a widespread tendency to look at diseases that are otherwise not well understood as in some way brought on by those who succumb to them. Susan Sontag (1977: 50–7) notes the similarity between, on the one hand, popular beliefs in our day about cancer as the outcome of personality disorders and, on the other hand, explanations given in the nineteenth century of what made people susceptible to tuberculosis, as well as the belief prevalent in the sixteenth and seventeenth centuries that 'the happy man would not get plague.'

Clearly, the assumptions that people do not suffer without there being some reason for it and that their suffering may be taken as a sign that they have done something they should not have done can be sustained without the belief that the world is governed by a superhuman judge who metes out punishments and reward. But the belief in such a superhuman judge can make these assumptions much more compelling.

3.3   God's will

The impatience of Job and the submission of al-Ash'arī

Religion may be defined as a cultural system that combines beliefs about the powers that govern the world (at least those bearing on human well-being or fulfillment) with a set of ritual practices informed by that system of beliefs. Where a religion is integral to the structure of a culture or subculture, the climate of attitude that sustains its ritual and that in turn is informed and given a basis in its belief structure will evidently constitute a concrete morality. Many systems of religious belief involve one or more superhuman (divine) personalities, who are either responsible for the existence and the order of the world around us or have influence within that order.

There are scholars who hesitate to treat as a religion any system of beliefs that appears to involve no superhuman persons who have this influence. The Confucianism practised over the centuries in China involved rituals in which the emperor functioned in a role mediating between society and the wider order of the world, and was treated as exercising moral and political authority, which rested on the 'mandate of heaven.' But the source of this wider order was not personified in any determinate way, and many have hesitated to classify Confucianism as a religion.[8] Buddhism accepts the existence of various divinities, but as the salvation that it offers (termination of the cycle of rebirth), as well as the concrete moral practices that it promotes, involves neither the agency nor the approval of these divinities – the Buddha was an exemplary person, not a god – questions are sometimes raised about its status as a religion. Both Confucianism and Buddhism count as religions under the definition given above.

Religions that do involve superhuman persons commonly hold that these persons have an interest in human beings and their prosperity, or their salvation from some deeply flawed condition, and want humans to conduct their lives in specific ways. In these religions, tradition and charisma mediate between God and ordinary human beings by underwriting directives or imperatives (what has to be done or what must be avoided), which are taken to represent what a, or the, divinity desires. Whatever moral authority is claimed by a human representative of such a being will thus be grounded in divine will.

In a polytheistic belief system, such as that found in the Greek and Roman myths, human relationships to the gods are modeled on the relationships of ordinary persons to influential human beings; deities are praised (flattered) and offered gifts (bribes) to gain their favor and protection. People learn by listening to either traditional or charismatic representatives of the gods (priests, oracles and seers), not only the forms of praise and sacrifice required to gain the gods' favor but also to do and approve what it is believed the gods want and approve, and to avoid and condemn what the gods forbid and disapprove of. Obedience to and acceptance of this moral authority is often regarded as part of a bargain. In exchange for correct conduct, right attitudes, ritual praise and appropriate sacrifice, the gods are expected to help their devotees to prosper.

Portions of the Old Testament appear to reflect a similar relationship between Yahweh and his people. In Genesis 39: 2–3, it is stressed that Yahweh made all that Joseph 'did to prosper in his hand.' In Genesis 28: 20–2, Jacob offers a vow in the form of a bargain:

> And Jacob vowed a vow, saying, If God will be with me, and will keep me in this way that I go, and will give me bread to eat, and raiment to put on, so that I come again to my father's house in

peace; then shall the Lord be my God: And this stone, which I have set *for* a pillar shall be God's house: and of all that thou shall give me I will surely give the tenth unto thee.

(Genesis 28: 20–2)

After a defeat in battle, Joshua points out to Yahweh where events seem to be leading and appeals to Yahweh's sense of his own reputation: 'For the Canaanites and all the inhabitants of the land shall hear of it, and shall environ us round, and cut off our name from the earth: and what wilt thou do unto thy great name?' (Joshua 7: 9).[9]

Later books of the Old Testament reflect a growing belief that the gap between God and man is too great to be bargained across in this way. The Book of Job is bracketed by the story of a prosperous servant of God, Job, whose devotion is tested by the loss of his fortune, his children and his health. In the prologue (Job 1–2), Job remains steadfast and refuses his wife's advice to 'Curse God and die!' He declines to utter one sinful word. What is commonly associated with the figure of Job is unconditional devotion (loyalty and obedience) to God and acceptance without question or protest of what God wants from us or gives to us.

The concrete morality that issues from such a conception differs importantly from that lived as a form of bargain in which obedience to a superior is exchanged for immediate aid and comfort. Here the value of obedience is supposed to take precedence over that of immediate prosperity (or perhaps real prosperity is taken to lie in obedience, regardless of what immediate discomfort this may involve). Failure on the part of God's servants to prosper would not take away their reason for obeying God; rather, they are supposed to trust that God will ultimately reward their unquestioning obedience. In the epilogue to the Book of Job (42: 7–17), Job has children, wealth and health restored. A more extreme version of a devotion ethic would discount even the expectation of ultimate reward and treat devotion as an end, a reward, in itself and despise any form of material or psychological compensation for loyalty and obedience.

This phenomenon of making an absolute value of devotion appears elsewhere in history – even where the object of devotion is not a transcendent deity – when a system of mutual support between superiors (divine or human lords) and inferiors persists but its necessity or effectiveness has become hard to discern. Instead of abandoning the system, inferiors, who do not want to live in and acknowledge its empty shell, fixate on it objects and elevate the performance of their roles to the level of an absolute value. Thus, during the peace of the shogunate period in Japan (1603–1867), the loyalty of a warrior (*samurai*) to his liege lord (*daimyo*) ceased to have the importance that it had had during the bloody conflicts of the previous centuries. It was during this period that a retired *samurai* articulated the ethic of *bushido* in the classic *Hagakure* (Yamamoto 1716), which valorized unswerving devotion to one's *daimyo* and a willingness to die without hesitation in his service.[10]

The Book of Job is not, however, primarily concerned to articulate an ethic of unswerving devotion to God. The prologue and epilogue of Job are prose; this distinguishes them from the Hebrew of the main part of the book, which is poetry. It is suggested that together they retell a popular form of tale about the tribulations of a prosperous and pious man, analogous to stories found in Babylonian literature (Habel 1975: 4–5), a storyline that provided the narrative theme for the creative work of a Hebrew poet. In any case, the Job of the intervening poetic chapters is hardly a paragon of unquestioning submission to the will of God or of faith that God will reward what is now known proverbially as 'the patience of Job.'

At the end of the prologue, three of Job's friends arrive to comfort him but lapse into silence when they see the awful state he is in (smitten 'with sore boils from the sole of his foot unto his crown. And he took him a potsherd to scrape himself withal; and he sat down among the ashes' (Job 2: 7–8).) The silence is broken by Job cursing the day he was born, and the first of his friends chides him for losing his patience and suggests that Job must have done something to deserve his misfortunes ('who *ever* perished, being innocent? or where were the righteous cut off? Even as I have seen, they that plow iniquity, and sow wickedness, reap the same' 4: 7–8.[11]) Job, however, is persuaded of his own innocence and asks to be shown what he has done wrong.

Job's second friend is shocked at the suggestion that God might 'pervert justice' (8: 3). But Job would like to have his case heard in court, the only problem being that there is no higher authority to arbitrate between him and God. ('Neither is there any daysman [from "day" in the sense of "day fixed for trial"] betwixt us, that might lay his hand upon us both' (9: 33).) Job's third friend accuses of him of arrogance in the face of the unfathomable wisdom of the Almighty, and in subsequent cycles, in which the friends take turns to remonstrate with Job and hear his replies, the accusations against Job escalate as his friends pressure him to accept responsibility for his situation and to throw himself on the mercy of God. Job throughout clings to his belief in his own innocence and the feeling that he has not been treated fairly.

Read in isolation, the prologue to Job appears concerned only with the contrast between on the one hand obedience to God's will in the expectation of prompt receipt of benefit and on the other a willingness to honor and obey God through an indefinite delay in the receipt of benefit. The body of the book is concerned with a contrast between unquestioning acceptance of God's will and the possibility that what God wants or has allowed to happen may be questioned on some independent basis, preferably one to be decided by an independent judge. The Job of the poetic chapters expects God not to allow such misery to befall him without at least making clear what he, Job, has done to deserve it.

But Job does not receive satisfaction of even this modest expectation. In the climax of the poetic portion, which comes at the beginning of Job 38, Yahweh speaks to Job 'out of the tempest' and instead of justifying His ways or explaining to Job what sins he committed to deserve what he has suffered, God asks Job a series of questions about the nature of the universe that He has created, questions that underscore the distance between them. In the face of this mighty theophany, Job admits that there is nothing he has any business saying and repents 'in dust and ashes,' whereupon the epilogue begins in which Yahweh rebukes Job's friends and restores his fortunes.

This picture of the relationship between God and human beings also appears in Islamic thought. During the two centuries after its founding (in 622 CE) there grew a practice – known as *kalām* (discourse, disputation, eventually synonymous with 'theology') – of using carefully argued exchanges of views to deal with questions of law and the interpretation of scripture. The Mu'tazilites, for a time the dominant school of *mutakallimūn* (as those who pursued the practice of *kalām* were known), appear to have thought that to speak of Allah as 'just' meant that He would not ask of mankind what was contrary to principles of justice or was contrary to conceptions of the welfare of His creatures that were independent of His will (Watt 1962: chapter 8).

In the tenth century CE, a man named al-Ash'arī initiated a movement that explicitly repudiated these Mu'tazilite views on the grounds that they failed to represent adequately the omnipotence of God. Al-Ash'arī regarded it as contrary to the Qur'ān to represent Allah as under any kind of constraint. That God was all-powerful meant that what constituted justice and injustice was determined by God's free choice. To say that God is just is in effect to say that He is the source of the very concept, and hence the standard by which its correct application is fixed. God had determined that an infinite amount of punishment should be inflicted for a finite amount of sin; as God is the author of everything, including what is just and unjust, this must be just. Had God decided that infants who died before they were old enough to embrace the faith should be consigned to hell, where pain would be inflicted on them, that would be just (McCarthy 1953: 99).

As a matter of Islamic belief, such infants – having not had an opportunity to 'sustain an act of worship after puberty' (the minimum required to qualify as a believer) – were assigned an inferior place in paradise. But as the length of one's life was thought to be determined by God, this raised further possible questions about God's justice. Al-Ghazālī, a follower of al-Ash'arī who flourished in the eleventh century, discussed the following imaginary case (said to have also been used by al-Ash'arī): three boys are born. The first dies in infancy and is assigned an inferior place in paradise; the second lives a full life as a devout believer and secures a high rank in paradise; the third, having reached maturity and embraced unbelief, is consigned to the depths of hell. The first boy complains to God about his inferior place, saying that he never had a chance to live the life of a devout believer. God, knowing all things, replies to the boy that had he not died in infancy he would have embraced unbelief and ended in hell. This silences the first boy, but the third now complains from the depths of hell:

> 'O Lord, You knew of me that if I reached maturity, I would embrace unbelief. Could You not, then, have caused me to die in my childhood? For I would be satisfied with the lower rank in which You have lodged the child who yearns for the sublime ranks.'
> At this point it remains for him who claims 'Wisdom' only to stop replying and venturing [any farther]!
> ... For the attributes of Lordship [Divinity] are not weighed in the scales of conjectures [suppositions], and God does what He will 'and is not answerable for what He does, but they are answerable' [Qur'ān 21.23] and by this it is clear that there is no obligation to send a Prophet.
>
> (McCarthy 1980: 242)[12]

Note that neither al-Ash'arī nor al-Ghazālī seriously entertains the idea that God may deal arbitrarily or capriciously with His creatures. Their point is that it is presumptuous to ask that God's ways be justified.

Responding to the challenge to justify the ways of God is the task of a discipline known as 'theodicy' (Greek: *theo* = God; *dike* = justice). The attitude of al-Ash'arī and his followers is that theodicy should not be undertaken. Wisdom consists of knowing when it is inappropriate to press for answers to questions. ('At this point it remains for him who claims "Wisdom" only to stop replying and venturing [any farther]!') What God does is not to be weighed on any scale that a human can comprehend. By virtue of His greatness, God is above being bound in any reciprocal relationship to human beings, while humans remain unconditionally bound to obey God's word. The only appropriate response for a human being, whatever the conditions of his or her life, is submission to the will of God – which is what the Arabic word *islām* means.

3.4 Reason

The lex talionis *and reason's aesthetic*

As was noted at the beginning of Section 3.1, the third of Weber's pure types of authority, 'rational', is very closely identified in his mind with certain well-developed bureaucratic and legal institutions – roughly, those with characteristics found in late Roman law (1978: 975). We will look into this in Section 4.3. Here we will consider the way in which rationality affects the way people deal with practices that are shaped largely by tradition and charisma as well as deal with one another within the institutions that govern such practices.

Let us begin with what emerges at the climax of the poetic portion of Job and in the Ashʿarite tradition in Islam, the idea of God as a source of authority so exalted that it is inappropriate to demand any accounting from Him, certainly not one that answers to principles we might expect to be applied to relations between one human being and another. Humans whose actions adversely affect other human beings are expected to listen to complaints, answer (provide justification) for what they are doing and discuss whether the *reasons* they offer are adequate. The whole process is sometimes called 'listening to reason.' Job was shown (as the Ashʿarites later insisted) that it is inappropriate to expect God 'to listen to reason.'

Human beings are able to ask for and provide reasons for what is done because they are language-using creatures. The Latin word *ratio*, which is the source of our words 'rational' and 'reason,' has a range of meanings very similar to the Greek word *logos*, the source of our words 'logical' and 'logic.' *Logos* may in different contexts be translated as (1) words or discourse; (2) 'reason' in the sense of words that provide an explanation or justification for something; or (3) 'reason' in the sense of a general capacity to offer and understand 'reasons' in the second sense.

People manifest the capacity that is 'reason' in the third of these senses in a number of different ways. Reasons may be given for something that happens naturally (an explanation), for believing something, for feeling disposed (favorably or otherwise) toward something or for doing something. When someone understands the connection between a reason and what it is a reason for, we commonly say that that person 'sees the reason.' Inanimate objects, animals and small children seem to lack whatever 'eyes' give people this capacity. This is a theoretical (from a Greek word meaning 'to watch') use of the human capacity known as reason. Providing reasons, contriving them from one's own resources, is a practical (from a Greek word meaning 'to do' or 'accomplish') use of reason. A common reason for doing something is that it is a means to achieving some end. It is a theoretical use of reason to appreciate that something serves as a means to an end, and it is a special use of practical reason, an instrumental use, to come up with means to serve a proposed end.

It is also a function of reason as a human capacity to evaluate reasons, to appreciate that some are more satisfactory than others. The least satisfactory situation is when reasoning results in conflicting outcomes, contradictory conclusions. Avoiding this situation is one way of conforming to the demand ('of reason') for consistency. Another form of (the 'demand of reason' for) consistency is that similar considerations must not be treated differently unless it is possible to detect some relevant difference between them. It is not possible to say precisely and comprehensively what is to count as a relevant difference (and hence what constitutes similar considerations); this has to be worked out between the individuals who are using their rational capacities to resolve some matter before them. What has to happen for these individuals to reach a resolution of the matter before them is that there must be a shared sense of what is to count as similar and different. This shared sense will be shaped by what shared understanding they have of what they are jointly trying to achieve and by whatever cultural background they share.

Without the ability to achieve this shared sense, people will be unable to use language to resolve conflicts or to make right (to complete) situations felt to be unsatisfactory (incomplete) in some way. Finding an appropriate name for this second use of reason is not easy. It often involves sensitivity to formal features of a situation, but stress needs to be put on the word 'sensitivity' rather than 'formal' because the latter suggests a predetermined outcome to many people. It may not be inappropriate to refer to this crucial function as 'aesthetic' (from a Greek word meaning 'to sense' or 'feel') manifestations of our rational capacities.

As well as the urge to maintain some kind of consistency in what is done, another 'aesthetic' manifestation of reason is the urge to strike some kind of balance, create or restore some kind of reciprocity to situations. When this sensitivity is applied to relations between human beings, we find the effort governed by words like 'just' or 'fair.' For example, if one person is making life difficult for another, 'reason demands' that the second person have done something that provides a counterbalance to (or justification for) this distress; otherwise it is not 'fair,' it is not 'just.' This is what Job wants from God – some idea of what he, Job, did to merit the misery he is suffering. Where the second person has done nothing that earns or merits being afflicted, the first person should desist and maybe do something to compensate the second (another demand for a kind of counterbalance) for the distress that was caused.

At a very basic level, the feeling for consistency will cause people to continue in the manner in which they began (custom becomes a reason for itself); the feeling for balance will cause people to bargain in an effort to exchange what are regarded as things of equal value; and the feeling for reciprocity will make people retaliate, where they can, for injuries suffered. The problem is that retaliation may not be accepted as due, especially if it more than counterbalances the injury received, and may spark counter-retaliation, thereby initiating a cycle of escalating violence. The boast of Lamech, a descendant of Cain, illustrates the tendency for the exchange of injury to escalate: 'For I have slain a man to my wounding and a young man [a man's son] for the hurt I received. If Cain shall be avenged sevenfold, truly Lamech seventy and sevenfold' (Genesis 4: 23–4). This tendency for reciprocation to escalate can be understood if one remembers (see Section 2.1) that in earlier periods in history the main basis of security for persons and property was the credibility of one's capacity to retaliate for injuries received, and the more forceful the retaliation, the more credible the threat and the more effective the deterrent. If it could be carried out, sevenfold (or seventy and sevenfold) retaliation would purchase greater security in the future.

One way to put an end to the dreadful cost of an endless cycle of blood letting is to forbid retaliation that involves more than the original wrong. This appears in the earliest written laws of Rome (the Twelve Tables), where it is known as the *lex talionis* (law of retaliation), and in the Old Testament as 'an eye for an eye, a tooth for a tooth' (Exodus 21: 24).[13] The principle sounds barbaric (putting out the eye of someone who has caused the loss of an eye), and historically it has in most cases given way (if not to the practice of turning the other cheek (Matthew 5: 38–42), then at least) to the practice of paying compensation *proportionate* to the injury received. One should, however, before dismissing the *lex talionis* as barbaric, recognize the advantages of stopping when a balance of distress has been achieved rather than allowing an escalating cycle of violence.

The *lex talionis* thus comes as a limitation placed by the feeling for what is reasonable (just or fair) – *no more than* an eye for an eye – on what in some societies was a fundamental imperative of instrumental rationality seeking security of life and property: that vengeance must be sought. To be sure, another imperative of instrumental rationality arises from the fact that escalating cycles of revenge damage and impoverish the lives of those caught up in them. The feeling for reciprocity that works toward equality on each side offers a way out of these cycles that reconciles the conflicting imperatives of instrumental rationality.

To have no more than a total of two eyes or two teeth lost is preferable to escalating mayhem, but it seems even better for the loss of irreplaceable lives and organs to stop at one. Improvements on the strict *lex talionis* would thus involve seeking to balance something of value, but not irreplaceable, for the lost life or organ: compensation in the form of payment, proportional to the injury. Thus in archaic German and Anglo-Saxon law there was the institution of *wergild*, the price one paid to a person's family for taking that life inadvertently or in a quarrel. But how ever obvious the advantages of such a system may be to our way of thinking, a person raised in the tradition that only blood can compensate for blood will not find the arrangement satisfactory. An eighth-century Norse poet, Egil, left a moving lament for his dead son, which also contains the less than progressive sentiments: 'No one can be relied on, for men nowadays lower themselves and are glad to accept payment instead of revenge for the blood of brothers' (Grönbech 1931: 28).

It may well take charismatic leadership to move a culture with a revenge ethic to the point of accepting some agreed number of cattle or sheep in payment for an eye or tooth rather than another eye or tooth. The Prophet Muḥammad was instrumental in moving the Arab society of his day from the *lex talionis* to a system of compensation for death and injury (Watt 1968: 6ff). What will serve eventually to compensate a personal or family loss will in turn have to be settled by custom. We have here a good illustration of ways in which validity based on tradition, charisma and reason interact.

An important theme in the Western philosophical tradition from classical Greece onward has been the attempt to locate the ultimate source of authority in the principles that govern rational thought, consistency, balance or reciprocity in some form or other. The deities of Greek mythology were often quite capricious, but as the Greeks never thought to exalt any of their pantheon to the level of an incorruptible, infallible source of moral authority, any capriciousness could be set against some independent idea, how ever vague, of reasonableness. Gradually, the Greek polytheistic belief system was supplanted (among the educated and sophisticated) by an abstract conception of a single divine principle; but the exemplary qualities of this Being consisted in His adherence in all He did or approved to rational principles independent of His will. Plato tends to speak of the divinity as a single thing and to insist that it function as a moral exemplar – myths in which gods misbehave are scandalous (*Republic*: 377ff). The Stoics were pantheistic monotheists whose God, Zeus, was as unlike the philandering figure of mythology as could be.

During the second century CE, as proselytizing on the part of Christians and Jews came to encroach on pagan culture, pagan authors such as Galen and Celsus began to make adverse observations about the kind of deity that Christians and Jews believed in:

> According to Celsus, the Judaeo-Christian belief that God deals with the universe and mankind simply by His will or pleasure, is both absurd and blasphemous. God does not arbitrarily dispose of anything, since all his activity is perfectly rational. This rationality indeed is the source of divine power, justice and goodness.
>
> (Dihle 1982: 7; *cf.* Hoffman 1987: 86)

Pagan thinkers in late antiquity took for granted that the universe is ordered – both in what happens by nature and what should happen in human society – by principles 'which the human mind can understand as reasonable, good and salutary' (Dihle 1982: 4) through its capacity to reason. In the biblical framework, the Creator is the source of the order in things and thus transcends that order; that His creatures can understand the most important of the principles of this order is not because they share a rational nature with God and Creation antecedent to both but because of God's benevolence toward mankind through revelation.

To rest the authority or validity of attitudes and practices in something accessible to the human capacity to reason, as did leading thinkers of classical antiquity, is to make humans responsible for clarifying uncertainties, resolving conflicts and adapting their customs to changing situations, in part through developing their understanding of the principles by which their own thought works. To rest the authority or validity of attitudes and practices ultimately in the inscrutable will of a superhuman being, a god, forces people to rely on (charismatic) individuals who can claim to speak for this superhuman being when difficulties arise. It is to terminate questions about validity in a source that may well be opaque to human understanding.

Our age is the heir of a perplexing sequence of historical events that has taken place in the history of Western Europe. First, during late antiquity, reliance on the will of a superhuman being supplanted the belief that humans had resources in their own thought processes to clarify, resolve and adapt their concrete moralities. Then, as leading thinkers over the past three centuries have sought with less than complete success to re-establish confidence in innate human resources, this belief in a superhuman being decayed, leaving many with the belief that the only available sources of moral authority were the unconstrained wills of individual human beings, each finite but modeled on God's unconstrained will.

Further reading

On Weber's pure forms of authority, consult Weber (1978: 212–55). The contrast between *nomos* and nature (*phusis*) was commonplace in early Greek philosophy: see Guthrie (1971: chapter IV). On 'law' and literacy in the Greek world, see Robb (1994: chapters 4–6). For more on the *nomoi* of the Spartans, see Morrow (1960: chapter II). On Indian caste customs, in addition to O'Malley (1932) and Hutton (1963), see Dumont (1980). On pollution and purification in the belief system of the ancient Greeks, see Burkert (1985: 75–84). On *karma*, see Aiyar (1935: chapter IX), and on incest, see Hopkins (1980). Habel (1975) provides a good starting point for study of the Book of Job. Mishima (1977), a twentieth-century Japanese writer, indicates something of the significance of the early-eighteenth century *bushido* text *Hagakure* (Yamamoto 1716) for Japanese living in this century. For a comprehensive view of al-Ghazālī's ethics, see Quasem (1978), and for a survey of Islamic ethics generally, see Fakhry (1994). For pre-modern attitudes to revenge in Japan and China, see Mills (1976).

Notes

1 Cited in Bellah (1985: 140) from an unpublished lecture.
2 Weber indicated that the details of the concept had been worked out by scholars concerned with the history and social theory of religion, and he insisted that it was 'nothing new' (1978: 216).

3 That is boys of the citizen class:

[The Spartan citizen] was a member of a small dominant group in the midst of a subject and hostile population many times larger. Surrounded by enemies who might rise and attack them at any time, the Spartans knew that they could survive only by standing together and by ruthlessly subordinating individual interests and ambitions to the good of all.

(Morrow 1960: 50–1)

For the information in the remainder of this paragraph see *ibid*. (p. 53), especially 'Above all the boys learned to live not as individuals, but as members of a herd.'

4 As in many matters in many societies there is one standard for men and another for women. A woman who has 'illicit relations' with a man of lower caste is automatically 'degraded to the level of her lover' (O'Malley 1932: 64).

5 This is a quote by O'Malley from E.C. Chandler, *The Sepoy*, 1919: 129–30.

6 Hopkins (1980: 325), quoting K. Mather, *Genetical Structure of Populations*, London, 1973: 33.

7 Hopkins reviews documentary evidence that marriage between brothers and sisters was an acceptable practice in Egypt among ordinary people during the first two centuries BCE. This provides a striking counter-example to the common claim that the only exceptions to the otherwise universal taboo on incest are found among royalty in Hellenic Egypt, Hawaii and the Incas of Peru (and in such exceptional cases as between fraternal twins of the opposite sex in Bali). For an example of this claim, see Hoebel (1949: 191–2).

8 A dispute broke out between different orders of Catholic missionaries in China during the seventeenth century. 'The Chinese Rites Controversy' was over the question of whether in the light of the supporting belief system Confucianism could be regarded as a system of civil rituals (comparable with the rituals that attend the opening of the British Parliament) so that to convert to Christianity a Chinese person did not have to foreswear Confucianism. See the editor's introduction to Mungello (1994).

9 The appeal is like that which might be made to a feudal protector known to be concerned with the honor tied to his reputation. According to Hillers (1969), the relationship between Yahweh and His people was modeled on the feudal agreements between imperial powers and client peoples throughout the Middle East, and the commandments that governed relations between individual Israelites conformed to the regulations an imperial power would impose on how its client states dealt with one another.

10 For a caution about the inadequacy of the picture of the comprehensive Japanese virtue of *giri* (the concern to repay one's debts) that is offered by the cult of *bushido*, see Benedict (1946: 175).

11 Recall the tendency, noted at the end of Section 3.2, to assume that people who are afflicted must have done something to deserve it. This is strengthened here by the conception of an all-powerful God who personally carries out punishment and reward.

12 The question of whether God is responsible for making salvation accessible to everyone also brackets al-Ash'arī's discussion; see McCarthy (1953: 97). The two agree that whatever favors one receives from God, including the opportunity to find salvation through belief under the guidance of the Prophet, are entirely gratuitous acts of mercy on His part.

13 To reconcile the Confucian demand that a son average his father or a younger brother, his older brother with the need for public order, provincial officials in Japan prior to the Meiji Restoration (1868) would issue licenses authorizing family members to carry out revenge, but they would not authorize secondary revenge (Mills 1976).

4

CONFLICT AND THE SEARCH FOR STANDARDS

Behold the beginning of philosophy: a recognition of mutual conflict among men and an inquiry into the origin of that conflict, a distrust and rejection of mere opinion and an investigation to determine whether opinions are rightly held and to discover a standard like the balance scale for determining weights, like the carpenter's rule for determining straight and crooked.

(Epictetus (first century CE); Oldfather 1925: II.11.13)

The will of Heaven is like the compasses to the wheelwright and the square to the carpenter. The wheelwright tests the circularity of every object in the world with his compasses, saying: 'That which satisfies my compasses is circular. That which does not is not circular.' Therefore whether an object is circular or not is known, because the standard of circularity is established. The carpenter also tests the squareness of every object in the world with his square, saying: 'That which satisfies my square is square; that which does not is not square.' Therefore whether any object is square or not is known. Why so? Because the standard of squareness is established.

(Mo Tzu (fifth century BCE); Mei 1929: 149–50)

Recapitulation: The customs that constitute a concrete morality are taken by participants to have a validity that lies in some combination of (1) human authority (traditional or charismatic); (2) ways the natural world is taken to be ordered and thus to constrain what is possible for humans to do; and (3) rational characteristics such as consistency, balance and reciprocation. Some (but not all) concrete moralities that are interwoven with a system of religious beliefs see the validity of attitudes and practices as dependent on (4) the will of one or more superhuman beings. These sources of validity are frequently combined with one another. The legendary sources of tradition are figures with charismatic qualities. Charisma involves standing in a special relationship to nature or to the will of God. Adherence to tradition is a form of consistency. For a culture to change to customs that involve more elaborate forms of consistency, i.e. reciprocation between actions or balance between states of affairs – e.g. from no more than an eye for an eye to some form of proportional compensation – may require charismatic leadership.

Prospectus: To attempt to give an account of the sources of validity that might be claimed for one's own concrete morality is to begin to engage in ethical theorizing. People are moved to give such accounts when they face uncertainties over which attitudes or practices they approve and which they condemn. Such uncertainties occur when individuals within a given society come into conflict with one another, or a society finds itself in tension over changes that may come about through environmental stress (famine or population pressures), internal social or economic forces (e.g. evolving from an agrarian to an industrial society) or through coming into contact, and possibly into conflict, with other cultures. When uncertainty persists or comes to appear endemic, a number of quite diverse cultures have drawn upon the same image to express what is felt to be needed: the sort of standards (reliable ways of assisting judgment) that have a variety of uses in the building trades.

4.1   Conflict

The anguish of Arjuna and the arrogance of Euthyphro

Most of the time, people live within their concrete moralities as comfortably (or otherwise) as they live in their houses or tents, and they do not feel called upon to justify their practices and attitudes or to examine what if any basis these might have. Having learned how it is appropriate to feel and conduct themselves toward family and friends, neighbors and strangers, their responses appear to them to have much the same status as those that enable them to cope with the natural world. People who come into contact with other groups having very different economies or cultural traditions find themselves confronting possible ways of relating to one another and conducting their daily affairs that would otherwise not occur to them. Groups of people following very different ways of life can exist side by side in relative peace, sometimes becoming mutually dependent on one another through trade, while viewing one another's customs with anything ranging from curiosity to disdain.

Often, however, there will be competition for economic resources and a struggle for dominance. Sometimes a group that achieves dominance, through conquest or colonization, will seek to impose a concrete morality

– its own or a variation that will help it to maintain dominance – on a subject population. There have been some instances of what might be called 'cultural colonialism,' in which a nation convinced that it has a set of beliefs and practices that would benefit other peoples sends its representatives to live in foreign parts with the aim of convincing foreigners of the value of its religion and concrete morality. If its representatives arrive with no interest in military conquest or economic domination – e.g. the Buddhists who took their religion from India to the Far East in the early centuries CE – they are known as 'missionaries.' Often efforts to 'convert' others come in the wake of conquest or economic colonization, as in the histories of Islam and Christianity.

Cultural colonization includes efforts to change the concrete moralities that converts live by. Thus Christian missionaries have not only sought to change people's beliefs about God and their forms of worship but they have also sought to change attitudes to dress, to sexual practices and to marital institutions (such as polygamy). Christians have not been unique in this respect. Converts to Islam must, among other things, give up drinking wine and (men must) reduce the number of their wives to four. Adherents to certain religions ('peoples of the book') in regions conquered by Muslim armies were not forced to convert to Islam, but they were not allowed to worship openly, and their customs (of dress or drink, for example) were not to scandalize Muslims (Schacht 1964: 41, 131). The practice of brother–sister marriages in Roman Egypt became unlawful when full Roman citizenship was conferred on all the male inhabitants of the empire (including Egypt) in 212/13 CE. (This was more than a century before Christianity was made the official religion of the empire.) Such marriages were not only not recognized as legal, but they were condemned by pagan writers as contrary to propriety and holiness (Hopkins 1980: 353–4).

Confrontations of this kind raise questions regarding what basis there might be for the practices of one society to be approved of or condemned or accepted with indifference by another. But for the participants in such historical events these questions would normally be lost beneath more pressing matters, questions of personal and cultural survival. If people accept pressure (economic, military or less coercive forms of persuasion) to change their attitudes and practices – feelings of shame related to customs of dress, feelings of guilt related to customs of diet, feelings of anxiety related to personal pleasures, feelings of propriety related to marriage, aggression or oppression – the continuity of their culture will be disrupted and their identity as a people may be called into question.

The smaller and more isolated a group of people is, the less likely are its members to be called on to justify their concrete morality or to reflect on its basis. Larger groups of people who do not happen to have experience of cultures that differ from their own may nevertheless generate enough internal diversity of interest to lead their members to challenge one another's claims to economic goods, or enough internal diversity of roles to bring them to question their own or another's role in society. Conflicts between families or between branches of the same family over inheritance, claims to the use of certain areas for hunting, grazing or gathering, care of widows and orphans, etc. can present a society with problems in restoring or maintaining social harmony. The problems may not have arisen in a similar form before (or within living memory), so current attitudes and practices offer no immediate guidance.

Conflicts that compel people to reflect on the validity of claims may arise without there being two distinct parties (cultures or individuals) involved in conflict. Societies that possess enough size and complexity to assign people more than one role (e.g. family member and citizen) can place individuals in painful dilemmas, which may bring them face to face with questions regarding the basis of the complex of attitudes and practices that they have acquired from their culture. These dilemmas provide some of the most salient motives to undertake ethical inquiry, and it will be instructive to consider two classic illustrations in some detail. The first is from the literature of ancient India, which includes a relatively small but extremely popular work, the *Bhagavad Gītā* (*Song of the Lord*), built around a situation perceived by its central character to be intensely and painfully problematic.

The *Gītā* appears as an episode of a large epic (the *Mahābhārata*) about a war between two branches of a ruling family, the Kauravas and the Pandavas. The former had deprived the latter of their share of the kingdom, and when attempts to settle the dispute by negotiation failed, the two sides collected large armies and prepared to settle the dispute by combat. The *Gītā* opens as the two sides, drawn up in formation, confront each other across the battlefield. The fortunes of the Pandavas rest to a considerable extent on the skill, strength and valor of a champion named Arjuna. But as Arjuna surveys the two armies from a chariot positioned between the opposing sides, his resolve falters.

There are brothers, friends, in-laws, fathers and sons, teachers and pupils standing on opposite sides about to try to kill or maim each other. In addition to his kinsmen, Arjuna faces two of his own teachers, whom he regards as worthy of veneration; how can he try to kill them? Arjuna believes his opponents have cheated his branch of the family and are blind to the destruction that they are bringing on the whole family and the society it governs because they have been overpowered by greed. But is the desire of his side for its rightful share a motivation more worthy than greed? Whichever side wins the battle the result will be lawlessness, the defilement of the women of the family, the neglect of the spirits of ancestors and a general undermining of the social hierarchy. Would it not be better to die without resistance or live as a beggar than to enjoy the bloodstained spoils of war?

Arjuna confesses his misgivings to his charioteer, Krishna, and indicates the effects they are having on him: 'My limbs falter, my mouth goes dry, my body shivers and my hairs stand on end' (I.29).[1] At the end of his confession, he casts aside his bow and arrows and sinks onto the seat of the chariot in despair. Arjuna's charioteer is, as it happens, an incarnation of the god Vishnu. His first response to Arjuna, however, is in the character adopted for his incarnation, that of a foreign-born counselor to, and sometime envoy on behalf of, Arjuna's family. He begins by trying to shame his friend: despair in the hour of crisis is unbecoming a nobleman; it is disgraceful, unmanly. Arjuna recognizes that pity or compassion is a weakness in a fighting man, but his perception of the consequences of the battle about to be fought leaves him confused about what he should be doing. 'I am afflicted with the defect of pity; my mind is perplexed about my *dharma*. I ask you to tell me definitely which is better. I am your pupil teach me' (II.7).

Recognizing that Arjuna needs to be told more than simply 'Pull yourself together and act like a man!' Krishna begins a lengthy effort to dispel his friend's misgivings by observing that Arjuna is trying to speak as a wise man would, but he lacks sufficient wisdom. Over the remaining seventeen chapters Krishna's efforts to persuade Arjuna draw increasingly on his own knowledge and power as a major deity; in the eleventh chapter, he reveals his majesty to Arjuna in an awesome theophany not unlike that at the climax of the poetic portion of the Book of Job. The general direction of the argument is that to achieve the wisdom that would allow him to see his situation correctly, Arjuna would need to develop forms of discipline and detachment. And once he has done so, Arjuna will see why it is indeed right for him to participate in the battle about to commence. This part of Krishna's argument will be used in Section 11.4 to illustrate the phenomenon of worldly asceticism. Here it will be sufficient to assess how far Krishna gets, as he urges Arjuna to fight, before he plays trump cards accessible only to a god. Krishna does not at any point pretend to be conducting a dispassionate inquiry about how Arjuna should resolve his perplexity, but the considerations offered that would be available to a sympathetic, wise but completely human charioteer do not entirely square with one another let alone answer Arjuna's concerns.[2]

Krishna begins (II.11–25) by claiming that wise men do not grieve for the dead or for the living, as Arjuna is clearly grieving for those about to die in battle, for no one is really going to die. According to the doctrine of the cycle of rebirths (*saṃsāra*; see Section 3.2) only the body perishes; the 'eternal embodied [soul or self]' has always existed and always will exist, casting off worn-out bodies and taking on new ones, just as a person throws away old clothes and puts on new ones. For good measure, Krishna adds (II.26–8) that if Arjuna did not accept the rebirth of souls, death for humans is in any case unavoidable, so there is no cause for grief. But that everyone is destined to die and either be reborn or not (as the case may be) does not offer any reassurance about the effects that the impending battle will have on Arjuna's family and on the social fabric. Might Arjuna not insist that he is grieving in part that the souls of those about to be reborn will enter a socially impoverished world as a consequence of the battle?

Krishna next appeals to Arjuna's *dharma* (see Section 2.2) as a member of the warrior class. At this point, the emphasis is on the glory he will earn with victory, the automatic reincarnation into heaven should he be killed in battle, the dishonor he would suffer if he declined to fight, the painful ignominy of being spoken of by others with contempt. But Arjuna is already considering whether living as a beggar might not be preferable to killing his own teachers (II.5). In subsequent chapters, he will be told repeatedly (VI.7, XII.18–19, XIV.24–5) that he should be indifferent to honor and dishonor.

In the third chapter, an appeal is made to the role of Arjuna's social class in maintaining social order[3] and the poor example he will set by refusing to fight: in failing to perform the function assigned to warriors, he will thereby encourage members of other classes to fail to do what is proper to their roles. But are such functions to be carried out regardless of the circumstances and probable consequences? Has not Arjuna expressed the worry that by performing his role he will contribute to lawlessness, perhaps contributing more than if he simply sets a bad example?

Krishna's efforts are directed toward closure of the question that Arjuna raises and in favor of one course of action. In the literature that survives from ancient Greece there are by contrast examples of an effort to open questions of this sort and to prevent their resolution before a carefully thought out way of answering them has been found. The origin of this effort is credited to Socrates, as he is represented in the writings of Plato and Xenophon (for he left no writings of his own). An example of someone facing a problem as acute as that facing Arjuna occurs in one of the shorter dialogues of Plato, the *Euthyphro*, although one significant difference is that the eponymous Euthyphro, unlike Arjuna, does not feel he has a problem. In fact, the dialogue represents Socrates as finding it difficult to persuade Euthyphro to suspend his self-righteous self-confidence long enough to think about the basis on which he should be proceeding.

The dramatic setting of the *Euthyphro* is the day that Socrates is to make his initial appearance to answer charges of religious impropriety (3b), which led to his being sentenced to death (see Section 3.1), and opens as Socrates encounters Euthyphro, a young man known for and proud of his observance of religious propriety. Euthyphro is, as it happens, engaged in prosecuting his father before a religious court on a charge of negligent homicide. His concern is that murder and association with a murderer are ways to incur serious (ritual) pollution (see Section 3.2). 'The pollution is the same if, knowingly, you associate with such a man, and do not cleanse yourself, and him as well, by bringing him to justice,' he says (4c).[4]

Euthyphro may have gone overboard in his zeal to cleanse his family of pollution. He appears to be able to speak on questions of religious propriety with some (mostly self-proclaimed) authority, but Plato contrives the circumstances of the case to stress the difficulty of the judgment Euthyphro has so confidently made. The victim, who had been working for Euthyphro's family in a remote region, had himself committed a murder and had been bound and left in a ditch by Euthyphro's father while a messenger was sent to seek advice on how to deal with him. In the time it took the messenger to return, the man had died of hunger and exposure.

Euthyphro may well have been right that his family had as a result of the second death incurred pollution and needed to be cleansed, but his view of what is required by religious propriety is disputable. An Athenian of his day might well have assumed that the death of a slave who had himself committed murder was an atonement for the pollution incurred by the first death and left the family purified. In any case, would the gods not frown upon the lack of respect shown by a man who drags his father into court? As Plato represents him, Euthyphro is well aware that people around him regard his action against his father with profound contempt, and when he appeals to myths that tell of gods taking action against their fathers (as precedents that justify what he is doing), Socrates suggests that such myths are not only dubious but distasteful (5e–6c).

The *Euthyphro* and the *Bhagavad Gītā* both turn on conflict that is possible in almost any society, between the interests of one's immediate family and some wider conception of what is right or best for everyone regardless of how closely related they may be. Euthyphro is prepared to commit what looks like an assault on his father in the name not merely of ritual purity but of a concept of justice that takes account of the interests of even lowly members of society. Arjuna fears that the cost of pursuing the interests of his own branch of the family may be too great when the effects on society at large are taken into account. It is clear what each is likely to hear if he consults what serves as public opinion in his society; for the interlocutors, Socrates and Krishna, each begin by calling to mind what people around them say – about a son who drags his own father into court, about a warrior who is not man enough to fight. Euthyphro appears to lack sensitivity to what people will think, Arjuna to lack the resolve to carry out what people expect.

4.2 Standards

Straight thinking and right-angled conduct

If either Euthyphro or Arjuna took his case to a court or tribunal that saw itself as responsible for the interests of all members of the society regardless of who they were or were related to, the decisions might or might not favor the impulses of these two characters to think more widely than their immediate family loyalties. It would depend to a large extent on the composition of the tribunal and the conventional attitudes that governed its deliberations. If the tribunal thought that there was a kind of propriety which could override the obedience to parents expected of a son (or override a call to arms issued to a warrior), they might well speak like the Stoic philosopher Musonius Rufus, who, five and a half centuries after Socrates died, is reported to have said 'Do not let your father be an excuse to you for wrong-doing whether he bid you do something which is not right or forbids you to do what is right' (Lutz 1947: 105). Musonius would no doubt have endorsed the statement that resulted from replacing 'father' by 'duty as a soldier.' He suspects that people will regard as disobedient 'the man who, having a money-loving father, is ordered by him to steal or make away with money entrusted to him, but does not carry out the order.' Musonius nevertheless insists: 'he is in no way disobeying, inasmuch as he does no wrong nor fails of doing right' (*ibid.*: 103).

If, like Confucius, the members of the tribunal viewed legal proceedings as an inferior way of achieving a properly functioning society and believed instead that filial loyalty (or class *dharma*) was the ultimate basis for proper conduct, they might well urge Euthyphro and Arjuna to think again, or better, not to think beyond what their roles as son and warrior require. One should bear in mind Confucius' doctrine that society needs to be structured throughout and at all levels on the model of the relationship obtaining between dutiful son and caring father to appreciate the following passage from the *Analects*.

> The governor of She said to Confucius, 'In our village there is a man nicknamed "Straight Body." When his father stole a sheep, he gave evidence against him.' Confucius answered, 'In our village those who are straight are quite different. Fathers cover up for their sons, and sons cover up for their fathers. Straightness is to be found in such behavior.'
>
> (Lau 1979: XIII.18)[5]

What advice one receives when taking counsel will depend a great deal on the culture and conventional attitudes of one's counselors. Compare Musonius on parents that one believes are intending wrong with

> The Master said, 'In serving your father and mother you ought to dissuade them from doing wrong in the gentlest way. If you see your advice being ignored, you should not become disobedient but remain reverent. You should not complain even if in so doing you wear yourself out.'
>
> (*ibid.*: IV.18)

Ideally, one would like to consult someone who could be relied on to be above this conflict between the requirements of family and the requirements of wider society.

Religious beliefs commonly involve representations of superhuman beings who in transcending the human condition can take this sort of right unbiased perspective. The gods are often believed to speak through oracles, and although Euthyphro appears not to have consulted an oracle, he might have done so. The messages given to the devout by an institutional oracle, such as that at Delphi, were, however, notoriously open to a variety of interpretations. Euthyphro is in any case confident that the gods support his conception of justice and that they would treat the negligent homicide of a lowly murderer as just as polluting as the death of anyone else. In the light of his extensive experience of ritual and myth, the gods appear to advise Euthyphro unequivocally about what he should be doing. Other religious experts might well reach a different conclusion; indeed – as Socrates reminds him at one point in the ensuing discussion (7b) – the gods themselves do not always appear to agree on what humans should do.

Arjuna has no need of an oracle, for under the conventions of epic poetry he has the voice of God with him in his chariot. The message about what he should do is unequivocal, and to dispel his misgivings Arjuna is encouraged to detach himself from his natural concerns, carry out the conduct conventionally associated with his role and assume no responsibility for deciding whether that conventionally expected conduct is in present circumstances really appropriate to that role. This might in the end be exactly what a human should do. But before exploring this advice further, it is important to consider how questions might arise about the conduct appropriate to a given role. Is it obvious what a man whose role is to 'maintain or guard the social order' (see note 3) should do in Arjuna's circumstances? Can we say that if a son 'who did what was right and expedient even when his parents did not counsel [want, wish] it, was [really, in spite of appearances] obeying his parents' (Lutz 1947: 103)?

The character of Euthyphro is not sketched very sympathetically, and Plato himself may well have viewed Euthyphro's taking his father to court with some distaste, but the point of reminding Euthyphro how his action will be viewed by other people is not to persuade him to change his mind but to motivate a line of inquiry that Socrates wishes to open. Euthyphro has made a contentious decision; on what basis was it made? Euthyphro claims that his action is required by religious propriety (*to hosion*, 4e), but not everyone accepts that what Euthyphro is doing is religiously proper. As Euthyphro appears confident of his judgment and as Socrates has himself been accused of religious impropriety, Socrates adopts toward Euthyphro the role of one seeking expert advice. How do we tell the difference between what is religiously proper and what is not? Socrates puts the question in this form: 'What do you say religious propriety and religious impropriety are?' (5d)

Euthyphro does not understand that he is being asked to specify the general criteria he used to determine what he should do to conform to the demands of religious propriety, so he replies by offering his current action against his father as an example of something that is religiously proper. Socrates, however, is not going to be helped by having a disputable example of religious propriety pointed out to him. If what Euthyphro is doing is religiously proper, what does it share with other (less disputable) examples? Give me 'the religiously proper itself . . . the form (*idea*) by which all things that are religiously proper are religiously proper,' Socrates insists, 'so that by keeping my eye fixed on it, I may use it as a pattern or exemplar [*paradiegma* has both meanings] and determine whether anything you or anyone else does is religiously proper or improper by seeing whether it agrees with it' (6d–e).

What Socrates appears to want when he asks for a 'pattern or exemplar' is something that would work like a straightedge or try square in the building trades. One holds a straightedge up to a piece of wood to see if it has been planed flat or to a course of bricks to see if it has been laid evenly. Indeed, where Socrates is made to ask for a 'definition' of a term like 'religiously proper' or 'just' using a word, *horos*, that originally meant 'boundary marker' or 'limit' and also 'rule,' 'standard' or 'measure,' it became common within two or three generations following Socrates' death for Greek philosophers to use a term, *kanōn*, – used in the building trades for a straightedge – to speak of anything that served as a standard of judgment. The two quotations at the head of this chapter illustrate how widespread is the impulse to use this metaphor. Epictetus speaks of discovering something that will work as a balance scale or carpenter's straightedge to assess the conflicting opinions of men.[6] In China at about the time that Socrates lived, Mo Tzu expressed confidence that the standard he referred to as 'the will of heaven' could be used like a pair of compasses or a carpenter's try square.

It is important to note that these images, which we have found in both Greek and Chinese traditions, are not about choosing a unit of measure, which may differ in different places – a yard in one place, a metre in another or the Imperial gallon on one side of the Atlantic and the American gallon on the other. Three of the four examples involve no quantitative notions at all. The use of a balance scale does allow objects to be compared and judgments made to the effect that one thing is so many times heavier than another, but this refinement, although possible, is not required to use the balance scale to aid in making simple qualitative comparisons to the effect that one thing is heavier than another. The other three examples also allow of judgments of more and less (straighter, closer to 'true,' etc.) but no convention-independent notion of one thing being so many times straighter or truer than another. These are examples of qualitative not quantitative measures, devices to aid in circumstances where the eye cannot see by looking or the hands determine by hefting.

Two of the 'measures' – compasses and balance scale – involve no exemplars, just procedures for assessing the qualities of objects. The other two – straightedge and try square – involve the use of objects that have the desired qualities and a simple procedure of holding the exemplar up to the object being assessed so that the eye can see whether there are gaps between them. Behind these two are procedures for generating the exemplars with the desired qualities. Procedures for generating straightedges and try squares are available to all cultures. One procedure for generating straightedges is to make three simultaneously and – so long as the way of fashioning them allows them to be modified as they are compared with one another – comparing them pairwise with one another until each pair fits together flush, i.e. allows no light to shine through gaps. (The point of comparing pairwise is that a convex and a concave object, even if they fit flush, will not both fit flush with a third object.) A similar procedure can be used to generate right angles, once three pairs of straightedges are available. These procedures are adequately justified and can be refined to meet whatever level of accuracy is required, so the question of why one should trust a carpenter's rule or try square can be settled by finding out how it was made and how well it was cared for after it was made, or going back to the procedures that generate such devices. Simple devices such as these are not culture-specific, and these images of testing whether something is straight or square all encourage the idea that the validity of conventions may not need to be assessed from within a culture or concrete morality.

These images, however, have apparent limitations as pictures of what we are after when we ask of some action, 'Is that really right or proper?' (Is it really proper to give evidence against one's father? Is it really right to ignore or to help to cover up his criminal activities?) Even if we had a procedure that would generate or confirm that what we have possesses some quality, how do we know our test is for the relevant property? If the people of She devised some procedure that confirmed the straightness of 'Straight Body,' might Confucius not dismiss it as irrelevant? Might he not also be able to accept the procedure and insist that it has been misapplied?

The answer to the first question appears to be that this image of applying a measure assumes that the parties have a common understanding of what is in dispute, perhaps a common purpose to which the disputed judgments contribute. One party is not laying a course of bricks and the other shaping a wheel, with the two trying to identify a quality common to the satisfactory completion of both tasks. Both are engaged in an enterprise in which the disputed judgments have similar functions. If the hope held out by the image of the measure can be fulfilled, Confucius and the people of She must share enough of a common purpose in making their assessments of people as 'straight' (or as we more commonly say 'upright [citizens]') for one to show why a procedure correctly identifies what they are interested in.

The answer to the second question is, 'of course he might find that a procedure had been misapplied.' Someone might be able to understand the point of the procedure well enough to detect this even if that person did not accept that the procedure was relevant to present concerns. Procedures do not apply themselves. Some may take less skill and understanding to apply than others, but no procedure is absolutely idiot-proof. The point of asking for a 'standard' or 'measure' should never be to obviate altogether the need to make judgments or to invest thought; the point is to find a tool that increases the 'leverage' of our judgments. There are those who will insist that a standard or measure provide a mechanical decision procedure (an algorithm), but they are commonly in search of substitute authority figures to whom we can surrender responsibility for our decisions. A device that serves successfully as a measure may well take more than average skill and intelligence to apply. In that case, those with the required skill and intelligence acquire authority in proportion to the importance of the determinations they are able to make.

It is clear from the way in which the character of Socrates is made to proceed in dialogues like the *Euthyphro*, which are assigned to Plato's early period, that being able to come up with a pattern or exemplar to guide assessment is only the beginning of a line of inquiry that is designed to test the expertise of the individual being cross-examined. People with expertise, with the authority to assess the qualities that elicit approval and condemnation, are clearly expected to be able to articulate what they use to guide their assessments. When, as in Euthyphro's case, they find it difficult to provide a pattern or exemplar, Socrates suggests one that looks plausible and then turns around and shows them that they really do not understand its principles or know how to use it. A famous example occurs near the beginning of the first book of Plato's *Republic*, where Socrates engages a wealthy old man named Cephalus in a conversation about the advantages of being wealthy.

Cephalus, near the end of his life, claims that his wealth has enabled him to keep his promises and discharge his obligations to the gods and his fellow men so that he need not fear punishment in the afterlife.

> 'For wealth contributes very greatly to one's ability to avoid both unintentional cheating or lying and the fear that one has left some sacrifice to God unmade or some debt to man unpaid before one dies. Money has many other uses, but taking one thing with another I reckon that for a reasonable man this is by no means its least.'

'That fair enough, Cephalus,' I said. 'But are we really to say that doing right consists simply and solely in truthfulness and returning anything we have borrowed? Are those not actions that can be sometimes right and sometimes wrong? For instance, if one borrowed a weapon from a friend who subsequently went out of his mind and then asked for it back, surely it would be generally agreed that one ought not to return it, and that it would not be right to do so, nor to consent to tell the strict truth to a madman?'

'That is true,' he replied.

'Well then,' I said, 'telling the truth and returning what you have borrowed is not the definition of doing right'.

(Lee 1974: 331c–d)

As in his discussion with Euthyphro, Socrates is interested in the basis on which Cephalus decides – decides in this case not religious propriety but the sort of propriety that is spoken of as making something 'just' or 'right' (*dikaios*, both 'punishment' and 'wrongs' translate words that are cognates of *dikaios*).

As a way of opening this inquiry, Socrates extracts two criteria from what Cephalus says – being a man of one's word and repaying one's debts – and asks if that is what doing right amounts to. One might offer these two as simple criteria for doing the right thing: 'always tell the truth and pay back what you owe.' The difficulty with this is that there are cases where following these rules will appear to lead one to do the wrong thing. Socrates' example turns on having borrowed weapons and being asked for their return when the owner will be likely to cause himself and other people undeserved injury. (Imagine being asked to return a hunting rifle to a man who, you fear, is intent on killing his wife's lover.)

Plato nowhere dwells on it, but this brief exchange illustrates an extremely important point about what may be called efforts to 'externalize criteria.' A 'criterion' (from a Greek verb originally meaning 'to separate' and which acquired the sense of 'to discriminate,' 'to judge') is a standard, rule or test for reaching a correct judgment. To externalize, to make explicit, that by which one judges should be regarded as merely a preliminary step in the examination of a practice. The external representation is by itself inert, it does not apply itself, it does not anticipate its own limitations. Commonly, even a simple general prohibition is used with an implicit understanding of conditions under which it does not apply. Most people who regard themselves as bound by the biblical commandment 'Thou shalt not kill,' do not regard it as forbidding them to kill another human being in self-defense or while serving in wartime in the armed forces. Many who accept it support the death penalty and do not regard this commandment as applying to the people designated to carry out a judicial execution.

An externalized criterion does not by itself settle disputes or conflicts. A number of people accept the sixth commandment in a less restricted way and see it as entailing pacifism, as incompatible with violent measures to defend oneself as well as with the death penalty. The point here is not to determine the correct interpretation of Exodus 20: 13 (= Deuteronomy 5: 17) but to stress that no standard can be applied without interpretation. (Even those who read this commandment as an absolute prohibition against taking a human life into their own hands have been known to accept the risk to human life of driving an automobile on the highway.)

4.3   Rational authority

Two ways to straighten the use of words

Dramatic portrayals of Socrates asking supposed experts or authorities for criteria – usually of the application of one of their key terms of evaluation but occasionally of the name for the expert's own area of expertise – appear in dialogues other than the *Euthyphro* and *Republic I*. All but one, the *Theaetetus*, are assigned to an early period in Plato's life. Thus we find Socrates asking for accounts of excellence in general (*aretē*, see Section 1.1), of courage (or manliness), of moderation (or intelligent self-control), of what merits admiration (*to kalon*). It is also part of this pattern that each proposed account or definition is shown by Socrates to be unsatisfactory, and the dialogue ends without finding an answer to Socrates's question.

In dialogues reckoned to have been written at a later period, Plato turns from dramatizing fruitless quests for such accounts and in several places – in particular the central books of the *Republic* – Socrates is made to sketch out the method of a kind of intellectual discipline, called 'dialectic' (from a Greek word meaning 'conversation'), which if pursued carefully and diligently is supposed to generate the required accounts. The products of the dialectician's efforts are then recommended (see e.g. *Cratylus* 390c) to the legislator (*nomothetēs*, one who puts *nomoi* in place) so that the latter can proceed to craft the customs and laws that would realize the standards identified by the former. By holding up the account of what is right or just (embodying a conception of how society is properly constituted and governed and of the character of individuals who deal with one another as they should), the legislator will be able to determine whether any given legislative proposal – indeed, whether any aspect of culture (including works of art, see *Republic* 401e) – should be adopted or rejected.

The idea behind this at first sight curious division of labor makes good sense and can be applied generally to any project governed by deliberate thought. If you are doing something – whether it be legislating, managing, training fighting men or producing an artifact – it is best to be clear about what you take yourself to be trying to achieve (a just society, a well-managed operation, combat-worthy soldiers or serviceable artifacts) and then assess each thing you propose to do in terms of a clear and precise grasp of what you are trying to achieve. Specifying, defining, giving an explicit account of what a law giver is supposed to achieve is the task that Plato assigns to the dialectician. 'Law giver' is in fact a term applied to anyone exercising governance or control over some affair, e.g. a physician managing the recovery of a patient or a trainer managing the development of an athlete (*Statesman* 295b–e). Dialectic is also a method for refining the conception of health that should guide a physician, the conception of athletic fitness that should guide a trainer, even of the governing conception that should guide the efforts of mathematicians. It probably mattered little (or not at all) to Plato whether distinct people undertake the two tasks of specifying the goal and finding ways to realize it; what mattered was that the two tasks be recognized as distinct and be carried out in the proper relation to one another.

Plato, at least in the dialogues credited to his middle period, appears to have thought that satisfactory criteria for the application of key terms of appraisal, such as 'just,' 'courageous' ('manly') and 'temperate,' would be reached by a systematic process that began by laying down a criterion in the form of a definition, that is of some way of specifying the limits of the concept being examined. This definition was to be treated as a hypothesis to be criticized by finding in it the sort of flaws in proposed definitions that Socrates brings to light in the early dialogues. Having had its weaknesses exposed, the proposed definition would be replaced by a better one and the process repeated until no further criticism was possible.

There are several obvious questions about this process that need to be addressed. What constitutes an improved definition? Is there any reason to think the process will terminate? And if there is, is there any reason to think the process will terminate in exactly one way? The first question is easy to answer: an improved definition is one that does not have the flaws found in any of the proposed definitions considered so far. Plato's confidence that the process of improving definitions will terminate seems to have arisen from the idea that the attempts to define various terms will be carried out in a co-ordinated fashion under the effort to define a comprehensive term of evaluation known as 'the Good.' Once we have satisfactory definitions of all our key evaluative terms co-ordinated with one another, there will be no further reason to modify our accounts, as it will not be possible for one particular good (desirable quality) to reveal limitations in our account of another particular good. But because Plato resorts to the use of images to explain the role that 'the Good' has in his project, he is not led to confront the third question; he simply assumes that there is only one account to be given of the way everything should be, not several equally coherent but incompatible accounts.

There is only one example in the works of Plato of a definition that is not shown to be inadequate, although it is acknowledged not to be securely established until a satisfactory definition of the Good is reached (*Republic* 435d; *cf.* 504b–d). This is the definition offered in the *Republic* of the notion at the center of its inquiries, the just (*to dikaion*) or justice (*dikaiosunē*). Whatever its limitations might prove to be as the definition of the Good is pursued, if this definition can be taken as indicative of the sort of thing that would satisfy Plato, it is clear that he did not expect a definition to serve on its own as any kind of decision procedure. The cryptic formula, 'the having and the doing of one's own and what belongs to oneself' (434a), does not make sense and cannot be used except in the context of the socio-psychological theory (three social classes reflecting three parts to the human soul) that is developed in Books III–IV. The upshot of this theory is that an individual human, as well as society as a whole, functions properly only when it is governed by rational authority, and this cannot be readily conveyed simply by a definition of a key term.

Dialectic and the use of its products, definitions, give rise to rational authority in a refined sense of 'rational.' Definitions not only provide reasons for applying key concepts, but are also intended to be abstract (without details that distinguish individual cases from one another), general (comprehending as many individual cases as possible) and consistent (free of internal conflict). It is this perspective, afforded by standards or measures with these characteristics, that is supposed to enable those who can grasp and apply definitions to avoid mistakes, anticipate difficulties and perceive otherwise obscure possibilities. Plato's dialectically guided law givers have a form of authority that is rational in this special sense: their policies are based on the most refined uses of human capacities to reason; their directives are guided by abstract and general principles and have been forged in a furnace of intense critical scrutiny aimed at discovering their limitations.

Unlike the kind of rational authority that Max Weber had in mind when he identified his third pure type of authority, the 'rational authority' that Plato has in mind is not vested in institutional forms but remains vested in human individuals (in the 'Guardians' of his ideal city-state). It is not externalized in a legal system or a bureaucracy but remains in the character of those who exercise it. People with the sort of authority that Plato recommends do not derive it from the procedural rules of the system they follow, even if the rules are recognized to have been worked out with maximum consistency, abstraction and generality. Plato's rulers have authority because of the grasp they have of standards to be applied when discriminations are to be made, a grasp that is firm and unerring because of its consistency and comprehensiveness.

If we were to compare the two by asking where the standard or measure resides, the answer for Weber would be in the institutions, the explicit rules, legal and administrative, that should govern people's lives. For Plato, the properly ordered and governed (i.e. just) society does not consist of institutions, of customary and conventional behavior abstractly conceived, whether it be consciously or unreflectively regulated, but in the actual dispositions of its people. It is the character of individual people that gives rise to their conduct, and it is this rather than the institutions that a political leader, a statesman, is trying to shape. What should function as a standard, then, is not an ideal institution but an ideal of character. This is clear from what Socrates usually seeks to have defined, qualities of character, and when he asks for an account of someone's expertise, it is an opening to explore what a person with that expertise will do to the character of one who follows him. The desirable quality of a political order, its being '*dikaios*,' just or right, which is explored in the *Republic*, is patterned after, and shown to be dependent on, the qualities of the people who live in that form of social structure.

The ultimate measure is not the definition but the person who knows what to do with it. If you lack the knowledge and want to know what courage, self-control or fair-mindedness require in a given situation, put a person known to be courageous, self-controlled or fair-minded in that situation and see what happens. (Compare: if you want to know what is required to plane an edge straight, place the straightedge alongside it.) And if we follow this analogy and think in terms of the ideal, excellent or virtuous person as a standard, the weight of the whole enterprise comes to rest on *how we generate that person*. People acquire their characters through experience; the control of that experience takes the form of either education or personal (self-)cultivation. Thus the crucial part of this project becomes the description of a regime that will generate ideal persons.

Approached from this direction, it should come as no surprise that most of *Republic* II–VII, is devoted to outlining an educational program that is designed to generate people with ideal habits and intellectual capabilities and to place them, the 'Guardians' of the city-state, in positions of leadership where their qualities will determine how society is structured and governed. To ensure that the character of these exemplary people is undistorted, Plato insists that they live without luxuries – almost literally a Spartan existence, because the model here appears to be the *nomoi* of Sparta (see Section 3.1). But more importantly, they will live without the distorting influences of private concerns, either property or family. To ensure that the minds of these exemplary people will be equipped to function properly, they will study mathematical disciplines (those that define and apply concepts like 'straight,' 'square,' 'circular' and 'equal in weight') as a preparation for undertaking dialectic, where their task will be to define the qualities that they use to assess everything in the culture of their society.

To appreciate more fully the force of 'rational' in the kind of authority that Plato wants his Guardians to have, it is instructive to compare the direction that Confucius and his followers took from a very similar starting point. Confucius, like Plato, recognized the importance of how people use words when employing crucial evaluative concepts. There is but one (unusually long) passage in the *Analects* where Confucius takes up this theme, and it initiated what has proved to be a perennial topic of discussion in Chinese philosophy, *cheng ming*, 'the rectification of names.' The passage, XIII.3, begins with a disciple named Tzu-lu asking Confucius what is the first thing he would do if the Lord of Wei asked him, Confucius, to govern (or bring order to) his state and Confucius replying that his first step would be to govern (bring order to, rectify) names. Tzu-lu is dismissive in his response, and Confucius is unusually forceful in putting Tzu-lu in his place:

> How can you be so coarse [dense?]! An exemplary person (*chün tzu*) remains silent about things that he does not understand! When names are not properly ordered, what is said is not attuned; when what is said is not attuned, things will not be done successfully; when things are not done successfully, the use of ritual action and music will not prevail; when the use of ritual action and music does not prevail, the application of laws and punishments will not be on the mark; and when laws and punishments are not on the mark, the people will not know what to do with themselves. Thus, when the exemplary person (*chün tzu*) puts a name to something, it can certainly be done. There is nothing careless in the attitude of the exemplary person (*chün tzu*) toward what he says.
>
> (Hall and Ames 1987: 269–70)

In this passage, a number of things are said to depend on the correct use of names; these will be discussed more fully in Section 8.2. What interests us here is how Confucius would go about ensuring that names are used correctly.

There are no definitions in the *Analects*, no suggestion that anything that would serve as a standard or criterion to guide the application of a term would be of any use, and no subsequent Chinese philosopher, Confucian or non-Confucian, who took up the theme[7] takes this topic in the direction indicated by Plato. What we find instead are indications that instead of a single general criterion or standard, Confucius assumed that ensuring the proper use of names required a lengthy process of minor adjustments, all contributing to instilling a practice of correct identification. An important evaluative term, for example, occurs in the passage above. '*Chün tzu*' is also translated 'gentleman' and 'superior person'; Confucius clearly wants it applied only to people who deserve to exercise authority, to direct and to set an example for others to follow. Tzu-lu aspires to be this sort of person, and Confucius uses the occasion reported above to correct Tzu-lu's application of the term, but not in a way that produces a general characterization of it.

There are numerous passages in the *Analects* where Confucius makes particular observations on what he takes to be a correct use of this term. Often these come in the form of a contrast with an inferior or 'small' person (*hsiao jen*). What observations like these afford is an incremental process of building up a grasp through particular aspects of the intended ideal.

> The superior man understands righteousness (*yi*), the inferior man understands profit.
>
> > (Chan 1963: IV.16)

> The gentleman is easy of mind, while the small man is always full of anxiety.
>
> > (Lau 1979: VII.37)

> The superior man is conciliatory but does not identify himself with others; the inferior man identifies with others but is not conciliatory.
>
> > (Chan 1963: XIII.23)

> The superior man is dignified but not proud; the inferior man is proud but not dignified.
>
> > (*ibid.*: XIII.26)[8]

This is characteristic of the Confucian approach. As in Plato, there is an interest in seeing that words, particularly those that guide conduct, are applied only in ways that (it is felt) they should be applied; as in Plato, there is particular interest in the development of proper habits of feeling, attitude and response, in short of character; and as in Plato reliance is ultimately placed on people with properly developed character. But there is no hint in Confucius or his followers that attempts to develop the right character will be helped by abstract and general formulations of any kind.

Building character is, like acquiring the ability to use a word accurately, a long-term incremental process. It requires a dedication to a form of self-cultivation. The Confucian approach does not rely on explicit general guides that can be applied consciously but seeks to forge a reliable complex of sensitivities and habits of response. What this calls for is suggested by a phrase attributed to Henry James – 'successive accumulations of "endless" amounts of history, and tradition, and taste.'[9] The claim would be that to develop the judgment needed to make difficult decisions about one's conduct and roles or the practices and institutions of one's society, it is not necessary to employ rational thought that makes use of abstractions, generalization and comprehensive representations that have been carefully checked for consistency. Rather, what is needed is extensive familiarity with history and its many particular examples, with tradition and the art and literature it preserves, and with taste, that is with the attitudes embodied in the refined artifacts of a culture.

If we added to this list constant practice in rituals of courtesy and appropriate conduct, the result would sum up reasonably well the attitude of Confucius and his followers. Although they discuss in some detail values and excellences of character, Confucius and his followers do not identify forms of rational thought as essential to the development of the ability to make sound judgments about how to conduct oneself or govern public affairs. Instead, the emphasis is on unending self-cultivation involving two principal activities, learning (*hsüeh*) and ritual (*li*). The former consists of becoming familiar with and reflecting upon the classics of Chinese culture; the latter consists of practising diligently the ritual forms of conduct that Chinese tradition prescribes. The cognitive excellence that the standard of judgment (the exemplary person) embodies is pretty much what James described, a successive accumulation of 'endless' amounts of history, tradition and taste, where the last of these is shaped as much by practice as by examples found in literature.

Faced with a problem or a conflict, well-cultivated Confucians do not respond mindlessly. They have resources available, models in literature and patterns of response in ritual, that they can adapt. Adapting does not proceed either thoughtlessly or unintelligently just because it does not proceed through abstraction and generalization, any more than does drawing on one's training and experience to adjust one's tennis game to new opponents proceed thoughtlessly or unintelligently. On behalf of the direction Plato took, it can be argued that the drives to consistency, abstraction and generalization provide resources too valuable to overlook. They afford new perspectives that reveal new possibilities as well as limits to the usefulness of old patterns of response. In reply, it can be countered that abstraction decreases one's sensitivity to the particulars of the situation in which one has to act, that generality may obscure relevant differences and that consistency may tie one's response to habits that create rather than dissolve problems. Rational authority, that is personal authority informed by the refined uses of reason that Plato favored, has, it may be argued, drawbacks that authority informed by the refinements of culture can remedy.

4.4 Reason and reality

Seductive and authoritative objects

We have so far uncovered two very general kinds of thing that might serve to redeem the promise held out by the image (see Section 4.2) of tools for measuring qualities, like a straightedge or a try square. One kind of device for determining the quality of a response – e.g. can what X is doing (or feeling) be characterized as courageous, fair-minded, religiously proper, etc.? – would be an abstract and general criterion. Another kind of device would be to identify individuals with the right qualities of character and compare their responses. In this section, we will introduce a further kind of device, one similar to the first but standing in a different relation to practical reason. In subsequent chapters (beginning with Chapter 6), we will examine accounts of devices of these three kinds and look more closely at what value there is in dealing in abstractions and generalizations and at the claims of concrete particulars to serve in lieu of, or as a necessary supplement to, abstractions and generalizations. But before adding to the kinds of device we might need to examine, we must consider more carefully the connection that measures or standards have to the authority of a directive, the validity of a convention and the basis of an attitude of approval or disapproval.

The terms that Plato wanted to have defined and Confucius wanted to have applied correctly are terms that normally signal approval, and their opposites normally signal disapproval. Each term, moreover, specifies a different kind of approval, not a different specific qualitative feel to, but a different sphere of application for, the approval or disapproval. The sphere of application of the terms 'generous' and 'stingy' is where people have opportunities to share their resources and differs from that of 'courageous' and 'cowardly', which have to do with the way people deal with their fears. What a standard or measure for the application of words like these would offer is a way of distinguishing where among similar cases we should bestow approval or disapproval.

To seek such a standard is to assume that it is possible to misapply, or at least to do better and worse at applying, such terms. If there is no basis for their application other than the facts about what people usually do with these words, then the discovery that other people are uncertain about these cases is the discovery that it is not possible for anyone to get it wrong or to do better or worse. There is in this case no validity, none at least that can be properly called 'objective,' in the sense that it calls for attention to more than the facts about what is done. Where there might have appeared to be a convention in Weber's sense, there is merely a custom with the force of a fashion – a matter of *mere* fashion or etiquette (see Section 2.3) – and no exercise of authority can claim legitimacy.

As it happens, the important connections here were first probed in a passage of Plato's *Euthyphro*. Occasionally one comes across the phrase 'the *Euthyphro* problem'. This refers not to the question of whether Euthyphro should prosecute his father but to a question that Socrates asks in the course of exposing Euthyphro's inability to provide a satisfactory criterion for religious propriety. The religiously proper, Euthyphro has suggested, is what all the gods love (9d). Socrates then asks whether the gods love what is religiously proper because it is religiously proper, or whether it is religiously proper because they love it (9e). The implication is that if the latter is the case, there is no basis for religious propriety beyond whatever benefits follow from being in the good graces of the gods. If the former is the case, then the criterion that Socrates is seeking, the account of what it is that constitutes an act as religiously proper, will make clear what it is that draws the gods to love it and (hopefully) will make clear why this is a reason for us to follow their authority and perform the act. Euthyphro responds in a way that conforms to the presuppositions of his culture – he accepts that the actions and attitudes of the gods conform to standards that are independent of their attitudes and desires (see Section 3.4 on Galen and Celsus) – and thus accepts that there is something distinct from the love of the gods, something 'objective,' that renders an act religiously proper and gives the gods reason (draws them) to love it.

It might be tempting to infer from this that, for there to be an 'objective' basis for climates of approval and disapproval, i.e. a basis beyond the mere facts of the existence of these climates, there have to be features of the world that in and of themselves ('intrinsically') call for, require or demand from us approval or disapproval. The model that gives rise to this temptation is that of perceptual judgments. The basis of the judgment that there are seventeen chairs in room 302 – the reason it would be a mistake to judge otherwise – is the presence of exactly that many chairs in room 302. ('Go in and count them.') This is independent of what anyone or everyone may fancy to be the number of chairs in that room. However, this model seems inappropriate to the phenomena of approval and disapproval. Objects may require our thoughts to conform to them if our judgments are to be true or false, but our approvals and condemnations, our desires and rejections are not the sorts of things that have to conform to the world. Instead, we try to make the world conform to our desires and rejections; our approvals and condemnations are, if judgments at all, judgments about how well the world conforms to what we at some level desire or reject.

Now we came to these considerations from situations where there were conflicts over what to approve and try to bring into effect, and over what to disapprove of and take care to avoid doing. The question was premised on the assumption that our present patterns of approval and disapproval may need adjustment – at the very least refinement and quite possibly wholesale revision. The perceptual model taken by itself leaves us with a very peculiar picture of what would have to be the case if there were a basis (for approving and disapproving) of the sort that allows us to make sense of a need for refinement or for wholesale revision. There would have to be objects in the world that called out to us for our approval with an authority that could not be rejected or resisted.

The metaphor of objects calling out to us, exerting a pull on our affections, is not without foundation. The desire to eat a doughnut, possess a trinket or comfort a child may be experienced as calls or pulls from objects, but there may be reasons (a diet, a budget, a need to discipline) to reject each of these and to override the desires that lead us to feel these calls or pulls. What we seem to need, if there is to be an objective basis for our approvals and disapprovals, is objects whose call we should hear and not ignore, whose pull we should feel and not resist. Something like this does obtain in the cases where we recognize the need to override a desire. What someone's mind hears when it ignores the call of the doughnut are the demands of a diet that excludes doughnuts. There is an object that provides the basis for our disapproval of what calls out to our appetite; it is our health or appearance, whatever the diet serves to advance – and the basis of that disapproval is in that sense 'objective.'

The model that gives rise to this sense of 'objectivity' is that based on the use of our practical reason, which connects our present acts to our longer-terms goals; what it adds to the model based on perception is the way in which perception may be informed by the connections that we have discovered obtain between one thing and another. This is not a 'thin' sense of objectivity that reduces to the fact that this is what people happen to approve or disparage. To the thin sense in which what people happen to approve or disparage may be said to be objective, we now have a more robust sense that allows facts about the way people actually feel to be seen to embody mistakes. People can be seen to be mistaken when it is clear that by approving this, and disparaging that, they are led to pursue or avoid what will frustrate projects central to their lives.

For many, this is not an adequate sense of objectivity. What is truly objective, it is held, must be independent of what we think or feel or hold to be central to our lives. That we happen to value highly something like reduced risk of heart disease or a slender figure does not give the disapproval of eating the doughnut any basis worthy of the term 'objective.' 'Objectivity,' according to this view, requires that there be real properties of things or states of affairs in the world around us with real power to demand approval and disapproval from us. This attitude is characteristic of one form of what has come in recent years to be known as 'moral realism.'

A realist attitude does not entail the belief that there are such properties; an attitude of this sort may be part and parcel of a rejection of the whole idea that climates of attitude have any basis beyond their own existence as social phenomena. This 'skeptical' position, as it is called, this doubt that there is any objective basis (see Section 5.3), is fed by the confidence – which is perhaps an overconfidence – that many of our factual judgments about the world around us are not dependent on our desires or on the purposes served by the judgments that we make. This comes from ignoring the extent to which purposes served are buried in the context in which a judgment is made. That there are seventeen chairs in room 302, for example, depends on our being interested, perhaps, in how many can be moved to room 310 for the crowd we expect there rather than how many people can be seated in 302. In the latter case, the fact that three people can sit comfortably on a counter top might raise the relevant number to twenty.

Those with a realist attitude, and who embrace the view that there are such properties, commonly approach these questions from the standpoint of 'the morality system' (see Section 1.1) and take the refinement or revision of our customs of approval and disapproval to be based on an obligatoriness that can be discovered in the world by a 'cognitive' process modeled on perception. We examine a situation with our minds as we look over the contents of a room with our eyes and discover, instead of so many pieces of furniture, overriding obligations to act in certain ways (including acts of expressing approval and disapproval). What recommends this model is on the one hand the extent to which our talk about our obligations is conducted using grammatical forms (indicative sentences and conditional clauses) that purport to state facts and on the other hand the way it supports the idea that obligations and the attitudes of approval and disapproval may be unconditional. The basis for refining or revising our attitudes of approval and disapproval in response to the workings of practical reason is, however, conditioned by the objectives that have been adopted. No disapproval is called for unless and until some goal like health or appearance has been adopted.

The view that there are properties such as the realist claims does little, it should be noted, to help to settle questions about what our obligations are or how we are called on to refine or revise our attitudes of approval and disapproval. It is a view about how things have to be in order for us to accomplish something (refinement or revision) that we hope to accomplish, but it does not add to our capacity to accomplish it. It is a 'metaphysical' picture comparable to that which Plato used for a somewhat different but closely related purpose.

Plato's interest, we have seen, was in finding abstract and general statements that could guide the use of terms that mark discriminations between different qualities of acts, character traits or institutions. To underwrite the authority of these definitions to guide discriminations, Plato spoke of them as though they described non-physical objects, which he referred to using terms that are translated as 'Form' and 'Idea' (often with an initial upper case letter to indicate the special authority that Plato accorded these objects). Plato also wrote as though there was access to these objects through a kind of mental vision, a speculative or theoretical use of reason, and that dialectic is merely a way of prompting the required use of our rational capacities.

The claim that there are such objects serves to underscore the authority and objective validity that definitions are supposed to have, but whether the claim is true or not does not further the project of finding standards to guide our discriminations or settle which measures have been correctly fashioned. At most, it affects the seriousness with which we undertake the activity of dialectic and the use of its products – a seriousness that might equally well be sustained by the belief that dialectic is a form of intellectual technology producing cognitive implements for a better way of life.

Plato was a realist about definitions and spoke of the corresponding realities, Forms or Ideas, as separate from the world around us. He laid no stress on the independent reality of the qualities of acts, characters and institutions found in the natural world and may well not have embraced that form of realism had he encountered it. Modern realists, who stress the independent reality of properties of things or states of affairs in the world around us, normally reject Plato's claim that there is a reality corresponding to abstract and general accounts of terms of appraisal. They differ among themselves over whether the required real qualities in the world are natural or non-natural qualities. Realism, even moral realism, is not one thing.

Plato's pupil and for a time junior colleague, Aristotle, took up the idea that a person with certain ideal dispositions constituted a standard and wrote into his definition of an ethical excellence the requirement that those with any fully developed ethical excellence make their choices through reasoning in the manner of a person who possesses the key intellectual virtue of *phronēsis* (commonly translated 'practical wisdom'). *Phronēsis* involves the ability to deliberate well, i.e. settle on a course of action in the light of a goal, not merely in the light of some particular goal that may be before one, but in the light of the goals that contribute to a good life in general (1140a25–30).

Aristotle distanced himself from Plato in a number of respects. He emphasized that the ethical excellences did not rest on the use of theoretical reason but on the practical employment of our rational capacities. Along with his stress on the importance of deliberation, he assigned far less importance to dialectic. He rejected the idea that there were realities corresponding to abstract and general accounts of terms of appraisal. He offered what guidance he could through accounts of particular excellences rather than seeking for general criteria for the application of terms of appraisal. He did not follow Plato in treating 'good' as a term of appraisal on the same level as 'courageous' ('manly'), 'generous' or 'fair-minded' ('just'). 'Good,' he argued in effect, is a schematic notion. It is what things aim at (1094a2) and will be different for different things in different contexts.

Aristotle's approach still places high value on the use of our rational capacities to deal in abstraction and generalization. Although it would be a mistake to try to give an account of the good in general (there is no single thing here, 1096a20f), it is possible to develop a general account of a good life for a human being and an account that should guide the deliberations of a *phronimos* (one who possesses *phronēsis*). Because he proceeded as though there was but one account to be given of this 'good for humans insofar as they are human,' it is common to treat Aristotle as a realist about this good. But there is no suggestion that we have access to this particular good by any route modeled on simple perceptual apprehension. Anyone who wanted to argue that there is more than one possible 'good for humans,' or none at all, would not find that Aristotle thought there were *metaphysical* obstacles to doing so.

In Aristotle at any rate, we find suggested a third kind of standard or measure, one to be employed by practical reason as it determines appropriate responses to situations: how well a response 'measures up' depends on what contribution it makes to our ultimate objectives. The validity of a custom and of the attitudes people take to ways of behaving, the authority of a directive and of anything held up as exemplary, will all be assessed relative to the contribution to our most comprehensive goals that will be made by following them. The most general terms used in English for judging in this way, in terms of some end, are 'good' and 'bad'; assessments made in these terms may be referred to as using 'a measure of the good.' The most general terms used in judging character are 'virtuous' and 'vicious,' and this kind of measure may be referred to as 'a measure of virtue.' When judging whether a performance measures up to previously specified criteria, the most general terms of appraisal are 'right' and 'wrong,' and this may be referred to as 'a measure of right.' In the later chapters, we will look in more detail at standards or measures of all three sorts: criteria for applying terms of appraisal (in particular those that have come to be institutionalized in legal systems); the character traits of human beings (especially those that can be held up as exemplary); and accounts of goals or objectives (those that offer a unified direction for a human life) – all of them different devices for evaluating the ways in which humans conduct themselves.

It should not be assumed that there is but one standard or measure to be sought and that we must find it in precisely one of the three types that we will be examining in more detail. Craftsmen do not rely on a single measuring tool; it would be folly to dispense with try square and calipers because one has a satisfactory straightedge on hand. Intelligent craft requires assessing problems and progress in many qualitative dimensions. It should not be assumed that we can assess the quality of conduct and ignore the contribution of character and goals, or assess people and pay no attention to what they aim at and what they steer by, or assess practices relative to ends and ignore what kind of people this will involve and what criteria might serve to guide their endeavors.

Before we look in more detail at the use of standards or measures and what they can tell us about the basis we have for our attitudes and practices, we need to consider a variety of claims to the effect that we do not need and cannot successfully devise such tools. One of these claims comes in a somewhat paradoxical form, no doubt for rhetorical effect: we do not need to measure, since each of us is his or her own measure of what things are and of how they ought to be.

Further reading

Zaehner (1972) provides a full-scale commentary on the *Bhagavad-Gītā*; Sharma (1986) offers a good account of current Indian views of this famous text, and Sinha (1986) contains some interesting heterodox speculation on what might possibly have been the first version of the text. Hamilton and Cairns (1961) and Cooper (1997) are comprehensive collections of translations of Plato's works. For a well-motivated discussion of Plato's project and the metaphysics that grew out of it, which is centered on the *Euthyphro*, see Allen (1970). Robinson (1953) is a careful study of how the method of Plato's early period grew out of the practice dramatized in the early dialogues. Further reading on Confucius will be given following Chapter 8, but for a discussion of rectifying names, see Makeham (1994: chapter 2). For a naturalist version of realism, see Brink (1989), chapter IV of which addresses the question of what difference one's metaphysics might make to one's approach to ethics. For a non-naturalist version, see Dancy (1993), chapter IX of which contains an extremely useful discussion of objectivity.

Notes

1   Quotations from the *Bhagavad Gītā* will be from the translation of Sarvepalli Radhakrishnan in Radhakrishnan and Moore (1957: 102–63), but occasionally will be modified in the light of those given by Zaehner (1972) and Deutsch (1968).
2   It has been suggested (Sharma 1986: introduction) that apparent inconsistencies and ambiguities in the *Gītā* are the product of its having been added to and adapted in the course of being transmitted over the centuries. (Its first formulation is thought to have occurred some time between the fifth and second centuries BCE.) This view is repudiated by traditionalists, and there is not even limited consensus among Sanskrit scholars (as there is among biblical scholars) about the probable evolutionary structure of the text as we have it.
3   III.20, 25, *lokasaṅgraham* 'connotes maintaining or guarding the social order' (Deutsch 1968: 146).
4   The translation will, as in the case of the *Crito* (see Section 3.1), depart from that in Fowler (1914).
5   References to the *Analects* of Confucius (early fifth century BCE) will be by book (Roman numeral) and chapter (Arabic numeral) as they appear in the translation (Lau 1979). Various translations will be used. Those of Chan (1963) are preferred, but his selection is incomplete.

6 Epictetus, who lived five centuries after Socrates, and his teacher Musonius were members of a philosophical tradition, Stoicism, (so-called because its original members held forth in a colonnade in Athens known as the *Stoa Poikilē*), which regarded Socrates as one of its important intellectual forebears.

7 E.g. Hsün Tzu (Watson 1963–4: 139–57); Tung Chung-Shu (Chan 1963: 273–4); Kuan Chung Tzu (Hall and Ames 1987: 274).

8 The choice of English words to render these contrasts is fraught with difficulty. Lau (1979) translates the last two thus: 'The gentleman agrees with others without being an echo. The small man echoes without being in agreement.' 'The gentleman is at ease without being arrogant; the small man is arrogant without being at ease.'

9 The attribution to James is made by W.A. Oldfather (1925, Vol. I: xviii). It has not been possible to find Oldfather's source in the works of James.

5

MAN AS THE MEASURE

Man is the measure of all things. Of the things that are, that
they are and of the things that are not that they are not.
(Protagoras (fifth century BCE); as reported by Plato
(*Theaetetus* 152a))

Recapitulation: The occurrence of chronic uncertainty about
what attitudes to adopt, actions to take or practices to follow has
given rise to a perceived need – in the minds of people from
widely separated cultures – for something that could function like
the devices used in the building trades that serve as standards for
assessing or 'measuring' various qualities (straight, circular, level,
right-angled). A number of 'moral measures' have been suggested.
These have fallen into these kinds: (1) a measure of right that is
something to serve as a pattern to guide simultaneously the application of a word that evaluates and the performance that would
be evaluated by it (for example a definition); (2) a measure of
virtue, the identification of exemplary types of human beings
(people whose lives are worthy of emulation or whose judgment
can be relied upon in difficult circumstances); and (3) a measure
of the good, i.e. accounts of comprehensive goals in terms of
which to assess patterns of conduct or character traits. It should
not be assumed that chronic uncertainty can be dealt with satis-
factorily by employing measures of only one kind.

Prospectus: The same image that expresses hope for the resolution of uncertainty is also used to undermine the impulse to
seek a standard by suggesting that any attempt to undertake ethical
inquiry will reach only the conclusion that there is no basis for
the validity of attitudes and practices beyond that which etiquette
and fashion have. The sources of these negative claims about the
outcome of ethical inquiry include an unwillingness to grant that
one person's judgment can have any more authority than that of
any other, a deep suspicion of human efforts to control conduct
by using articulate thought (rather than unmediated impulse or
direct guidance from God), and a lack of faith that humans can

101

achieve the necessary knowledge or intellectual authority to under-write standards of attitude or measures of conduct. The most recent arguments along these lines have appealed to the nature of the linguistic activity that is used to express moral attitudes and to conduct ethical inquiry.

5.1 Relativism

Protagoras, conventionalism and tolerance

In two of Plato's dialogues, an important role is given to a prominent intellectual of a previous generation, a man who was already well-known when Socrates was relatively young, Protagoras of Abdera. There is little surviving evidence of Protagoras' views that does not come to us via Plato's writings, but the lines at the head of this chapter purport to be a direct quotation from something he wrote and are the epitome of his intellectual legacy. They are said to be found in a text that Protagoras wrote titled 'On Truth' and clearly involve the image of a 'measure' (*metron*, that by which anything is measured). It is clear from the discussion of this claim in the *Theaetetus* what Plato thinks they mean. Plato takes Protagoras to be claiming that each individual constitutes a standard or measure of what is true and what is false – including claims about what are correct attitudes and what is proper conduct.

Taken in isolation, the quoted words do not suggest this doctrine to everyone. Protagoras might have meant 'man' in the sense of mankind as a species and claimed not that every individual constituted a standard but that what is true and false has to be determined relative to mankind in general and to human nature. It is not relevant here to inquire what Protagoras *really* meant or to consider whether Plato misrepresented him; there is in any case insufficient historical evidence to settle these claims. Protagoras has come to represent what Plato interpreted him as saying, a doctrine sometimes called 'Protagorean relativism,' which can be restated in all these ways:

- There is no basis ever to prefer the judgment of one person over another.
- There is no truth ('how it really is') independent of the judgment of individual human beings (of 'how the matter appears to each person').
- Each person's judgment is true for that person, and if one judgment conflicts with another, each judgment must be accorded equal authority.

Protagoras' thesis, it should be emphasized, comes in a very general form and is developed primarily using examples of sense perception. To take a paradigm that makes Protagoras' view seem plausible: if a person entering a sauna feels the air outside to be warm and a person leaving the sauna feels the air to be cool, there is no true degree of warmth of the air that one or both may be mistaken about; the air is truly warm for one and truly cool for the other. This is also intended to apply to the attitudes of an Englishman who views a plate of roasted horse meat as disgusting and a Frenchman who views the same plate as appetizing, or the third-century CE Roman who views marriage between brother and sister as contrary to propriety and holiness and a contemporary from Egypt who views the same arrangement as perfectly acceptable.

An analysis of the way in which Plato develops Protagoras' position for him (Burnyeat 1979) reveals that the argument for there being no true or correct view of any situation is based on the fact that people's views conflict and the inference from this that insofar as they conflict there cannot be a single (objective) truth of the matter. The principle here, however, is equivalent to the claim that if there is a single truth about some matter, then all people will view that matter the same way. In other words, there cannot be such a thing as a misleading or distorting perspective leading to a false judgment on anything about which there is a single objective (i.e. independent of what people happen to think) truth. Put this way, the argument has very little plausibility. We can all appreciate what it would be for there to be a single objective truth about the warmth of the air outside a sauna and have no difficulty understanding why two people should offer conflicting assessments of it. Conflict is not by itself sufficient to undermine the claim that there is an objective truth.

Plato noted several difficulties with maintaining a consistent relativist position. One (*Theaetetus* 170a–171d) is the status that the relativist position has in the light of the claim it is making. (This way of looking for a weakness in a position is known nowadays as applying self-reflexivity; in the ancient world it was known as a 'turning around,' *peritrope*, argument.) Protagoras' thesis says that there is no judgment that can claim to be more authoritative than any judgment that appears to conflict with it. What is the standing of this thesis in the face of someone who thinks that it is not true, who thinks that for some judgments that are made there is a single objective truth of the matter? It seems to follow from Protagoras' theory that it can only be true for those who, like Protagoras, are prone to believe it and must be false for those who disagree with it.

Another difficulty is over the claim to expertise that Protagoras makes alongside his claim about the nature of truth. How could someone like Protagoras charge a fee for training or advising people (as he did) if the authority of what he had to say could not claim to be greater than that of anyone else? Plato fashions a reply on Protagoras' behalf (166e–167d) that has Protagoras say that he does not receive payment for telling people how it really is, rather he is paid to help them to experiences that are more satisfactory for them. But Plato has Socrates point out in reply

(178b–179b) that unless the conditional statements of the form 'If you take this medicine you will get relief from your headache,' or 'If you add this ingredient to your cake you will find it tastes better,' have objective truth, there is no basis for anyone to claim to be an expert of the kind that Protagoras claims to be.

If in spite of the difficulties we find ourselves drawn to accept Protagoras' thesis, we need to consider how, if there is no correct or authoritative view of any matter and people's perceptions of the same situation may conflict radically, people manage to communicate with one another. The answer appears to be that it is simply the case that enough of the time people's judgments do not conflict; we have agreement in judgment (and fortunately when enough of us look at people's judgments we generally agree that what we see is agreement). It also appears (to enough of us) that when there is a group of people who agree about certain matters, especially attitudes about conduct, and a few people do not, the group as a whole will apply direct and indirect pressure to those few to make them at least conform outwardly to what the rest say. In other words, agreement in judgment on any matter has no more validity than that possessed by a fashion or a custom of etiquette.

The view about the validity of concrete moralities that follows from Protagorean relativism is sometimes called 'conventionalism.' The word 'convention' is used in this context in a sense that differs from that of Weber (see Section 2.1). 'Convention' is often associated in people's minds with an agreement, deliberately reached, on the part of a group of people to conform to some rule or principle. Most customs were never established as conventions in this sense, and conventionalists usually acknowledge this. But, they will insist, there is no reason why people could not discuss any custom they become aware of and agree to change some aspect of it. This applies as much to a prevailing concrete morality as to any other custom. Conventionalists believe that there is no reason to prefer one system of attitudes and practices to another, so when people become aware of how they are affected by living within the framework of a concrete morality, they could agree to alter it in any way they prefer. It is in this sense that moralities – established as they usually are by historical accident – are alleged to have a conventional status: they can be modified by agreement.

The conventionalist outlook that arises from Protagorean relativism is viewed by many as a consequence of the individualistic way it is formulated – it has been implicitly understood to claim that 'there is no basis for holding any preferences or beliefs of any individual to be superior to those of any other individual.' Not all relativists, however, are comfortable with formulating their position within an individualist framework. As a consequence of reflecting on the social dimension of human nature, a number of people, both relativist and non-relativist, have drawn the conclusion that it is a mistake to consider individuals in isolation from the society in which they acquire their dispositions and habits. For the customs of their society not only equip them with a moral outlook, they also provide them with ways of understanding and coping with their environment as well as with a range of possibilities within which they can form personal aspirations. Thus it is alleged that the very idea that people might stand back from the prevailing concrete morality of their culture as individuals, or as collections of independently thinking individuals, and treat that morality as a set of conventions that can be altered if everyone agrees, is itself a cultural phenomenon accessible only in a limited number of (mainly modern North Atlantic) peoples and reflects assumptions specific to their cultures.

Instead of adopting the individualist formulation, relativists who are responsive to these claims acknowledge that, as people's preferences are shaped by their social environment, there are only limited occasions and limited respects in which it is coherent to think of a morality as a conventionally agreed expression of individual preferences. This alternative, which is commonly designated 'cultural relativism,' would reject altogether the notion that a concrete morality is something that people might restructure as a *means to a preferred way of living*. But having accepted the claim that preferences for ways of living are themselves (largely) a product of socialization, the relativist thesis can be restated in terms of culture and concrete moralities: there is no basis for holding the concrete morality of any culture to be superior (preferable, more valid, more authoritative) to that of any other.

Relativism of the individualist sort is often assumed to lead to tolerant and liberal attitudes toward other people or cultures. A Protagorean relativist, for example, is believed to have no alternative but to let people decide for themselves what to do on whatever basis they choose – or on no basis at all, if that is what they choose. However, this depends on whether relativists hold the view (whether, that is, they judge for themselves) that tolerance and its effects are more important to them than realizing some other preferences. Relativists with personal preferences for living in a stable society – and who believe, as it is plausible to believe, that this requires people around them to share a common set of dispositions to condemn and avoid what law or custom forbids and to approve and adopt only what law or custom allows – have a personal preference for there being a concrete morality of some kind or other. For the most part, what law or custom requires may be a matter of as much indifference to relativists as whether people drive on the lefthand side of the road or on the right. It is not, however, a matter of indifference whether there is a common concrete morality, just as it is not a matter of indifference whether or not people drive on the *same* side (left or right) of the road.

A relativist who prefers a quiet life in a stable society may thus find it more readily in a society of people who believe that there is good reason to obey the law than in a society of people who believe there is no better reason to conform to the law than to break it. Giving people good reasons to obey the law might well involve the provision of draconian punishments and a brutal and repressive police force. Consistent relativists could thus support whatever repressive measures were deemed necessary to make possible the sort of life they wished to lead. Some people seem to prefer living in a repressive society, especially those people who derive privileges from the system that maintains the repression. Relativists are not by definition selfish, they do not have to be motivated exclusively by some conception of their own advantage, but relativists who are thoroughly selfish and derive personal advantage from behaving in intolerant and illiberal ways have (in their own terms) the best reason for doing so and no reason to change.

That someone may hold a contrary view, either about the best sort of life or about the sort of society (open or repressive) needed to live it, does not affect this conclusion. It is consistent for people to hold that what they would like to see has no claim to be preferred to what other people want and at the same time to take steps to see that their desires are more likely to be fulfilled than those of other people (e.g. by supporting a political party with repressive tendencies). Relativists might therefore accept that to live the sort of life they prefer, they should not be tolerant of people who believe that there is no reason to obey the law rather than break it. To believe that a society of people who accept relativism will be aware of the advantages for themselves of a law-abiding society and will as a result be generally law-abiding requires an optimistic view of human beings that is not entailed by the relativist thesis alone. Indeed, a certain amount of faith in the goodness of human nature (see Section 5.2), rather than specifically relativist views, appears to be a necessary buttress of liberal and tolerant attitudes.

As individualist relativism is assumed to entail tolerant and liberal attitudes, cultural relativism is assumed to respect and encourage traditionalism within each culture. What a culture offers to its members is, according to this view of cultural relativism, indispensable to the humanity of those people, namely values, aspirations, the ability to cope with their environment and the framework of a common social life. People should therefore seek guidance from the traditions of their culture, although (since this is a relativist form of traditionalism) there is no basis for claiming that their culture and its concrete morality are superior to any other. But as individualistic relativism is liberal and tolerant only if it draws heavily on optimistic assumptions, cultural relativism supports traditionalism only if relativism is compromised to some degree.

To see this, recall that cultures and their concrete moralities (as we observed in Section 4.1) come under pressures to change. In response to these pressures, a culture may resist change altogether, it may draw on

106

resources from its past and evolve a new way of life in which the pressures to change are integrated with its traditions, or it may abandon its traditions and develop in a way unconstrained by its past. All of these outcomes would be the culture of a human society, and cultural relativism entails that none of the outcomes can be said to be superior to any other. So if there is any basis for preferring the first or second outcome (reactionary traditionalist resistance or a considerable degree of cultural continuity) to the third (cultural discontinuity), it cannot come from the doctrine of cultural relativism alone.

5.2   Anarchism

Intuitions, optimism and the tao of Chuang Tzu

Relativism undermines claims to any kind of intellectual authority, but as we have seen it is compatible with the support for vigorous and repressive forms of political authority. Its tendency is 'anarchistic' only within the intellectual sphere. There is a widely held belief that if every person is allowed to follow his or her own view in matters affecting other people, the result will be chaos. Once again, Mo Tzu furnishes an example of how old and widespread this belief is.

> Mo Tzu said: In the beginning of human life, when there was yet no law and government, the custom was 'everybody according to his own idea.' Accordingly each man had his own idea, two men had two different ideas and ten men had ten different ideas – the more people the more different notions. And everybody approved of his own view and disapproved the views of others, and so arose mutual disapproval among men. As a result, father and son and elder and younger brothers became enemies and were estranged from each other, since they were unable to reach any agreement. Everybody worked for the disadvantage of the others with water, fire, and poison. Surplus energy was not spent for mutual aid; surplus goods were allowed to rot without sharing. Excellent teachings (*Tao*) were kept secret and not revealed. The disorder in the (human) world could be compared to that among birds and beasts. Yet all this disorder was due to the want of a ruler.
>
> (Mei 1929: 55–6)

We have seen that even Protagorean relativists can consistently support repressive policies; political authority does not need to be underwritten by claims to intellectual authority merely for it to exist. We have also seen that those who value tolerance and a comprehensive principle that no one should interfere in the affairs of anyone else must possess optimism that people can survive and thrive without anyone claiming or exercising authority over anyone else (either that or they must be prepared to live with the consequences).

In assigning ethics the task of seeking a basis for our concrete moralities, we have assumed that it is worth having a source of intellectual authority for our attitudes and practices, if one can be found, and we have committed ourselves to using a form of thought that may be described as 'discursive.' Relativism, whatever its motivation, repudiates the need for any kind of intellectual authority. One possible motivation for this repudiation is lack of faith in our ability to use discursive thought to achieve anything as momentous as well-founded intellectual authority.

The word 'discursive' suggests that at a minimum thoughts are joined together or 'articulated' (e.g. 'this should be done because of that') and may or may not include the use of abstract definitions and generalizations. It stands in contrast to the notion of 'intuitive' thought, where people, although aware of what is going on and of what they are doing, react as they are stimulated, without drawing consciously on the past or engaging in any form of deliberation. Even those, like Henry James or Confucius, who propose to rely for guidance entirely on 'successive accumulations of "endless" amounts of history, and tradition, and taste' (Section 4.3) will consciously and deliberately bring instances from that accumulation to bear on current problems or decisions; it does not require abstract concepts or general statements to do this, but it does require putting thoughts together in a way that renders them 'articulate.'

One form of resistance to the project of seeking standards, then, is to insist that people do much better at resolving their conflicts and dilemmas if they do not attempt to apply discursive thought of any kind (rational or otherwise) but simply rely on some form of intuitive thought. Thoroughly consistent advocates of intuitive thought will decline to offer any discursive justification for their position and will consequently not make interesting responses if attempts are made to draw them into conversation. Those unwise enough to offer to explain their position, however, often rest it on a belief that all humans are born with sound instincts of response and that social and intellectual influences tend to distort these responses. If people are just left alone to develop naturally, they will lead fulfilled lives in harmony with one another and will not find themselves facing conflicts or dilemmas.

It would be appropriate to apply the term 'nativism' to the belief that we are born with 'native dispositions,' dispositions that have determinate forms prior to cultural influences. Reliance on intuition has to be based on an 'optimistic' nativism, i.e. the belief that these native dispositions are positive. 'Pessimistic' nativism, which holds that these natural dispositions tend to work against human flourishing in general and human social life and co-operation in particular, often portrays these natural inclinations as conflicting with the guidance given by discursive thought.

Those who favor applying discursive thought to the assessment of conduct, character and attitudes – those 'rationalists' who advocate using abstract definitions and generalizations, as well as those who wish to rely only on accumulations of history, tradition and taste – do not necessarily have a view on the question of whether there are native dispositions and whether, if there are, they are in general a positive or negative influence on our lives. Plato took a pessimistic view of natural inclinations, especially those associated with the body, its desires and pleasures. Aristotle appears not to have been drawn to nativism; he held that we do not automatically acquire excellence of character, but when we do it is not something contrary to our nature (1103a19–25). Confucius likewise reveals no nativist tendencies, stressing as he does the need for strenuous efforts at personal cultivation if we are to earn the status of a superior individual (*chün tzu*) and to achieve authoritative humanity (*jen*). However, one of Confucius' influential followers, Hsün Tzu, was a decidedly pessimistic nativist:

> A warped piece of wood must wait until it has been laid against the straightening board, steamed, and forced into shape before it can become straight; a piece of blunt metal must wait until it has been whetted on a grindstone before it can become sharp. Similarly, since a man's nature is evil, it must wait for the instructions of a teacher before it can become upright, and for the guidance of ritual principles before it can become orderly.
>
> (Watson 1963–4: 157–8)

Another Confucian, Mencius (Meng Tzu), appears to have been a more optimistic nativist: 'Humanity, righteousness, propriety and wisdom are not forced on us from outside. We originally have them with us' (Chan 1963: 54). Mencius objected to images that suggested that ritual and learning had the effect of mutilating humans and offered instead the picture of human tendencies as moving of their own volition in a positive or healthy direction as water seeks low ground (*ibid*.: pp. 51–2). But Mencius was not so optimistic as to suggest that humans could live fulfilled and harmonious lives without the Confucian disciplines of learning (*hsüeh*) and ritual practice (*li*).

Optimistic nativism surfaces from time to time in educational reform movements (often identified as 'progressive'). For the most part, efforts to prevent the 'distorting' influences of culture from spoiling 'sound' instinct consist of forms of schooling (or deschooling) that avoid educational practices thought to interfere with the natural healthy development of children. Some Westerners inclined to optimistic nativism find inspiration in Taoism, a tradition that functioned at times as a counter-culture in China – a focus of resistance to the dominant influence of Confucianism and the Confucian call (in effect) for 'successive accumulations of "endless" amounts of history, tradition and taste.' Taoist philosophical texts express profound skepticism about the value of learning and urge instead the value of skillfully executed spontaneous action. An anecdote from a classic Taoist text, the *Chuang Tzu*, uses a craftsman's tacitly acquired skill to highlight the futility of 'learning.'

> Duke Huan was reading a book at the top of the hall; wheelwright Pien was chipping a wheel at the bottom of the hall. He put aside his mallet and chisel and went up to ask Duke Huan,
> 'May I ask what my lord is reading?'
> 'The words of a sage.'
> 'Is the sage alive?'
> 'He is dead.'
> 'In that case what my lord is reading is the dregs of men of old, isn't it?
> 'What business is it of a wheelwright to criticize what I read? If you can explain yourself, well and good; if not, you die.'
> 'Speaking for myself, I see it in terms of my own work. If I chip at a wheel too slowly, the chisel slides and does not grip; if too fast it jams and catches in the wood. Not too slow, not too fast; I feel it in the hand and respond from the heart. The mouth cannot put it into words. There is a knack in it somewhere which I cannot convey to my son and which my son cannot learn from me. This is how through my seventy years I have grown old chipping at wheels. The men of old and their untransmittable message are dead. Thus what my lord is reading is the dregs of the men of old, isn't it?
>
> (Watson 1958: 152–3)

Other passages in the *Chuang Tzu* illustrate a similar message with the skill of a cook in butchering an ox (*ibid.*: 50–1) and the skill of a swimmer who can negotiate waterfalls and rapids (204–5).

All of these skills involve discrimination. The wheelwright has to feel his way between chipping too slowly and chipping too quickly. The cook seeks to disjoint the ox through the natural articulations of its skeleton without blunting his knife on the bone, but he sometimes comes upon a complicated articulation and has to work slowly with his eyes on what he is doing. The swimmer has to 'go with the flow' but has to discern which way the flow is going. In none of these activities is discrimination helped by the use of words, let alone abstractions and generalizations, or by the influence of immersion in the classics of one's culture. Even the needed discriminations must not be given undue authority.

> Those who divide fail to divide; those who discriminate fail to discriminate. What does this mean, you ask? The sage embraces things.

Ordinary men discriminate among them and parade their discrimi-nations before others. So I say, those who discriminate fail to see.

(*ibid.*: 44)

Thought interferes with accurate perception, especially thought driven by personal preferences:

HUI TZU said to CHUANG TZU: 'Can a man really be without feeling?'
CHUANG TZU: 'Yes.'
HUI TZU: 'But a man who has no feelings – how can you call him a man?'
. . .
CHUANG TZU: 'When I talk about having no feelings, I mean that a man doesn't allow likes or dislikes to get in and do him harm. He just lets things the way they are and doesn't help life along.'
HUI TZU: 'If he doesn't try to help life along, then how can he keep himself alive?'
CHUANG TZU: 'The Way gave him a face; Heaven gave him a form. He doesn't let likes or dislikes get in and do him harm. You, now – you treat your spirit like an outsider. ... Heaven picked out a body for you and you use it to gibber about "hard" and "white"!'[1]

(*ibid.*: 75–6)

The tendency to prefer one thing to another is natural. It takes a form of cultivation to preserve oneself from this natural but in Chuang Tzu's view ultimately damaging tendency, so that one can respond naturally without the distortions introduced by acculturation or efforts to develop one's own capacities.

One plausible interpretation of what Taoists aim for (if they can be said to have aims or objectives) is to function smoothly within the world as a healthy organ functions within the body and to receive what guidance is needed (to adhere to the *Tao* or 'Way') from the natural world in a form unmediated by discursive thought of any sort. Religions such as Judaism, Christianity and Islam, which conceive the world as governed by an all-powerful being who transcends the natural world, may seek a similar form of unmediated guidance, but it will not be conceived as coming through natural perception but rather through some direct channel to a transcen-dent realm. To be prepared to receive this guidance, it is commonly thought, requires special periods of withdrawal from interaction with the natural world in which devotees engage in prayer or meditation in order to close out distractions and open themselves to charismatic inspiration. To be open to God's guidance, in other words, may require intense forms of personal cultivation of the sort that seeks to disconnect the practitioner from the influences of 'the world' (at least of the world of human beings and often of the demands of the body).

If God reveals to a devout believer what should be done in some circumstance, that person does not usually feel it necessary to seek reasons behind the guidance, either through abstract and general thought or through knowledge of history, tradition or taste. There may well be a feeling that seeking justification for such a course of action or form of conduct will only obscure or confuse the guidance received, and that the better (more exemplary) a person is, the more that person will be willing and able to place trust in God's guidance. In a similar spirit, the better Taoists see themselves as more willing and able to respond to the world around them, if they can disengage their tendencies to form likes and dislikes.

Religious belief, it must be stressed, is not incompatible with a discursive reliance on either tradition or reason. Not all religious traditions seek guidance directly from God. Many believe that God's guidance is embodied in tradition or available through the use of reason – rather than, or as well as, charismatic sources – and many expect to find at least limited understanding of whatever guidance they receive.

Optimistic nativism, insofar as it calls upon us to trust in people's natural goodness, appears to many people to be naïve, while reliance on intuition and revelation appears foolish to those who lack faith in the soundness of human nature or the accessibility of God. It is far from clear that reliable guidance can be derived from one's native impulses or that (as more pessimistic nativists insist is implausible) humans can live in sufficient harmony with one another without thought being invested in devising (at times coercive) forms of social control. What optimistic nativism advocates is 'anarchism,' i.e. the recognition of no special authority, rational or traditional. What it relies on instead of discipline is a democratized form of charisma, a 'gift' from God or from nature that is available to us all.

5.3 Skepticism

From peace of mind to 'queer' entities

Relativism, like doctrines that rely on intuition or revelation, rejects any attempt to articulate the basis on which one institution or form of conduct may be preferred to another and also rejects any attempt to articulate an authoritative standard by which to determine how to respond to difficult situations. Unlike doctrines that rely on intuition or revelation, however, relativism does not claim a superior, more direct, route to *the* answer (than is offered by the use of discursive thought); it declares that there is no answer. It is in this respect, however, every bit as much a declaration of (negative) faith as any religion.

A closely related position – but one that is *less* vulnerable to the accusation of being based on unsubstantiated faith – declares, not that there is *no* basis, but that *we* have no *knowledge* of whether there is one or of what it is. Claims that take this form are expressions of 'skepticism,' and they can support tendencies that are intellectually anarchistic in a way that differs only slightly from that of relativism. Relativism claims that no view may be treated as superior to any other, because all are *equally* good; skepticism claims that no view may be treated as superior to any other because none *is able to show* its superiority.

Skeptical tendencies can be identified in the views attributed to philosophers at least as far back as the third century BCE, when, two generations after Plato's death, members of the Academy he had founded adopted a position that later came to be known as 'skepticism.' The term 'skeptic' was not introduced until near the beginning of the Common Era, and long after it was, an 'academic' continued to mean (someone who thinks like a member of the Academy of Athens and hence) a skeptic. To ancient skeptics, any position that involved commitment to some belief or attitude was 'dogmatic.' Nowadays, this word applies to people who are unusually resistant to having their beliefs or attitudes changed. In the vocabulary of the skeptics of the ancient Greek world, the word 'dogmatic' applied to anyone who thinks there is reason to hold a belief or attitude in preference to its opposite.

This raises the question of whether skeptics can – without being exposed to the charge of being dogmatic themselves – think there is reason to hold their view in preference to a view they would disparage as 'dogmatic.' It is clearly difficult for them to maintain that no belief or attitude will ever be able to show its superiority to any belief or attitude incompatible with it. Even if we grant that no such view has so far shown its superiority, there is, nevertheless, as yet no rigorous proof that one view cannot some day be shown to be superior; to hold that no view will ever be able to establish its superiority would be a very dogmatic posture. Can skeptics even maintain that there is no reason for accepting a particular belief or attitude without becoming stained by the dogmatism they deplore in others?

Skeptics clearly need to exercise caution if they do not wish to be vulnerable to the accusation that they practise what they condemn in others. The ancient skeptics managed the required caution in this way: rather than claim (come forward as believing) that any given belief or attitude was without adequate support, they listened to reasons in favor of it and then offered reasons for holding the opposite view. Thus if someone were to defend the custom of expressing emotion in public, praising perhaps the willingness of men in eighteenth-century England to weep openly and copiously (White 1962: chapter 13), the skeptic would point to advantages of the uncomplaining decorum in hardship displayed by the Japanese, whose self-respect is built on their capacity for quiet and temperate behavior (Benedict 1946: 148). The point would not be to recommend one or the other custom but to show that where there were reasons for holding or approving of one thing, equally weighty reasons could be found for holding or approving of the opposite.

Skeptics did not claim that they could not know; rather, they tried very hard not to believe (hold opinions). Recognizing that belief is a natural human tendency (rather like the natural tendency to form preferences), they disciplined themselves to suspend belief by examining – the verb at the root of the Greek word *skeptikos* means to examine or inquire into – each claim that they were tempted to believe or disbelieve. The aim of this examination was not to determine toward which side the balance of reason (or discursive thought in general) tilted but to balance evenly the reasons in favor of each side with the reasons against it. Skeptics employed many of the arguments based on conflicting appearances that were offered for the general relativist position attributed to Protagoras in Plato's *Theaetetus.* These were not used to reassure any people that their beliefs and attitudes were as good as those of anyone else but as ways ('modes') to help to cultivate the suspension of belief – the best-known of these are the 'Ten Modes' (of argument) preserved by the second to third century CE writer Sextus Empiricus (Bury 1933: 1.40–1.163).

Even if skeptics undertook time and again to show that there was no more reason to hold something than to hold its opposite, the point was not to mount a proof that we could not know anything but to bring about the state of mind of not believing, of not being committed to the truth or validity of anything. This was recommended as the most honest and effective way of achieving the same peace of mind or imperviousness to emotional turmoil offered by competing schools of philosophy. (For the competing schools of Epicurus and the Stoics, see Sections 10.1 and 11.3, respectively.) As Chuang Tzu aspired to make discriminations without having preferences (likes and dislikes), ancient skeptics aspired to live without commitment to either beliefs about the natural world or beliefs about how humans should conduct themselves. As a consequence, they faced the same sort of challenge that Hui Tzu put to Chuang Tzu in the last quotation in Section 5.2: How can you live without belief? The reply was that they lived by responding unreflectively to appearances, that is without deliberation, without commitment to any goals or principles. This is what in effect Chuang Tzu appears to have recommended.

Skepticism, like relativism, is believed to encourage tolerance of opposing views. Again this is not necessarily the case. Skepticism reflects a loss of confidence in the sort of rational discursive activities that Plato and Aristotle recommended as sources of guidance. In the hands of the skeptics, the intellectual tools recommended by rationalists were turned against themselves and developed into a practice for avoiding any guidance that the use of generalization and abstraction might generate. Once the use of reason, or of discursive thought in general, is discredited, however, there is scope for more to emerge than quiet and tolerant souls who believe that we are all equally ignorant of whatever truth there may be. If skeptical arguments are taken to have shown the impotence of discursive thought, there is also scope for dogmatism in the more familiar sense, especially the kind based on non-discursive routes to the truth. Indeed, during the Reformation and Counter-Reformation in Europe, religious sectarians of all kinds adopted methods, tactics and arguments from the ancient skeptical tradition to use against their opponents in an effort to clear the ground for their own brand of faith (see Popkin 1964: chapter 1). Skepticism could be used in this way in an age when living without religious belief was regarded as unthinkable and the basis of religious faith (and the concrete moralities that accompanied it) was often held to be independent of the reach of discursive thought.

Modern manifestations of what is known as 'skepticism' are not linked to the pursuit of peace of mind through non-commitment and do not cultivate the practice of balancing reasons for with reasons against in an effort to achieve the suspension of commitment. They consist instead of claims to the effect that we do not have, and appear to have no prospects of attaining, knowledge of some specified kind. The first part of this sort of claim is an often healthy response to the claims of enthusiasts, who might well be charlatans; it is always advisable to consider claims carefully and consider what basis there is for making them. The second part – claims that we have no prospects for attaining knowledge of some kind – are often risky, because it is hard to anticipate the ingenuity of those who are interested enough to press their inquiries.

Modern philosophical skeptics sometimes mount claims that knowledge is not possible by holding up a standard of knowledge established in some favored area, usually science or mathematics, and arguing that some other area cannot be investigated, or claims within it established, using the methods comparable with those of science or mathematics. Aristotle anticipated (or perhaps had first-hand experience of) arguments along these lines and insisted that there were different standards of precision (or 'rigor') in different areas of investigation. As judgments about what actions are admirable or right 'admit of much variety and fluctuation,' it is simply inappropriate to demand the same precision in ethics that one demands in, say, geometry, 'for it is the mark of an educated man to look for precision in each class of things just so far as the nature of the subject admits' (1094b13–28).

A strategy that sidesteps the accusation of inappropriate demands is to argue that contrary to appearances, the discourse that is of interest to the systematic study of ethics functions in ways that simply cannot yield the sort of authoritative pronouncements that people hope to see established. One way to execute this strategy is to argue that if the judgments about what is and is not to be done did express knowledge, this would have to be knowledge of something wholly unlike anything else in our experience.

This argument appears plausible if one makes familiar realist assumptions (see Section 4.4), e.g. that the form of judgments about what is or is not to be done (is to be approved of or condemned) is the predication of properties like 'right' or 'wrong,' 'virtuous' or 'vicious,' in such a way as to attribute them to an action or person's character. We then not only have to answer questions about the aspects of the world by virtue of which these predicates apply – are they like colors and shapes? how do we recognize when they have been correctly applied? – we have to explain how these properties come to be able to constrain our decisions, affect our motivations.

Having concluded that entities of this 'queer' sort were required if there was to be such a thing as objective moral judgments, the self-professed moral skeptic J.L. Mackie felt confident that he could go beyond the usual skeptic's caution and, dispensing even with familiar arguments designed to show that discourse that presupposed these kinds of things must be meaningless, he declared flatly that such statements were false (1977: 40). Mackie perhaps stretched the term (moral) 'skepticism' when he included under it not merely doubts about the existence of the moral objects or properties in question but also downright disbelief. But what needs more careful examination is not Mackie's right to his dogmatic-sounding confidence that something does not exist but the assumptions that he made about how the discourse that interests ethics is supposed to function and what in general it takes for discourse to function objectively or authoritatively.

We will take up these assumptions and their source in the next section, but before concluding this section, it is important to consider a consequence that Mackie insisted did not follow from his position:

> The denial of objective values can carry with it an extreme emotional reaction, a feeling that nothing matters at all, that life has lost its purpose. Of course this does not follow; the lack of objective values is not a good reason for abandoning subjective concern or for ceasing to want anything.
>
> (*ibid.*: 34).

Where the ancient Greek skeptic hoped to be relieved of the burden of subjective concern and Chuang Tzu hoped to eliminate preferences, Mackie's skepticism leaves a clear space for both preferences and subjective concerns. But what does follow from his position is that what does not matter is how hard one thinks, that concern to assess conduct and attitudes critically and objectively is misplaced, and that the preference for engaging in practices and pursuing projects that can withstand rational scrutiny is simply a peculiar taste like that for starched shirts or shaken, not stirred, martinis.

5.4 Non-cognitivism

Emotivism, prescriptivism and distant views

Since the 1930s, questions about the language of moral discourse have been widely taken to have a crucial bearing on how systematic ethics can be properly conducted. This approach was initiated by a group of philosophers and scientists known as the Vienna Circle, who held that natural science provides not just a standard of precision and rigor for what it is to have well-established claims to know, but a model of what it is for people who may be in dispute to know what they are arguing about. The discursive practices in the natural sciences, the ways in which language works in these fields, show us, it was alleged, what it is to engage in genuinely meaningful communication. In natural science a claim may not be well established, but it is not properly a subject of scientific discussion unless it is clear what would count in its favor and what would count against it. Disputes in many other fields go on interminably because those involved have no clear idea of what actual experience would support a position and what would undermine it. These people have, it was alleged, no clear idea of what they mean; their disputes and the language in which they conduct them must be meaningless.

This rough way of dismissing issues – those raised not only by alleged pseudo-sciences (Theosophy, Freudian psychology, Marxian history) but by metaphysics, theology, and art criticism – was regarded as scandalous. The meaning of ethical disputes seemed, moreover, not to involve matters that could be settled in ways whereby empirical science is accustomed to settling its questions. None of the facts about abortion, it was noted in Section 1.4, are in dispute. Both parties agree that human life begins at conception and that at early stages in its development a human embryo is distinguished from primitive life forms only by its potential to become a human being. Can disputes that go beyond such facts be dismissed as meaningless?

The first response to this challenge was to acknowledge that moral discourse is informed by another source of meaning. In addition to experiences that count in favor of the truth of a belief and those that count against it, people make emotional investments in certain states of affairs; they are pleased by, and pained at, them. Disputes arise when people express opposite attitudes, some approving and wishing there to be, and others condemning and wishing there not to be, some state of affairs. So in addition to disputes about what states of affairs actually obtain, there are also disputes about how to regard a given state of affairs, disputes that arise from people's emotional responses to them. This was the starting point of what is known as the 'theory of emotive meaning,' and those who insist that this is all there is to moral discourse, *viz.* the expression of a personal (subjective) attitude toward some states of affairs, hold one (radical) version of what is known as 'emotivism.'

This radical version, sometimes known as subjectivism, still has difficulty explaining how it is possible for there to be disputes over matters like abortion, assisted suicide or repressive policing practices. That a state of affairs elicits an internal response from one person and the opposite from another does not put the two in dispute. Williams (1972: 16) shows the weakness of the subjectivist thesis by comparing the case of two passengers on a boat, one of whom feels seasick while the other does not; the two cannot be said to be in conflict about any state of affairs. Stevenson (1944) offered an emotivist theory that tried to address this difficulty by appealing to the fact that people who have an attitude toward something commonly want others to share it and will approve of those who do and disapprove of those who do not. (The passenger with his sea legs may, however unreasonably, feel a species of moral contempt for the 'landlubber' who is overcome by nausea.) This more sophisticated emotivism presents moral discourse as consisting of combined acts of expressing an attitude and encouraging others to maintain or adopt a similar attitude. Those who persist in holding the opposite attitude are those with whom one is in dispute.

Emotivism is couched in terms that raise directly the central question that has been posed in this book: what basis, if any, is there for shared attitudes of approval or disapproval? Is there, in other words, any basis that would allow us to say that those who shared some attitude are mistaken and need to adjust (refine or revise) their attitudes? If someone does not share an attitude or conform to its demands, could that person be wrong? The emotivist tendency was to deny that there was any such basis. It provided succor for relativism and – if one held that discourse could only be objective if there were external objects by virtue of which linguistic expressions could be determined to be correct or incorrect – it fueled moral skepticism. External objects ('values') in terms of which the expression of an attitude could be determined to be correct or incorrect would somehow have to elicit the correct attitude. That there would have to be such 'queer' objects is what gave J.L. Mackie (see Section 5.3) his confidence that there is no objectivity in moral discourse.

The situation does not change significantly if the theory shifts its weight from the 'expressing emotion' (feeling) function to the 'making demands' function of language. In the theory of R.M. Hare (1952), known as 'prescriptivism,' the principal linguistic function of moral discourse was taken to be to 'prescribe' how things should be rather than to express feelings about how they are or might be. Hare distinguished ordinary imperatives (commands, directives, prescriptions) from those that qualified as 'moral' by the further requirement that those who professed commitment to a prescription (or uttered it intending it be followed) be committed to a universal prescription from which that particular prescription followed, i.e. one that applies to themselves as much as to everyone else.

The roles that universal requirements of this sort play in ethics will be considered in subsequent chapters. For now, what is important is that this imposes a structure on the commitments that individuals can treat as their moral commitments (they have to be, or have to follow from, consistent general commitments), but it does not provide a basis other than inconsistency with or among universal prescriptions for saying that a particular prescription is incorrect, and it provides no basis, other than failing to conform to a prescription, for saying that something is wrong. Ultimately, the quality of conduct, attitudes and character traits is judged only against an individual's fundamental attitudes. 'A [hu]man' remains 'the measure.'

Emotivism and prescriptivism are classed as 'non-cognitivist' theories of moral discourse. The basis of this classification lies in a widely shared assumption that discourse has (at least) two independent ('orthogonal') dimensions and that all linguistic acts can be projected onto these dimensions and thereby resolved into their components. The two dimensions are marked by grammatical moods: where there is a lack of fit between the world and something said in the indicative mood, the mistake lies in the linguistic act since its function is to say how the world is; where there is a lack of fit between the world and something said in the imperative mood, the mistake lies in the world since the function of the linguistic act is to say how the world is supposed to be. An assessment, for example saying without irony that a certain act was 'generous,' contains a descriptive component and a prescriptive component. In this case, the former component identifies the act as revealing the agent's willingness to give away material possessions and the latter endorses the act and recommends it, and those relevantly like it, to everyone else (including the speaker). The descriptive component expresses the speaker's beliefs about the facts, and the prescriptive component expresses the speaker's values.

The separability of the two components, descriptive and prescriptive, and their independence from one another is, moreover, reflected in a pervasive metaphysical distinction, a distinction between *fact* and *value*. If one is a non-cognitivist, the facts that constitute the world as it is independently of us (which for many is the only standpoint from which objectivity is possible) are motivationally inert. They are not capable of moving us to act or of determining how we are to act independently of our having some impulse, desire, passion, emotion or aspiration – something that reflects a value. Values are what we bring to the world of facts, and that world constrains us only through the means it makes available or unavailable for realizing those values. One consequence of accepting this distinction is that it will appear impossible to draw inferences about what should be the case from statements purely (strictly and entirely) about what is the case – not only impossible but a piece of folly on the same level as drawing a conclusion about how things are from statements about how they ought be. Nothing contained in statements about what is the case can constrain how anything ought to be, just as nothing contained in statements about how things ought to be guarantees the truth of any statement about how they actually are.

Inferences from fact to value or from (statements involving only) 'is' to (a conclusion involving) 'ought' are scouted by non-cognitivists for committing the 'naturalistic fallacy.' One version of cognitivism that would make inferential traffic from 'is' to 'ought' perfectly legitimate is the moral realism sketched in Section 4.4. If the world is not motivationally inert, if the idea that states of affairs outside us make demands on us can be accepted as literally true, so that the statement 'X ought to be done' can be treated as correct or incorrect by virtue of the way the (value part of the) world is, then there is no fallacy that consists simply and solely of inferring an 'ought' from an 'is.'

Whether every kind of cognitivism has to be some version of this kind of realism depends on how the term 'cognitivism' is to be applied. The term is clearly tied to descriptive uses of language and to mental activity ('cognition') that determines which descriptive uses are correct and which incorrect. It would be misleading to apply the term where there is reliance on prescriptive uses of language and the mental activity ('preference') that gives rise to these. The question is whether, if we continue to treat the world apart from human beings as though it were motivationally inert, there is any sense in which prescriptions, inclinations or aspirations can be true or false, correct or incorrect. Could a person's inclinations, for example, be treated like descriptions, and it be determined that the lack of fit between certain inclinations and things in the world be regarded as mistakes like those found in descriptions? Could a person's character be treated as flawed because it did not respond to situations in the world with an appropriate set of feelings and aspirations?

We do conclude in some cases that there is something wrong with (a flaw in) a person's discriminatory capacities. If a person cannot distinguish between red and green, we say that that person is color-blind. Now there are philosophers who conclude from phenomena like color-blindness and from the way that colors depend on lighting and context that colors are not real features of the world, only products of the way in which our perceptual apparatus reacts to the world. Some non-cognitivists then compare our visual experiences of color to the attitudes that we take in response to people's conduct and character and say that neither the colors nor the moral qualities we attribute to situations are really there; rather, both arise within us and are 'projected' by our minds onto the world. This doctrine is known as 'projectivism.'

This way of talking about colors might give the impression that we color a colorless world in the way a person suffering from delirium tremens populates the world with pink elephants. Experiences of color are, however, systematic responses to objective features of the world and are accessible to people with normal visual apparatus in specifiable conditions of light and context. The projectivist likewise acknowledges that our finding conduct and character objectionable or praiseworthy is also related to the world in systematic, if culturally mediated, ways. However, the distinctively moral aspects of our responses to these discriminations do not, according to projectivism, answer to anything in the world, and apart from being in agreement, or in conflict, with those of people in one's community, they cannot be said to be correct or incorrect. This is what makes projectivism a form of non-cognitivism.

Nevertheless, could it be that in a manner similar to a diagnosis of color-blindness we could diagnose individuals or even whole communities as being deficient in the way they respond to situations that elicit their approval or disapproval? If the determination of what constituted (objective) deficiency were to be made by cognitive means, we would have a form of cognitivism that at least did not have to invoke 'queer' objects.

To explore a little further the possibility of a cognitivism that does not involve the sort of realism sketched in Section 4.4, it will be helpful to consider the views of the eighteenth-century Scottish philosopher David Hume, who anticipated in a fairly thorough fashion what is now called 'non-cognitivism':

> Take any action allow'd to be vicious: Wilful murder, for instance. Examine it in all lights, and see if you can find that matter of fact, or real existence, which you call *vice*. In which-ever way you take it, you find only certain passions, motives, volitions and thoughts. There is no other matter of fact in the case. The vice entirely escapes you, as long as you consider the object. You never can find it, till you turn your reflexion into your own breast, and find a sentiment of disapprobation, which arises in you, towards this action. Here is a matter of fact; but 'tis the object of feeling, not of reason [sc. 'cognition']. It lies in yourself, not in the object. So that when you pronounce any action or character to be vicious, you mean nothing, but that from the constitution of your nature you have a feeling or sentiment of blame from the contemplation of it. Vice and virtue, therefore, may be compar'd to sounds, colours, heat and cold, which according to modern philosophy are not qualities in objects, but perception in the mind.
>
> (Hume 1739–40: 469)

Hume is credited by many with having identified what is now called the 'naturalistic fallacy' in a passage that follows closely on the one above:

> In every system of morality, which I have hitherto met with, I have always remark'd, that the author proceeds for some time in the ordinary way of reasoning, and establishes the being of a God,

or makes observations concerning human affairs; when of a sudden I am surpriz'd to find, that instead of the usual copulations of propositions, *is*, and *is not*, I meet with no proposition that is not connected with an *ought*, or an *ought not*. This change is imperceptible; but is, however, of the last consequence. For as this *ought*, or *ought not*, expresses some new relation or affirmation, 'tis necessary that it shou'd be observ'd and explain'd; and at the same time that a reason should be given, for what seems altogether inconceivable, how this new relation can be a deduction from others, which are entirely different from it. But as authors do not commonly use this precaution, I shall presume to recommend it to the readers; and am persuaded, that this small attention wou'd subvert all the vulgar systems of morality, and let us see, that the distinction of vice and virtue is not founded merely on the relations of objects, nor is perceiv'd by reason.

(*ibid*.: 469–70)

The phrase 'naturalistic fallacy' was introduced much later by G.E. Moore (1903: 10–14), and as Moore's exposition of the alleged fallacy was riddled with difficulties, those of a non-cognitivist bent found it convenient to attach the phrase to Hume's formulation.

Hume's argument is, moreover, premised on a doctrine about how language has to work for it to be the proper object of 'reason' (his word for what is now referred to as 'cognition'). 'Reason is the discovery of truth or falsehood' (Hume 1739–40: 458), and for something to be capable of truth or falsehood, it must 'agree with' or 'disagree with' (correspond to or represent) something beyond itself. A passion (motive or volition) 'contains not any representative quality, which renders it a copy of any other existence or modification' (415). 'A passion is an original existence' (*ibid*.).

But one thing in the world (original existence) can represent another without even having to resemble it (as a dark cloud represents impending rain, or a flag represents a nation), and Hume does not in any case wholly exclude the possibility that a passion may need to be corrected. Our feelings for things near to us in time and space tend to be more intense than for things remote from us. People frequently avoid things that will produce a little distress (a trip to the dentist), even though they recognize that the long-term consequences of doing so will be a great deal more distress – but the prospect of a little distress today is felt more keenly than the prospect of a great deal of distress in the distant future.

Hume compares (*ibid*.: 582) an affection for a servant 'if diligent and faithful' and one for 'Marcus Brutus as represented in history.' As Brutus' ultimately unsuccessful attempt to save the Roman Republic was regarded as heroic by Hume's contemporaries, he expects that if we could somehow approach as near to Brutus as we are to our servant, the former would inspire admiration of much greater intensity than the latter. Even if we are not actually able to correct our feelings, we are able to judge that this would be the case, and this is why we are able to say (and this is what it means, as we now say, to judge 'objectively') that Marcus Brutus is a greater man than our servant. Judging that this is the case requires us to adopt what Hume refers to as 'some distant view or reflexion' (583). Likewise, hostility toward someone may make it difficult for us to appreciate the pleasure afforded by the fine qualities of his voice 'and give praise to what deserves it.' To reflect on the qualities of this man's voice from a viewpoint distanced from our particular interests and arrive at such an undistorted assessment of pleasure requires not only 'a person of a fine ear [but one], who has command of himself' (472).

So we can to some extent correct our feelings and attitudes and offer a judgment that discounts some of them as misleading. We might say, although Hume's doctrine would treat this 'strictly and philosophically' (415) as nonsense, that some of these original existences misleadingly represent other original existences. The standpoint from which we make the assessment that the intensities of certain passions, motives and volitions have to be discounted before we act (even merely to express approval or disapproval) is one that only a creature with rational or cognitive capacities can adopt, the 'distant view or reflexion.'

The idea that this is not a cognitive function is hard to credit, but noncognitivists are not persuaded by this to abandon their doctrine. The 'distant view or reflexion' is available to creatures sufficiently equipped (as most humans are) with cognitive capacities, but to take that view, rather than leave it, requires some 'determining motive of the will.' For this purpose, Hume introduced 'calm passions' so that he could avoid saying that reason makes demands on us (or were he writing two and a half centuries later, avoid saying that cognition discovers motives outside us).

> 'Tis seldom men heartily love what lies at a distance from them, and what in no way redounds to their particular benefit; as 'tis no less rare to meet with persons, who can pardon another any opposition he makes to their interest, however justifiable that opposition may be by the general rules of morality. Here we are contented with saying, that reason requires such an impartial conduct, but that 'tis seldom we can bring ourselves to it, and that our passions do not readily follow the determination of our judgment. This language will be easily understood, if we consider what we formerly said concerning that *reason*, which is able to oppose our passion; and which we have found to be nothing but a general calm determination of the passions, founded on some distant view or reflexion.
>
> (*ibid.*: 583)

Hume goes on to acknowledge that we are led to seek a 'standard of merit and demerit' of the sort provided by that distant view, because we would otherwise find 'many contradictions to our sentiments in society and conversation and ... an uncertainty from the incessant changes of our situation.' One might consider a distant view and in deciding whether to take it or leave it, decide that like the taste for starched shirts or shaken, not stirred, martinis (end of Section 5.3), it is something that one can leave – but to leave it altogether is to leave the society that shares it.

Those who tend toward skepticism about the possibility of objective assessments of value tend to hold that objectivity is possible only if we can achieve a standpoint that is in no way a partial perspective and that is wholly without any subjective aspects. Should one share the skeptics' pessimism about achieving this, but not think that this is sufficient reason to abandon the effort to look at things objectively, it is open to insist that it ought to be enough if we can take a *more* distant view of things, if we can overcome some (any) limitations of perspective without having to overcome all of them. A person wrapped up in his feelings for those around him can learn to feel for people in distant places and admire people who lived long ago. A person whose animosities incline her to overlook the good qualities of her enemies can learn to suspend her spiteful feelings. Those impervious to the long-term consequences of present indulgence can develop a more vivid imagination to amplify the weak impact that the long term has on their decisions.

Moreover, we have seen that, Hume's initial position notwithstanding, it is at least coherent to treat attitudes (passions, emotions, desires, volitions, aspirations) as subject to cognitive evaluation and to look for respects in which such attitudes need to be adjusted (refined or revised wholesale). For present purposes, it is sufficient to note that adjustments of this kind are made relative to what a community provides in the way of a 'distant viewpoint,' so that individuals can successfully communicate and co-operate with others. Functioning within a community does not require total conformity of attitude to a community standard, and, yes, it is conditioned by the strength of an individual's desire to function at some level in his or her community.

'Distant viewpoints' that make community possible are, to be sure, partial and heavily conditioned. If we do not insist on reaching an unconditional standpoint in one decisive step, we can go on to investigate the possibility that we may be able to find a perspective from which to assess the attitudes shared by a whole community and discover that they need adjustment. We will in Chapter 7 consider an institution widely accepted throughout history that our own culture would reject and will examine whether we can identify a basis for saying that the attitudes that supported this institution need adjustment (indeed wholesale revision). In the next chapter, we will approach Hume's observation about the function of standards of assessment in a community from a different angle by exploring the institutions of law and the extent to which they must be based on 'some distant view or reflexion.'

Further reading

For the view that Plato misrepresented Protagoras, see Margolis (1991). For an excellent account of the importance of the argument from conflicting appearances, see Burnyeat (1979). For an analysis of the (non-Weberian) notion of convention, see Lewis (1969). On the relationship of Chuang Tzu to relativism and skepticism, see Kjellberg and Ivanhoe (1996). On the ancient skepticism see Burnyeat and Frede (1997) and Nussbaum (1994: chapter 8). The modern *soi-disant* skepticism in Mackie (1977) appears in a very accessible form. For a penetrating analysis of the difficulties in Moore's (1903) use of the term 'naturalistic fallacy' see Frankena (1939), and for a cluster of issues around the fact/value distinction (including scholarly disputes over the relationship of Hume to twentieth-century developments of non-cognitivism) see Hudson (1969). Ayer (1936: chapter VI), Stevenson (1944) and Hare (1952) are the main points on the trajectory of twentieth-century non-cognitivism. Dewey (1939) contains an early and interesting response to non-cognitivism. Blackburn (1984: chapter VI) sets out the doctrine of projectivism. On Hume's 'distant view or reflexion,' see Tiles (1992).

Note

1   Hui Tzu counts logic (arguments about 'hard' and 'white') as among his preferred forms of personal cultivation.

6

LAW AS MEASURE

Law is a rule and measure of acts whereby man is induced to act or is restrained from acting: for *lex* is derived from *ligare* (to bind), because it binds one to act. Now the rule and measure of human acts is *ratio* which is the first principle of human acts ... since it belongs to *ratio* to direct to the end, which is the first principle in all matters of action ... It follows that law is something pertaining to reason.

(St Thomas Aquinas (thirteenth century CE); 1911: IaIIæ Q90 A1)[1]

Recapitulation: As we saw in Chapter 4, measures of qualities that are important to the building trades have provided a model of what is needed to resolve conflicts and uncertainties in the moral sphere. In Chapter 5, we explored four general reasons for thinking that it would be pointless to look for similar measures of moral qualities: (1) relativism, the doctrine that there is no authority above that of the attitudes and beliefs of individual human beings (or, the cultural variant of relativism, of individual societies); (2) anarchism based on optimism about human beings, the doctrine that in the absence of distorting influences every individual can be relied upon to form socially appropriate attitudes and beliefs; (3) skepticism, the doctrine that if moral measures were possible, we would not be able to discover them or establish their credentials; and (4) non-cognitivism, the doctrine that there cannot be measures of the required sort because of the way language works or because of the way our minds would be required to use them.

Prospectus: Authoritative pronouncements of what binding custom is serve to clarify and stabilize shared understanding, both of what custom requires of the conduct of individual members of society and of what it provides by way of procedures for resolving uncertainties and disputes. Such pronouncements are the beginnings of legal institutions. Tensions may arise between explicit pronouncements (positive law) and a shared sense of justice or

126

appropriateness regarding how people are to deal with one another. There continue to be related tensions between the use of intuitive judgment and judgment that relies on abstract and general rules, tensions that come to the surface in disputes over how properly to conduct moral deliberation and how legal and bureaucratic institutions should respond to hard cases. What sense of justice forms a part of a given concrete morality will depend on the social formation and institutions that provide the context for the judgments involving this sense of justice. This is not an argument for relativism or skepticism but a preliminary to examining what basis, if any, there may be for the sense of justice specific to a social formation or institution.

6.1   The lawful and the just

Lex *and* ius

In communities without specialized legal institutions, law and valid custom amount to pretty much the same thing. One meaning of the word 'law' in English that points to this stage in social history is 'binding custom or practice of a community.' Pressure toward the development of distinct legal institutions, however, builds wherever conflict arises over what exactly are the established customs and how they are to be followed in particular circumstances. Where there is uncertainty and where the understanding of different groups or different private individuals differs, then there is need for an authoritative determination of what established custom requires, and the addition of 'an authoritative determination' generates a concept closer to more familiar senses of our word 'law.' This concept of 'law' normally includes, and sometimes extends more widely than, the sphere where coercion to enforce compliance is regarded as valid or legitimate (see Section 2.4).

In societies without any literacy (purely oral cultures), 'law' in this sense is stored in the memories of individuals; in partly literate societies it may be stored in documents accessible only to (the few) literate individuals. What is stored includes both what is expected of the behavior of members of the community and what procedures are to be carried out, e.g. trials, for dealing with conflicts and uncertainties. As examples of individuals whose roles were to serve as authoritative sources, Weber (1978: 768) mentions the *lag sagas* among the Nordic tribes and *rachimburgi* among the Franks. Because anything of this importance was commonly treated as a sacred affair, these roles were often filled by priests, e.g. the Brehons in Ireland and the Druids among the Gauls (*ibid.*). Disputes in early Roman society were taken to a group of priests known as the college of pontiffs (Stein 1966: 4–5), and holy scriptures (the Old Testament and the Qur'ān)

127

are often repositories of law. In some cases, individuals or families in dispute would seek mediation services from private individuals known and respected for both their sound judgment and their knowledge of custom. Schacht (1964: 7–11) gives the instance of the role of the *ḥakam* in Arabic society in pre-Islamic and early Islamic times.

Tension might arise between a dominant social class (such as the patricians in Rome, exclusively the source of members of the college of pontiffs) that reserved for itself the right to make such authoritative pronouncements and the rest of the community, especially if the latter suspected that group memory was being manipulated in the interests of the dominant class. Law and concrete morality start to part company at this stage (see Section 2.4). What gives people the idea that what is 'lawful' in the sense of an authoritative pronouncement is not 'lawful' in the sense of valid custom is memory (or hearsay) of how things used to be done, a memory that is usually shaped by a shared understanding of how things are supposed to be done.

There is commonly a vocabulary, similar in force and function to the English words 'just' and 'unjust,' that gives expression to that understanding and allows contrasts to be drawn between the quality of social arrangements that do obtain and those that it is felt should obtain. In ancient Greece, closely corresponding terms were *dikē* and *adikia*. In Arabic (and hence throughout the Islamic world), *'adl* contrasts with *jwar*, and each has multiple near synonyms expressing different shades of meaning (Khadduri 1985: 6). Native Hawaiians apply the term *pono* to appropriate conduct and relations between people in general and *pono'ole* to what was not (Pukui *et al.* 1972: Vol. 1, 60–78). In ancient Rome, the term *ius* (*iuris*) expressed what it was for matters to be as they should between households or private individuals, and *iniuria* was something contrary to that state of affairs.

As legal systems develop, this vocabulary often expresses what the law is (at least in intent) as well as what it should be. In urbanized Rome of later centuries, for example, the *iura prædiolum* (laws of small holdings) governed relationships between people living in dense housing in cities or villages A jurist of the second century CE wrote of

> the *ius* of building houses higher and obstructing the light of neighboring houses, or not doing so, because it obstructs their light; the *ius* of streams and gutters, that is, of a neighbor taking a stream or gutter overflow through his yard or house; and the *ius* of admitting into one's property someone else's drains.
>
> (translated from the *Institutes* of Gaius in Tuck (1979: 9))

In most cases, there was no 'law' in the sense of statutes governing any of these arrangements; what was right (*ius*) and wrong (*iniuria*) for neighbor to inflict on neighbor was preserved in the memories and memoranda of legal specialists known as jurists.

Traditions in Rome and historical evidence in Athens indicate that tensions over what was 'lawful' in the sense of authoritative declaration and what was 'lawful' in the sense of 'just' gave rise to pressure to have a public written record of the law in order to ensure stability. In Rome the outcome was the 'Twelve Tables' (mid-fifth century BCE), but in allowing this much codification, the patricians conceded relatively little. The Twelve Tables provided a code that was by no means comprehensive, presupposing rather than formulating Roman institutions such as the legal powers of a father (*paterfamilias*) over his family, and many of its 'rules' were little more than concrete paradigms (to kill a person caught thieving on one's property at night is lawful) or ways of settling doubtful points of procedure (such as that following failure to respond to a summons) (Stein 1966: 7–8). The vast bulk of Roman private law and legal procedure remained unwritten, or at least unpublished, and controlled by jurists, who remained until late in the republican period priests of the college of pontiffs. Even when the role was secularized, it was filled almost exclusively by members of the patrician class. These individuals were private citizens in the sense of holding no public office but were consulted at all stages of litigation, and their authoritative pronouncements on interpretation of the Twelve Tables, on procedure and on precedent had far more influence over the outcome of cases than any action by a magistrate (*ibid.*).

When the law is declared, the community as a whole or its senior members (elders, sometimes of both sexes, sometimes all adult males) might, depending on the authority structure of a society, be asked to acknowledge a public declaration as authoritative. In Rome, the power to formulate *leges* was jealously guarded by members of the patrician class, who formed the senate, but once formulated *leges* were put to ('asked of') the *populus* (adult males with sufficient property to have the right to bear arms; Weber 1978: 772) and if accepted the result was a *lex rogata* ('law that has been asked'). This procedure was not, at least in its initial stages, thought of as legislation in our understanding of the term, i.e. as 'law making'; rather it was law finding, determining what the law (custom) already was and had always been (Stein 1966: 24).[2]

To understand the force of the word *lex* (plural: *leges*) and its relation to *ius*, both of which, like the German words *Gesetz* and *Recht* (see Section 2.1), may in some contexts be translated as 'law,' it is important not to overestimate the importance of written texts. Stein (*ibid.*: 9–10) mounts a convincing case for rejecting the etymology offered by St Thomas Aquinas in the quotation at the head of this chapter and for accepting instead that the root of *lex* is the verb *legere*, meaning to read (out loud) or to declare, and he argues that public declaration is at the heart of the Roman concept of *lex*:

The characteristic feature of *lex* as a form of *ius* was not only that it formulated the *ius* into a rule but also that it authoritatively declared that formulation to the public. A statement by a private person of what he conceived to be *ius* was liable to be questioned. In a *lex* the whole group have committed themselves to a definite statement of *ius*, which can no longer be challenged. It has passed out of the exclusive possession of a particular group.

(*ibid.*: 13)

What is or is not *ius* is an objective state of affairs, about which individuals may make mistakes, but a publicly agreed formulation is authoritative.

A public declaration, written or otherwise, of what is deemed to be correct conduct or procedure (positive law) has the utility and the drawbacks of a rough and ready measuring device adopted by a crew on a building site. At least there is a common standard with which to work, and for some purposes (having a stable unit of length in terms of which to express relations between various dimensions of the intended project) this is good enough. For other purposes, shortcomings in the standard (e.g. of straightness) may interfere with achieving a common purpose and have to be rectified. Normally, however, such a standard is not open to the suspicion that some members of the crew have fixed it to their advantage.

Statements of the law are likewise human artifacts and can be recognized as such by people whether they believe such statements represent discoveries (law finding) or decisions (law making). For some purposes, it is enough that people all do something in a similar fashion (e.g. all drive on the same side of the road, whether left or right); in some cases, it would seem that departure from a norm should not be acceptable, even if everyone departs in the same way (e.g. awarding contracts to the highest briber instead of the lowest bidder). What is the status of the concepts like 'just' or '*ius*' or '*adl*' that are used to point out shortcomings in the prevailing legal standards (in positive law)? Are they, like fashion or etiquette, a sense of what things should be like that simply happens to be shared by most members of a community? Or are they, like 'circular' and 'right-angled,' concepts that transcend culture? And even if they do transcend culture, are people required to live by them; or could a society dispense with them, as it might dispense with 'circular' and 'right-angled,' if it had no use for round wheels and square corners?

Authoritative pronouncements about what is binding custom are (end of Section 4.4) a species of measures of right. Conduct that conforms to the pronouncements is right; conduct that does not conform is, relative to the pronouncements, wrong. But such pronouncements may in turn be assessed relative to local variants of similar concepts that are found in a variety of cultures and the pronouncements found wanting. What sort of measure are people reaching for? The evaluative concepts commonly assess both conduct and character; there are just and unjust people, as there is just and unjust conduct. Is the related 'measure of virtue' what is involved here?

It may be that when people reject an authoritative pronouncement as 'unjust,' they are appealing to what a person with an exemplary character would have said or done. As we will see in the next section, more emphasis is traditionally placed on the characters of judges in Islamic legal thinking than on procedure, and in the end reliance on the 'measure of virtue' may be unavoidable, but if we are to clarify the basis for criticizing authoritative pronouncements, something needs to be said about what just and fair-minded judges and legislators can be expected to do and not do. Perhaps judges and legislators can be expected to look out for the common good or the public interest, apply a 'measure of the good,' and if they are manifestly not doing so, their pronouncements can be criticized.

Both Christian and Islamic thinkers took human pronouncements of what is lawful to be assessed in terms of how well they served the end of promoting true religion and general welfare. St Thomas Aquinas (thirteenth century) endorsed the view of St Isidore of Seville (early seventh century) that the law should foster religion, be helpful to discipline and further the common weal (IaIIæ Q95 A3). Islamic jurists, according to Khadduri (1984: 135–41), took the point of law to be, besides that of indicating the path (*shāri'a*, also the word for Islamic law) to God's justice, that of promoting public welfare and protecting public interest, and the development of good character. However, secular legal thinkers not only exclude any goals or values based on religious belief but are also nowadays reluctant to appeal to conceptions of the common good on the grounds that in complex societies these are not sufficiently widely shared, are open to fundamental disputes and belong in the arena of politics rather than the institutions of justice.

Another possibility is that authoritative pronouncements of law are to be assessed by a further 'measure of right,' one internal to the concept of law. Some developments in legal institutions seem to appeal to what feels right to our rational capacities, based on the formal (but nevertheless aesthetic) principles of consistency, balance and reciprocity (see Section 3.4). Is this perhaps the source of the measure that is indicated by the words 'just' and 'unjust'? This suggestion is reinforced by the close association of words like 'just' with words like 'equal' as well as the familiar Western icon for justice, the balance scale. The Arabic *'adl* includes the meanings 'equal,' 'equivalent,' 'equalize,' 'balance' and 'counterbalance,' along with 'straightening' and 'correcting,' (*ibid.*: 6). *Æquus* in Latin includes the meanings 'level,' 'equal,' 'fair' and 'just'; *iniuria* (an injustice) has *iniquitas* (meaning 'unequal' – root of the English word 'iniquity') as a near synonym. In trying to identify the trait of character indicated by the broad sense of the word 'justice' (*dikaiosunē* in Greek), Aristotle remarks:

131

both the lawless (*paranomos*) man and the grasping (*pleonekēs*) and unequal (*anisos*) man are thought to be unjust (*adikos*), so that evidently both the law-abiding (*nomimos*) and the equal (*isos*) man will be just (*dikaios*). The just, then, is the lawful and the equal, the unjust the unlawful and the unequal.

(1129a34–b1)

Just retaliation (the *lex talionis*; see Section 3.4) is achieved when harm done to one party is balanced equally by harm done in return, even if it would be preferable to balance harm with some form of compensation.

If the urge to seek balance and reciprocity in human relations is a product of our capacity for rational thought, might refined uses of those capacities generate a precise and substantive concept of justice in the way that refined uses of the same capacities have turned 'straight,' 'right-angled' and 'circular' into geometric concepts? Aristotle reports that an earlier school of mathematically oriented philosophers, the Pythagoreans, had defined justice (*dikaiosunē*) as the simple form of reciprocity found in the *lex talionis* (1132b22–23). The appeal of this simple concept, Aristotle noted, was that many think that a man should 'suffer what he did' (1132b26), a principle that he attributed to a Cretan source ('the justice of Rhadamanthus'). Aristotle himself thought that this was an inadequate definition and offered one using the more sophisticated mathematical concept of proportion (1131a29). This proposal would have appeared to Aristotle's contemporaries as the product of a more refined use of reason, for another meaning of the Greek word *logos* (discourse, reason) is 'proportion,' the ratio of two numbers, and the Latin word *ratio*, which gives us our word 'ratio,' has a similar range of meanings – it is both the ratio of two numbers and the human capacity for the kind of thought we call 'reasoning.'

The reciprocity that sustains social solidarity, Aristotle explains in the *Ethics* (1132b30–5), is that on the basis of proportion, not of equality. Proportion provides the basis of fair exchange (barter or for money), but it not only allows for proportional compensation instead of strict application of the *lex talionis*, it also allows only equals to be treated equally. The proportionality between what people high in the social hierarchy can demand from those beneath them and what those beneath can expect by way of reciprocal return is determined (and in part sustains) differences in rank. The biblical statement of the *lex talionis* goes on (Exodus 21: 26–7) to specify that if a man strikes a servant so that the servant loses an eye or a tooth, the man does not suffer the loss of an eye or tooth but is required to free the servant. In Rome, the Twelve Tables prescribed half the compensation for personal injury for a serf as for a freeman (Kunkel 1973: 8). Aiyar (1935: 93) compares ancient Hindu law, which fixed compensation for the life of a member of the warrior class (*kshatriya*) at

132

a thousand cows, that of a trader or cattleman (*vaishya*) at a hundred cows and that of a servant (*sudra*) at ten, with laws of the Bretons and Scots, which put a value of a thousand cows on the life of the king of the Scots, a hundred cows on the son of an earl or thane and sixteen cows on the life of a peasant (villein). For social unequals, unequal remedies are prescribed. In a more egalitarian society, this appears to be a travesty of justice.

What counts as reciprocity, how a balance is to be struck, does not, initially at least, seem to be something like 'equal in weight' that transcends culture. Before drawing conclusions, however, we need to look more closely at the procedures that lead to authoritative pronouncements of what the law in general is or what is required in disputed cases.

6.2 Procedures, rules and particulars

Oracles and kadis, precedents and statutes

Law begins as binding custom, and an ostensibly authoritative pronouncement of what such custom requires (in general or on particular occasions) can be challenged not only by claiming that conforming to the pronouncement would not result in justice but also on the grounds that it is capricious or self-serving. Such challenges can be forestalled by procedures that demonstrate the pronouncement's connection to what it is supposed to represent, binding custom. This might be done by attempts to connect directly to sources (gods or founders) of the tradition, by valid living embodiments of the tradition (people who are 'true' in the way wheels are round) or by appeal to (usually written) records of the tradition.

Weber, whose writings on the sociology of law are a rich repository of details about a variety of legal traditions, created a classification of legal orders, or ways in which law is determined, based on four ideal types (1978: 976–7). It did not matter whether any actual legal system fitted comfortably into one of Weber's types; his classification served as a means of identifying the relevant features of actual systems, which might well have the features of more than one ideal type. The type that Weber regarded as most primitive was characterized by its use of procedures, such as oracles and ordeals, to connect directly to the sources (natural, divine or historical) of its tradition. For example, in a classic anthropological study from earlier in this century, Evans-Pritchard (1937) describes the poison oracle of the Azande of Central Africa. These people produced a substance from a forest creeper with a toxicity that varied in a highly random way and administered this poison to chickens (and occasionally to humans) to settle questions. 'No important venture is undertaken without authorization of the poison oracle. [It is used] in important collective undertakings, in all crises of life, in all serious legal disputes, in all matters strongly affecting individual welfare' (*ibid.*: 261). Ancient Romans studied the behavior of birds (*auspices*) and the entrails of sacrificial animals (*harupices*) in a similar spirit. Stein (1966: 4) suggests that the etymology of *ius* (*iuris*) derives from the oaths sworn by parties on such occasions – *iurare* is to swear an oath – both to ensure by invocation and to bear solemn witness to the fact that the outcome would represent the will of the gods.

Such procedures appear superstitious, although if we subtract the background belief that the outcome reflects the will of the 'powers that be,' a random device such as tossing a coin or drawing straws is, in circumstances where competing claims are agreed to have equal weight, accepted as a fair or just way to resolve an issue. But where there is no agreement that competing claims have equal weight, the parties have to believe that somehow the oracle or ordeal determines the relative merits of their claims. The parties involved, it should be noted, would see only that 'the powers that be' favored one side over the other, not the reason why, and the procedure is thus not 'rational.' If either a judge or a jury in our courts were to look at an individual case and pronounce a verdict without having reasons that relate the verdict to other cases or general principles, they would function in much the same way as an oracle, and where the verdict in court is the outcome of emotional appeals on behalf of plaintiff and defendant, the outcome has much the same standing as that of a trial by ordeal.

A similar observation applies to the second of Weber's four types. Here, instead of rituals designed to communicate directly with the sources of tradition, certain individuals, such as the elders of the tribe or the old Arabic *hakam* (see Section 6.1), are consulted because they are regarded as living embodiments of the tradition and the qualities (e.g. of justice) that it is taken to sustain. But for their accumulated experience, a pronouncement from them in the absence of any reasoning in support of it would be little better than a oracle. However, if these specialists are believed to have acquired, through a long education or process of self-cultivation, a stable disposition imbued with the traditions of their culture, the result might not qualify as 'rational,' but it would certainly not be rank superstition to believe that the outcome accurately reflects tradition.

Weber (1978: 976) applied the term '*Kadi*-justice' to this type of adjudication. The term derives from the title of an early Islamic magistrate, a *qāḍī*, established by the Umayyads (seventh–eighth centuries CE) to perform the role traditionally filled by the *hakam* – in effect bringing a hitherto private institution under government control (Schacht 1966: 24–5). That a *kadi* speaks from an extraordinary accumulation of history, tradition and taste (see Section 4.2) – in this case better characterized as the accumulation of scripture (the Qur'ān and *hadīth*), Islamic law (*shāri'a*) and personal piety – is what distinguishes his pronouncements from a charismatic source in the strict sense of a 'direct line to god.'[3]

If, instead of simply pronouncing a verdict or recommendation, legal experts cite identifiable concrete precedents as reasons for their decisions or draw analogies between previous cases and those before them, Weber (1978: 976) called this 'empirical justice.' Actual *qāḍī*s did engage in this form of reasoning to support their adjudications, although a great deal more emphasis was placed on a *qāḍī*'s reputation for being a just judge (*qāḍī ʿadl*) than on the process by which the decision was reached (Khadduri 1984: 145). If records of precedents are carefully kept and systematically used, the practice of empirical justice could be, Weber said, 'sublimated and rationalized into a "technique"' (*ibid.*). This technique forms an important part of any sophisticated legal institution, and its mastery (both of the body of precedent and how to use it) is a key constituent of the education of legal professionals.

Although actual *qāḍī*s did practice 'empirical justice,' the practice does not necessarily presuppose or build on '*Kadi*-justice.' In Weber's ideal typography, each of the two provides a different axis, relative to which actual practice may be located. '*Kadi*-justice' is based on an individual developing sensibilities for the application of general evaluative concepts without any systematic treatment of how the particulars to which they apply differ. 'Empirical justice' is based on an accumulation of experience of concrete differences and may involve a minimal degree of generalization – the way in which analogies are drawn between different particulars may be entirely unsystematic. Weber thought a legal system that did not combine both of these features to the fullest extent possible was not fully rational.[4]

The key to the fourth of Weber's ideal types, rational justice, and the third of his ideal types of authority (see Section 3.1) was the use of abstraction and generalization. Like Plato (see Sections 4.3 and 4), Weber wanted the use of terms crucial in evaluation to be carefully controlled using abstract and general definitions, but he placed even more emphasis on a device that Plato did not emphasize, abstractly formulated general imperatives – what are commonly called 'rules.' The most common meaning of 'rule' in our vocabulary is a statement to the effect that all persons of a certain general class should perform or not perform some act characterized in general terms in circumstances also characterized in general terms. The connection to a measuring device – a straightedge is sometimes referred to as a 'rule' – appears accidental, but the etymological history as related by Stein (1966: 51–73) suggests that the connection is far from adventitious.

'Rule' derives (via French) from the Latin *regula*, a rule, standard, pattern or model; in the vocabulary of a classical writer like Cicero it was equivalent to the Greek *kanōn* (straightedge). The word *regula* began to incorporate some of the sense of 'rule' as general prescription when it and *kanōn* were applied by grammarians first to tables of inflections and

135

then to statements of the regularities represented in those tables. This usage influenced jurists, who in the first centuries BCE and CE associated '*regulae*' (rules) very closely with '*definitions.*' Initially, the latter were brief descriptions of what a complex legal custom involved, and the former were brief statements of normative principles taken to be something like the intention behind a complex custom. The notions tended to merge as jurists took sides in disputes over whether any such brief account could prescribe rather than merely describe legal practice.

A definition is a rule for using words, a rule in the sense that a general imperative guides conduct. What conforms to the imperative is right; what does not conform is wrong (and what has nothing to do with what the rule is about is neither right nor wrong relative to that rule). Is this not simply the 'measure of right' that authoritative pronouncements on law provide? Is law a system of rules? Weber appears to have thought that ideally this is what law should be, but as many practitioners of law will attest, not only is law not merely rules but it arguably could not be replaced by a set of rules or a code. No matter how thoroughly law is expressed in general imperatives (how thoroughly it is reduced to a 'code'), it will never be able to dispense with that technique which Weber associated with refinements in empirical justice, that is with a body of examples to serve as precedents or with the dispositions required to use those precedents correctly.

Socrates was scripted in Plato's early dialogues to drive his interlocutors toward a general definition, or a rule for the application of the concept under discussion, by rejecting concrete instances of the concept – as when Euthyphro offered as a model of 'religious propriety' his own act of prosecuting his father on a charge of manslaughter (5d). The challenge to someone who offers examples as guidance is always, 'How do I know that is an example of what I am trying to do?' But if a rule is formulated, there is a corresponding challenge: 'Here is a case that apparently fits a rule, but how do I know I should follow the rule in this case?' For as we saw at the end of Section 4.2, once a rule has been formulated, it is possible to come up with cases that fit it but where the indicated guidance should be rejected. 'When requested, everyone who has borrowed something should return it to its owner. I have borrowed X and the owner of X is requesting its return. How do I know that this is not a case where I should decline to follow the rule?' The general advice to ignore the rule whenever it would be wrong (or even 'defeat the purpose') to do so is not very definite guidance.

The answer may be that the rule has not been fully spelled out; the cases in which it does not apply have not been specified. The commandment not to take the life of another human being needs more than the not very informative addition 'without good cause'; it needs to have exceptions specified in a precise fashion: 'unless doing so in defense of your own life or you are authorized to carry out a death sentence legitimately pronounced by a court or you are a soldier and the life is that of a enemy combatant, etc.' The 'etc.' indicates that there may be more exceptions. Will there ever be an end to the need to specify exceptions as new circumstances arise? And how would we recognize that we had reached that end? That a rule might not settle all cases does not render it completely useless, but it does argue that the rule cannot function by itself.

Between emphasizing that examples are not sufficient and (on one occasion) suggesting that general formulae cannot guide on their own, Plato was probably indicating the need to have, or to rely on the guidance of people with, understanding and integrity. Is there any way to acquire the understanding that discerns the limits of the guidance that rules may offer? Those in the legal profession who recognize the inadequacies of the idea that law is nothing but a system of rules (statutes or a legal code) point in the first instance to the function of precedents, records of individual decisions, in determining decisions in new cases, and of the need of every legal professional to know, and know how to use, case law. The claim is that without the backing of a system of precedents and training in their use, without the techniques of Weber's 'empirical justice,' a system of rules cannot provide the basis of an adequate legal system.

Weber's own education as a legal scholar was shaped by a tradition dominant on the continent of Europe that took as its model the late (sixth century CE) codification of Roman law known as the *Corpus juris civilis*. A revival of interest in Roman law beginning in the fifteenth century ensured that for a long time portions of the *Corpus juris* were used as a textbook in the training of almost every continental lawyer. This training provided Weber with the paradigm of his idea of 'rational law,' which was 'conceptually systematized on the basis of "statutes," such as the later Roman Empire first created with a high degree of technical perfection' (1978: 975). England, for reasons having to do with the organization and education of its legal specialists, never 'received' Roman law with anything like the enthusiasm with which it was taken up on the continent. As a result, English law remained, as Roman law had been before the sixth century, 'empirical,' uncodified, based far more on precedent than on the guidance of statutes.

Weber joined, on the continental side, the mutual contempt with which legal traditions of English and American 'common law' and continental European 'civil law' viewed one another. The lack of logical articulation, conceptual explicitness and systematic codification struck Weber as signs of an incompletely developed tradition, while common law theorists viewed the idea that every legal decision was the application of an abstract general principle to a concrete situation as a theoretician's pipe dream. A 'common' lawyer would insist that the meaning of a statute remained unclear until it had been applied to a number of cases. A 'civil lawyer' would shudder at the lack of rigor and the scope for inconsistency that deciding cases by comparison to other cases allowed.[5] A 'common lawyer' would insist that the strength of his tradition lay in its flexibility. The 'civil' lawyer would retort that this flexibility left the judicial process open to illegitimate distorting influences.

The dispute here is important because moral deliberation is very commonly modeled on legal reasoning. General rules – as in the dispute between the civil and common law traditions – have both been assigned an essential role in moral assessment and been scouted as insufficient, unnecessary or even positively deleterious to moral reasoning. The 'prescriptivism' of R.M. Hare, it was noted in Section 5.4, treats a moral judgment as belonging to the genus of prescription, distinguished as a species by being or following from a universal prescription. A universal prescription applies to everyone, e.g. 'No son should ever treat his mother with disrespect.' A merely general prescription might apply to only one person. A father who told his son 'Don't you ever treat your mother with disrespect' because of holding his wife in far higher regard even than his own mother would not have issued a moral prescription in Hare's sense. (Hare was adapting a doctrine found in Kant, which will be examined in the next chapter.)

From time to time, resistance surfaces to the assumption that moral judgments or attitudes must involve commitments to general rules or principles. One recent manifestation of this resistance is known as 'particularism' and is supported by the argument, a species of 'holism' (Dancy 1993: chapters 4–6), that what counts as a reason in one situation, and how it counts, is not guaranteed to be the same in other situations. To judge correctly, one has to respond to the relevant particulars of each situation, not subsume the situation under a general rule and follow the consequences of doing so just because the situation happens to fall under the general circumstances that the rule is supposed to cover.

Part of what particularism is resisting is undeniably a mistaken conception about how one reaches a correct decision (moral or otherwise) comparable to the mistaken idea that a legal judgment is reached by placing the facts of a case under rules and deducing a verdict and a sentence. Part of what particularism supports is the important truth that general statements, being human artifacts, cannot guarantee to anticipate correctly all that may fall under them (a point, it will be seen in the next section, recognized by Aristotle and turned into an important legal concept with a long and interesting history). We might indeed generalize the point that emerged from Socrates' brief exchange with Cephalus (see end of Section 4.2) and say that it may not ever be possible to specify a rule that should always be kept; for any rule there are circumstances that may arise in which the rule should be set aside.

But the cost of extreme particularism – one that makes a rule out of never making a rule – should not be underestimated, for to carry the doctrine to the extreme would be to abandon an evidently useful mode of thought. With what would we be left? If we strictly eschew generalization, there is very little left to articulate thought – at most comparison between particular situations but without the means (general terms) to articulate relevant similarities. Judgment would ultimately be made *Kadi*-style, better or worse depending on the sensibilities of the person doing the judging, but again we would be without the means to articulate in general terms what leads to better sensibilities. In its purest form, particularism has to fall back on intuitive thought, and unless an appeal is made to a form of nativism (see Section 5.2), 'intuition' will reflect only the way in which the person intuiting has been brought up. One might assemble records of particular cases (real and fictional) to provide intuition with an empirical leavening, but the principles of selection could not be articulated in general terms.

If we find ourselves threatened by a 'tyranny of principles (rules)' (see Section 6.3), it is because having created artifacts to help us to think, we are prone to expect our artifacts to do our thinking for us. It may be salutary to remind ourselves from time to time what it is to think without relying on artifacts, but forswearing useful devices because we may misuse them is folly. A more sensible approach would be to remind ourselves constantly that a rule (general imperative) is a device to aid thought like a rule (straightedge) is a device to aid perception – a device that may need improving or replacing when it is applied in new or unusual circumstances. Rules should be treated as scientists treat hypotheses, engineers treat design specifications and managers treat budgets: devices to guide and to be amended or abandoned when they are clearly not providing the guidance that is needed.

6.3 Equity and casuistry

A mute divinity, the Lesbian rule and the tyranny of principles

The tension between authoritative pronouncements made in the form of rules and the qualities (justice, appropriateness) that we look for in the outcome of an adjudication was familiar to Aristotle. He observed (1137a32–1138a3) that laws have to be stated in general terms, even though general statements cannot always anticipate correctly all the cases that they are meant to cover. This, Aristotle said, was not the fault of the law or of the law giver; it is the nature of things that particulars do not always fit under universals in this way. Where this occurs, we make a distinction between what is fitting or appropriate and what the law says is to be done. 'Fitting' or 'appropriate' translates Aristotle's Greek word *epieikēs*; the Latin translation as *æquitas* and the English translation 'equitable' carry connotations of 'equality' that are not present in the Greek.

However, having to make this distinction puzzles people, Aristotle observes, because they want to know whether the lawful is what is just (*dikaios*) or whether the equitable is what is just. Aristotle's response was to avoid giving a simple answer. The equitable is a form of justice and is preferable in circumstances where the letter of the law is defective owing to its universality, although it is not preferable to justice without this qualification. Aristotle went on to insist that the indefiniteness of particular circumstances called for an indefinite measuring device like the lead strip used by builders from Lesbos to check the uniformity of the shape of the molding they were crafting.

This view of the limitation of law as a guide arises from the problem touched on in the previous section that rules cannot be formulated in such a way as to anticipate all the cases to which they might apply. When St Thomas Aquinas discusses Aristotle's notion of equity he uses Plato's example: the law requires us to restore deposits, but it is good to set aside the letter of the law in cases like that of a man in a state of madness who, having put his sword on deposit, demands it back (IIaIIæ Q120 A1). This is not passing judgment on the law but on the particular case, Aquinas said; and in response to the principle of late Roman law that only the sovereign (the emperor) has the authority to interpret the law, he replied 'when the case is manifest there is need, not of interpretation, but of execution' (*ibid.*). But whether to trust one's measuring device on the one hand or a judgment that one forms independently of using that device on the other is something that itself calls for judgment. What action is called for in a particular case may not be equally obvious to everyone.

The eighteenth-century philosopher Immanuel Kant treated matters of justice (and right, *Recht*, in general) as tightly circumscribed by what it was reasonable to expect laws and courts of law to enforce. The problem that he saw with claims of equity was that they involve appeals to grounds which the law has not recognized and hence a judge is not able to consider. (They appeal, as he put it, to a 'mute divinity who cannot be heard'; 1797: 234.) If a man enters a business on equal terms with partners and then pours additional resources of his own into the venture in a vain attempt to save it from failure, he can by the law of contracts claim only an equal share of the proceeds when the business is finally liquidated, although it can be argued on grounds of equity that he should receive a share proportionate to his total investment. Appeals to equity, however, cannot and should not be thought able to affect what can be enforced against his partners. Likewise, if a man agrees to work as a servant for wages to be paid at the end of a period of time and discovers at the end of that period that inflation has significantly reduced the value of what he will receive, the courts cannot enforce a claim for more from his employer to cover inflation, unless that provision was part of the contract. Kant would agree with Aristotle that particulars are indefinite, but he rejects the idea that a judge may apply an indefinite standard: 'a judge cannot pronounce in accordance with indefinite conditions' (*ibid.*).

Kant does not suggest that the partners or the employer should be deaf to the 'divinity,' who must remain 'mute' in court. Where the judge's own rights are involved, he should listen to equity. Now normally it is not proper for judges sitting in court to hear cases that involve their own interests, but ordinary people frequently 'judge' matters relating to their own interests, and if in doing so they pay attention to what is equitable and act accordingly, Kant would recognize their merit as much as did Aristotle, who evidently thought well of the 'equitable man,' who 'tends to take less than his share though he has the law on his side' (1138a2).

In some judicial systems, the highest court of appeal is also the sovereign power, and decisions made by a king, or on his behalf, cannot avoid being involved in the king's interests. The model of a monarchical system is commonly that of a private householder, and where 'the Crown' is the owner of government property and the agent in governmental transactions, it makes sense that the judge 'should listen to equity, as, for example, when the crown itself bears the damages that others have incurred in its service . . . even though it could reject their claim by strict Right' (Kant 1797: 234–5). Thus, although Kant declares 'that a *court of equity* (in a conflict of others about their rights) involves a contradiction,' he would not have rejected as nonsense the task of hearing appeals based on equity, which English kings assigned to their lord chancellors[6] so long as the complaint to be heard was against the Crown.

What Kant seems to have thought incoherent was the idea of an impartial (disinterested) court that heard cases on the grounds of equity. Kant conceived right (*Recht*, which it was the duty of the courts to uphold) as requiring the application of rigid, universal standards, not Lesbian lead strips, which can be bent to accommodate circumstances. Kant did not claim that there was no basis for the judgment that 'the Right' might be wrong in some circumstances, merely that such judgments were out of place in courts of law. Kant probably would have agreed with Weber's assessment of

> the role played in the development of the law by purely 'emotional' factors, such as the so-called 'sense of justice.' Experience shows . . . that the 'sense of justice' is very unstable unless it is firmly guided by the *pragma* of objective or subjective interests. It is, as one can still easily see today, capable of sudden fluctuations and it cannot be expressed except in a few very general and purely formal maxims. . . . Being mainly emotional, that 'sense' is hardly adequate for the maintenance of a body of stable norms.
>
> (1978: 760)

Whether Weber would have encouraged people as Kant did to follow a 'sense of justice' in private affairs is unclear. His main concern was with what is appropriate for institutions, and here the overriding value was stability. People need to know what to expect in order to plan their affairs. It not only leads to general inefficiency but is also not fair (it is a species of injustice) if they cannot rely on the letter of the law to form accurate anticipations.

Are rules that do not allow exceptions the only way to ensure stability? If we all had the same 'sense of justice,' we would not need procedures to settle disputes; at most we would need mechanisms to enforce what everyone would agree was right. We might try to achieve a stable common sense of justice through education and training, although this might be thought to require greater discipline of the emotions than would be regarded as healthy, and it might be argued that it would destroy the independence of thought that provides a useful source of correction to a distorted sense of propriety that might otherwise prevail in a community. We could follow the example of the English Court of Chancery and set up a judge to hear appeals on the basis of equity in the manner of a *kadi*, but the problem is how to identify *kadi* judges with a reliably 'superior' sense of justice. Such a court would in any case probably begin to follow its own precedents and find that its categories and general principles were hardening into something indistinguishable from the 'legal justice' to which it was supposed to be an alternative – as indeed happened historically in the Court of Chancery (Pound 1922: 25).

It may be that law courts should simply be left to follow rules and precedents without appeal to a 'sense of justice' and that we recognize this is a necessary expedient given that we want to function together in the sort of complex society that has evolved around us. Nevertheless, it does not take a particularist to recommend that we resist the pressure to follow this institutional model in everyday life. If Kant and Aristotle disagreed about the appropriateness of a court hearing an appeal on the basis of equity, they at least agreed that ordinary judgments about how to interact with people should be tempered by a sense of equity. But if we come to a situation where we do not know how to proceed and find that our individual senses of justice do not provide similar guidance, are we forced to 'go to law,' where the rules and precedents will allow consistency and stability to override everyone's sense of what is appropriate in the circumstances? Are we caught between on the one hand trying to function each as a *kadi* and on the other surrendering our lives to unfeeling institutional mechanisms?

Albert R. Jonsen and Stephen Toulmin have mounted a sustained critique of what they call 'the tyranny of principles' (1988: 5)[7] and identified a historical resource for bringing about its overthrow. To illustrate the hold of this tyranny, they cite a case where bureaucratic inflexibility had caused intense and needless distress to a disabled person, leading to her eventual suicide. The response of a reporter covering the story was to declare 'there should be a *rule* to prevent this kind of thing from happening' (*ibid.*: 8–9). The reporter did not regard it as an option that officials should be given *kadi* authority to use their own judgment to achieve a fitting or appropriate (equitable) result where rigid application of existing rules would not achieve this. So the response was to suggest that the ill effects of rigidly applied rules be corrected by means of more rules.

Jonsen and Toulmin recommend instead a practice of determining how best to deal with individual cases that was widely used in the sixteenth and seventeenth centuries to help priests to give pastoral advice to parishioners. This 'empirical' method of dealing with particular moral decisions, known as casuistry, became corrupted (allowing wealthy parishioners to be treated with scandalous indulgence) and following a devastating satire on the practice by the French cleric, philosopher and mathematician Blaise Pascal (1657), fell into disrepute. The bad odor associated with the name 'casuistry' for the past three centuries, Jonsen and Toulmin contend, is undeserved. That the practice was once abused is not sufficient grounds for continuing to abuse the potentially useful techniques that it offers.

Jonsen (1991) subsequently set out a fresh articulation of the method and recommended its adoption in the new field of clinical ethics. Specialists in this field function as consultants to medical practitioners, who find themselves without rules or precedents to guide them toward satisfactory resolutions of ethical dilemmas created by advances in medical technology. If one applies the common image of a professional specialist, one might imagine that resident specialists in medical ethics (as there are now a considerable number) would function as oracles or *kadis* on matters of ethical right and wrong in clinical deliberation. What they do provide to a clinical team is access to a professional network (with a published literature and in recent years Internet bulletin boards and chat rooms) that has developed its own empirical rationality for dealing with the ethical dilemmas that arise in clinical practice. Their function is not unlike that of the Roman jurists, who, in spite of having no official standing or government office, were largely responsible for the justice that Roman courts dispensed.

Jonsen proposed that a version of casuistry would serve to refine the methods of medical ethicists (as it might well have served to refine the institutions of empirical law at points in its history) by deriving guidance from cases that have already arisen. The first step in the method, which Jonsen refers to as creating a 'morphology,' is to identify the relevant features of cases on record. Then a range of possible cases can be organized in such a way that the clearest cases of appropriate and inappropriate conduct are identified, and the relative distance of doubtful cases from these can be determined. Jonsen calls this creating a 'taxonomy.' Finally, to reach a decision, judgment has to assess to what extent the clear (paradigm) cases 'impart a kind of moral movement to other cases.' Hence this part of the method is called 'kinetics.' 'In casuistry, the motion is a shift in moral judgment between paradigm and analogous cases, so that one might say of the paradigm, "this is clearly wrong" and of an analogous case, "but, in this case, what was done was justified, or excusable"' (*ibid.*: 303).

Where Jonsen's method goes beyond the use of precedent and analogy in empirical reasoning is in the explicit identification of relevance and the synoptic view of possible cases that is provided by the taxonomy and which the simple use of precedents may not afford. This synoptic view serves as a measure; by locating within it cases as they arise, guidance is offered as to how to dispose of these cases. There remains, however, a question about the calibration of this device: how do its users go about selecting relevant features ('morphology'), arranging possible cases in some order of appropriateness ('taxonomy') and assessing how much moral momentum paradigms impart to other cases ('kinetics')? Is this to be done intuitively, *kadi*-style, in the way that judgments of equity appear to be reached?[8]

Although this highly methodical approach to dealing with cases does not rely on or seek to formulate universal principles or definitions that impose sharp and rigid lines of demarcation, it does not in the spirit of extreme particularism dispense altogether with the use of abstractions and generalizations. Acknowledging a need at various stages to employ at least 'a brief rule-like saying,' Jonsen introduces the concept of a 'maxim:' 'A maxim was, for the rhetoricians, "maxima sententia," a leading or important proposition. Sometimes, they referred to them as *gnomoi* or wise sayings, because they seemed to distill, in a pithy way, experience reflected upon by wise men' (*ibid.*: 298). (The Greek *gnomōn* is another of the family of words for measuring devices; it means, among other things, a judge or interpreter, the index of a sundial, a carpenter's try square or a guide of life.) Maxims are not intended to function as exceptionless principles. One might pick out as a relevant factor of a case whether the patient has requested or accepted treatment, doing this by reference to the maxim that 'competent persons have a right to determine their fate' (*ibid.*). For the taxonomy one might select as a paradigm of what should not be done the unprovoked killing of one person by another and do this by reference to the maxim 'thou shalt not kill' (301–2). The exercise of prudent judgment in the 'kinetics' stage of the process 'apprehends the fit of maxims and circumstances' (304).

Are these examples of the 'very general and purely formal maxims' that Weber was quoted above as dismissing? Do they do any real work other than create a space in which 'the *pragma* of objective or subjective interests' can exert influence? Jonsen and Toulmin cited experience (1988: 16–20) which suggests that people from quite diverse moral traditions can agree fairly comprehensively on the appropriate disposition of cases, even though their respective attempts to theorize the bases of the agreements they have reached often lead them into sharp disputes that are difficult to resolve. This shows that, having set aside the use of rules that provide guidance, they can co-operate with one another in constructing a new artifact for guiding decisions that does not conflict in immediately obvious ways with their old practices of receiving guidance. Does this mean that the new device is superior or merely that profession, religious teaching and theoretical commitment are less important in shaping a climate of moral attitude than wider cultural factors, so that if the former can be effectively suspended (as in this methodical exercise), the latter can surface and allow consensus to form around a measuring device?

If our objective is consensus, casuistry as a method seems to be a very useful tool. If our question is what, if any, basis there is for the judgments and attitudes that are validated by appeal to the devices generated by casuistry, we appear to be left with no answer. This empirical device aids in the clarification of a shared sense of justice or appropriateness by showing how to extend it to cases where the shared sense gives uncertain guidance. Rather than try to identify a *kadi* with exceptionally well-developed sensibilities, we can exercise our own kinetic sense, which has been honed on the taxonomy that we created from our morphology. This is no mean achievement, but it does nothing to equip those who use it to respond to criticism of the judgments it supports.

This would not be a problem, except that someone standing outside the cultural presuppositions that shape the exercise (by giving content to its use of otherwise 'very general and purely formal maxims') might find the outcome utterly baffling. It will be worth devoting some space (the next two sections, in fact) to sizing up the problem that this leaves, so that attempts (taken up in subsequent sections) to tackle the problem directly by an appeal to our capacity to make laws (in the sense of universal rules) for ourselves will appear well motivated.

6.4   The diversity of justice

Equality, self-determination and collective responsibility

Authoritative public declarations are, as we have seen, devices for stabilizing the binding customs of a society and making conformity easier to perceive. As fallible human pronouncements (*leges*), they can be assessed against a shared sense of how it is proper for members of a society to relate to one another (*ius*). In considering the tensions that may surface between these different embodiments of a society's notion of what is 'lawful,' we have, for the most part, proceeded abstractly. Apart from an allusion (see Section 6.1) to differences in what may strike hierarchical and egalitarian societies as appropriate ways to balance one act against another, not much reference has been made to the particular kinds of institution and social formation that shape people's perceptions of what is 'lawful.' But whether a society is hierarchical or egalitarian, what notions of property it has and how it conceives individuals to be related to groups within the society may affect what people are prepared to accept as 'lawful.'

Aristotle observed two different senses of the words *dikaios/adikos* in Greek, one involving a very general assessment that made *dikaios* almost synonymous with ethical excellence in general (1129a27–30a13), except that it clearly retained the connotation of pertaining to interactions between human beings (1129b26). This appears in translations as 'universal justice' because 'universal' is a traditional translation of the Greek term (*katholou*) for 'according to the whole.' There is also a narrower sense, which appears as 'particular justice,' i.e. the justice that is part of virtue rather than the whole of it (1130b30ff.)

The narrow sense applies to two specific aspects of human interactions, one of which is the distribution of benefits and hardships among members of the community. This is still commonly known as 'distributive' justice, and its focus in our society tends to be on taxation policies – whether it is just to tax wealth or income or purchases. What constitutes a just distribution will depend on a combination of attitudes toward social hierarchy and the prevailing institutions of property. What is distributed is a function of what can be owned and how.

Judicial institutions are primarily concerned with the process of rectifying wrongs (punishment and compensation) for what one person may do to another. Aristotle referred to this aspect of particular justice as 'corrective' or 'rectificatory' (1131b25ff.) Injuries arise in the course of transactions that are voluntarily undertaken (e.g. contracts) and also occur in interactions not voluntarily undertaken. What constitutes corrective justice will also depend on whether hierarchy is taken for granted, what constitutes someone's property (what cannot be owned cannot be stolen) and how one conceives agency and the locus of injury where more than one individual is implicated. If an injury is regarded as serious enough (murder, theft) it may be an offence against the whole community and treated under the criminal law; if it is not regarded as a matter of concern for the whole community, it will be treated under private or civil law as a 'tort' or 'delict.' This line is not always drawn in the same place; we treat theft as a crime, but in Roman law it was a delict (Watson 1981: 13), a civil matter like slander and personal injury in our law.

A single 'general and purely formal maxim' covers each of these spheres, distributive and corrective. The aim in each is to give every person what he or she is due. As Cephalus in *Republic I*: 331d (see Section 4.2) breaks off the discussion that he has been having with Socrates in order to keep an appointment, his son, Polemarchus, intervenes and appeals to this maxim, which he credits to the Greek poet Simonides, to explain why it would be right or just not to return borrowed weapons to a manic friend. Give each his due: to a friend is due good and not evil; to return the weapons before this friend has calmed down would be an evil, to withhold them a good. Doing what is right or just clearly requires the exercise of intelligence, especially in cases like this. This is partly why Aristotle did not like the idea that the reciprocity involved in justice was a matter of simple equality. Far better, Aristotle suggested (see Section 6.1), to use the general and purely formal notion, that based on proportionality, even if it requires more thought to apply. This means, as we have seen, that equality is only for equals, but we have not yet addressed the question of who are to count as equals.

Aristotle recognized that who counts as equals for the purpose of determining questions of 'particular' justice depends on the nature of the society in which the concepts 'just' and 'equal' are applied. Different social formations have different ideas of both. Aristotle saw societies as differing largely over what proportion of the populace were eligible to participate in government – what proportion of the free adult males, that is, for livestock, slaves and women were not constituents of a city but of its wealth. Rule by a wealthy few, oligarchy, produced one idea of justice; rule by the many or the *dēmos* (the poor majority), another. Both views began correctly:

> For justice is thought by them to be, and is, equality – not equality for all, but only for equals. And inequality is thought to be, and is, justice, neither is this for all, but only for unequals. . . . [But] the one party, if they are unequal in one respect, for example wealth, consider themselves to be unequal in all; and the other party, if they are equal in one respect, for example free birth, consider themselves to be equal in all.
>
> (1280a11–24)

Both of these views, Aristotle declared, were imperfect. The point of a political society is not merely living together but acting admirably, and it is those who contribute most to such a society that deserve the greatest share in it (1281a4–5). However, it is far from easy to extract a clear picture from Aristotle's writings of what he would count as a political society that facilitates acting admirably or what exactly it would mean to have a greater share in one.

Modern developments have divided the democratic pole of Aristotle's opposition in two, so that a recent writer (Watson 1981: 21) offers a threefold classification of ideas of justice, an 'aristocratic-fascist' notion, which corresponds to Aristotle's oligarchical notion and insists that it is proper for inequalities between different people to be reflected in the law. Individuals' rights and responsibilities, even the legal value of their persons (their *wergild*, if such an institution exists), should reflect their social standing. Aristotle's democratic concept is divided into a 'liberal-democratic' notion, which insists that all individuals be treated as having equal standing before the law, and a 'socialist' notion, which denies the possibility of people being treated equally before the law if there are vast inequalities in their economic power. In other words, the 'socialist' conception, unlike the liberal-democratic conception, does not assume that corrective justice can operate independently of distributive justice.

A further division between different substantive concepts of justice is created when account is taken of two possible attitudes that a moral tradition may hold about whether individuals are in general competent to determine and pursue their individual and collective interests, or whether human nature is weak and most individuals stand in need of external discipline and the guidance of either exemplary human, or superhuman, authority (Khadduri 1984: 1–2). (See Section 5.2 on 'optimistic' and 'pessimistic' nativists.) A fascist-aristocratic attitude will normally involve the latter, as the superiority of the few establishes their fitness to govern the rest, although some will see authority structures as unfairly restricting the better sort of person and advocate minimal collective governance to allow the superior type to emerge and claim their stations above their fellow human beings and their privileges before the law.

Those who operate within a liberal-democratic conception may also incline toward disciplinary and elitist forms of authority rather than allowing as much self-determination and free choice as possible – in effect not treating self-determination, either individual or collective, as something that should be distributed widely. Much depends on the relative values placed on equality, self-determination and the institution of property. Some liberals take the most important freedom to be that which gives people the security to use what is theirs as they see fit, and if because of human frailty those with little to call their own are perceived as posing a threat to property, their lives will be tightly regulated. Depriving those of what is rightfully theirs is treated as a more serious injustice than large inequalities in the means and opportunities available to people to make their own lives. Other liberals require inequalities to be justified in terms of benefits that they make possible for all. The formulation given by John Rawls (1971: 14–15) bases the concept of justice on two principles, the first requiring equality in the assignment of basic rights and duties and the second allowing inequalities of wealth and authority only if they benefit everyone, including the least advantaged.

Those with a socialist orientation may see the human impulse to individual appropriation as a weakness that inevitably needs authoritarian measures to control. Those who believe this impulse to be a cultural phenomenon look to the day when 'bourgeois attitudes' to property have been eliminated and there are relatively few pathological individuals whose urges to excessive private appropriation pose a threat to the self-determination that everyone enjoys. Those who operate within a theologically based conception of justice and support religious (Hebrew, Christian and Islamic) as opposed to secular states have often favored the pessimistic view of human beings and used it as justification for imposing what guidance they found in the revelations of their respective religious traditions. Others place a premium on the free choice to believe and live as God has willed and prefer to rely on exhortation rather than imposition.

So far, we have seen different conceptions of what is just encompass different attitudes toward equality, toward the inviolability of property rights and toward the extent to which people are allowed to make their own choices. There are also different attitudes toward what are proper procedures when holding people responsible for their crimes and misdemeanors. It might, for example, seem obviously improper (unfair) for people to be punished for what they did before there was an explicit law making it illegal. But if one lives in a society that treats its laws as statements of what has always (or for as long as anyone can remember) been valid, then it is illegal to do whatever is against the law, whether or not the law has been proclaimed, and there is no reason not to regard offenses committed before the law was formulated as punishable.[9]

It will also seem obviously unfair (unjust) that persons be held responsible or made to suffer for actions they did not commit, as when the *lex talionis* is observed by exacting an eye or a tooth from a member of the offender's clan rather than the offender himself. But the idea that the agent of an offense should be assumed to be the individual or individuals who carried it out, and not any wider group to which they might belong, does not always appear natural to people. Many societies do not think of themselves as organizations of individual human beings but rather as organizations of households, and the identity of a person may be so closely tied up with a group of immediate relatives that the acts of an individual are regarded in the first instances as acts of that group. If we are to understand a society of this kind, Grönbech explains,

> we must begin with the kin, the race or family; a gathering of individuals so joined up into one unit that they appear incapable of independent action. ... the individual cannot act without all acting with and through him; no single individual can suffer without affecting the whole circle. So absolute is the connection that the individual simply cannot exist by himself.
>
> (1931: 31)

A society may thus feel it appropriate to punish a whole household for the crimes or follies of one member. For this to appear fair or fitting, just or reasonable, it is not necessary to assume that those close to the culprit must have been guilty of complicity or were responsible for ensuring that the culprit did not misbehave; it is enough to think of the boundaries of the perpetrators of a crime as extending beyond their bodies to the whole of the group that they represent.

An incident chronicled in the Old Testament illustrates this. Following a humiliating defeat in battle, Yahweh informs the Israelites that He has permitted this to happen because one of their number behaved improperly after the conquest of Jericho and until they 'destroy the accursed from among' them, Yahweh refuses to be with them (Joshua 7: 13). Upon investigation, it is found that a man named Achan had (mis)appropriated from the spoils of Jericho 'a goodly Babylonish garment and two hundred shekels of silver and a wedge of gold of fifty shekels weight,' and he duly suffers the consequences:

> And Joshua, and all Israel with him, took Achan the son of Zerah, and the silver, and the garment and the wedge of gold, and his sons, and his daughters, and his oxen and his asses, and his sheep and his tent, and all that he had: and they brought them unto the valley of Achor. And Joshua said, Why has thou troubled us? the Lord shall trouble thee this day. And all Israel stoned him with stones, and burned them with fire, after they had stoned them with stones.
>
> (7: 24–5)

Thus when Achan is condemned along with 'all that he hath,' this appears to entail the destruction not only of what he looted from Jericho together with his tent and animals but his sons and daughters as well. While serving as Archdeacon of Hong Kong during the mid-nineteenth century, John Henry Gray wrote extensive memoirs of his observations of Chinese laws, manners and customs. He tells (1878: 237–9) of exceedingly severe punishment being visited not just on culprits who committed assault against their parents but also on their relatives and neighbors, for in this Confucian society such acts were seen as striking at the very foundations of the social order.

How people deal with strangers also reveals different conceptions of what is just or fair. Part of the concrete morality governing our commercial practices is the expectation that the same level of honesty may be expected in dealings with the general public as with close friends and relatives. Historically, this has not been a common expectation. With members of their immediate group (ethnic, religious, occupational), people were expected to ease up on the relentless pursuit of personal gain and not resort to sharp practice of any sort. People expected to be able to trust their close associates not to take advantage of them, but with outsiders it was *caveat emptor*.

In discussing the practices of the Jews following the conquest of their land by Babylonia and the beginning of what has become known as the *diaspora*, Max Weber stresses that their attitudes were entirely typical of commercial and financial dealing until developments among Protestants in Europe in the seventeenth century: 'whoever practised usury as a tax farmer in the services of a godless Jewish prince or, worse, of a foreign power against one's own people was deeply objectionable and held by the rabbis as impure. However against foreign people this way of acquisition was ethically adiaphorous [indifferent]' (1952: 344–5). Weber (*ibid.*) maintains that seventeenth-century Quakers and Baptists were the first to incorporate into their concrete moralities the same standards for fair dealings with outsiders as with members of their own religious communities. Our assumptions (which arguably are a necessary condition of the size and complexity of our commercial culture) derive from the influence of these early capitalists. At other times in history, paradigms of fair dealing would be quite different, and even the maxim that honesty is the best policy would meet with incredulity.

This illustrative catalogue of differences in attitudes and assumptions about what is fair, just or appropriate in dealings between people might be taken to support the relativist and skeptical views examined in the previous chapter. The conclusion that can be drawn so far, however, is that these concepts depend on the social formations and institutions that provide contexts for their application. The attitudes and the differences between them may depend on these formations and institutions, but we have yet to raise questions about what bases, if any, there may be for sustaining the formations and institutions rather than working to change or abolish them. The next chapter will begin with one long-standing institution that in recent history has come to be widely and sincerely opposed and then consider what basis there might be for this opposition.

Further reading

The portion of Weber (1978) that along with the editors' notes provides a rich source of details about the sociology of law was originally published as Weber (1954). On Roman law, in addition to Stein (1966), see Kunkel (1973) and Watson (1992; 1995). Schacht (1964) and Khadduri (1984) together provide a good introduction to Islamic legal traditions. On the contrast between the common and civil law traditions, see Pound (1922) and Watson (1981). On the role of precedent and the limitations of the conception of law as statutes, see Llewellyn (1930) and Levi (1949). Dancy (1993: chapters 4–6) is the main source for contemporary particularism. Yack (1993: chapters 5–6) provides a useful discussion of Aristotle on justice and equity. Jonsen and Toulmin (1988) is an excellent recent source on casuistry. Alongside the egalitarian liberal notion of justice of Rawls

(1971), consult Nozick (1974), who develops a concept of justice more in the tradition of classical liberalism. On overcoming the bourgeois notion of property, see Marx and Engels (1846: 79–81).

Notes

1 Citations of the *Summa Theologica* or (*Theologiæ*) will be given by part (this one is to the first, la = *prima*, part of the second, IIæ = *secundæ*, part), number of *Quæstio* and number of *Articulus*.

2 'the subjective conviction that one is applying only norms already valid is in fact characteristic of every type of adjudication which has outgrown the age of prophecy' (Weber 1978: 767).

3 The term *Kadi*-justice has come to be applied by specialists to specific social phenomena, somewhat in the way 'taboo' is used in ordinary speech. David Buxbaum (1968: xviii–xx), for example, uses it to characterize procedures of adjudication in pre-literate societies throughout Asia.

4 This interpretation owes a great deal to – but develops rather than follows – Trubek (1972: 728–30).

5 *Cf.* Levi (1949: 2–3) on the 'doctrine of *dictum*': whatever reasons a judge might give for deciding a case on the basis of precedents are not binding on subsequent decisions (is merely *dictum*, something said); only the actual decision is binding, and judges can devise their own rationale to explain how that decision and earlier precedents point to a decision in the subsequent cases before them.

6 The *Encyclopedia Britannica*, 1959: Vol. 8, p. 675 explains: 'The king, as *pater patriae*, had a duty to see that none of his subjects was denied a remedy where conscience required that he should have one, and this duty he delegated to his chancellor who became the keeper of the king's conscience.' The office of chancellor had this judicial role from the twelfth to the nineteenth century; in 1873, the Court of Chancery became a division of the British High Court of Justice, and the institutional distinction between courts of law and equity ceased.

7 In terms of Dworkin's (1967) distinction between rules and principles (see Section 2.4), this would be the 'tyranny of rules', as Dworkin's principles, unlike ideal laws conceived as rules, are not specific, occasionally conflict, and are not intended to be applied without exception. They are what Jonsen (1991) refers to as 'maxims.' Dworkin's principles, it should also be noted, were not to be used to avoid travesties of justice where the law is clear and an appeal is being made to equity, but to guide where the law is unclear.

8 For the connection between Jonsen's methodological recommendations and Aristotle's notion of 'equity,' see Jonsen (1991: 304).

9 Stein (1966: 21–3), at any rate, appeals to the existence of the belief that it is improper for new *leges* to entail penalties for past actions as evidence that the Romans had by that point reached the conception of law as something made rather than (or as well as) discovered.

7

THE MEASURE OF LAW

True law (*vera lex*) is right reason (*recta ratio*) in agreement
with nature (*naturae congruens*); it is spread everywhere,
constant and everlasting; it calls to service by its commands
and deters from wrong-doing by its prohibitions. It does not
command or prohibit good men in vain although it has no
effect on the wicked. It is not right (*fas*) to try to alter or
try to repeal any part of it and impossible to abolish the
whole of it; indeed neither the Senate nor the *Populus* can
cancel it. There is no need to look to anyone else for an
expounder or an interpreter of it, nor will there be different
laws at Rome and at Athens, or different laws now and in
the future, but one everlasting and unchangeable law will
hold for all nations and all times. And it will be as if one
master and ruler, God, is over us all, the author, proposer
and promulgator of this law. Whoever does not obey is fleeing
from himself and spurning his own human nature.
(Cicero (first century BCE); Keyes 1938:
Republic III.xxii, 33)[1]

Recapitulation: Although the norms of a legal system may not
be fully congruent with the concrete morality, especially the shared
sense of justice, of the people who live under them, the institutions of law serve to clarify, make explicit, reinforce and on
occasion modify concrete moralities. The failure to be fully
congruent may be the inevitable result of the fact that laws are
expressed using general rules, which cannot anticipate the variability of particulars and thus cannot provide unerring guides to
what should be done (what is fitting) in all circumstances. Even
legal practices that rely more on the application of precedents
than of statutes can deliver decisions that are not sufficiently sensitive to the variability of circumstances. From a more distant
standpoint, both accepted legal practice and the sense of justice
of a community may appear to have been distorted by the social
formations and institutions that shape the attitudes and assumptions in that society.

Prospectus: Slavery as an institution appears in many cultures throughout history. It has been supported by the concrete moralities of societies that recognize the roles of master and slave, roles that have been enshrined in, refined and enforced by prevailing legal systems. Slavery is now so widely condemned that it is sometimes difficult to understand how it was possible for people to take it for granted and why it took so long for attitudes about slavery to be viewed with the current level of loathing. Slavery will serve as a useful example of what is involved in the criticism from a moral standpoint of an entrenched institution, and the lessons may be applied to other entrenched institutions that appear deeply objectionable (such as those canvassed in Sections 1.3 and 1.4). The ethical theory of Immanuel Kant suggests a basis in the distinction between persons and things and the insistence that a person should not be reduced to being merely the means to another's ends.

7.1   Persons, rights and roles

God, slaves and corporations

In making his complaint against God see (Section 3.3), Job might have appealed to what Albert Jonsen (see Section 6.3) would call a 'maxim,' *viz.* that people should not be *made* to suffer unless it is at the very least made clear to them what they have done to deserve suffering. (People who suffer because of the operation of blind causes are a different matter.) This maxim would certainly have widespread, if not universal, support; it seems to be one of those aspects of what it is for one person's dealings with another to be fair or 'fitting.' Job thus has a claim that, if it had been made against another human being, would be upheld by most people, who heard it, as valid and deserving to be enforced (insofar as that is possible). That is to say, Job would be recognized by these people as having a *right* to be shown adequate reason for what was being done to him or a right that the perpetrator should desist and suffer retribution and/or make amends. To say that Job has a *right* (or a rightful claim) is to say that the perpetrator has a *duty* to respond in this way to his claim, and that it would be appropriate to coerce the perpetrator in some way to fulfill this duty. But God is not like another person, not merely in being inaccessible to coercion. The point of the climax of the poetic portion of the Book of Job was that the disparity between God and man is too great for maxims like this to apply to dealings between such different beings.

As Kant saw it, the idea of God is the idea of a being who has rights and no duties (1797: 32–3). That is, God can make rightful claims on us, but we can make no rightful claims on Him; no request that God grants us, no reward for merit, can be our due but must rather be reckoned to be an act of His mercy. Human beings, unlike God, normally have both rights and duties – they can make claims and have claims made upon them that will be recognized as valid. At the opposite extreme to God would be a being who had duties and no rights. This being, Kant says (*ibid.*), would be a slave or a serf. People would stand toward this being as a god, able to make rightful claims on it but not subject to any rightful claims by it. Kant declared that there were no such beings, but this has not prevented people treating some of their fellow humans as though they were beings without rights.

To be clear about this we need to distinguish a servant from a slave. People render services to one another individually ('in the service industries') or collectively ('public service'), and we would obviously live poorer lives if we never did anything of this sort for one another. Having our liberty and freedom of choice constrained by, for example, terms of employment or military discipline is a form of servitude that we find, if not wholly convenient, at least worth the benefits that arise from accepting it. 'Servant' (public, domestic) is an occupational category; 'slave' is (among other things) a legal condition, that of being without certain important rights – in the extreme case, as Kant put it, having no rights, only duties. Slaves have been employed as both public and domestic servants as well as laborers. Moses Finley writes of 'slave societies as distinct from societies in which there were slaves.' In the former, slaves are an important source of productive labor (in mines and factories, on plantations). There have been many of the latter, relatively few of the former: Finley identifies ancient Greece, ancient Rome, and the US South, the Caribbean and Brazil in modern times as slave societies (1980: 79).

Some slaves in ancient Greece and Rome performed in highly responsible and by no means arduous roles, but the good fortune of some should not obscure the depravity of the legal condition. Finley identifies three important components of the slave's condition: 'the slave's property status, the totality of the power over him, and his kinlessness.' As property, slaves had the status of (marketable) commodities with no control over their own labor, their bodies or their persons. Being kinless meant they could be sold and separated from any spouse or children they might have been allowed to have and thus had no stable kinship identity or network of kin support. The power over their bodies included sexual exploitation by their masters (*ibid.*: 96) and being subject to corporal punishment. As a rule, corporal punishment in antiquity was restricted to slaves (93). In Rome, slaves were required by law to give testimony under torture; the worthlessness of testimony given under torture was beside the point:

If a slave is a property with a soul, a non-person and yet indubitably a biological human being, institutional procedures are to be expected that will degrade and undermine his humanity and so distinguish him from human beings who are not property. Corporal punishment and torture constitute one such procedure.

(ibid.: 95)

Methods that would now be labeled 'state terrorism' included the Roman 'ancestral custom' that if a slave murdered his master, all the slaves 'under the same roof,' including women and children, were put to death as punishment. In a case in 61 CE, this happened to more than four hundred in the household of a murdered prefect, Pedanius Secundus (102–3).

Being unable to act in any public capacity except through their masters, slaves had in effect no public personality, and the control exercised over their daily lives allowed them only a very restricted private personality. The notion of personality has come to be central to ethics as a systematic study, and it is important to understand the sense of the term that is involved and useful to know something about its origin. Kant defines 'person' as 'a subject whose actions can be imputed to him' (1797: 223) and 'civil personality' as the 'attribute of not needing to be represented by another where rights are concerned' (314). Where women must be represented in legal matters (in court, in property transactions, etc.) by their husbands or some other male relative, they lack civil personality *(ibid.)*. The idea of a source of action was once the main sense of the term 'person,' which derives from Latin *persona*, a mask worn in a drama identifying a character and hence the source of the actions performed. Compare Hobbes: '*a person is he to whom the words and actions of men are attributed*,' (1658: 83, italics in original). Kant defines the now more common psychological notion as 'merely the ability to be conscious of one's identity in different conditions of one's existence' (1797: 223).

We assume that the number of persons involved in some affair can be counted by counting heads. But the idea that a group of people should receive punishment for acts done by one or a few members of the group (examples of which have appeared above and in Section 6.4) has the effect of treating the group as the agent – in effect one person with many heads. At some points in history this idea may well have been taken quite literally (see the quotation from Grönbech in Section 6.4), but the idea may also have functioned as a useful fiction, as in the case of the slaughter mentioned above in the household of Pedanius Secundus. Another way of denying the personality of the individuals of a class is to treat them as simply parts of a larger whole.

However, in the case of Rome this was not a fiction devised solely for the purpose of oppressing the slave class. The Roman household was literally an extension of the legal personality of the male head of the household. The Roman *paterfamilias* had the legal power of life and death over the members of his household: that is, he could kill his slaves or children

156

without becoming liable to prosecution for murder. By late in the republican period a father who exercised this power over his children would have come into conflict with prevailing Roman concrete morality and been subject to severe condemnation by his peers (Dihle 1982: 139); any similar feeling about his treatment of his slaves, however, would be nowhere near as severe.

No doubt transactions within a household had to take account of the independent agency of its members, but outside a household only its head was an independent agent (person). A grown man could not validly enter into contracts so long as his father was alive and he fell under his father's *manus* (hand). This proved inconvenient for fathers and sons whose joint business affairs required that the son act as an independent legal entity, but instead of changing this customary law by new legislation, Romans adapted to this inconvenience by manipulating a different part of the institution. Fathers had always had the power to sell their children into slavery. If the son's new master freed him, he fell back under the *manus* of his father again, but if he were sold three times by his father and freed each time, he became a legal person in his own right. So father and son called upon a family friend to participate in a formal (publicly declared) ceremony in which the friend bought the son as a slave and freed him three times (*ibid.*: 139–40).

To us, treating individuals as part of larger wholes in these ways denies them rights, and indeed it does. Instead of recognizing individual human beings by the rights they can claim, individuals will be recognized by the roles they are assigned – male or female, husband or wife, father or mother, parent or child, noble or common, free or slave, etc. Roles are defined by what is expected of an individual, what obligations that individual is under, what duties that individual has to perform. An individual in such a society is much more a locus of responsibility than a source of claims, because roles are far more socially relevant than anything that depends on the claims that might be made upon others – especially such claims as would be appropriate to back up by force. Such claims will in any case be largely the responsibility of that individual's household or other primary group. What will be immediately sought when confronting another human being will be the role, place or standing of that being. What expectations may reasonably be formed follow from the recognition of this role, place or standing; there may or may not be corresponding rightful claims that the individual can make.

As long as human beings are conceived as inseparable from the roles they are assigned and roles are not merely differentiated but hierarchically structured, there will be a bottom step in the hierarchy. In the ancient Greek and Roman worlds, there were no rightful claims that those at the bottom of the hierarchy could make. Some slaves became objects of genuine affection (such as 'masters' and 'mistresses' still develop for their dogs and cats), others became objects for venting spleen; some were valued for exceptional skills, others as confidants and advisors. These factors may mask what the slave's legal standing contributes to the texture of the relationships, but at the foundation of all modifications remained the fact that slaves had no legal autonomy or public personality, could not leave their master's service by their own choice, and had to 'answer with their bodies for all offenses' (Finley 1980: 93). Legally, a slave had a standing little better than one of our domestic appliances. As Aristotle puts it:

> the servant is himself an instrument [or 'tool' or 'appliance,' *organōn*] for instruments. For if every instrument could accomplish its own work, obeying or anticipating the will of others . . . if the shuttle would weave and the plectrum touch the lyre, chief workmen would not want servants, nor masters slaves.
>
> (1253b33–1254a1)

The only reason that a master has not to maltreat or undernourish his slaves that is linked to their roles is the effect it will have on their usefulness to him.

Recent students of intellectual history have recognized that during the seventeenth century CE European thought crossed a watershed. Looking back, it is possible to discern assumptions about the nature of society that are prevalent now but were almost non-existent in ancient and medieval thinkers, and ideas once taken for granted that are now more than a little hard to understand. In a work published early in this century, the German historian of social theory Otto Gierke distinguished the two notions of human association involved in this conceptual transformation as 'corporation' (*Gemeinschaft*) and 'partnership' (*Gesellschaft*) (1934: Vol. I, 45). The first conception, Gierke indicated, would correspond to the Latin notions *universitas, communitas* and *corpus*, the second to *societas* – a *socius* was a military ally or a business partner. The latter notion, which has become dominant in the modern period, looks at human association (particularly at the political level) as a coming together of independently existing individuals who constitute a political environment by agreeing to co-ordinate their activities with a view to some mutual benefit. The former notion, prevalent in earlier times, had a variety of forms, but in all of them it was taken for granted that humans were not fully human outside a political environment, and hence it did not make sense to view the political environment as constituted by the agreement of (possibly) independent individuals.

It is not that pre-modern people did not use the concept of a partnership (temporary or long term); what they did not do was conceive all human interactions as at bottom partnerships. But at the same time it should not be assumed that they always understood the image of the 'body-politic' as involving a thoroughgoing organic unity. The variety of ways of conceiving 'corporations' or 'communities' that older thinkers might advocate ranged from literal applications of the metaphor of an organic body to somewhat looser forms of unity. Under the former, people were conceived entirely in terms of the more permanent of their roles and could not, any more than can the organs of a body, have lives and/or human capacities independently of their function in the 'body politic.' While never dispensing altogether with roles, less strictly organic models allowed more weight to be placed on voluntary agreement.

In the course of criticizing what he saw as a hankering after an inappropriate degree of social unity in Plato's thought (evident most prominently in the *Republic*), Aristotle distinguished three degrees of unity: that appropriate to a biological organism; that appropriate to a family; and that appropriate to a *polis* (city-state; 1261a15–22). Aristotle's argument rested on the principle that the more unity an organization has, the less self-sufficient it is; the *polis* is more self-sufficient although more of a plurality (less of a unity) than a family and the family more self-sufficient and more of a plurality (less of a unity) than a single human being. A *polis*, however, did not achieve its self-sufficiency by being a collection of *undifferentiated* parts (like a military alliance; a23–5). 'The elements out of which such a unity is formed differ in kind. That is why reciprocity preserves *poleis*, as it was said earlier in the *Ethics*' (a29–31). People still have roles, but in constituting a *polis* more reliance is placed on agreement, contract and mutual claims that entail (in effect, if not identified as such) mutual rights. But not everyone is a player, as the *Ethics* explains:

> For it is by proportionate requital that the city holds together. Men seek to return either evil for evil – and if they cannot do so, think their position mere slavery – or good for good – and if they cannot do so, there is no exchange, but it is by exchange that they hold together.
>
> (1132b34–1133a2)

Customs of exchange based on some idea of reciprocity have the effect of forming people into a *polis*, but no reciprocity need obtain between individuals if the differences in their roles place them in widely separated places in the social hierarchy.

With the decay of the framework built around the notion of community, human beings came to be thought of in terms other than their social roles; their relationships to one another came to be thought of, if not as partnerships of their own making, then as partnerships at least susceptible to being remade by agreement. What then became relevant to those (now thought of as contractual) relationships were the claims that 'partners' or 'associates' might reasonably ask to have enforced against one another. It became possible to reduce roles to the claims that they entailed, to rights and correlative duties, founded on voluntary commitment.

The replacement of the notion of *communitas* with that of *societas* is not by any means a well-understood phenomenon. A number of prior and concurrent changes in institutions like that of property can be observed. The sense in which a slave was a piece of personal property in the ancient world is not quite what it would be today if it were permissible to 'own' someone. The notion of the power, *dominium*, of a head of a household was modified in several ways before it came to express something like our notion of property. It was both extended to cover what men had under their control by the grace of a superior (emperor, feudal lord) and also extended to cover such abstract items as fame and liberty. In groping toward a foundation for the institution of slavery that incorporated the idea of a status voluntarily entered into, the Portuguese Jesuit Luis de Molina, poised on the watershed that was mentioned above, argued that

> Man is *dominus* not only of his external goods, but also of his own honor and fame; he is also *dominus* of his own liberty, and in the context of the natural law can alienate it and enslave himself. ... It follows ... that if a man who is not subject to [any civil law restricting voluntary servitude] sells himself unconditionally in some place where the relevant laws allow him, then that sale is valid.
>
> (translated in Tuck (1979: 53–4) from Molina's *de Iustitia et Iure*, Mainz, 1614: cols 162–3)

The sort of obligations that entailed no correlative rights, associated with roles not voluntarily entered into, were becoming less important and have now become for us much less salient.

7.2   Natural slaves and natural law

Contours of nature and the flow of rhetoric

The only record of a defense of the institution of slavery by an ancient thinker is that offered by Aristotle. He addresses the claims that slavery is 'contrary to nature,' exists only by custom (*nomos*; 1253b21) and is neither very good nor just (*dikaion*; 1254b19), although it is not clear who may have formulated these arguments. The key premise of Aristotle's argument is that some people do not possess a capacity for initiating discursive thought, only a capacity for perceiving or complying with it (1254b21–4). Part of this premise is the assumption that nothing can be done by way of education to develop the missing capacity. This is how Aristotle tries to 'naturalize' the institution of slavery (see beginning of Section 3.2).

The inference from this seems to be that it is reasonable and proper for people who have only enough intelligence to do what they are told but not to figure out for themselves what needs to be done to be assigned the 'logical and juridical' (as Finley (1980: 77) puts it) condition of slave.

Given what we saw in the previous section, it should come as no surprise that missing from Aristotle's defense is any attempt to explain why the incapacity to initiate discursive thought should be correlated with an absence of important rights. We accept that in some cases capacities are prerequisites for possessing rights; one must be able to see well enough to have the right to drive a car and must have acquired certain knowledge and abilities to have the right to practise law or medicine. What is not obvious is why lacking a capacity for figuring out what needs to be done should entail being required to 'assist with [his/her] body the necessities [of the master's life]' (b26). What may have helped Aristotle over this step was the way in which societies in which there are slaves categorize them as children, calling a slave 'boy' or 'child', e.g. Greek *pais*, Latin *puer*. As it is not unreasonable to expect children to contribute to the household economy in a manner commensurate with their abilities, it would be reasonable to expect those who were going to remain in a permanent state of immaturity, as it were, to contribute in what ways they could to the household that feeds and shelters them. The assumption about the permanence of their immaturity follows from the assumption that 'naturalizes' the institution, but this still does nothing to address the question about what rights the immature (permanent or otherwise) should or should not be acknowledged to have.[2]

The problem is that there is nothing in Aristotle's vocabulary that corresponds directly to 'right,' and it would not occur to him to frame the question in anything like this way.[3] Masters directed, it was their role to deliberate about what was to be done and this gave them rightful claims. Slaves carried out directives; that was their duty and it was not their role to reason why or their right to hear reasons. The supposed ability of the former to initiate discursive thought and the congenital inability, as Aristotle saw it, of the latter was no doubt little more than a projection and underscoring of the roles assigned to them by society. Nevertheless, the value of having people who were supposed to be able to think well completely direct the lives of those who could not was taken to be obvious – the rightful claims and duties entailed by these differences of function did not seem to call for justification.

Sixteen centuries later, St Thomas Aquinas offered much the same justification for the existence of slavery, although his version at least acknowledged the slave's standpoint: it was 'useful to this man [the slave] to be ruled by a wiser man, and the latter to be helped by the former as the Philosopher [Aristotle] states' (IIaIIæ Q57 A3). The justification given concentrates on the advantages of the arrangement, and although Christian morality, which Aquinas helped to articulate, recognized slaves as having in effect more rights (to sustenance, to their own families and to freedom from physical abuse and sexual exploitation) than they were granted in the ancient world, the advantage of having the lives of the cognitively less well endowed under the comprehensive control of a more talented master (or tied to his land), rather than a matter of mutual agreement between them, was not addressed. Roles seemed to have a unity that made such justification unnecessary.

One thing that may still surprise, after the relative unimportance of rights and roles is appreciated, is that rhetoric about basic equality and natural freedom was not unknown in the ancient world, but it did not work as we would expect it to work against slavery as an institution. This is the watershed effect: no matter how high the rhetoric falls, if it does not fall on the right side, it does not flow in the expected direction. Talk of a fundamental equality among all men and the idea that all men are born free appear long before the institution of slavery was ever seriously challenged. The writers who used these expressions were, moreover, well equipped to distinguish what a society regarded as lawful and what it ought to regard as lawful.

Cicero (first century BCE) articulated the Roman attitude to law in such a way that it appeared to answer to something more universal than the Roman sense of *ius*. Connected to this doctrine that what is lawful is a universally recognizable natural property, which appears at the head of this chapter, is a striking statement of the fundamental similarity of all human beings: 'No single thing is so like another, so exactly its counterpart, as all of us are to one another' (Keyes 1938: *Laws*, I.x.29). Conclusive proof of our common human nature, according to Cicero, is that we all satisfy the same definition; indeed, all humans are sharply distinguished from beasts by possessing a capacity for *ratio* (30).

> For those creatures who have received the gift of reason (*ratio*) from Nature have also received right reason (*recta ratio*) and therefore they have also received the gift of Law (*lex*), which is right reason applied to command and prohibition. And if they have received Law, they have received *ius* also. Now all men have received reason; therefore all men have received *ius*.
>
> (33)

(On the range of meanings of *ratio*, see Sections 3.4 and 6.2.)

Where Aristotle thought some members of the species were deficient in the capacity that distinguishes humans from other animals, Cicero reckoned that we all had the beginnings of intelligence (*intellegentia*) imprinted on our minds, and with the right nurture we could all reach an acceptable, even somewhat demanding, level of competence in its use. What prevents people reaching an acceptable level is another aspect of our fundamental equality: we are all subject to the same influences, 'troubles, joys, desires and fears' (32), which generate 'bad habits and false beliefs' that 'twist weaker minds' (29). Thus we find, in the end, that some people's natural capacity for *ratio* is so damaged that (as a fragment of Cicero's *Republic*, III.xxv, suggests) it is not improper to exercise *dominium* over those who are not capable of governing themselves.

Cicero thus needs to answer some of the same questions that Aristotle left unanswered: what does it take to govern oneself? Is it proper to treat those who cannot govern themselves as marketable commodities? However, Cicero had not set out either to attack or to defend the institution of slavery when he insisted on the similarity of one human being to another. He was considering rather the basis of law, and he claimed that it is a consequence of our common capacity for discursive thought that 'We are so made by nature that we share with one another, and pass on to all, (a sense of) *ius*' (*Laws* I.12.33). This appeal to our common humanity might sound to us like it ought to issue in rejection of the practice of slavery, but what Cicero apparently thought followed was that all would recognize the authority of certain legal institutions, which enshrined among other things the practice of slavery.

Roman legal experts writing two to four centuries after Cicero felt comfortable living in a slave society while embracing the thesis that Aristotle had tried to refute, *viz.* that the institution of slavery has no natural basis. Ulpian, explaining the Latin term for freeing a slave, *manumissio*, writes 'whereas one who is in slavery is subjected to the hand (*manus*) and power of another, on being sent out of hand (*manu* + *missio*), he is freed of that power,' and adds 'of course everyone would be born free by natural *ius*, and manumissions would not be known when slavery was unknown.' Florentinus, a few decades after Ulpian, states flatly 'Slavery is an institution ... whereby someone is against nature made subject to the ownership of another' (Watson 1985: I.1.4, I.5.4).[4] Florentinus and Ulpian did not, however, any more than did Cicero, suggest that slavery should be abolished.

As a group, the Roman jurists of this period distinguished the customs and institutions that might be endorsed and enforced in any given kingdom or city-state (*ius civile*) from customs and institutions that all nations (clans, peoples, *gens*) observed. The latter they designated either *ius gentium* or *ius naturale*.[5] Once it became possible to think and speak of slavery as a violation of a person's natural rights, scholars traced the antecedents of this back to Cicero and to the jurists represented in Justinian's *Digest* – 'natural right' being, after all, a possible translation of *ius naturale* (for example, Carlyle 1930: 5–13). But there is no indication anywhere of reservations about the institution of slavery. We find what may strike us as humane and enlightened attitudes toward the treatment of slaves expressed using cognates of *ius*:

> But let us remember that we must have regard for justice (*justitia*) even toward the humblest. Now the humblest station and the poorest fortune are those of slaves; and we are not given bad guidance by those who bid us treat our slaves as we should our employees: they must be required to work; they must be offered fair dealings (*iusta præbenda*).
>
> (Cicero, *De Officiis*; Miller 1913: I.41)

But there is no suggestion that the institution itself might be contrary to what is *ius*.

Early and medieval Christianity has the same perplexing (to us) features. The salvation of every human being was equally important. In St Paul's words: 'There is neither Jew nor Greek, there is neither bond nor free, there is neither male nor female: for ye are all one in Christ Jesus' (Galatians 3: 28). But this lack of distinction between human beings in relation to God did not translate into sustained attempts to subvert these distinctions in everyday life. That there is neither male nor female in Christ Jesus did not mean that different social roles could be abandoned, even in church. St Paul insisted that women maintain their traditional submissive roles and 'keep silence in the churches: for it is not permitted unto them to speak; but they are commanded to be under obedience, as also saith the law' (I Corinthians 14: 34). Like the more humane pagans, Christians acknowledged the humanity of their slaves and thought it proper to treat them fairly: 'Masters, give unto *your* servants that which is just [*to dikaion*] and equal [*tēn isotēta*]' (Colossians 34: 1). But servants were equally under instructions 'to obey *your* masters according to the flesh not in eyeservice, as menpleasers; but in singleness of heart, fearing God' (*ibid*. 3: 22). Social differences between master and servant were insignificant in the light of the relation that all people should have to God: 'For he that is called in the Lord, *being* a servant, is the Lord's freeman; likewise also he that is called, *being* free, is Christ's servant' (I Corinthians 7: 22). But the social differences remained intact.

Although not as important to the economy of medieval Europe as it had been to the Roman world, slavery as an institution continued to exist. The Church accepted and participated in it – Church law (known as 'canon law') up to the thirteenth century was based on the assumption that the Church owned slaves[6] – although it insisted on humane treatment of them. Where St Thomas Aquinas (thirteenth century) would return to an Aristotelian position and rationalize the institution of slavery in terms of its utility, St Augustine (fourth to fifth century) had treated the condition as a consequence of man's sinful nature (the lust for domination), a just punishment for sin and an instrument of God's judgment (Bettenson 1972: XIV.13, XIX.15).

Christians from St Paul onward also used the vocabulary of natural law and natural justice to articulate the idea that the laws of God stood above the laws of men. One sees in Latin authors increasing use of the term *lex naturale* instead of *ius naturale*, reflecting, no doubt, the idea that the standard against which human (positive) law was to be judged was embodied in something with a linguistic form, God's word. In considering whether natural *law* (*lex naturale*) was subject to change, Aquinas allowed (IaIIæ Q94 A5) that it was possible to add to natural law but not to remove anything from it. Additions to natural law could still be natural, since it was essential (of its nature) to law that it promote the common good (Q90 A2), so an institution could be treated as naturally lawful if humans discovered by using their minds that it promoted the common good:

> A thing is said to belong to the natural law in two ways. First, because nature inclines thereto: e.g. that one should not do harm to another. Secondly, because nature did not bring in the contrary: thus we might say that for man to be naked is of the natural law, because nature did not give him clothes, but art invented them. In this sense, *the possession of all things in common and universal freedom* are said to be of the natural law, because, to wit, the distinction of possessions and slavery were not brought in by nature, but devised by human reason for the benefit of human life. Accordingly the law of nature was not changed in this respect, except by addition.
>
> (Q94 A5)

This is a revealing gloss: to say that all humans are born (their natural condition is) free is to say about as much as to say that they are all born naked. Social custom sanctioned by God's law will see to it that they are dressed in clothes and assigned social roles – some of them lowly indeed.

By the seventeenth century (at the 'watershed'), slave labor had, because of its use in colonies in the New World, once again become central to the European economy, but as we noted in the previous section a new way of thinking about liberty began to the replace the idea of a natural nakedness to be covered by a social role (including whatever forms of servitude went with a given role). It was now possible to conceive of *libertas* as a possession that, like an artifact or a piece of land, could be disposed of in whatever manner would contribute to an individual's welfare or survival.

Not everyone was comfortable with putting this much of an individual's destiny in his or her own hands, but one of the pivotal figures in the transformation of European social thought, the early seventeenth-century Dutch legal scholar Hugo Grotius, suggested that lifelong service in exchange for lifelong maintenance was for many people an advantageous bargain (1625: 255). He regarded the basest form of voluntary subjection to be that resulting from having staked one's liberty on the throw of dice – as Tacitus reported the practice among the Germans of the first century CE

– but he nevertheless accepted even the outcome of such a wager as binding (*ibid.*). Grotius also recognized the right (*ius*) of conquerors to enslave their captives (690). That we are born free (the traditional doctrine of the individual liberty of primitive man) does not mean that humans 'have the right never to enter slavery' (551). Moreover, those legitimately enslaved (not captured in an unjust war, or not simply kidnapped) are not permitted to resist their masters, e.g. by trying to escape. The condition of slavery and its attendant rights and duties are traced by Grotius to acts for which a slave is responsible (contracting into slavery or going to war).

Much of the concern with these issues at this time hinged on their application to a subject's obligations to obey a sovereign ruler. Grotius cited Roman and Hebrew law, which permitted voluntary slavery in order to underwrite the suggestion that a people might surrender all their *iura* to a king and have no more right to restrain those who abused the office of sovereign than a slave can restrain an abusive master (103). The basis of obligations that arise within human institutions generally (not merely those involving political authority) are in Grotius and in subsequent thinkers increasingly seen as the products of voluntary acts, promises, agreements and contracts.

Subsequent thinkers, however, were wary of the dire consequences (as well as the somewhat paradoxical nature) of a voluntary act that constrains all scope for future voluntary action as severely as does contracting into slavery. Sixty years later, Locke appears to have moved a considerable distance from Grotius on these matters, for he insists that people do not have the power to enslave themselves, that the condition of slavery is tantamount to the state of war between master and slave and that slaves are under no obligation not to resist their masters (Locke 1689: *Second Treatise*, §§22–4). However, Locke had a very narrow understanding of the condition of slavery: it was being under 'Absolute, Arbitrary Power,' the 'Arbitrary Will of another Man' (*ibid.*). Grotius did not regard masters as having arbitrary power of life and death over their slaves (1625: 256) nor even the power to order them to commit a crime or to act against the state (589). Limits like these on a relationship meant that it did not count as slavery for Locke, but rather as 'drudgery,' a condition that individuals could, he allowed, contract into.

The significant difference between Locke and Grotius lies not in the practical difference that their views made to the institution of slavery (which by then had become the basis of the economy of large parts of the world) but in the relocation of the constraints on the exercise of power by one person over another. Grotius found classical sources (e.g. 'humane' Romans such as Cicero and Seneca) for these constraints and in effect read them as part of the *ius naturale* in the sense of ideal legal constraints on the laws and concrete morality of any particular nation that practised slavery. Locke continued the trend of transforming these constraints into the natural property of individuals: rather than natural law constraining those who exercise power over others, everyone could claim, as Locke did, to be born with 'A Liberty to follow my own Will in all things, where the Rule prescribes not. . . . As *Freedom of Nature* is to be under no other restraint but the Law of Nature' (1689: §22).

Moreover, Locke began to identify a kernel of that liberty as something that one could not contract to surrender, or bargain with, as one might a commodity. People have their lives as possessions which they cannot alienate or divest at will, 'For a Man not having the Power of his own Life, *cannot*, by Compact, or his own Consent, *enslave himself* to any one, nor put himself under the Absolute, Arbitrary Power of another to take away his Life, when he pleases' (§23). Grotius had recognized no principle that constrained consent in this way, and thus had offered no basis for the notion of an 'inalienable right.'

Locke, however, appears to be more in agreement with Grotius when he allows that people who had committed capital offenses, or been taken prisoners of war, might be reduced to slavery in the strict sense, since they had already forfeited their lives. He also appears to have assumed that negro slaves in the colonies had been 'justifiably enslaved because they were captives taken in a just war, who had forfeited their lives "by some Act that deserves Death"' (see Laslett's note to Locke 1689: 302–3). Grotius had also treated the conqueror's right to enslave the vanquished as a consequence of his right to kill them. The momentum of the new conceptions of natural freedom and natural rights, however, brought Jean-Jacques Rousseau in the eighteenth century to challenge this supposed right of a conqueror and to deny vehemently that it provided any rightful basis for slavery (1762: 144–7).

7.3 Kant's canon

Reason and its imperatives

What we have just seen of the history of the evolution of ideas of natural law in relation to the institution of slavery illustrates the extent to which those who believe that the basis of our moral judgments lies outside us – in nature or in God – tend to find there reflections of familiar attitudes and institutions. For a long time this did not make anyone suspicious, as our minds were assumed to be tuned to nature's wavelength. What Cicero added, under the influence of his contacts with Stoic philosophers, was the suggestion that to obtain a better reception we should tune our reason. For the Stoics were pantheists and took the natural world to be a thinking, purposive being (an immanent god) and human thought to be correct to the extent that it conformed to the ends of that being (God or nature). The result of combining Stoic theology with Roman attitudes to law is the heavy emphasis on *ratio* in Cicero's statement of the fundamental equality of human beings quoted in the previous section. St Paul more than a century later took it that salvation required (among other things) conforming to a law that at least some gentiles already obeyed because it was 'written in their hearts' (Romans 2: 12–15). St Ambrose and St Augustine (late fourth century CE) identified what Paul had said was written in human hearts with *lex naturale*.[7]

This bi-polar natural basis of what is lawful – something outside us and something within us that receives or represents it – also underwent a transformation in the seventeenth century. One can discern the direction of this transformation in the cautious steps that Grotius took toward thinking through the principles by which we might criticize existing legal institutions without appealing to how God expected human beings to conduct themselves and their interactions with one another. 'What we have been saying would have a degree of validity even if we should concede that which cannot be conceded without the utmost wickedness, that there is no God, or that the affairs of men are of no concern to Him' (1625: 13). Grotius thus moved in the direction of thinking about what was natural without thinking of it as an expression of God's will.

But what then is the source of the validity of the fundamental principles of law? It would have to lie in what is written in our hearts or be found using the native resources of our minds. Grotius was impressed by the way mathematicians used their minds to reach enough clarity about very simple and basic concepts to guarantee the correctness of definitions that were expressed using these concepts. He believed that the same techniques could be used to articulate his version of the doctrine of natural law:

> I have made it my concern to refer the proofs of things touching the law of nature to certain fundamental conceptions which are beyond question, so that no one can deny them without doing violence to himself. For the principles of that law, if only you pay strict heed to them, are in themselves manifest and clear, almost evident as are those things which we perceive by the external senses; and the senses do not err if the organs of perception are properly formed and if the other conditions requisite to perception are present.
>
> (*ibid.*: 23)

Grotius was not claiming to have used his external senses to come up with the fundamental conceptions of law but to have used a faculty (mental ability) that yielded a degree of evidence every bit as good as that of the senses, and superior for being abstract and general. 'With a truthfulness I aver that, just as mathematicians treat their figures as abstracted from bodies, so in treating law I have withdrawn my mind from every particular fact' (30). Grotius was not alone in believing that mathematics could serve as a model of how to use the mind in other areas; his French contemporary, René Descartes, recommended this strategy as a way to advance the sciences of nature.

Even Locke, who thought that abandoning the senses in an effort to understand the natural world was a serious mistake, recognized the special certainty afforded by mathematics and thought that the principles of law, politics and morals could be established on the same basis. Our knowledge of morals, like that of mathematics, was knowledge of our own ideas, 'hence it follows that moral knowledge is as capable of real certainty as mathematics' (Locke 1690: IV.iv.7). The fact that morals is based on our own ideas did not mean, Locke insisted, that moral principles can be anything we like, no more than it follows that, if mathematics is knowledge of our own ideas, mathematical principles can be anything we like. '[A] man [may] have the idea of taking from others without their consent, what their honest industry has possessed them of, and call this *justice* if he please' (IV.iv.9), but the idea of justice should not be confused with the word 'justice':

> As in mathematics, [we have to] keep to the same precise ideas, and trace them in their several relations to one another without being led away by their names. If we but separate the idea under consideration from the sign that stands for it, our knowledge goes equally on in the discovery of real truth and certainty, whatever sounds we make use of.
>
> (*ibid.*)

Murder by any other name, Locke believed, still deserves the death penalty (*ibid.*: IV.iv.8).

However, one might hesitate to follow either Grotius or Locke in adopting their faith in reason if it issues in such disputable claims as that a conquering power acquires over the vanquished the right to determine whether they are to live or die and the right (if their lives are spared) to enslave them. Definitions and axioms with consequences like these are bound to strike many people as in no way 'beyond question' or 'the discovery of real truth and certainty.' Even though neither Grotius nor Locke succeeded in executing the program each had outlined for the use of reason, this does not mean that their faith was baseless, merely that neither had sufficient talent, analogous to the talent required to be a creative mathematician, to carry out the program.

Arguably the philosopher who, close to a century after Locke, made the most convincing attempt to carry out something like this program was Immanuel Kant. However, Kant sharply distinguished the use of the mind in the creation or discovery of mathematics from the use needed to provide a rational foundation for morality or provide rational principles for the criticism of a legal institution (like slavery) or a concrete morality (e.g. that takes slavery for granted). Reason (*Vernunft*) for Kant is strictly speaking our ability to deal with what must universally be the case, that is judgments or statements that apply necessarily and universally (A75n/B100n). Since experience can reveal that a thing is so, but not that it is necessarily so (B3), this means that reason deals with what we can know prior to experience, that is *a priori*; the criteria of *a priori* knowledge are necessity and strict universality (B4).[8] Reason is not by any means the source of the most important items of the *a priori* knowledge that we are entitled to accept in mathematics and natural science, but when it comes to determining what should be done, reason can set a goal for itself (i.e. for us) entirely in terms of characteristics proper to itself, that is specify the goal entirely in terms of its *rational* features.

This comes about in the following way: everything we do deliberately is governed by one or another explicit or implicit general principle of the kind that Kant calls a 'maxim.' This technical use of the term 'maxim' should be carefully distinguished from that of Jonsen (1991; see Section 6.3). A maxim, Kant explains, is a subjective principle of volition, that is a general rule that it seems to us, as individual agents, is a good idea to follow. If we thought of this rule as an objective principle, as something that everyone should follow, Kant would say we are thinking of it as a 'law' (1785: 400n, 421n). Now insofar as we are rational creatures we should aspire to think and act in terms of principles that are universal and necessary; it should not be good enough merely to act on principles that suit us as particular individuals. That is to say, it suits us far better *as rational creatures* to conform to a law, that is to a principle that applies universally to all rational creatures and binds them by a kind of rational necessity. To achieve this we must, at the very least, reject any maxim that (or refuse to follow a subjective principle if it) cannot be made into a universal law. In Kant's view, this gives rise to the one supreme rational principle of action, the 'categorical imperative': 'act only on that maxim which you can at the same time will that it should become a universal law' (*ibid.*: 421).

Kant offers a number of illustrations of how this apparently refined aspiration to be true to one's nature as a rational creature is supposed to have quite specific practical consequences. One of them, the most convincing, involves a man in a tight spot who sees that he can get out of his difficulties by borrowing money and promising to pay it back within a fixed time, knowing full well that he will never be able to keep his promise. The maxim of his action, Kant says, is 'Whenever I believe myself short of money, I will borrow money and promise to pay it back, though I know that this will never be done.' The problem with this maxim is that if it were made a law, that every one believing himself to be in need can make any promise he pleases with the intention not to keep it[, this] would make promising, and the very purpose of promising, itself impossible, since no one would believe he was being promised anything, but would laugh at utterances of this kind as empty shams.

(*ibid.*: 422)

Here we see a constraint of reason (the outcome contradicts the intention behind the maxim) standing in the way of a maxim becoming a universal law applying to all rational creatures. The result, that one should not make a lying promise, coincides with the concrete morality that operates in our society as well as in Kant's – indeed, in any society in which there is a recognized institution of promising. It makes plausible the claim that by trying to be as true to their rational nature as possible, people would be led to conduct themselves honestly.

Another of Kant's illustrations is of a man who, as a consequence of a series of misfortunes, feels that life has nothing to offer him and is contemplating suicide. His maxim, Kant says, is 'From self-love I make it my principle to shorten my life if its continuance threatens more evil than it promises pleasure' (*ibid.*). This, Kant claims, cannot become a universal law of nature, because there is a contradiction in having a feeling (self-love) whose function is to stimulate the furtherance of life produce the very opposite, the destruction of life.

The argument here strikes many people as unconvincing. Why should self-love be directed solely toward the preservation of life, regardless of the quality of that life? Is it not at least as plausible (at least as 'reasonable') to say that the function of self-love is to direct people to make the most of what life offers and that if it appears that nothing can be made of it except misery, not to prolong it? The point here is not whether suicide is ever justified, but that Kant's principle does not offer an indisputable resolution of the question – not, however, because there appears to be anything wrong with the demand to universalize, but because it is possible to challenge the maxim that Kant applies to the situation before subjecting it to this demand.

Kant offers two more illustrations, which involve complications; discussion of them will therefore be taken up in Section 8.1. We have seen enough to begin to appreciate how Kant proposes to lay the groundwork (*Grundlegung* in the title of 1785) of this theory. His answer to the long and widespread tradition that looks for a standard by which to assess conduct is to offer the categorical imperative as 'the general canon for all moral judgment of action' (424). (On 'canon' as straightedge see Section 4.2.) For something to serve to determine what we ought to do (as a canon by which to determine what our duty is), it has to be a command ('imperative') that is not conditional on something we happen to want. A

171

conditional command, 'If you want to reduce your chances of getting lung cancer and heart disease, do not allow yourself to become a heavy smoker,' is an example of what Kant calls a hypothetical imperative and applies only to people who happen to desire to reduce their chances of getting lung cancer or heart disease. An imperative that does not depend on any condition of this or any other sort is 'categorical' as opposed to 'hypothetical.'

It might seem from the way in which Kant's argument has been presented so far that what he calls 'the categorical imperative' is really based on the implicit condition, '*If you want to be rational, then* act only on a maxim that you could, if you were doing the legislating, make a universal law of nature.' Kant, however, takes himself to be addressing human beings insofar as they are rational, and that if the imperative applies to them, it does so because it applies to all rational beings. The only thing that Kant believes he has so far still left problematic (a matter of 'if . . .') is whether there is an imperative that applies to all rational creatures. *If* there is, he believes he has shown that it will be 'act on that maxim, etc.' (425). But what will show that there is a law that applies to all rational beings?

The answer lies in the concept of the will of a rational creature (426):

> For the purpose of achieving this proof it is of the utmost impor-
> tance to take warning that we should not dream for a moment of
> trying to derive the reality of this principle [the existence of this
> law] from *the special characteristics of human nature*. For duty
> has to be a practical, unconditioned necessity of action; it must
> therefore hold for all rational beings (to whom alone an impera-
> tive can apply at all), and *only because of this* can it also be a
> law for all human wills.
>
> (425)

A rational want (not necessarily a pure rational want) is one that has been informed by the idea of a law. When the idea that there is a law connecting habitual smoking with lung cancer and heart disease is joined to the desire to remain healthy, the result is a rational want not to smoke habitually. However, this is a rational want based on a subjective end – the desire to stay healthy may be valid for human beings (in most circumstances) in view of the special characteristics of their nature, but not for every rational creature. For a want to be fully rational, it must be directed toward 'some-thing *whose existence* has *in itself* an absolute value, something which as *an end in itself* could be a ground of determinate laws':

> Now I say that man, and in general every rational being, *exists*
> as an end in himself, *not merely as a means* for arbitrary use by

this or that will: he must in all his actions, whether they are directed to himself or to other rational beings, always be viewed *at the same time as an end.* All the objects of inclination have only a conditioned value; for if there were not these inclinations and the needs grounded on them, their object would be valueless. . . . Beings whose existence depends, not on our will, but on nature, have none the less, if they are non-rational beings, only a relative value as means and are consequently called *things.* Rational beings, on the other hand, are called *persons* because their nature already marks them out as ends in themselves – that is, as something which ought not to be used merely as a means – and consequently imposes to that extent a limit on all arbitrary treatment of them (and is an object of reverence).

(428)

Therefore, to treat rational beings as ends in themselves is an uncondi-tioned end for a rational creature and to want this above all else is a fully rational want.

The connection between this formulation of the categorical imperative (treating rational beings as ends in themselves) and the earlier one (act only on maxims that can be universalized) becomes somewhat clearer as Kant goes back over his illustrations in terms of the new formulation. To borrow money knowing that one cannot keep to the terms of the loan is to treat the lender as a means of getting oneself out of difficulty rather than as an end in himself (429–30). The reason that adopting this means would contradict its own end, if its maxim were made a universal law of nature, is that rational creatures would be able to form an idea of this law and adjust their conduct accordingly (i.e. laugh at the empty sham). Likewise, to take one's own life because life offers only misery is to treat oneself (a rational creature) merely as a means to what Kant regards as a contingent, and therefore conditioned, end, *viz.* having a certain quality of life, a life that is at least minimally agreeable to the person living it.

Kant's argument might be summarized in this way: to rational creatures the imperative 'Be rational' is both real (objective) and unconditioned. To obey this imperative, rational creatures must want, whatever other wants may be valid for them in view of their particular natures, to show respect to all rational creatures by treating them as ends, not as means – for such creatures are (objectively and without condition) ends in themselves. To conform to this demand to treat rational creatures (persons) as ends in themselves, the maxims that rational creatures (persons) act upon must conform to the requirement that they can consistently be willed to be universal laws of nature by the persons acting on them. The requirement to treat persons as ends, not as means, is in fact simply another formu-lation of the categorical imperative (p. 436).

7.4 Taking legal measures

Respect for persons and the limits of coercion

Kant's canon for moral judgment makes our ability to recognize and live by universal laws the touchstone of what it is to be rational, but it includes reference to the motive behind the action. Whether conduct is morally worthy depends on whether it issues from the intention that the maxim that guides it can be made a universal law or (equivalently) from the intention that one show respect for every rational creature by not treating any of them merely as means. To have a will with this overriding objective is to have a good will, and a good will, Kant asserts, is the only thing in the world that can be said to be good without qualification (1785: 393). We saw (Section 2.1) that for Kant the domain of *Recht* (sometimes translated 'law', in other contexts 'right' and 'justice') is the domain where it would be appropriate for human beings to apply coercive measures to one another. As motive is the key to the moral qualities of human conduct, legal institutions in the sense of procedures that channel rightful coercion cannot be set up to enforce morally worthy conduct without introducing motives that are irrelevant to – and tend to interfere with – the motives that are relevant to its moral standing. Conduct motivated by the intention to avoid penalties rather than to show respect for persons is not by Kant's criterion morally worthy.

But the principle that rational creatures should be treated as ends in themselves gives rise to a 'principle of right,' which can be detached from reference to motives and used as a straightedge to assess both what legal institutions facilitate and what they impose on people:

> Any action is *right* if it can coexist with everyone's freedom in accordance with a universal law . . . If then my action or my condition generally can coexist with the freedom of everyone in accordance with a universal law, whoever hinders me in it does me *wrong*, for this hindrance (resistance) cannot coexist with freedom in accordance with a universal law.
>
> (Kant 1797: 230)

The law may thus rightfully command each of us (on pain of penalty) to act in such a way that our choices can co-exist with the freedom of everyone else and take no account of motives behind our actions (231). On the other hand, laws that permit one person to limit the freedom of another unilaterally (non-reciprocally), e.g. to enslave another, are wrong.

Thus, although we have so far traced only the outlines of the foundations of Kant's theory, it is clear that it offers an unequivocal basis for saying what is wrong both legally and morally with the institution of slavery. The basis – at last we come to a basis that does not reduce to the mere fact that some climate of attitude exists – resides in a distinction between two fundamentally different kinds of entity, persons and things. Persons are sources of actions in ways that things cannot be. In discussing personality (see Section 7.1), we saw Kant define 'person' as 'a subject whose actions can be *imputed* to him'; in the same place, Kant says 'A *thing* is that to which nothing can be imputed.'

Now we can in a loose manner of speaking 'impute' a hole in a roof to the tree that fell through it and the tree's falling to the high wind that uprooted it, but this is not what Kant means by 'impute.' A sense of agency, 'natural agency,' is involved here that Kant would reject as metaphorical. He would not allow that what we say the wind and the tree 'did' were 'deeds' in the strict sense, that is actions that could be 'imputed' to these objects. He would deny that the tree was the 'author' of the hole in the roof or the wind the 'author' of the tree's being uprooted. To be deeds or actions that can be imputed, the events have to be considered in terms of freedom of choice, which for Kant involved the agent who is the author of its effects being 'subject to no other laws than those he gives to himself (either alone or at least along with others)' (223).[9]

Ultimately, this distinction turns on the ability of some (but not all) beings in the world to think and act rationally, which Kant defines in terms of a capacity to represent laws and make one's actions conform to those representations. 'Everything in nature works in accordance with laws. Only a rational being has the power to act *in accordance with his idea* of laws – that is, in accordance with principles – and only so has he a *will*' (1785: 412). In Kant's view, this fundamental distinction calls for special treatment for all rational beings from all beings capable of recognizing the difference (that is from all rational beings). Because a rational being is a special source of action, not to acknowledge this – not to acknowledge that a rational being has freedom to frame its own ends ('under moral laws') – and instead to treat it as though it were merely a thing and use it merely as the means to one's own ends, is wrong.

This is the basis on which we apply the version of Kant's canon known as 'the formula of the end in itself.' Slavery as an institution is to be condemned, because to render human beings liable to physical and sexual abuse, to deal with them as marketable commodities, to deny them family and control over their labor, their movements and their personalities, is to treat them as *things* rather than as *persons*, as mere means or mere instruments to one's own ends rather than as beings that have their own ends. Aristotle was quite explicit about a slave's status as an instrument. We have seen that he viewed slaves as unnecessary if domestic appliances could be given motor attachments. The condemnation of slavery on the basis of the distinction between things and persons does not even, as does Kant's illustration of the lying promise, depend on the existence of an institution like that of making promises. Neither the presence nor the absence of any institution alters the judgment that to treat people as marketable commodities or otherwise reduce them to non-persons is to do something that we ought (are duty bound) not to do and should not be allowed by law to do.

Kant's theory gives us a rigorous formulation of what under his influence has come to be spoken of as the principle of respect for persons. Being ends in themselves gives to rational creatures a 'dignity' (*Würde*) (1785: 435) and the limitation of 'our self-esteem by the dignity of humanity in another person' is 'respect (*Achtung*) in the practical sense' (1797: 449). It is only necessary to think back over the history surveyed in this chapter to imagine where a challenge to this principle might come from. Anyone who views humanity as consisting of creatures of varying degrees of worth that extend down to the level of farm animals will not be able to see the validity of Kant's formulation, or of the condemnation that follows from it.

It was not Kant's influence by itself that changed attitudes. The new attitudes, as we have seen, have roots in both pagan and Christian traditions of natural law, but they do not come together to challenge the institution of slavery until the time of Kant. The first Christians to dissociate themselves from holding slaves were Quakers *circa* 1760; organized anti-slavery agitation first occurred in the 1780s as Kant was formulating his ethical theories (Davis 1984: 107, 109). Kant can nevertheless be credited with having given a particularly rigorous formulation to a new set of attitudes that had started to emerge in the seventeenth century in Europe and since Kant's time have become familiar, at least to educated people, throughout the world.

There are two principal components to the new set of attitudes. One is what is known as *respect for persons*, for the value that resides in the capacity for being the author of one's own actions; the other is the belief that *all humans are persons*. Respect for persons is the foundation of rightful claims, claims that it is believed people can make on one another simply by virtue of being persons; the belief that all humans are persons is that which qualifies these rightful claims as *human* rights. These two principles together allow us to measure positive law and concrete morality in the way that earlier traditions imagined it possible to appeal to natural law or God's intentions in order to determine whether actual human practices are as they should be.

The application of such principles is, however, never completely straightforward. Steven Lukes folds these two principles together under the phrase 'respect for persons' and insists that the result presumes that we are equal to one another in a strong sense:

> What is worth stressing here is that this principle [of respect for persons] is strongly egalitarian, since it asserts that respect is

equally due to all persons – in virtue of their being persons, that is of some characteristic or set of characteristics which they have in common ... Thus respecting persons contrasts with, for instance, praising or admiring them, for we distribute praise and admiration unequally. This is necessarily so, since we praise or admire people for characteristics which single them out from others. We praise someone for his particular achievements and we admire someone for his particular qualities or excellences; whereas we *respect* him *as a human being*, in virtue of characteristics which he shares with all other human beings. It might be objected that, since individuals may possess these characteristics to different degrees, they are therefore persons to different degrees. But to this it may be replied that it is the existence of the characteristics, not the degree to which they are possessed or actualized, which elicits the respect.

(1973: 125–6)

How strongly egalitarian is this principle? We cannot restrict the freedom of anyone unless doing so can be shown to make possible greater freedom for everyone, and that means everyone equally. But does this mean that everyone will be socially and economically equal?

Kant went on (1797) to appeal to the principle of right to justify the institution of property and gave no hint that legitimate appropriation need be even roughly equal. People acquire and hold property in order to realize their individual goals (conditioned or unconditioned), and as long as in doing so they do not interfere with the activities of others in pursuit of their goals, it would be wrong to interfere with them. Advantages accrued through unevenly distributed property cannot therefore be challenged unless these can be shown to limit the freedom of someone.

This is not to say that it is easy to distinguish when exclusive ownership by some person or persons of the means to an important component of people's livelihoods constitutes a restriction of their freedom. Nor is it clear when human relationships that fall short of the condition of slavery – forms of dependency created by unequal relations of social and economic power – are contrary to Kant's principle that humans, insofar as they are rational, are not to be treated merely as means but always also as ends. This is not to say that doing this is never permitted, for Kant allows that people may be condemned to the status of being 'another's tool' (*servus in sensu stricto*), just as people can forfeit their lives through committing crimes; this status of *servus in sensu stricto*, however, unlike the status of a slave, cannot be inherited (1797: 330). If this is carried out in accordance with Kant's principle of right, this will happen only to people who have seriously interfered with the freedom of others or who constitute a clear and present danger to that freedom.

Apart from those who forfeit their rights, there are temporary roles and relations that people may enter in which they serve as someone else's instrument. Obtaining their agreement, hiring them before using them, acknowledges their freedom, their capacity to determine their own ends. It is not treating them *merely* as a means. But obviously if one obtains an agreement to function merely as means from people by use of a credible threat to kill or make them miserable, this is precisely the condition of slavery. If circumstances are such that no threat is necessary, because they will simply die of starvation or be reduced to abject poverty if they do not agree to function purely as someone's instrument, is the condition any better than slavery? There might be scope here for an interesting exercise in Jonsen's version of the method of casuistry (see Section 6.3): set up a continuum of cases from these two versions of slavery to a market in which labor is freely exchanged in a way that allows those functioning as instruments of others to integrate their performances in these roles into their own life goals, then try to determine where along this continuum agreements no longer fail to measure up against Kant's canon.

David P. Ellerman (1995: chapter 4) has argued that there is a violation of the Kantian principle of respect for persons wherever people exchange their labor for wages instead of the products of their labor for a fee, wherever they are employees instead of self-employed providers of goods and services. Ellerman exaggerates the similarity of slavery to a lifetime of wage labor by suggesting that the only difference is that in the case of a slave, a lifetime of labor is owned, whereas in the case of the wage laborer the employer buys not a lifetime but determinate increments of a lifetime – days, weeks, months, depending on the contract – and the sum of the increments of the time one is treated as an instrument is equivalent to a lifetime of slavery. One crucial difference turns on the fact that a human being's life is more than the sum of the laboring that that person does. Unlike a slave owner, one's employer does not (normally) own the rest of one's life or decide what will be one's occupation, whom one can marry, how much leisure one has and how it is to be spent, what one will wear, or whether one will have to endure extreme discomfort or sexual exploitation.

Nevertheless, there are questions to be raised about the extent to which people in many occupations and in many structures of authority are treated in ways commensurate with their humanity. Ellerman uses his explicitly Kantian analysis of the relations of production current in our society to argue for participatory democracy in the workplace.[10] People who have a share in decision making have a share in the product and are thus represented by their humanity (as consciously choosing beings) in the exchange that earns them their daily bread. They are not bare instruments used by another conscious being.

According to Kant's principle of right, we are entitled to restrict the freedom of people who in act or intention deny freedom to others. We are arguably entitled to (we are acting rightfully when we) do this if the denial of freedom is a consequence of employers denying the humanity of those who work for them, or of owners denying access to what other people need, or of producers degrading the environment in which others seek to live their lives. Otherwise no one – neither a state that monopolizes the means of coercion nor private individuals taking what matters they can into their own hands – is right to restrict the freedom of another. This is a liberal principle: restrictions on people's freedom to act, applications of coercive force, must be justified. Forceful restriction, which is applied just because it can be applied and because those who have the power feel like applying it, is not rightfully applied.

It is not always obvious when the activity of one person impedes the freedom of another in a way that justifies restraining the first. There are no cut and dried answers to such questions as: are we right to tax the privileged in order to create opportunities for the underprivileged? To regulate manufacturing enterprises to make them safer for employees and more environmentally friendly for the neighboring community? To limit the activities of banks and multinational corporations because of their effects on working people in both developed and underdeveloped countries?

An alternative to Kant's appeal to the difference between persons and things as the basis for restricting the freedom of others is found in a well-known principle propounded by John Stuart Mill:

> The object of this Essay is to assert one very simple principle, as entitled to govern absolutely the dealings of society with the individual in the way of compulsion and control, whether the means used be physical force in the form of legal penalties, or the moral coercion of public opinion. That principle is, that the sole end for which mankind are warranted, individually or collectively, in interfering with the liberty of action of any of their number, is self-protection. That the only purpose for which power can be rightfully exercised over any member of a civilised community, against his will, is to prevent harm to others. His own good, either physical or moral is not a sufficient warrant.
>
> (1859: 72–3)

What constitutes harm is not any easier to determine than what constitutes restricting freedom. It is not enough to establish that A has harmed B if A has merely done something that B does not like; ultimately, to establish harm, it has to be shown that B suffered some loss of function as a result of something A did. The notion of harm, however, applies equally to persons and things – both in different ways can be harmed through suffering loss of function – and one does not need to appeal to the basis identified in Kant's ethical theory, the distinction between persons and things, to apply Mill's principle of harm.

Nevertheless, there appears to be a need to assess harm to a human being relative to a specific notion of human function. The notion of human function was first suggested by Plato and made into a key component of ethical theory by Aristotle. We will examine Aristotle's notion of human function and the use he made of it in Section 9.2, but it is possible to indicate here how Kant might appeal to this notion of function to trump Mill's principle. Kant's challenge would be: 'how can we assess harm to human beings except relative to their function of determining and acting in accordance with universal laws, in other words of acting in accordance with freedom?' So the principle of harm, because it is being applied to human beings, must reduce to the (Kantian) principle of right.

The two principles competing in this dispute are extremely general, and whichever is adopted will have to function very much as one of Jonsen's maxims (see Section 6.3) or as one of what Dworkin calls 'principles' (see Section 1.4). Precisely because what counts as 'freedom' and 'harm' cannot be specified in advance of particular circumstances, neither principle provides a comprehensive decision procedure for determining when we would be justified in restricting someone's liberty to act. Making an assessment to determine this might on some occasions be straightforward, but on many occasions it might take a special degree of sensitivity, imagination and ability to foresee the consequences of many possible courses of action. Someone who could do this well would deserve not merely our respect but our admiration and our praise (as Lukes put it in the passage quoted above); the ability to bring this off successfully might not be equally distributed among all human beings – it might call for exemplary human beings, human beings who excel, who have good moral qualities in abundance, who are virtuous in the manner of virtuosos.

Kant presents the 'groundwork' of his ethical theory (1785) in a way that suggests that ethical questions can be settled in a mechanical way. All that is required to determine one's duty is to apply the universalization test to the maxim on which one proposes to act and what duty requires will emerge unambiguously. But to anyone familiar with Kant's *Critique of Pure Reason* (1781/1787), it should not come as a surprise to discover that Kant is prepared to concede quite a bit to particularist concerns. His discussion of the role of judgment ('the faculty of subsuming under rules'; A133/B172) acknowledges that

> though understanding is capable of being instructed, and of being equipped with rules, judgment is a peculiar talent which can be practised only, and cannot be taught. It is the specific quality of so-called mother-wit; and its lack no school can make good.
>
> (*ibid.*)

When Kant turns to developing his theory, he allows scope for choice in the performance of some duties and allows that better and worse choices can be made. In spite of initial appearances, Kant's ethical theory does have room for a notion of moral excellence or virtue, and he leaves scope for the kind of judgment that could earn one praise or admiration. To see how much Kant's canon leaves unmeasured, we will have to take up the notion of virtue in the next chapter; Kant's own treatment will provide a convenient entry point, although once we have surveyed its shortcomings, we will have to look further back into the tradition of conducting the systematic study of ethics as an inquiry into the nature of virtue.

Even if Kant's canon does not allow us to measure all the qualities of character and conduct, practices and institutions, that we need to assess, the achievement it represents and the basis it articulates rigorously should not be underestimated. For the better part of two centuries now, it has been possible to receive a hearing for the claim that people deserve (are rightfully entitled) to a minimum of consideration from others. The minimum precludes the enslavement of the weak by the powerful and some other forms of exploitation,[11] and if it is not clear how far this minimum should extend, it may be because it is not always wise (as we will see Confucius and his followers argue in the next chapter) to try to order all our affairs by taking legal measures, even carefully measured legal measures.

Further reading

On the practice of ancient slavery, see Finley (1980); on the development of ideas of rights in connection with slavery and property, see Tuck (1979: chapter 1). On Aristotle's access to the concept of rights, see Miller (1995: chapter 4), and on his attitudes to slavery, see Brunt (1993: chapter 11). For Cicero's social and legal philosophy, see Wood (1988: chapters IV and V). For a useful collection of material on natural law theory, including its relation to slavery, see Carlyle (1930), but as a corrective to Carlyle's reading of ancient and medieval anticipations of modern attitudes, see d'Entrèves (1951: chapter 1). For the anti-slavery movement in modern times, see Davis (1984). On current forms of exploitation that amount to slavery in all but name, see Bales (1999). For more detailed expositions and further on the political implications of Kant's ethics, see van der Linden (1988), O'Neill (1989) and Korsgaard (1996). On the role of judgment in Kant's ethics, see Herman (1993), especially the title essay. The issues surrounding the justifications and limits of legal coercion are explored in a four-volume series by Joel Feinberg, the fourth of which Feinberg (1988) begins with a useful synopsis of the first three volumes.

Notes

1 This passage survives only as a fragment of a lost book of Cicero's work preserved by a Christian writer, Lactantius, of the early fourth century, who thought that Cicero, although a pagan, had written this passage under divine inspiration (see McDonald 1964: 412–13). A part of what Lactantius presents as quotation is treated by scholars as spurious, i.e. a reference to a Roman consul who flourished fifty years after Cicero's death. How much of the rest represents Cicero's precise words is open to conjecture.

2 The gradual extension of the notion of rights first to men without property, then to females, has only recently reached children (see Freeman and Veerman 1992).

3 Miller (1995: chapter 4) argues strenuously that Aristotle had and used the notion of a right. It is not being claimed here that Aristotle cannot express the idea of a rightful claim, merely that the vocabulary used to do this (e.g. *to dikaion*) will in other contexts have nothing to do with rightful claims. Rights are not for Aristotle central, as they are in our way of thinking.

4 These two citations are preserved in the *Digest of Justinian*, originally assembled and published under the auspices of the Byzantine emperor Justinian in 534 CE as part of the *Corpus Juris Civilis*, which (see Section 6.2) is the foundation of the continental civil law tradition.

5 The jurists represented in the *Digest of Justinian* (Watson 1985) commonly use only two categories – distinguishing *ius civile* from either *ius gentium* (e.g. Gaius at I.i.9) or from *ius naturale* (e.g. Paulus at I.i.11). Ulpian is unusual in offering a basis for the threefold division of *ius*: *naturale* is what is common to all animals (such as the practices of procreation and the rearing of young), *gentium* is what is common to all groups of people and *civile* what is specific to a state. Slavery is taken by Ulpian to be an illustration of a practice common to all groups of people and hence sanctioned by *ius gentium*.

6 For citations, see Carlyle (1930: Vol. II, 120–2), among which is a ninth-century canon of a Council of Toledo strictly forbidding a bishop to emancipate slaves who belonged to the Church unless he replaced their value from his own property.

7 Carlyle (1930: 105) provides citations of Ambrose from *Ep.* lxxiii.2 and of Augustine from *Contra Faustum Manichaeum*, xix.2.

8 Kant assigned to metaphysic(s) the task of establishing *a priori* principles, which is what lies behind the phrase that appears in the titles of his 1785 and 1797 works: 'Metaphysic of Morals.'

9 'Subject to no other laws' here will have to be glossed in the light of the next paragraph as meaning 'having to make actions conform to' rather than 'working in accordance with.'

10 Ellermen's theory, however radical, is not Marxian. He argues on the basis of a labor theory of property (1995: 94) rather than, as Marx did, a labor theory of value.

11 It is interesting to compare Mo Tzu's measure: 'The will of Heaven abominates . . . the strong who plunder the weak, the clever who deceive the stupid, and the honoured who disdain the humble . . . it desires people having energy to work for each other, those knowing the way to teach each other, and those possessing wealth to share with each other' (Mei 1929: 142–3).

8

THE QUALITIES OF
EXEMPLARY PERSONS

The believing lay-sister when rightly admonishing her only
son, dear and beloved, would thus admonish him: 'See, my
dear, that thou become like Citta housefather and Hatthaka
of Āḷava.' *These, brethren, are the standard, these are the
measure of my lay disciples, even Citta and Hatthaka.* 'If
thou, my dear, go forth from home to the homeless, see that
thou become like Sāriputta and Moggallāna.' *These, brethren,
are the standard, these are the measure of my ordained disciples, even Sāriputta and Moggallāna.*

> (The Buddha (sixth century BCE); Rhys Davids and
> Woodward 1922: 159)

The compasses and square are the ultimate standards of the
circle and the square. The sage is the ultimate standard of
human relations.

> (Mencius (fourth century BCE); Chan 1963: 73)

Recapitulation: Kant generated what he claimed was 'the
general canon for all moral judgement of action' by insisting that
we would be true to our nature as rational creatures if we not only
lived by general principles (maxims) but by those that were capable
of being made universal laws. This meant that our general principles applied to everyone without exception, in particular without
exceptions made for the person who applied them. This also
required that special regard, *respect*, be accorded to other creatures with the capacity to universalize in this way. And it entailed
a number of quite specific duties, *viz.* not to make promises one
knows cannot be kept, not to take the life, restrict the liberty or
inflict gratuitous discomforts on rational creatures – except where
'doing so can co-exist with the freedom of all' (e.g. applying coercion to people whose actions would restrict the freedom of others).

Prospectus: Kant may have initially overestimated his achievement when he suggested in 1785 that his categorical imperative

was the only canon needed and that it served 'for all moral judgement of action.' Two of the four illustrations he gave of how the canon was to work, the two that we have so far not examined, suggest that, strictly applied, the canon can generate only negative duties. When in 1797 Kant published the superstructure that he had intended to build on his 'foundation' (*Grundlegung*) of 1785, the issues raised by these two illustrations are placed in the context of a new division of duties under the heading 'duties of virtue' and appear in a significantly different light. The concept of virtue (moral excellence) is, as we will see, multifaceted and has a long history during which attempts have been made to use the responses of virtuous persons as a canon of moral judgment, in other words as a moral measure. Who is recognized as virtuous, however, differs in different cultures; partly this is a reflection of different demands on people in different social environments and partly this is a reflection of different ideas of what kind of thinking is required to respond well to problematic situations.

8.1 Duties of virtue

Perfection of self and duties of beneficence

Kant gives four illustrations in his 1785 *The Foundation of the Metaphysic of Morals* to show how the categorical imperative serves as 'the general canon for all moral judgement of action.' The four are divided into perfect and imperfect duties, a division found in natural law theories from Grotius onward (Schneewind 1990: 49–50) that Kant acknowledges he is adopting largely for the sake of convenience. The only explanation he offers is that a perfect duty 'allows no exception in the interests of inclination' (1785: 421n). The perfect duties among Kant's illustrations are the ones we considered in the previous chapter, the duty not to make a lying promise and the duty not to commit suicide. The other two are the duties to develop one's talents and to help others.

The first is an imperfect duty, because if someone were so inclined – the 'exception in the interests of inclination' – there would be no contradiction in proposing a maxim of 'lazy self-indulgence' as a universal law. That is, a person could think, 'I won't work to develop any talents I might have and I won't expect anyone else to do so.' There is nothing inconsistent in a world in which all rational creatures obey a law that has them devote their lives ('like the South Sea Islanders') 'solely to idleness, indulgence, procreation, and, in a word, to enjoyment,' as Kant puts it (423). Likewise, someone prone to self-preoccupation – the 'exception in the interest of inclination' – might propose as a universal law the maxim of (to give it a name, since Kant does not) 'looking out only for number one.' This person might think, 'I will not help anyone else and will not ask anyone for help. There is nothing inconsistent in having the whole world behave this way; my maxim is universalizable.' Kant suggests that the will to follow the 'law of looking out only for number one' conflicts with itself when a person needs help from others. The universalization of the maxim is still not inconsistent: we will naturally want to be helped when we need help, but one could extinguish that natural want.

The formulation of the categorical imperative that recognizes rational beings as ends in themselves yields the same result. People who fail to develop their talents are not treating anyone solely as a means, and this is, as Kant says, 'compatible with the *maintenance* of humanity as an end in itself, but not with the *promotion* of this end' (430). People who make it a principle not to help others are not using anyone solely as means if they then for the sake of consistency do not seek help and reject all offers of help. What Kant says in effect is that the world will be a poorer place if people universalize the maxim of lazy self-indulgence or the maxim of looking out only for number one, but he does not show that universalizing either involves a contradiction as obvious as that involved in making a lying promise. Kant's discussion of these two examples assumes that people will have certain desires and that universalizing these maxims will be inconsistent with those desires, but he does not show that it would be contrary to reason to try to live without those desires or impossible to succeed.

However, when Kant comes to build a superstructure (his *Metaphysic of Morals* of 1797) over his *Foundation* (*of the Metaphysic of Morals* of 1785), he takes special care to spell out how reason can determine goals or 'ends' for us, 'ends that are also duties' (1797: 385). There is little doubt that in doing this Kant has in mind the two imperfect duties from his earlier four illustrative examples, for the goals have to do with developing one's talents and helping others. Furthermore, these are said to be 'wide duties' and 'the wider the duty . . . the more imperfect is a man's obligation to action' (390). We will look at what the notion of 'wide' adds to the idea of an 'imperfect' duty shortly.

The first of Kant's 'ends that are also duties' is that of seeking to perfect ourselves. Perfecting ourselves means cultivating the gifts that nature has given to us as individuals. The gifts or talents we have are nothing we can take credit for; our merit derives only from our efforts to build on our natural predispositions. Why must we strive to do this? Our intrinsic value rests on our ability to set ends for ourselves, but it is our cognitive (understanding) and conative (will) capacities that allow us to do this, allow us to free ourselves from our inclinations, so that our duty can become the sole motive of our action, i.e. so that we do what is our duty for its own sake (387). Another way to put this would be to note that through the exercise of reason we are capable of the freedom (in the sense of self-governance); that is the basis of our dignity and of the respect due

185

to us from other rational beings. As the actual degree of the freedom that each of us has is a function of the development of certain of our capacities, we each have a duty to develop those capacities.

Perfection for Kant is not happiness in the strict sense, which is psychological satisfaction with what nature (and our circumstances) happens to have given us. The qualification 'strict' is a consequence of Kant's reluctance to call 'happiness' (*Glückseligkeit*) any satisfaction that a person derives from doing his duty for the sake of duty ('from mere consciousness of his rectitude': 388). Used in this strict sense, reason cannot endorse the principle that we should strive for happiness. What happiness is for each of us can, moreover, only be discovered empirically, not *a priori* by reason (215). In the *Foundation* (1785: 418), Kant claims that as a consequence of this a person cannot say 'definitely and in unison with himself what it really is that he wants and wills.' So we have only a derivative duty to work for enough happiness for ourselves to ensure sufficient psychological health not to be overly susceptible to the temptations of vice – that is a duty to seek our own happiness as a means to a more important end. 'It is not my happiness but the preservation of my moral integrity that is my end and also my duty' (1797: 388).

Now we cannot work directly for the perfection of others, since that involves the use they make of their own freedom; perfection of free rational agents can only arise from their own spontaneous activity (not determined by outside influences). No other agent can bring that about; individuals themselves are the only ones who can take responsibility for their own personal development. But as this development does depend on their achieving some degree of happiness (in the strict sense), i.e. enough mental satisfaction to sustain a healthy mind, Kant claims that the happiness of others is an end that is also a duty,

> The reason that it is a duty to be beneficent is this: since our self-love cannot be separated from our need to be loved (helped in case of need) by others as well, we therefore make ourselves an end for others; and the only way this maxim can be binding is through its qualification as a universal law, hence through our will to make others our ends as well. The happiness of others is therefore an end that is also a duty.
>
> (*ibid.*: 393)

Kant distinguishes 'beneficence' (etymology: 'good deeds'), 'which is the maxim of making others' happiness one's end' from 'benevolence' (etymology: 'well-wishing'), which is 'satisfaction in the happiness (well-being) of others' (452).

This end that is also a duty is presented as though it stands on the same level as the duty to work for one's own perfection, but the argument rests on the need to be loved by, and to call upon the aid of, others – a need giving rise to maxims that must be universalized. When Kant reiterates the argument for the duty to help others, it is clear that it rests explicitly on universalizing the maxim that expresses the desire to be helped by others when in need.

> To be beneficent, that is to promote according to one's means the happiness of others in need, without hoping for something in return, is everyone's duty.
>
> For everyone who finds himself in need wishes to be helped by others. But if he lets his maxim of being unwilling to assist others in turn when they are in need become public, that is, makes this a universal permissive law, then everyone would likewise deny him assistance when he himself is in need, or at least would be authorized to deny it. Hence the maxim of self-interest would conflict with itself if it were made a universal law, that is, it is contrary to duty. Consequently the maxim of common interest, of beneficence toward those in need, is a universal duty of human beings, just because they are to be considered fellowmen, that is, rational beings with needs, united by nature in one dwelling place so that they can help one another.
>
> (453)

Pressed by the possibility that a person might successfully universalize the maxim not to help others by consistently refusing help, Kant appears ready to say that this is not consistent with the principle of self-interest. If one is really interested in oneself one will need (and have compelling rational grounds to seek and accept) the help of others, and if others do not perceive one's preparedness to help them in time of need, they will refuse help.

Kant appears to think that he has established that it is everyone's duty to be willing to help people in need 'without hoping for something in return' (*ibid.*). The argument, however, does not appear to secure the whole of this claim. Why, if the duty rests on self-interest of this sort, is it not possible to universalize the maxim of helping others just enough to secure credibility for when one needs help in return and for that reason alone?

The duties of beneficence and self-improvement are both wide duties. That means that how they are to be fulfilled is difficult to specify, and there is latitude for free choice. No such latitude exists in the case of narrow duties, e.g. people who make promises must believe that they are able to keep their word, and there is no latitude for choice in the matter – but how and when they are to help others, and which and to what extent they are to develop their capacities, are all left up to them. This does not mean that they may make exceptions for themselves, merely that they will have to reconcile and respond to a number of possibly conflicting claims, e.g., to aid their parents as opposed to their neighbors (390). The claims of imperfect duty cannot be ignored altogether, but one can respond to them more or less well. It is not 'culpability' (*Verschuldung*; *demeritum*) to fail to respond well to this panoply of claims on one's time and resources, merely deficiency in moral worth (*moralischer Unwert*).

For those who think of Kant as providing the 'purest, deepest and most through representation' of the morality system (see Section 1.1), this recognition of a role for sensitivity to the particulars of one's situation, this concession to what, as we will see shortly, is the primary motivation of classical virtue theory, must be somewhat perplexing. Kant provides the purest representation of the morality system, partly because attention has traditionally (in the English-speaking world, at least) been focused selectively. Translations of the *Foundation* of 1785 are popular as undergraduate textbooks; translations into English of what Kant built in 1797 on that foundation have not been common – translations of each of the two parts were published independently but were not widely used, and a translation of the whole appeared only in 1991.

But Kant himself invites this view of his ethics, for virtue, from what he says about it, does not adequately fill the need identified in the discussion of wide or imperfect duties. Kant assumes that what it takes to do well in response to the claims of imperfect duties is nothing more than strength of resolve, and having defined 'virtue' as the fortitude (*Tapferkeit*; *fortitudo*), i.e. the resolve, to withstand what opposes our moral disposition (380), he declares that imperfect duties are the only 'duties of virtue' (390). One might wonder whether doing well or badly in response to the claims of imperfect duties depended on more than merely strength of resolve.

Does it not require judgment to determine whether one's parents (given their circumstances) have greater claims on one's time and resources than one's neighbors (in their circumstances)? How one chooses an occupation (392) to allow scope for the cultivation of one's talents takes judgment; so do competing claims from occupations that might better serve mankind but allow less scope for self-improvement.

In general, the contribution that the skillful use of cognitive capacities makes to the success of the moral enterprise is not given much attention in Kant. His *Foundation* begins with the famous claim (beginning of Section 7.4) that it is not possible to conceive anything good without qualification 'except a *good will*.' This means that the will to do the right thing (which for Kant is the will to do one's duty) is sufficient to qualify as good, regardless of how inept a person may be in pursuit of the aim of doing the right thing. Kant's gloss on this claim is equally famous:

> Even if, by some special disfavour of destiny or by the niggardly endowment of step-motherly nature, this will is entirely lacking in

power to carry out its intentions; if by its utmost effort it still accomplishes nothing, and only good will is left (not, admittedly, as a mere wish, but as the straining of every means so far as they are in our control); even then it would still shine like a jewel for its own sake as something which has its full value in itself. Its usefulness or fruitlessness can neither add to, nor subtract from, this value.

(1795: 394)

If it is clear what duty requires so that we can make sense of the claim that a person is trying to do his or her duty – so that we can recognize the person as 'well-meaning' or 'having good intentions' – this doctrine seems plausible.

However, the impression that what duty requires is always clear is the result of the way Kant treats as unproblematic the choice of maxim in any given situation so that the only question is whether it can be made a universal law of nature (or whether people are treated as ends as well as means). We have seen (in Section 7.3), however, that it is possible to challenge the maxim which Kant attributes to someone contemplating suicide. We can, moreover imagine a number of actions that if everyone did them (made them universal laws of nature) it would contradict their intentions, but that appear in very different lights depending on which circumstances are included in the maxim. For example, a person walks in a wooded area or across a grassy stretch for pleasure, and if everyone did the same, the area would be ruined and no one could take pleasure in it. But might it not be a relevant consideration that there are in fact not enough people nearby who would or could cause enough traffic to ruin the spot? A couple decide that raising children will interfere with doing what they want with their lives. If everyone did so (making this maxim a universal law), there would be no one to sustain the economy during their old age. But does it not matter what it is the couple want to do with their lives (perhaps devote their time to helping the needy) and whether there are a sufficient number of other couples interested in sustaining the population?

These questions clearly take us into the territory of wide duties. The decision whether to raise a family is surely like that of what career one should choose. What maxim one applies, what circumstances are relevant to include in specifying the general conditions under which one is acting, is something that takes judgment. It also takes judgment to determine whether one is dealing with a question of narrow or wide duty. It is clear that once we confront questions about wide duties, it takes judgment as well as resolve to make good use of one's resources in response to all of the variety of claims that can be made on behalf of developing one's talents and helping one's fellow man.[1]

Those who discussed the concept of virtue (*virtus* in Latin; *aretē* in Greek) in antiquity would have assigned a larger role to judgment and given less of a role to resolve. Among the traditional virtues, resolve or moral strength might well not even count as a virtue. Aristotle, for example, did not regard (moral) strength (*enkrateia*) as a virtue or its opposite, weakness (*akrasia*), as a vice. People whose actions involve conscious resolve, who have to grit their teeth and fight contrary inclinations in order to do what they are supposed to do, do not for Aristotle have a sufficiently well-established disposition to count as virtuous. For Aristotle, the problem was working out what should be done in this or that circumstance, and the person with a particular virtue will be the one who can be relied upon to find the right response (of feeling or action) relative to the situation.

As was noted (Section 1.2), Kant and Aristotle represent the two different sets of assumptions that philosophers bring to ethics in general and excellence in particular. The former proceeds as though what is to be done is obvious and it takes only resolve to accomplish it; the latter proceeds as though the most pressing question is how to determine what is to be done. The former treats excellence as a disposition to make one's acts conform to (the right) rules; the latter tends to treat acts as reflections of character and rules as guidelines for people whose character is not well developed.

Among the other changes that took place as European thought crossed what in the previous chapter was referred to as 'the watershed' was an increasing tendency to emphasize acts and rules and play down the importance of a good character. Kant singled out for criticism (1797: 404) the feature of Aristotle's definition of virtue, the doctrine of 'the mean relative to us,' that explicitly marks out the area where multiple factors are reconciled in a fashion that cannot be reduced to rules (see Section 8.4). In doing this, Kant was following in the footsteps of Grotius (1625: 25) and other natural law theorists on our side of the watershed. Likewise, in using the concept of an imperfect duty to acknowledge the domain where judgment was required − even if he did not adequately acknowledge the qualities of intelligence and character needed to deal with it − Kant was in step with the same tradition (Schneewind 1990: 49ff).

Commenting on this aspect of the new direction that European thought had begun to take, J.B. Schneewind observed: 'The culture [of the seventeenth and eighteenth centuries] seems to have been hungry for a morality giving the kind of explicit guidance that rules and laws provide' (*ibid.*: 48). It was, it seems, hungry to rely on external artifacts, linguistic formulations, instead of internal resources, good reflexes of judgment shaped by sound habits of response. It was perhaps eager to adopt attitudes that make complex organizations (bureaucracies) possible and to resolve problems not by relying on the intelligence and integrity of individuals but by devising rules that could regulate in an efficient manner any collection of fools and knaves. Where attitudes to character were once the backbone of every European concrete morality, it is now common to rule out *a priori* any solution to a social problem that involves 'preaching virtue.'

8.2 Classical virtues and the rule of ritual

Elite and demotic virtues, setting a good example

In the literature of the classical cultures of China and Greece we find authors, Confucius and Aristotle in particular, who believe that we must seek to identify exemplary individuals (to be used as models we should follow) by attempting to specify the qualities that make them exemplary. If one formed a composite (a 'conceptual identikit') picture of the human beings whom Aristotle and Confucius would regard as exemplary – the individuals whom they would regard as fit to govern others, the individuals they would think of as deserving of admiration and emulation – the two pictures would differ in important ways.

While the Greeks admired men whose words and deeds squared with one another, Aristotle never suggests that reticence (arising from putting more effort into deeds than into speech, *Analects* IV.22, 24, XIII.3) might be a quality to look for in a man of virtue. While Aristotle insists that an important virtue consists in being neither too fond of nor too reluctant to enjoy the pleasures that accompany touch (*viz.* food, drink and sex: 1117b24–1119b18), Confucius does not give special attention to this kind of self-control. He remarks that when young a superior man should 'guard against the attractions of feminine beauty' (Lau 1979: XVI.7)[2] and steadfastness appears to be jeopardized by being full of desires (V.11), but these are not specifically desires for the pleasures of touch, since he views older men as prone to strife (bellicosity) and avarice (acquisitiveness) (XVI.7). Aristotle and Confucius both employ concepts translated as 'courage,' but Aristotle regards his (*andreia*, manliness) as connected to what is painful (1117a33–6), whereas Confucius allows his (*yung*) a wider application that places it closer to Kant's strength of resolve, 'Faced with what is right (*yi*), to leave it undone shows a lack of courage (*yung*)' (Chan 1963: II.24).

These differences alone do not tell against the suggestion that the good or 'virtuous' person might be treated as a standard by which to assess conduct and attitudes. It may be that in describing something as complex as an exemplary person Aristotle and Confucius have, because of their different styles and preoccupations, simply emphasized different features, or it may be argued that a virtuous person could hardly be expected to look the same in different cultural settings, just as an appropriately dressed person will look different in different climates. In terms of the image of measuring devices, which was first considered in Section 4.2, it may be that different straightedges and try squares – or, better, different devices and procedures for generating straightedges, square corners and circles – when adapted for different purposes will look different, although they reflect the same fundamental principles. If that argument is correct then we would expect that what would serve as an exemplary person in our culture will differ at least in superficial respects from the descriptions given by Aristotle (mid-fourth century BCE) or Confucius (early fifth century BCE), owing to the differences between our culture and either of theirs.

Some of these differences are due to the fact that Aristotle and Confucius both take the hierarchical (and 'corporate,' Section 7.1) nature of the social environment for granted and are thinking in terms of the characteristics of the 'better class of person.' If we speak of 'ethical virtues' at all we have in mind such qualities as honesty, self-control, modesty, generosity, friendliness and courage, and there is a tendency on our part to assume that most people will possess most of the qualities we are discussing. Possibly the last of these is something we regard as unusual – this is why there are awards for bravery for both soldiers and civilians, although often the 'virtue' of courage refers to that modest level of self-confidence that distinguishes normal people from the pathologically timid. As for the rest, few people would want to admit that they were in any respect deficient in honesty, self-control, etc.

Aristotle appears to be interested in what makes people exceptional, rather than merely acceptable, citizens. In the last chapter of the *Nicomachean* version of the *Ethics*, we find the following attempt at a realistic assessment of the power of argument or discourse (*logos*):

> As things are while discourses [arguments about ethics] seem to have power to encourage and stimulate the genteel[3] among the young, and to make a character which is well born, and a true lover of what is admirable, ready to be possessed by *aretē*, they [discourses] are not able to encourage the many to nobility and goodness. For the many do not by nature obey the sense of shame, but only fear, and do not abstain from bad acts because of the disgrace but through fear of punishment; living by passion they pursue their own pleasures and the means to them, and avoid the opposite pains, and have not even a conception of what is noble and truly pleasant, since they have never tasted it. What discourses would remold such people?
>
> (1179b6–16)

An *aretē* in Aristotle's Greek is literally an 'excellence,' a respect in which someone excels. For everyone to be expected to excel is something of a paradox. Nevertheless, it was possible for *aretē* to slide from the exceptional to the acceptable (a reasonably demanding level of acceptability to be sure) in Greek even before Aristotle.

In one of Plato's early dialogues, the *Protagoras*, a young man of a 'great and prosperous family' asks Socrates to introduce him to the famous sophist Protagoras in the hope that by associating with Protagoras he would learn how to 'make a name for himself' (Hamilton and Cairns 1961: 316c). Protagoras, under questioning by Socrates, professes to be able to teach the young man 'the proper care of his personal affairs, so that he may best manage his own household, and also the city's affairs, so as to become a real power in the city, both as a speaker and as a man of action' (318e), in other words a man to be admired, emulated and regarded as exemplary. Socrates understands this as the claim to teach *aretē*, and he expresses doubts that this can be taught.

Protagoras responds by elaborating a myth about the origins of mankind which argues that unless a sense of shame (which Aristotle held in the passage above to be rare) and fair play (justice) were widely distributed, society would be impossible (322c–d). A corollary of this is an explanation of the observation that Socrates made when he initially questioned Protagoras, which is that there appear to be no recognized experts on justice and civic *aretē*; everyone, Protagoras explains, is an expert. Protagoras adds to this an analogy (327a) based on the conceit of a society in which flute playing is regarded as the *sine qua non* of social acceptance, and he suggests that in such a society everyone would reach a very high standard of performance. This, he says, is the situation of Greek citizens with respect to the (moral) excellences; they all achieve a very high standard. There are no recognized teachers of the (moral) excellences, because like the Greek language everyone teaches the younger generation. What happens as Protagoras elaborates his response is that the sense of 'excellence' slips from meaning 'exceptional,' in Protagoras's initial claim, to meaning (a high standard of) 'acceptable.'[4]

Where this leaves Protagoras' claim to be able to teach civic leadership (produce the virtuosos of virtue) is unclear. Plato has his character Socrates pass to a different line of inquiry without comment. Plato may well have felt that the weakness of the response he put in Protagoras' mouth spoke for itself and would have been obvious to anyone who shared his assumption that some people are born to rule, so that attempting to acquire the qualities (the excellences) that qualify one to rule is a very doubtful enterprise. Aristotle for his part shared this assumption, the obverse of his belief that there are natural slaves; as he puts it in the *Politics*, 'Leading and being lead are not only necessary they are expedient; indeed some are marked from the hour of their birth for subjection, others for rule' (1254a22–4). In particular, Aristotle regarded it as natural for men to rule over the women and children of their households as well as over some men who (Section 7.1) were fitted by nature only to be servants (1254b15–25).

Similar attitudes are implicit in the words attributed to Confucius: 'Women and servants are most difficult to deal with. If you are familiar with them, they cease to be humble. If you keep a distance from them, they resent it' (Chan 1963: XVII.25). Both men accepted the connection between status and occupation: 'Certainly the good man, the statesman and the good citizen ought not to learn the work of inferiors except for their own occasional use, otherwise the distinction between master and servant ceases to apply' (1277b4–6). Confucius sounds apologetic for being able to do menial things: 'When I was young I was in humble circumstances, and therefore I acquired much ability to do the simple things of humble folk. Does a superior man need to have so much ability? He does not' (Chan 1963: IX.6).[5]

The notion of a superior man in Confucius – see Section 4.3 on the contrasts that Confucius used to identify this sort of person – and the corresponding notion in Aristotle are both moral and socio-political terms of assessment. The superior man, if not required to compromise himself in the process (XV.7), is clearly called on to participate in government (XVIII.7). Aristotle believes that a ruler ought to have the ethical excellences (1260a15), and when considering whether the excellence (virtue) of a good citizen and a good man coincide, concludes that they will wherever 'citizen' means someone who takes a turn holding office (a view that Aristotle favors: 1275a22) and he adds that not thinking of the lower classes as citizens is no more unreasonable than excluding slaves from citizenship (1277a13–78a14). When we consider the views of Aristotle and Confucius on the virtues, we are dealing in each case with qualities thought to be relatively rare, rather than common, highly desirable, rather than minimal qualifications (except perhaps for someone who is to wield political power).

While it is true that scandal has been known to ruin the careers of some of our politicians, we tend to be fairly cynical about our leaders. Confucius for his part was sensitive to the way in which certain people set the pattern for others to follow and insisted that those who wanted to rule should take into account the effects of inevitably being prominent as long as they are dominant. 'If a ruler sets himself right, he will be followed without his command. If he does not set himself right, even his commands will not be obeyed' (Chan 1963: XIII.6). 'The character of a ruler is like wind and that of the people is like grass. In whatever direction the wind blows, the grass always bends' (XII.19) (cf. 'setting an example,' XII.7, XIII.1, XIII.2).

This idea of the influence that a ruler can exert may appear exaggerated given the low esteem in which political leaders are often now held, but we should not overlook the influence that individuals (sports stars, media personalities, anyone regarded as 'successful') and groups of people (the wealthy and powerful, members of high-status professions, the outspoken and articulate) exert on our characters, our attitudes and what we value. We take our cues about how it is proper to conduct ourselves and what to expect in our institutions from individuals who are 'the prominent,' many of whom are not 'dominant,' i.e. have no power to command or direct us. Confucius hoped to use this mechanism of influence to correct what he perceived to be the breakdown of good order in society around him.

In this connection, his attitude to the possibility that people can be made to feel sufficient shame (*ch'ih*) when their conduct is perceived to be improper stands in marked contrast to Aristotle's.

> Lead the people with administrative policies and organize them with penal law, and they will avoid punishments but will be without a sense of shame. Lead them with *te* and organize them with ritual actions [*li*], and they will have a sense of shame and, moreover, order themselves harmoniously.
>
> (II.3, Hall and Ames 1987: 175)

Confucius may be read as addressing a problem closer to that of Kant in that he is more confident that he can determine what is the right way to behave and is concerned with how a moral elite can bring it about that enough people follow this. Aristotle had sufficient confidence in laws and punishments as a social mechanism and, as we will see (Section 8.4), was more concerned with how the right sort of elite can function to determine what is the right way to behave.

What Confucius recommends as a mechanism of social control instead of penal law is a cultural resource that is not commonly given similar emphasis in the West. *Li* is often translated 'ritual' or 'rites,' although by themselves these English words do not convey much of the force of *li* in Chinese – particularly its foundation in social roles and relationships. We have some of what the Chinese call *li*, that is rituals from graduation and wedding ceremonies through forms of dress appropriate on certain occasions (ball gowns, evening dress, military uniform) to recognized patterns of interaction (introducing people, waiting in queues, holding doors, sending greetings cards), but we are not in the habit of warmly recommending conduct in general simply because it conforms to these patterns and do not see our social identities as tightly bound to the roles we take in these rituals. The forms and patterns are often treated as necessary inconveniences, sometimes with contempt. Chan Wing-tsit uses 'propriety' to translate *li*, which conveys the moral force of the Chinese word, but unless one remembers the associations that *li* has with recognized forms (suggested by the word 'ritual'), much of its peculiar sense will be lost.

The concept of *li* covers ceremonies such as sacrifices (including live animal sacrifice, III.17), how to interact with social superiors and inferiors, how to show respect for one's parents (II.5), how to compete with one's equals amicably (III.7), how to channel emotional responses such as grief (III.4) and shame (II.3), and how to dress and conduct oneself on any occasion. The tenth book of the *Analects* is almost entirely devoted to the sort of example that Confucius himself set in matters of dress, conduct and the outward expression of attitude on various occasions and in various circumstances. Music formed a part of many rituals and was itself performed according to ritual (just as were archery competitions, III.7). Confucius' boast of having rectified the music of Lu (IX.15) and his criticisms of certain musical forms and styles ('Banish the tunes of the Cheng ... the tunes of the Cheng are wanton,' Lau 1979: XV.11) are of a piece with his concern for the proper conduct of ritual. (These are strikingly similar to the concerns that Plato expressed that not merely the representational content of the performance arts in his ideal city should be carefully regulated but also the harmonies and rhythms that were integral to their performance, *Republic* 398c–402a.)

Confucius recommended *li* as an important force both for forming character and for governing people:

> Unless a man has the spirit of the rites (*li*), in being respectful he will wear himself out, in being careful he will become timid, in having courage he will become unruly, and in being forthright, he will become intolerant.
>
> (Lau 1979: VIII.2)

> The superior man widely versed in culture but brought back to essentials by the rites (*li*) can, I suppose, be relied upon not to turn against what he stood for.
>
> (*ibid*.: VI.27)

> When those above are given to the observance of the rites (*li*), the common people will be easy to command.
>
> (*ibid*.: XIV.41)

> If [a man's] knowledge is sufficient for him to attain [a position of power], his humanity (*jen*) sufficient for him to hold it, and he approaches the people with dignity, yet does not influence them with the principle[s] of [ritual] propriety, it is still not good.
>
> (Chan 1963: XV.33)

A later Confucian, Hsün Tzu (fourth century BCE), summed up the place of *li* in Confucian thought in this way: 'He who dwells in ritual and can ponder it well may be said to know how to think; he who dwells in ritual and does not change his ways may be said to be steadfast' (Watson 1963–4: 95). For Confucians, *li* represents a grammar of action, the means by which individuals may use their conduct to communicate with one another, and as a vehicle of thought. By means of *li* a ruler does not have either to preach or to legislate proper conduct, providing he joins his subjects in the continual performance of activities carefully structured to reflect the social order and the conduct appropriate to each role within that order.

8.3   Where the standard resides

Rituals, laws and sage kings

Just as Kant did not regard external conformity to law as sufficient for merit, Confucius regarded mere devotion to music and ritual as not enough. 'If a man is not humane (*jen*), what has he to do with ceremonies (*li*)? If a man is not humane, what has he to do with music?' (Chan 1963: III.3). There are two different approaches to translating the character represented by '*jen*'. One rests on etymology. The Chinese character is a modestly elaborated version of that for human being; this suggests that it should function in the way we use 'a real man' or 'humane' to indicate someone who is in some way or other an exemplary instance of the human race. The way *jen* is tied to sensitivity to what other people want ('Do not impose on others what you yourself do not desire,' *ibid.*: XII.2) supports Chan Wing-tsit's choice of 'humane.' The other approach is to try from the use of *jen* in Confucius and later Confucians to identify a functionally similar term in English. Lau's choice of 'benevolent' combines a near synonym for 'humane' with a characteristic prized highly in Western cultures, that of 'being well intentioned' or 'having a good will' (being, that is, *bene volent*) – the characteristic that we have seen Kant prized above all others, if it informs intense effort ('the straining of every means'). The danger inherent in the choice of 'benevolent' to translate '*jen*' is that we will assume too readily that Confucius shares Kant's outlook. The safest approach therefore is to adopt Chan's translation, understanding 'humane' as 'whatever characteristic makes one an exemplary human being.'

Asked about *jen* on various occasions, Confucius says that a mark of being *jen* is that a man is loath to speak lest he fail to live up to his words (XII.3), that a person who is *jen* reaps a benefit only after overcoming difficulties (VI.22), that a man of *jen* never worries (XI.29), that only a man who is *jen* is capable of love and hate (VI.3), that only by setting one's heart on *jen* can one be free of evil (VI.4), that few people sustain being *jen* for any length of time (VI.7), but that achieving it takes nothing more than desiring it (VII.30). A wise man will be attracted to *jen* because of its advantages (IV.2), but no one can be considered wise unless dwelling in *jen* (VI.1); indeed, *jen* appears to be a necessary condition of wisdom (V.19), as well as a sufficient but not a necessary condition of being a superior person (XIV.6). There are lists of lesser excellences that a person with *jen* may be expected to possess, 'A man who is strong, resolute, simple and slow to speak is near to humanity (*jen*)' (XIII.27). Also, 'Earnestness, liberality, truthfulness, diligence, and generosity' (Chan VII.6; *cf.* 'respectfulness, tolerance, trustworthiness in word, quickness and generosity', Lau 1979). The closest that Confucius comes to a definition is 'To master oneself and return to [ritual] propriety (*li*) is humanity (*jen*)' (Chan 1963: XII.1).

It is interesting that the Japanese, who use an identifiably Confucian vocabulary to articulate their moral outlook, seem not to find much use for this trait of character, which to some extent softens and introduces flexibility into the otherwise stringent demands for unquestioning obedience to those above one in family (parents, older brothers) and society (the emperor). In Japan, Benedict reports (1946: 117–19), the *kanji* character pronounced '*jin*' and used in phrases referring to acts ('doing *jingi*') is that which the Chinese use for *jen*. But 'doing *jingi*' is used to refer to activity outside the law, either 'above and beyond' (charity, mercy) or in the sense of 'outlaw' – as in the honor ('among thieves') that binds people who are acting contrary to what law requires. In neither case does it attract much approval or admiration. 'The Japanese, [have] entirely reinterpreted and demoted the crucial virtue of the Chinese system and put nothing else in its place that might make *gimu* [unconditional obligation to the emperor, one's parents or one's work] conditional' (119). Only in Japanese Buddhism does *jin* have positive connotations, as in the phrase 'knowing *jin*,' which refers to the mercy and benevolence characteristic of an ideal person (119n).

In Confucius, much less is said about another evidently central quality of human beings, *yi*, commonly translated as 'righteousness.'[6] At one point, Confucius declares that the superior man regards *yi* to be supreme, at least over the quality of courage. 'When the superior man has courage but no righteousness, he becomes turbulent. When the inferior man has courage but not righteousness [*yi*], he becomes a thief' (Chan 1963: XVII.23). (Two further passages connect the superior man to an interest in and understanding of *yi*: VI.10, VI.16.) A Confucian of the second century BCE, Tung Chung-shu, suggests a connection between *yi* and correction or rectification, '[*yi*] consists in correcting oneself and not in correcting others. If one is not correct himself, he cannot be considered righteous (*yi*) even if he can correct others' (*ibid.*: 286, with 'correct' for 'rectify'). Understood in this way, *jen*, as mastering or 'controlling' (Lau: 'overcoming') oneself converges with *yi* as governing or correcting (rectifying) oneself. The former could be thought of as a goal (a state of character), the latter as a way taken to that goal, but what one will do to travel that road will be to practice the *li*. Asked to elaborate on 'mastering oneself and returning to *li*,' Confucius puts it this way: 'Do not look at what is contrary to *li*, do not listen to what is contrary to *li*, do not speak what is contrary to *li*, do not make any movement which is contrary to *li*' (Chan 1963: XII.1, with *li* for 'propriety').

This emphasis placed on *li* would appear to give it the role of standard or measure in Confucian thought. The fourth-century Confucian Hsün Tzu articulated this conclusion, *viz.* that the standard (*fa*) resides in the *li*.

If the plumb line is properly stretched, then there can be no doubt about crooked and straight; if the scales are properly hung, there can be no doubt about heavy and light; if the T square and compass are properly adjusted, there can be no doubt about square and round; and if the gentleman [superior man] is well versed in ritual, then he cannot be fooled by deceit and artifice. The line is the acme of straightness, the scale is the acme of fairness, the T square and compass are the acme of squareness and roundness, and the rites are the highest achievement of the Way of man.

(Watson 1963–4: 95)

But how does one determine which of the many possible ritual forms should govern our practice? Over a century before Hsün Tzu wrote, Mo Tzu and his followers challenged the Confucians on this point (Mei 1929: 123–34, 200–11). The Confucians, it was alleged, waste a great deal of time and resources on *li*.

Among the most contentious points was whether it was necessary to mourn the death of a father for three years. (Mourning involved dress, rituals and restrictions on activities that had undeniable economic and social costs.) Speaking of one, Yü, who had argued that three years was far too long a time to observe mourning, Confucius said, 'How unfeeling Yü is. A child ceases to be nursed by his parents only when he is three years old. Three years mourning is observed throughout the Empire. Was Yü not given three years' love by his parents?' (Lau 1979: XVII.21). In response, Mo Tzu might have noted that infants are helpless and need three years of fairly constant attention, while it is unclear what departed spirits need (a point that Confucius himself all but made, XI.12) and might also have drawn attention to Yü's own reported arguments (in XVII.21) that failing to practice music and (other) ritual for three years will seriously damage one's mastery of them.

Moreover, the appeal that Confucius makes to established practice throughout the empire might be dismissed as precisely what is in question: should we be doing what we are in the habit of doing, or should we change our practice? Confucius would insist that established practice cannot be dismissed as irrelevant; a regard for *li* is precisely a regard for established practice, and there must always be at least a presumption in favor of continuing established practice. When one of his followers suggested dispensing with the sacrifice of a sheep at the ceremony marking the new moon, Confucius replied that he himself regarded the preservation of the ritual as more important than (the cost of?) the sheep (III.17).

But how far does the presumption in favor of existing practice carry? Confucius insisted that he merely transmitted and did not innovate; he was devoted to the ancients (VII.1). But he himself observed what may be called 'drift' in established practice, a change in material used for ceremonial caps, a step moved from one part of the proceedings to another (IX.3). In one case, Confucius accepted the new practice because it was more 'economical' (Chan; 'frugal', Lau); in the other, he insisted that the older form of ritual was better because it was less 'arrogant' (Chan; 'casual', Lau). These judgments reflect at least a limited preparedness to evaluate practices and make deliberate choices. But on what basis does one make such choices? Hsün Tzu compared the *li* to standards like the plumb line, the T-square, the compass and the balance scale, and it is indisputable that compasses generate circles, that balance scales (properly hung) determine which of two things is heavier, that edges can be made straight and corners made square, but there appears room to dispute whether a ritual is properly carried out or is even necessary.

If we have faith that at some point in history there were certain truly exceptional individuals – not merely superior men (*chün tzu*), but sages (*sheng jen*) – who have reached an even more elevated level of achievement, and if we believe that these exceptional individuals established correct rites, then the standard does reside with these (truly) exemplary individuals. The quotation from Mencius at the head of this chapter is then the most accurate account of the situation. Indeed, Hsün Tzu concedes this: 'All ritual principles are produced by the conscious activity of the sages; essentially they are not products of man's nature. ... The sage gathers together his thoughts and ideas, experiments with various forms of conscious activity, and so produces ritual principles and sets forth law and regulations' (Watson 1963–4: 160).[7]

The anti-Confucian Han Fei-tzu (at one time a pupil of Hsün Tzu) also stressed the importance of standards (*fa*) but had the decrees of rulers (having the force of penal law) rather than ritual in mind when he wrote. Nevertheless, we still find him looking to the wisdom of the past as the source of *fa*:

> Though a skilled carpenter is capable of judging a straight line with his eye alone, he will always take his measurements with a rule; though a man of superior wisdom is capable of handling affairs by native wit alone, he will always look to the laws of the former kings for guidance. Stretch the plumb line, and crooked wood can be planed straight; apply the level, and bumps and hollows can be shaved away; balance the scale, and the heavy and light can be adjusted; get out the measuring jars, and discrepancies of quantity can be corrected. In the same way one should use law (*fa*) to govern the state, disposing of all matters on their basis alone.
>
> (*ibid.*: 28)

As two recent scholars of Chinese philosophy (Graham 1989: 273–8; Hansen 1992: 347–52) have stressed, *fa* is a concept that covers more than laws; it also applies to the standards used in the building trades.

As a result of his preoccupation with effective rule through penal laws, Han Fei-tzu is known as a 'legalist.' Obviously, if it were only a question of adhering to a standard embodied in law that had been established at some time in the past, difficulties would be posed by the possibility of drift just as for someone like Hsün Tzu, who sought standards embodied in ritual practices. Han Fei-tzu, however, appears to have been prepared to calibrate his standards on the basis of whether they served to preserve and enhance a ruler's power (Watson 1963–4: 16–34, 84–9). Mo Tzu, who at a much earlier date had rejected Confucian *li* in favor of *fa*, would seem to have wanted to calibrate his standards, his *fa*, on the basis of whether they served to enhance the prosperity and welfare of ordinary people (Mei 1929: 30–54).

The basis of Confucian validity appears to be tradition that validates itself by belief in the charismatic qualities of its founders (see Section 2.1), qualities to which tradition itself testifies. The problem, as we have seen, is that even if we accept the charismatic or exemplary status of the founders of the tradition, unless currently living individuals are capable of determining what is ritual propriety, there is nothing to guard against drift away from genuine ritual propriety, as established practices are reproduced from generation to generation. Han Fei-tzu puts the point against his opponents effectively:

> Since the death of their founder, the Confucian school has split into eight factions, and the Mo-ist school into three. Their doctrines and practices are different or even contradictory, and yet each claims to represent the true teaching of Confucius and Mo Tzu. But since we cannot call Confucius and Mo Tzu back to life, who is to decide which of the present versions of the doctrine is the right one? ... Now over seven hundred years have passed since Yin and early Chou times, and over two thousand years since Yü and early Hsia times. If we cannot even decide which of the present versions of Confucian and Mo-ist doctrine are the genuine ones, how can we hope to scrutinize the ways of Yao and Shun, who lived three thousand years ago?
>
> (Watson 1963–4: 118–19)

It would be as if we used try squares and straightedges inherited from our ancestors without any idea of how to check them to see whether over time they had become warped – unless, that is, from time to time a sage appears who is capable of (re)calibrating our practices to insure that by adhering to them faithfully we will do as we should.

Confucius was reluctant to claim the status of being a sage, in which case, if we take him at his word, he recommended what he transmitted from the past on the basis of his faith that the ancients had fashioned the standards embodied in *li* correctly. Might it still not be the case that Confucius has said enough about the characteristics of sages (or perhaps fully accomplished superior men would be sufficient) that we can recognize someone who has what it takes to assess our grasp of tradition and either reassure us or set us straight? We might of course (as subsequent generations in China thought they had) recognize that in spite of his modesty – or partly because of his modesty – Confucius was someone whom we could take as the standard of human relations. But has Confucius said enough to enable us reliably to recognize the qualities of the right sort of exemplary person?

8.4   The analysis of virtue

Choice, the mean, reason and practical wisdom

The qualities of exemplary persons are virtues (*aretai*; *virtutes*) in the traditions of the West. Although Confucius discusses a number of particular qualities of this kind, it is hard to identify a character in the Chinese texts that expresses the general concept of a moral virtue or ethical excellence.

There is a general notion, *te*, commonly translated 'virtue' in Confucian (and other ancient Chinese) texts. It appears in the *Analects* as a power to exert influence over people (II.1) and to say memorable things (XIV.4). It can be related to a more general sense of the Greek word *arete*, for Aristotle's analysis takes for granted a point made by Plato in one of the arguments of *Republic I* (353b–d) that whenever something has a function to perform, *arete* applies to whatever it is that enables it to perform that function exceptionally well. This puts *arete* in the general category of powers or dispositions or qualities thought to lie at the basis of powers or dispositions. (The word 'virtue' is still used in English in this sense, as in 'the virtue of this design'; now largely obsolete expressions speak of the virtues of certain chemicals.) The idea is applied by Plato and Aristotle so that the virtue (or excellence) of a knife – what gives its user the power to cut something easily – would lie in its sharpness, weight and balance. The virtue of an eye – what gives its possessor the power to see well – would (given our understanding of how the eye works) lie in the shape and clarity of the cornea and the sensitivity of the cells in the retina.

As Confucius uses the word *te* it appears to be something unequivocally positive, although in other texts of the period it can be applied in a negative sense, as when we speak of the 'virtue' of an instrument of torture. Confucius may have been prepared to apply *te* in a way that is relativized to function. An isolated rhymed couplet attributed to Confucius (XIV.33) says that a good horse is to be praised for its *te* rather than its strength, which may be read to imply that different kinds of things have different kinds of *te*. Compare Aristotle: 'The *aretē* of the horse makes the horse good to look at and good at running and at carrying its rider and at awaiting the attack of the enemy' (1106a19–21). *Te* is spoken of as something to hold in esteem and to try to promote not only in oneself but in the common people (I.9). Beyond this not much is said, except that few people understand it (XIV.4). The particular ethical excellences that Confucius discusses are not shown to be special cases of *te* in any systematic way.

Aristotle (Section 1.1) locates ethical excellence within a general category of habits or 'states of character' and, as we will see below, the sort of habits that make up one's (ethical) character are acquired dispositions to act or feel along a variety of dimensions, each of which involves responding or feeling either to the right degree or too much or too little. The different excellences or virtues are distinguished by a dimension of feeling or action: courage is the right location on a continuum of degrees of feeling fear; generosity is the right location on a continuum of degrees of sharing one's material prosperity. There is also an important 'intellectual virtue,' which, among other things, helps to co-ordinate these different dimensions.

Before we take up Aristotle's detailed definition of an ethical excellence in general, there is an apparent paradox to be resolved. This emerges when Aristotle considers what it takes to act well in some specific manner (e.g. justly) and the way in which we acquire the specific excellence (justice) that allows us to do so. In specifying (1106a30–b1) what it takes to do just acts, Aristotle mentions three things. To qualify as having done something just in the full sense, a person has to (1) act knowingly (not do it inadvertently); (2) choose it and choose it for its own sake (in other words do it *because* it is just); and (3) act from a firm and unchanging state of character. The second of these implies that actions characterized by an ethical excellence must be seen by a person with that excellence as worth doing precisely because they are what a person with that excellence would do, i.e. that person must act for the sake of doing what is just. This is close to Kant's requirement that we act for the sake of duty, but Aristotle makes this into a family of requirements under concepts of various virtues rather than a single requirement.

From the last of these, however, it seems that one cannot do what is just without already being just, having the virtue of justice. Nevertheless, we become just, Aristotle says, by doing just acts (1105a17; and he means to imply in general, where X is an excellence, that we become X by doing X actions). But in the light of (3) how can we do just acts without already being just? The answer appears to be by imitating, with conscious effort and perhaps some discomfort (i.e. not really acting justly), what a just man would do gladly and with ease. Eventually, our disposition to do such things (actions characterized by the excellence, X) will become established. And when it is established, only then will our actions qualify as excellent.

Aristotle's account of ethical excellence in general has four important clauses (1106b36–7a2):

> *Aretē* [*ēthikē*] is a stable disposition (*hexis*) [to act or be affected]
> 1 involving preference or choice (*prohairetikē*);
> 2 lying in a mean (*mesotēs*) relative to us (*pros hēmas*);
> 3 determined by discursive thought (*logos*);
> 4 as a man of practical wisdom (*phronimos*) would determine.

Note that the last of these rests our recognition of any particular virtue like courage or generosity on our ability to recognize a person who exemplifies the virtue of sound judgment. The hope that we have brought to this definition is that we will be able to identify exemplary persons in general by means of their qualities. To see whether this feature of the fourth clause will render Aristotle's conclusion useless for our purposes, however, will require considering carefully each clause of this definition in turn.

To turn, then, to the general account of an ethical excellence or moral virtue. The four clauses are to be understood as follows:

An ethical excellence is a stable disposition (*hexis*) . . .

1 . . . involving 'preference' or 'choice'

Of these two possible translations (of *prohairetikē*), the latter suggests the involvement of consideration or deliberation – 'the thing already selected from our deliberations is the thing chosen' (1113a4–5). Since deliberation is thus central to choice, what is said about deliberation in connection with *logos* and the man who has 'practical wisdom' in clauses (3) and (4) will bear on this notion. 'Preference' suggests that the settled state of character (the *hexis*) in question reflects the personality and commitments of the person who has it. Intentions and decisions which count as *prohairetikē*, for Aristotle, reflect a conception of what it is for a person to live well (Anscombe 1965). Because young children and animals do not operate with a conception of what it is to live well and are not capable of deliberating to anything like the extent that adults are, children and animals are said not to share in choice (1111b9; cf. 1226b21), although they are capable of acting for themselves ('voluntarily,' as it is commonly translated) and are praised and blamed, punished and rewarded, presumably because these have effects on the states of character that give rise to their behavior. Children and animals cannot therefore have ethical excellences in the strict sense.

2   ... *lying in a mean relative to us*

This second clause readily gives rise to a number of misinterpretations of Aristotle's position. 'Lying in a mean' is not a recommendation of moderation in feeling and action, nor in spite of drawing on mathematical terms to explain the idea does Aristotle believe that there is a decision procedure, involving either calculation or geometrical construction, for determining what one should do or how one should feel. Likewise, the phrase 'relative to us' does not entail that we all make a subjective determination of what to do or how to feel. 'Relative to us' means relative to the particular circumstances in which we find ourselves, circumstances that anyone can appreciate and attempt to evaluate so as to determine which responses would be overreactions and which would be insufficient. In some circumstances, almost any degree of response may be too much (for example when being annoyed by someone who wants to derive satisfaction from creating annoyance); in some circumstances, it may be appropriate both to feel intense distress and to make strenuous efforts to remedy the situation (as when outrages are being committed against close members of one's family).

The point of talking about a mean is to suggest how we should think about the general form of the situations that call for a response. Responses either in action or of feeling can be compared with respect to more or less. The different dimensions of response are what give rise to different particular excellences. The courageous person responds neither too little to the effects of fear (ignores danger, acts recklessly) nor too much (reacts to every threat, avoids the slightest hazard). Self-controlled people neither respond too much to the attractions of pleasure nor are they totally abstemious. In every situation, eliciting a response along one or another dimension of action or feeling (even in the cases imaged in the previous paragraph) it is possible to respond either too much or too little.

Confucius made a similar point: 'To go too far is as bad as not to go far enough' (XI.16, Waley 1938).[8] In XIII.21, Confucius considers what he would do if he could not find 'men who steer a middle course' (Waley); the choice is between 'the undisciplined . . . [who] are enterprising' and 'the over-scrupulous . . . [who] will [at least] draw the line at certain kinds of action' (Lau). (However, when Confucius praises the *te* of 'the Mean' (VI.29) and complains at how rare it is among common people, he appears only to be observing how rare it is for people to 'hit the mark (get it just right) in everyday affairs.') How to find the proper middle between too much and too little remains to be determined. This is why it would be premature if not inappropriate to complain that talk of the mean tells us nothing – that all either Aristotle or Confucius is saying is that doing what is right is doing neither too much nor too little, which is empty advice. Advice has to be given in the light of circumstances, and we are considering these matters at too high a level of generality to bring in details that would allow for advice to be formulated.

That talk of a mean is not entirely empty even at this level of generality is clear from the complaints of those who think Aristotle's doctrine of the mean is seriously mistaken. These complaints come from those who are not satisfied with being told that the right response depends on the particulars of the circumstances one is in and who instead 'hunger for a morality giving the kind of explicit guidance that rules and laws provide.' In the seventeenth and eighteenth centuries there were Grotius and Kant (see Section 8.1), and in this century one can cite Ross (1949: 206) and Kelsen (1960: 119). The mistake, it is claimed, lies in thinking that there are two ways to go wrong for every way to go right. That this is thought to be a mistake rests on thinking of standards of doing well as having the form of rules or laws from which one can depart in only one way – by failing to conform. Aristotle recognizes that there are many ways to go wrong, so that excellence involves doing or feeling 'at the right times, with reference to the right objects, towards the right people, with the right aim, and in the right way' (1106b21–2). But he also believes that this complexity can usefully and properly be reduced to a scale on which the right lies between too much and too little. He goes on immediately (b23) to say that getting it right is intermediate, and after a dozen lines he offers the definition we are currently considering. He does not think of guiding norms as rules but uses instead the model of someone who must steer a course between two hazards (see 1109a333 for this image).

Aristotle recognizes, to be sure, that everyone, the ordinary law-abiding and the outstandingly virtuous, should conform to certain straightforward rules. He defends his definition of ethical excellence against misinterpretation by acknowledging that some words label things to be found at extremes that should be strenuously avoided, such as 'spite,' 'shamelessness' and 'envy,' 'adultery,' 'theft,' 'murder.' One cannot commit adultery with the right woman, at the right time in the right way (1107a9–17; nor is one an adulterer[9] by exceeding in intercourse with married women, 1221b20–1). But people who did no more than conform to such rules could easily lapse into less egregious faults because they failed to appreciate that it is always possible to have too much of a good thing. Sometimes, one of two possible vices is either uncommon or not a serious annoyance to other people, so that, as Aristotle notes (1107b7), we lack names for them. We can imagine a person in our society so obsessed with fidelity that he regards otherwise innocent social interaction with women other than his own wife as improper. Obsessions like these are part of what stands between ordinary 'law-abiding' people and what Aristotle understands by ethical excellence.

3 ... determined by discursive thought

In Aristotle's account, the mean will be determined 'by *logos*,' which is commonly translated 'by reason.' The phrase 'discursive thought,' discussed in

Section 5.2, avoids connotations of abstract calculation while keeping the association that '*logos*' has with articulate speech. When considering the role that Aristotle assigns to *logos* in ethics, it is useful to remember why he says (in the *Politics*) that it is natural for humans to live in cities (*poleis*).

> It is apparent that the city is among the things that are by nature and that the human being is by nature a city [dwelling] animal. ... For man alone among the animals has the power of speech (*logos*); voice is used to indicate pleasure and pain and is possessed by other animals ... but speech serves to make clear what is useful and what is harmful and also what is right (*to dikaion*) and what is wrong (*to adikon*). For what distinguishes human beings from the other animals is their having a perception of good and bad, right and wrong and the other [things of this sort], and the sharing of these makes a household and a city.
>
> (1253a2–18)

The thought processes by which people exercise control over what they do – evaluating different courses of action as beneficial or harmful, right or wrong – take place when communicating with one another. Aristotle's most common word for the discursive thought process that goes on when people decide what to do, 'deliberation' (*bouleusis*), derives from a verb meaning to take counsel (see Section 1.1). This can be an activity engaged in by an individual alone, but the advantages of doing this as a collective enterprise are, Aristotle suggests, the reason why it is natural for people to live in cities.

It is noteworthy that the ritual practices that are central to the Confucian conception of an exemplary person are given no mention in Aristotle's definition. Both Aristotle and Plato recognized the place in human life of public rituals such as sacrifices and festivals, but neither gave them the importance that Confucians did. On the other hand, a discursive practice, that of deliberating, which is given prominence in Aristotle's discussion of virtues, receives hardly any attention in Confucian texts. Confucians stress the importance of something translated as 'learning' (*hsüeh*), which involves the study of classic texts of history, poetry, music and ritual, and which, it seems clear, are to serve as a resource in determining how one should conduct oneself. Poetry is recommended in these terms:

> My young friends, why do you not study the odes? The odes can stimulate your emotions, broaden your observation, enlarge your fellowship, and express your grievances. They help you in your immediate service to your parents and in your more remote service to your rulers. They widen your acquaintance with the names of birds, animals and plants.
>
> (Chan 1963: XVII.9)

This recommendation is in terms not only of the value of poetry as a repository of knowledge (of names) but also as a resource for functioning well in society. Confucius is traditionally held to have edited books of history as well as poetry, ritual and music, and a number of passages of the *Analects* discuss episodes of Chinese history and the lessons they offer (V.19, XII.22, XIV.14–17, XIV.19). What Confucians do not appear to recognize (or consider useful) is the process of clarifying one's goals, exploring the means to achieve them and evaluating available alternatives. It is this, as we shall see, that is particularly characteristic of Aristotle's exemplary person.

4 ... as a man of practical wisdom would determine

What should be done or felt on a given occasion by a person with the relevant excellence will not be determined merely by an exercise of discursive (i.e. deliberative) thought. The required thinking will have to be done *well* – done as a person possessing a particular excellence known as *phronēsis* would do it. The appeal to this excellence in defining ethical excellence does not – immediately at any rate – introduce a circularity, for this is an intellectual not an ethical excellence (1103a4–19), but its relationship to ethical excellence is far from straightforward, and it drew from Aristotle a further separate discussion taking up almost a whole book (common to both versions) of the *Ethics*.

At the very end of this further discussion, Aristotle briefly opens a new line of argument which illuminates the role that *phronēsis* is supposed to play. Something like the dispositions we prize, something like the ethical excellences, sometimes appear in children, even in wild animals. Aristotle seems to have courage in mind, which children sometimes display and of which certain animals stand as emblems. He might also have had the eponymous character of Plato's *Charmides* in mind. Young Charmides is presented by Plato as naturally disposed to the kind of quiet, thoughtful self-control that Greeks called *sōphrosunē*. Part of the irony involved in having Charmides engage Socrates in a discussion of *sōphrosunē* is that, as Plato's audience knows, when Charmides grew up, he became one of 'the thirty tyrants' who collectively instituted a reign of terror for a time in Athens – the opposite of what someone would expect from a person who possesses *sōphrosunē*.

Now one who is naturally inclined to do just or temperate or courageous things unreflectively no more has these excellences in the unqualified sense than do people who are earnestly making strenuous and sometimes painful efforts to become just or temperate or courageous by doing what they think, or have been told, a just or temperate or courageous person would do. People with a natural excellence already have something close to the necessary fixed disposition, but they may not be acting for the sake of doing just or temperate or courageous acts because they possess an ill-formed conception of the relevant excellence. But 'if a man once acquires thought, that makes a difference in action; and [if] his disposition remains [that of someone who has the natural excellences], then it will be excellence in the strict sense' (1144b12–13).

As Aristotle observes, what one might call the natural excellences are capable of leading someone astray 'as a strong body which moves without sight may stumble badly because of its lack of sight' (1144b11–12). What *phronēsis* gives our soul is an eye (1144a29). How does it do this? Aristotle begins his account of this crucial excellence by considering the sort of people who are said to have it:

> For we say that to deliberate well is the most characteristic activity of the *phronimos* . . . and the person who is good at deliberating without qualification is the person able in accordance with reasoning to attain the best of things to be done by a human being. Nor does *phronēsis* consider only generalities, but must also consider particulars, for it is concerned with actions and action deals with particulars.
>
> (1141b9–16)

In deliberating, we look ahead at the consequences of proposed courses of action – this is how our soul begins to acquire an eye. But being 'good at deliberating without qualification' needs to be distinguished carefully from mere cleverness:

> There is an ability which is called cleverness which enables us to do things that are conducive to a goal we have set ourselves and to attain it. If the goal is admirable the cleverness is praiseworthy, but if the goal is bad, the cleverness is mere villainy; thus we call both *phronimoi* and villains clever. *Phronēsis* is not this ability but it does not exist without it.
>
> (1144a24–9)

So being good at the sort of discursive thought that qualifies as deliberation, while indispensable to *phronēsis*, is not sufficient for it. To deliberate well without *qualification* requires more than the ability to figure out how to attain the objectives we set ourselves:

> Excellence in deliberation in the unqualified sense, then, is that which succeeds with reference to what is the end in the unqualified sense, and excellence in deliberation in a particular sense is that which succeeds relative to a particular end. If, then, it is characteristic of *phronimoi* to have deliberated well, excellence in

deliberation will be correctness with regard to what conduces to the end of which *phronēsis* is the true apprehension.

(1142b30–6)

Phronēsis transcends the sort of excellence in deliberation known as cleverness, provided that cleverness is directed at attaining the goal which *phronēsis* should discern for us.

So how does *phronēsis* discern the goal at which we should aim? Part of the answer involves a further exercise in discursive thought which involves deliberating about what human flourishing or human fulfillment is. In the next chapter, we will consider how Aristotle conducts this enterprise. Until we have a clear idea about how deliberative thought may be used to clarify and identify accurately what a person should aim for in life, we do not have a complete picture of practical wisdom and therefore do not have complete pictures of any of the ethical excellences, the qualities of exemplary persons.

But it takes more than simply being clear about what human flourishing is; people who know what humans should aim at, and even deliberate well about what it would take for them to achieve it, may fail to be ethically excellent individuals if they do not put forth their own efforts in that direction. And even efforts made in the right direction may not be enough to qualify for ethical excellence; one has to be correctly motivated, i.e. move in the right direction because one believes it is the right direction. Aristotle reminds his audience that to qualify as possessing an excellence such as that of justice one must not merely do what people with this excellence do, but knowingly choose to do it and for its own sake (1144a14–20). To qualify fully as a *phronimos* one must both deliberate well about what human flourishing is and deliberate well in an effort to determine the means to that end, *because* of a fixed disposition to do so and for the sake of living as a flourishing human being – whatever the use of discursive (deliberative) thought determines that to be. There is once again an element here similar to Kant's good will, wanting to do whatever it is one should do, whatever careful thinking determines that to be,[10] as well as something that Kant's good will seems to need once it confronts the task of fulfilling its wide duties, *viz.* a conception of doing well that will guide its choices.

But there remains a threat of circularity. It still has to be recognized that unless the excellences have developed along with the ability to think effectively (cleverly) about how to realize human excellence, a person's thinking may be led astray, 'for wickedness perverts us and causes us to be deceived about the starting-points of action. Therefore it is evident that it is impossible to be *phronimos* without being [ethically] good' (1144a35–7). It does not appear, after all, that we can be sure we have identified a practically wise person merely by trying to assess the skill with which that person has deliberated about both ends and means, for just as 'it is not possible to be good without being *phronēsis*, it is not possible to be a *phronimos* without *ēthikē aretē*' (b30–1). The difficulty is that if individuals do not already have the virtues, the account of the end that they seek to guide their deliberations may be distorted by wickedness – unless, that is, the activity of deliberation can by itself be relied on to locate and correct such distortions.

Further reading

The story of the eclipse of virtue in European ethics is told in Schneewind (1990). A revival of interest in the role of virtue in ethics was sparked by the work of Philippa Foot, collected in Foot (1978), and by MacIntyre (1981). By focusing attention on the concept of virtue, Sherman (1997) sees a greater convergence between Aristotle and Kant than is usually seen. For Confucian philosophy, consult Hall and Ames (1987), Graham (1989: chapters I.1, II.1, III.2), Eno (1990) and Hansen (1992: chapters 3, 5 and 9). On Han Fei-tzu, see Graham (1989: chapter III.3) and Hansen (1992: chapter 10). For Aristotle's concept of virtue, see Kosman (1980), on choice (*prohairesis*) Anscombe (1965), on the doctrine of the mean Urmson (1973) and Tiles (1996), and on *phronēsis* Sorabji (1974).

Notes

1 'The virtuous agent, for Kant, has no epistemological privilege: when she exercises her virtue she is simply choosing at her discretion among alternative ways of helping others or improving herself, she is not displaying insight as to the morally best things to do' (Schneewind 1990: 61).

2 See note 5 to Chapter 4 on citations of Confucius.

3 The word here, *eleutheros*, literally means 'free' and refers to the class of people with enough material means not to have to spend much of their lives laboring to stay alive.

4 Cicero provides an example of how the word *virtus* in Latin could slide from marking the exceptional to indicating merely a demanding standard of acceptability: 'In fact, there is no human being of any race who, if he finds a guide, cannot attain to virtue (*virtus*)' (Keyes 1938: *Laws*, I.x.30).

5 Lau (1979) translates this as 'I was of humble station when young. That is why I am skilled in many menial things. Should a superior man be skilled in many things. No, not at all.'

6 Hall and Ames reject the suggestion of Lau (1979: xxii) that *jen* applies primarily to agents and *yi* to acts, and they identify it as a disposition of a person which insures 'the disclosure of appropriate meanings. Such disclosures of meaning arising from *yi* acts serve as both cause and consequence of the maintenance of harmony within a social context' (1987: 105).

7 The denial that this comes from the 'human nature' of the sage is part of Hsün Tzu's dispute (Section 5.2) with Mencius over whether humans need the interference of artificial constraints in order to live together in harmony.

8 Lau (1979) translates this as 'There is little to choose between overshooting the mark and falling short.'

9 '*Moichos*'. The fault here lies not in spouses' infidelity to their spouses (this is to judge by a late Stoic and Christian norm), but in the violation of a man's (property) rights, 'the husband's claim to exclusive sexual access to his wife' (Cohen 1991: 109).

10 Lau (1979: 16) maintains that one of the qualities of exemplary humans identified by Confucius, *chung* (translated as 'conscientiousness' by Chan; see e.g. I.4, III.19, IV.15), should be read 'doing one's best,' even though it later came to mean 'loyalty' in the sense of blind devotion. If devotion is not blind, then it is the resolve to do what is proper however that is to be determined.

9

THE END AS A STANDARD

What choice, then, or possession of the natural goods –
whether bodily goods, wealth, friends, or other things – will
most produce the contemplation of god, that choice or possession is best; this is the most admirable standard,[1] but any
that through deficiency or excess hinders one from the
contemplation and service of god is bad; this a man possesses
in his soul, and this is the best standard for the soul – to
perceive the irrational part of the soul, as such, as little as
possible.

(Aristotle (fourth century BCE): 1249b16–23)

Recapitulation: Exemplary individuals are used in many moral
traditions as standards or measures of, conduct. Examining the
qualities that such individuals are supposed to possess to see
whether and how these individuals can be identified has revealed
an emphasis on ritual practice in the Confucian tradition and an
emphasis on a discursive practice known as deliberation in
Aristotle. To determine what is involved in good ritual practice
requires relying on tradition, which rests its authority on the charismatic or exemplary qualities of its (often legendary) founders.
Aristotle's analysis of the qualities of exemplary individuals
(ethical excellences) was found to rely on an intellectual excellence, translated 'practical wisdom,' for which being good at
deliberation was a necessary but not a sufficient condition.
Practical wisdom, however, when it was analysed, was found to
involve the very thing we had hoped to see defined, ethical excellence. For without ethical excellence it is possible for a person to
frame a distorted account of the goal or 'end' of human action,
i.e. what it is that deliberation and action should aim to achieve,
namely a flourishing or fulfilled life.

Prospectus: Without a discussion of how practical wisdom
undertakes to deliberate about this end, Aristotle's picture of an
exemplary person (in particular the person with practical wisdom)
is incomplete. The outcome of Aristotle's deliberations in the
Nicomachean Ethics, which are intended to clarify what it is that

constitutes living well (or flourishing) is the nomination of an exercise of our rational or intellectual abilities, 'contemplation,' which has little appeal to many people and appears to stand in considerable tension with both Aristotle's avowed doctrines and obvious tendencies in the ways he develops his ethical theory. The other surviving version of his *Ethics*, the *Eudemian*,[2] develops a number of crucial points in a quite different way and yields a very different account of what constitutes living well. This account bears comparison with that which might have been generated by Confucian philosophers, had they raised the sort of questions that shape the development of Aristotle's theory.

9.1   The role of reason

Teleology, deontology and deliberative rationality

Possessing an ethical excellence, according to Aristotle, rests on being able to moderate one's responses by means of a particular intellectual excellence, *phronēsis*. The reason given is that even the best natural dispositions (*hexeis*) are blind, and without this intellectual excellence, their possessor is likely to stumble. Stumble on what? What is so difficult about finding the mean between the extremes of stinginess and prodigality or between cowardice and rashness? The answer is that one's particular circumstances affect where the mean lies. Talents, prospects and responsibilities elsewhere affect how much of one's resources is proper generosity, how much risk to one's life and limb is proper courage. The reason here is not unlike that which made Kant admit that when it came to wide (imperfect) duties it was impossible to say exactly what they require of a person. One duty might properly limit another and affect what was an appropriate response to its demands.

One important difference, however, was that Kant did not acknowledge how much judgment (how much in the way of intellectual resources) might be involved in reconciling conflicting demands. Moreover, Kant, in repudiating Aristotle's doctrine of the mean (Section 8.1), did not see that it might well be appropriate to view the problem of the co-ordination of wide duties in the light of the schema of a continuum of responses, where 'too much' and 'too little' indicate responses to avoid. One has wide duties to one's family, to one's neighbors, to one's career, to develop one's talents. How much is enough to discharge one duty depends on how much is enough to discharge another. It is clearly possible to do too much if less is enough and another duty is neglected as a result. If, however, one thinks of duties in isolation from one another, as Kantians are prone to do, then whether one has discharged a duty looks as if it admits of only a 'yes' or 'no' answer – no question of 'too little' or 'too much.' And when one thinks in terms of fulfilling wide duties in relation to one another, there appears to be an important role for a concept of living well or flourishing, which informs all virtuous choices in Aristotle's framework, but which Kant and his followers overlook.

How does one judge 'too little' or 'too much'? One way is by a 'feel for the outcome,' an aesthetic response. What might be done to ensure a good, or at least adequate, aesthetic assessment of some possible outcome? One might rely on native (untutored) sensibilities (Section 5.2), or one might immerse oneself in a body of cultural resources in the hope of acquiring proper sensibilities by means of 'endless' amounts of history, tradition and taste – or, if one is a Confucian, endless amounts of history, poetry and rites (Sections 4.3, 8.2). A properly tutored sensibility can issue *kadi*-style (see Section 6.2) pronouncements on how much is too much and how much is too little. By and large, this is the way that art criticism proceeds.

Aristotle, as we have seen, would reject nativism as wilful blindness and would suggest that, whatever role the cultivating influences of history, tradition and taste might have, much can and needs to be done with deliberative thought to clarify where the mean lies in particular circumstances. To do this requires an explicitly articulated account of what we should be aiming to do with our lives and an accurate assessment of what contribution will be made to this end by a habit of responding in some characteristic fashion.

The idea that we assess possible courses of action (or general patterns of response) in terms of what they contribute to or detract from our achieving some desired outcome is known as *consequentialism*, and this general approach to assessing attitudes and conduct is also referred to as *teleological* (after the Greek word for goal or end, *telos*). Where the outcome or goal is assumed to be fixed, we have what may be called a 'rigid consequentialism' (or an approach that is rigidly teleological). Where a goal is believed to be of overriding importance (the single most important thing in human life), rigid consequentialism can arouse anxieties. An end that has overriding importance might justify adopting any means whatsoever, including the violation of the minimum standards embodied in respect for persons (see Section 7.4). However, Aristotle's consequentialism is not rigid. He does assume that it is part of the task of ethics to provide a specification of the most important things in life, of a life supremely worth living, but the specification he provides still leaves a great deal of detail to be filled in. It remains possible to argue (although Aristotle for historical reasons was not in a position to consider the matter) that this goal should, for example, preclude violations of the minimal standards embodied in respect for persons.

A theory, like Kant's, that proceeds by specifying what is needed, what we are bound to do, what is due from us (our duty), is known as a *deontological* theory (incorporating the Greek word for 'binding,' 'needful,'

'proper,' 'right,' *deon*).[3] The accusation commonly leveled at deontological theories is that they serve only to entrench prejudice and established
privilege and to prevent some or all of us realizing goods that are properly ours. Kant's theory, however, underwrites the enforcement only of
duties that enhance the freedom of all. In addition to such duties of right,
Kant does specify ends, the perfection of oneself and the happiness of
others, and they are 'ends that are also duties.' But the duties here are
'wide,' leaving scope for discretion. Arguably, to make a good job of
fulfilling one's wide duties, a person should try to frame a more detailed
specification of what it is for a human being to do well, as a human being
– in other words, try to carry out what Aristotle sees as an important part
of the task of ethics. It is clear, in any case, that there is no reason why
an ethical theory cannot combine both teleological and deontological
components (apply both teleological and deontological measures).

Kant and Aristotle are both ethical rationalists in that each treats the
human capacity for discursive thought involving abstraction and general
principles not only as the source of what is peculiarly human and what
gives humans special dignity but also as the main source for the guidance
and assessment of conduct. Kant relies mainly on formal uses of reason:
requiring maxims to conform to a rational requirement and testing
outcomes for consistency. Aristotle, on the other hand, relies almost entirely
on deliberative rationality; he appeals hardly at all to formal features like
consistency for guidance. Even working out the specification of what it is
to live well or flourish takes a deliberative form.

This is because Aristotle's deliberative rationality is not strictly instrumental; that is, it does not proceed by identifying a goal and then seeking
only instrumental means of achieving that goal. Deliberation does not
always start from a fully specified goal; part of what deliberation may
have to do is bring specificity to an unspecific goal. The 'means' that
deliberation comes up with when addressing this task are not instruments
but more adequate specifications of the *constituents* of the objective being
sought. Instrumental reasoning moves from effect to causes that will realize
that effect; constitutive reasoning moves from general to specifics that will
realize that general. (One of Aristotle's examples of practical reasoning
goes, 'I need a covering, a coat is a covering,' 701a18 – a clear, if somewhat lame, 'logic teacher' example of moving from the general to the
specific.) As one may have a choice of causes to realize some effect, one
may have a choice of specifics to realize some (general) end or goal.

The two aspects of the function of deliberative rationality, moreover,
may not be easily separable. It does not follow that if some dreadful plan
looks like it is the only way to achieve a goal (as specified) that deliberative rationality has to accept this plan. If 'deliberative rationality' meant
only 'instrumental rationality,' it might have to, since instrumental rationality must take its goal as fixed. But when, through deliberation, we have

216

appreciated the consequences of setting a certain specific goal, we can ask whether the goal, if it involves those consequences, was adequately specified. If to run our business in what we think of as a profitable or efficient manner, we find that we have to lay off half our workforce or pollute the environment, we may reconsider what profitability or efficiency involves or what it is we are in business to achieve. If the attempt to cure a patient involves side-effects that destroy the quality of the patient's life, we may reconsider our understanding of what constitutes a cure.

There is here the possibility that deliberation can locate and correct distortions (even those caused by wickedness: end of Section 8.4) in the specification of 'the starting points of action.' 'Starting points' here might refer either to ends one has set out to achieve or to the first actual step to take in realizing those ends, or both. To effect the correction, we have to keep open the question of whether our goal has been adequately specified and be prepared to acknowledge the full effects of courses of action that we have adopted. Wickedness, however, often consists of willful blindness to, or refusal to accept responsibility for, deleterious side-effects of policies one has adopted. Deliberation can perhaps only correct the effects of wickedness in people too honest to qualify as wicked. Aristotle's conclusion that without ethical excellence it is not possible to be good at deliberating in an unqualified sense may have left his analysis with an unsatisfactory circle, but its conclusion is profoundly truthful.

Aristotle was quoted in Section 8.4 (under (4), the passage 1142b30–6) as saying that excellence in deliberation in the unqualified sense, the sense that qualified as *phronēsis*, was that which succeeded with reference to (i.e. in finding the means to) the end in the unqualified sense. 'End in the unqualified sense' means 'something not sought for some further end.' A thing (e.g. food, a screwdriver) may be sought for some further purpose that it serves (to nourish, to turn a screw); that purpose may in turn serve a further purpose (health, attaching something to a wall). Something that is not sought for a further purpose would be an end without qualification. That is obviously not a sufficient specification of what a *phronimos* is supposed to direct deliberations toward, even if we add that it will be 'the best of things to be done by a human being' (1141b13). If the *phronimos* has to aim for that which is an end in the unqualified sense, he or she will need to make this more specific by engaging in the non-instrumental kind of deliberation.

That addition 'done by a human being' in the most recently quoted passage is, however, already an important specification. The *Nicomachean Ethics* begins by noting that everything we undertake, whether it be art, inquiry, action or choice, is aimed at some good (1094a1), and after three brief discursive chapters Aristotle identifies the object of his inquiry as the highest of all goods achievable by (human) action (1095a15), the specification that is explicit in 1141b13. This means that what a *phronimos*

217

aims to achieve does not need to be considered in the light of any more comprehensive end or notion of good, such as how (from the standpoint of the universe) everything should be, or what is God's will for mankind as a part of His plan for creation as a whole. Deliberately placing his notion of 'end in an unqualified sense' outside any more comprehensive end of this sort (see Aristotle's rejection of Plato's 'form of the good,' 1096a12–97a14) may be said to constitute a form of 'humanism.' This humanist stance, of course, opens Aristotle to objections from people who favor accounts based on religious doctrines or, more recently, from those who seek to subordinate human interests to some independent conception of what is good for our planet's ecology (for 'the biosphere').

Aristotle's next step toward specifying 'the end without qualification' is to observe that there is general agreement on what to call this 'highest of all goods achievable by human action.' Greek speakers (both 'the many' and 'the discerning') call it *eudaimonia* and have in mind living well and doing well when they use this word, although not everyone gives the same account of what it is. Some regard it as consisting of pleasure, some of wealth, some of honor; when ill, a person will think of it as consisting of health, when poor, of wealth. But in general people are not so confident that they know what *eudaimonia* is that they will not listen to someone who suggests that it is something quite beyond their comprehension (1095a20–6).

The standard translation of *eudaimonia* into English is 'happiness,' but this English word has a number of unhelpful associations. People who are content with their lot and at least moderately cheerful – *cf.* 'natural happiness (which consists in satisfaction with what nature bestows, and so with what one *enjoys* as a gift from without)' (Kant 1797: 388; *cf.* Section 8.1) – may claim to be happy, and there is no basis on which to contradict this claim. 'Happiness' is subjective to the extent that individual subjects (persons) are the final authority on whether the term 'happy' applies to them. Aristotle does not use the adjective *eudaimōn* in this way. His term is an external, objective form of appraisal; it means doing well or living well in a way very similar to the way the word 'success' means doing well or living well. Whether something or someone may be claimed to be a success is a question we can all discuss and dispute; no one can claim to be a success simply because he or she feels successful.[4]

Having much in life to enjoy (take pleasure in) or being highly regarded (honored) are recognized forms of success, but although Aristotle accepts that these are candidates for *eudaimonia*, he dismisses wealth (closely associated in our culture with success) as something one acquires not for its own sake but for the sake of something else. *Eudaimonia*, living well and doing well, has to be something pursued for its own sake. Aristotle acknowledges that we need external goods (friends, wealth, influence) to live well and do well (1099a32–b7), but these he says should not be confused with doing well; these are (in the language of the *Eudemian* version at 1214b11–26) 'indispensable conditions' of living well. Just as diet and exercise are indispensable conditions of health, but do not constitute health, external goods do not constitute doing well or living well. We are trying to determine what in life is to be sought for its own sake and not for the sake of something else. Pleasure and honor, at least, are not immediately disqualified from this competition. A third important candidate, 'contemplation,' is introduced briefly, but further discussion of it postponed (1096a5).

Before setting up a basis on which to judge the three main contenders, Aristotle sets out two characteristics that a candidate must possess in order to qualify as *eudaimonia*. Apart from being achievable by action and being for the sake of which everything else is done, *eudaimonia* will have to be 'final' (complete, perfect; *teleion*) and 'self-sufficient' (*autarkēs*). The second of these, Aristotle insists, does not mean that *eudaimonia* is something we can have all by ourselves: 'By self-sufficient we do not mean that which is sufficient for oneself alone, living a solitary life, but also for one's parents, children, spouse and in general for one's friends and fellow citizens, since humans are by nature city [dwelling] creatures' (1097b8–11; *cf.* the quotation from the *Politics* under (3), Section 8.4). What 'self-sufficient' means is that whatever *eudaimonia* is, it will when considered on its own make life desirable and not lack anything that will make life more desirable (b15–20). Being final is explained as being chosen (desirable) for its own sake and never for the sake of something else. We choose wealth and instruments in general not for their own sake but for the sake of something else, so they are not final. We choose honor, pleasure, thought and all the excellences for their own sake, but also for the sake of *eudaimonia* , so they are not final in the required sense. *Eudaimonia*, whatever it is, is something we think of as chosen for its own sake and not for the sake of something else.

As students of Aristotle's *Ethics* have come to appreciate, the text at this point reaches an important fork in the road – there are two importantly different ways in which Aristotle might seek to fill out the 'whatever it is' in the previous sentence. He might identify a number of things that we do for their own sake *and* for the sake of *eudaimonia* and try to determine what combination or combinations of these constituents could lay a claim to constituting *eudaimonia*. The relationship between things like honor, pleasure, thought and the excellences of character on the one hand and *eudaimonia* on the other might then be thought of as like the constituent activities of golf, driving from the tee, fairway strokes and putting.[5] As golf includes all these activities, *eudaimonia* is inclusive of a variety of constituent activities. This is known as treating *eudaimonia* as an 'inclusive end.' Alternatively, Aristotle might look for a single thing that by itself will make life worth living – the sort of attitude that one might get from a sports fan: *eudaimonia* is not *like* golf, it *is* golf! ('Golf is life, all the rest is details.') The problem then is to decide whether it is golf or fishing or philanthropy or scientific research, etc. that by itself makes life worth living. This is known as treating *eudaimonia* as a 'dominant end.'[6]

It is not easy to tell, from the passages that discuss the characteristics of self-sufficiency and finality, what exactly Aristotle has in mind. He says, 'if there is an end for all that we do, this will be the good achievable by action, and if there are more than one, these will be the goods achievable by action' (1097a22–4). And, within a few lines, 'if there is only one final end, this will be what we are seeking, and if there are more than one, the most final of these will be what we are seeking' (a38–30). A 'most final' end need not be a dominant end; it could be a composite of things done for their own sake as well as for their contribution to that combination of things that makes for a flourishing life.

The *Nicomachean* version thus leaves the matter unclear and goes on to develop a principle for determining what constitutes *eudaimonia* in a way that preserves the unclarity, even to the point of putting new claims in the form already used: 'human good turns out to be activity of soul in conformity with excellence, and if there is more than one excellence, in conformity with the best and most final' (1098a16–17). Might the most final be a composite or inclusive excellence? But at the end of the *Nicomachean* version (Book X, chapters 6–8), Aristotle returns to the question and unambiguously argues for the claim that there is one activity, which he calls *theorein*, usually translated 'contemplation,' which is what *eudaimonia* consists of – in other words, the *Nicomachean* version comes out in the end for the 'dominant end' view of *eudaimonia*.

The result is for many reasons not very satisfactory. There are problems, which we will take up later, with the relationship that this activity has to the moral excellences, the way the case for *theorein* appears to be mounted on the very sense of 'self-sufficient' that Aristotle repudiated in his initial discussion, and the fact that there is not much plausibility in the view that human fulfillment consists of what the word 'contemplation' suggests. The Greek verb *theorein* would be used to describe what spectators do at a theatrical event, but the best contemplation is, Aristotle says, of the highest and most permanent of things, God, the cosmos (order of the universe), etc. Can this be the only or even the best way for humans to find true fulfillment?

9.2 The appeal to human nature

For the standard of what it is to live well

The reasoning by which Aristotle attempts to adjudicate between his candidates (pleasure, honor and contemplation), and which leads to this questionable outcome, starts from the premise that what we want is the highest thing we can achieve by human action, and to specify this we will have to say something about what human beings are and what human action is. Knowing what a thing is and what it does are in Aristotle's view, inseparable. The nature of a thing, he says clearly (in one of his works of what would now be thought of as 'natural science,' 390a10–11), is to be expressed in terms of its *ergon* (work, function, characteristic activity). These two inseparable notions, nature and *ergon*, are in turn closely tied to our ability to evaluate a thing and its performance. If you want to know what a good X is, you have to know what an X does; a good X, then, does well what X's do. This applies to instruments including bodily organs: a good knife (eye) does well what a knife (eye) does, namely cut (see). It also applies to examples of natural species and kinds of stuff: a good example of a waterwort, *elatine hexandra* (a good, pure, sample of sodium bicarbonate) does well what a waterwort (lump of sodium bicarbonate) characteristically does, *viz.* lives through a cycle of life characteristic of waterworts (interacts with other chemicals in characteristic ways).

As human beings are a naturally occurring species, a good human being will do well what humans characteristically do, and it can be claimed that a human who lives and acts in this characteristically human way may be said to be *eudaimōn*. One reason for not translating *eudaimōn* as 'happy' is that it might well not seem convincing to say that a person who does well what humans characteristically do will be happy in the sense of 'will feel good about his or her life.' The kind of inquiry that Aristotle is conducting is not 'what will make one feel good about his or her life?' but rather 'what sort of a life would a person have the best reason to feel good about and have no reason not to feel good about?' Aristotle's assumption in answering this latter question is that whatever else we identify ourselves with or as, we should be prepared to identify ourselves as human beings and with whatever can convincingly be argued to belong to us as members of our species.

It is interesting that for all his deep suspicions of our natural condition, Kant's argument on behalf of the authority of reason has a formal similarity to Aristotle's. Kant in effect argues that, how ever our natural inclinations may lead us to think of ourselves, we should be prepared to identify ourselves as rational creatures and endeavor to live in a manner true to that condition. Rationality, as we will see shortly, is the characteristically human part of our physical nature for Aristotle. Rationality is for Kant also a characteristic of our essential nature, but one that may well stand opposed to our physical nature. The beginning of the *Foundation* contends that we are prone to misunderstand 'the purpose of nature in attaching reason to our will as its governor' (1785: 394–5). If it were only a matter of preserving mankind, seeing to human welfare and happiness, Kant suggests (probably with some irony), we would be served far better by instinct. Reason offers only such 'feeble and defective guidance' to satisfying our appetites that it must clearly exist for something else, for, indeed, the purpose of producing a will that is good, not as a means to something else but as an end in itself (396).

At the end of the *Nicomachean* version, Aristotle will also tend to make into an end in itself an exercise of our rationality that is possibly independent of our physical nature. But the line of argument at the beginning of that version goes on to connect living well with the excellences, *aretai*. Since what humans do arises from their dispositions (*hexeis*), humans who do well and live well must do so because their souls (*psuchai*, 'souls' in the sense of whatever it is that distinguishes them from inanimate objects) possess and exercise dispositions that count as 'excellences' or 'virtues.' Thus Aristotle sometimes offers as a definition of *eudaimonia*, 'activity of the soul in accordance with complete excellence' (1098a17–18, 1102a5). This formula is very uninformative; it does little more than distinguish Aristotle's view from those who are confused enough to want to treat *eudaimonia* as strictly identical with possessing excellence. (One can after all possess an excellence, be able to act well but never have occasion to use it; Aristotle insists that only actually doing well, actualizing an excellence, counts as *eudaimonia*.) To provide some genuine specificity for his conception of *eudaimonia*, Aristotle has to spell out what the *ergon* (or characteristic activity) of a human soul is.[7]

Although it might be reasonable to hope for more specificity than Aristotle actually delivers, he does take some interesting and suggestive steps toward clarifying the *ergon* of a human soul. The *ergon* of a human soul cannot be merely to live – that is something even plants do – nor can it be merely to experience the world around us with the senses, for animals are able to do that. What is peculiar to humans is that they have something that equips them to act with discursive thought (*logos*), both in the sense of obeying or conforming to something discursively articulated and in the sense of thinking something over or framing for themselves a course of action. So the *ergon* of human beings is the actualization of their capacities to live in a way informed by discursive thought, or at least live in a way that is not without discursive thought. And if this is the way we determine a good individual example of a given biological species – by picking out those which live well a certain kind of life – and if the life characteristic of human beings is to act with the help of discursive thought, then this will be 'the good belonging to human beings.'

Some translations render 'good belonging to human beings' as 'the good for humans,' which suggests that acting with the help of discursive thought is good for us in the way that dietary fiber is good for us (our health). Now this 'good belonging to human beings' (*to anthrōpinon agathon*) does play a role in determining what is good for us in the 'contributes to our well-being' sense of 'good for.' Anything which promotes acting with the help of discursive thought, e.g. education, adequate sleep, sufficient physical exercise, is good for us, since this formula ('acting with the help of discursive thought') specifies how our well-being as humans is to be assessed. But Aristotle does not recommend either discursive thought or moral virtue as good for us in this 'contributes to our well-being' sense. His interest is focused on specifying what well-being is (for a human), so that he will be able to say whether anything contributes to it.

Living well, that is in a way informed by discursive thought, is next identified as the actualization of our capacities to live (over a whole lifetime) in accordance with excellence. The *Nicomachean* version (as we have already mentioned) goes on from here to add the formula that is poised ambivalently between the inclusive and the dominant view of *eudaimonia*, 'and if there is more than one excellence, then in accordance with the best and most final' (1098a17). At the end of this version Aristotle will recommend, as the dominant constituent of *eudaimonia*, what appears to him to be the highest activity of the capacity for discursive thought. This is not, as in Kant, the activity of a refined capacity to desire, in other words a good will, but the activity of a refined capacity (*viz.* of theoretical wisdom, *sophia*) to contemplate, to appreciate with understanding, the world around us.

The development of the *ergon* argument in the *Nicomachean* version began (1097b21) with Aristotle resolving to say something more than the apparent platitude that *eudaimonia* is the chief good, but his conclusion moves back toward what we have already identified as an uninformative truism: the best a human can do is to realize the best possible human disposition(s). The development of the argument is logically more satisfactory in the corresponding chapter of the *Eudemian Ethics*, where Aristotle starts with the idea that *eudaimonia* is the actualization of complete excellence (1219a38), and moves toward the more specific claim that this will have to involve a specific type of discursive thought, *viz.* reasoning (*logismos* 1219b39). This, at least, is not uninformative, although it is hardly all that needs to be said.

Left like this, Aristotle's thesis invites an objection based on the fact that criminal activity frequently involves carefully considered (discursively articulated) plans of action. Does Aristotle not have to allow that a gang leader who worked out an efficient method of extorting money, and his accomplices who understood and helped him to carry out his plans, are all actualizing a (the) peculiarly human excellence? Would this not then make them not only good examples of the human species but also involve them in the very activity that (if there were enough of it in their lives) would make them *eudaimones*? It is likely that if pressed by this objection Aristotle would appeal to the difference between being *phronimos* and merely being clever (Section 8.4, under (4)). These criminals are clever; they have worked out an efficient means to obtain what they have set themselves to obtain, wealth. However, there is a question that which needs to be raised as part of the task to which their discursive thought should address itself, the question that opens the opportunity for deliberation that has been perverted by wickedness to correct itself, namely what should they be trying to accomplish? If they have not done this, then they have not deliberated well in the unqualified sense.

Is obtaining wealth by any means, so long as the process involves an investment of discursive thought (deliberative reasoning), what humans do that is peculiar to their species – so that doing it well is what is to count as *eudaimōn*? It is true that no other species of animal accumulates wealth in the way that humans do – behavior like that of squirrels stands to the human institutions of wealth as 'giving voice' stands to human speech (see the quotation from Aristotle's *Politics* in Section 8.4, under (3)) – but Aristotle has already argued that someone who treats wealth as an end in life is confused about the difference between means and ends. If our criminals have adopted efficient means of achieving an end that they have set for themselves, and they are not (as Aristotle would see it) confused about the role of wealth as a means, they will have some goal beyond acquiring wealth – something they will do with the wealth once they have acquired it. If there is a basis in Aristotle's framework for criticizing them, i.e. arguing that they do not, however successful they may be as clever criminals, count as *eudaimones*, it will have to lie in this further goal, since Aristotle has no basis for criticizing the means that someone adopts other than in terms of what it may lead to or fail to lead to.

The *Nicomachean Ethics*, as we have seen, contains a shortlist of possible candidates for the types of life that could claim to realize *eudaimonia* – the lives of pleasure, honor (politics) and contemplation (1095b14–19). The *Eudemian* version has a similar shortlist, the lives of pleasure, excellence and *phronēsis* (1215a35). The lists of both versions are too short; there is, for example, no mention of the lives of artistic creation, religious devotion or humanitarian service. Some of this is the result of Aristotle's social snobbishness – the performing and plastic arts were generally regarded as fit only for menials, although literary artists had standing in the better circles and the failure to mention their lives seems to have been an oversight on Aristotle's part. Nevertheless, the items on these overshort shortlists are inclusive enough to cover quite a number of things that people might aim at in life. The life of honor could conceivably be stretched to cover careers in professional sports, management or entertainment (it included military activities for Aristotle). In spite of the shortness of the list, it will be useful to consider how *Nicomachean* candidates fare in the light of the possibility that the criminals imagined above might have intended to use their ill-gotten gains in pursuit of any of the three – pleasure, honor or contemplation.

When Aristotle first mentions a life of pleasure as a candidate for *eudaimonia,* his attitude again sounds somewhat snobbish: 'Now the vast majority are evidently quite slavish, preferring a life suitable for cattle,' and while allowing that self-indulgent rulers frequently set bad examples, he contrasts this with 'active and discerning' people who regard honor as *eudaimonia* and seek it in public affairs. What Aristotle has in mind when he speaks of the slavish are pleasures associated with the body. After considering the topic of pleasure carefully and in some detail, he recognizes that pleasure belongs potentially to any activity, and the important question is not whether one experiences pleasure but what one takes pleasure in. So when at the end of the *Nicomachean Ethics* Aristotle takes up the question of what *eudaimonia* is, a life devoted to pleasant amusement (*paidia*, literally 'child's play', also sports and games) replaces the life devoted to pleasure as the first candidate (1176b8).

Aristotle's criticism of the pleasure-seeking life begins with the observation that what seems valuable and pleasant to children is not what seems valuable and pleasant to adults and that what bad people enjoy is not what good people enjoy. So it is not surprising to find him claiming that 'to exert oneself and work for the sake of child's play seems silly and utterly childish.' He does accept that amusement has an important function in providing relaxation ('we need relaxation because we cannot work continuously,' 1176b35), but this makes it, like wealth, a means ('to amuse oneself in order that one may exert oneself,' 1176b33–4) not an end, hence not a candidate for *eudaimonia*.

So our criminals cannot claim *eudaimonia* by virtue of their investment of thought in their activities, if their deliberations aim only at pleasant amusement. However, they may be interested in amassing wealth in order to possess the means of securing political power and influence and ultimately the honor sought by those 'active and discerning' people whose lives are lived in the public sphere. Aristotle's initial treatment of the life of honor stresses its dependence 'on those who bestow honor rather than on him who receives it' (1095b24). This dependency seems to disqualify it on the grounds that it is not 'self-sufficient' enough to count toward *eudaimonia*, but only if the sense of 'self-sufficient' is allowed to slide back toward the very meaning that Aristotle denied to 'self-sufficiency' (1097b8–11; see Section 9.1).

Aristotle suggests that people who seek honor are seeking to be assured of their own merit, and this means that they are really interested in excellence. Someone might well have gained honor by means that could not be openly recognized, because if people knew how he acquired the wealth to buy the influence to gain the office, etc., they would hold him in contempt. However, such a person would have to be deceiving himself if he treated the honor he received as a sign of his own merit. Of course, some people are not particularly concerned with their own merit and are simply gratified by being held in public esteem. This perhaps reduces their political ambitions to the level of pleasure seeking, and although this kind of gratification may not seem to be an obvious example of pleasant amusement, it is easy enough to imagine how Aristotle would dismiss this version of a life of 'public service' as a candidate for *eudaimonia*.

There are two main reasons offered in the final book of the *Nicomachean Ethics* for giving low marks to a life devoted to political (which for Aristotle included military) affairs. One is that the things it seeks are not desirable for their own sake (1177b17); the other, perhaps merely a corollary of this, is that they are not undertaken by people when they are masters of their own time – as activities 'they seem to be unleisurely' (b7). Aristotle is clearly thinking of politics merely as promoting some policy, say having to do with seeing there is enough grain to feed the populace or seeing that public revenues are managed properly. Instituting a policy of this sort, Aristotle indicates, seems to be done for some further objective related to creating the opportunity for leisure. (At any rate, fighting a military engagement is not, Aristotle wisely observes, done for its own sake, but for the sake of peace.) Now if public life consists of doing nothing that would be done for its own sake, but for the sake of something else, then this something else must be what *eudaimonia* consists of. So what is it we do when the necessities of life (food, shelter, state security and public services) have all been attended to? What do we do when we are at leisure?

Aristotle's third candidate seems to provide the only answer. Those who are not slavish in their tastes exercise their minds in contemplation of the highest or best of all the things that can be known. What is contemplation? The verb *theorein*, recall, applies to what spectators at a 'theater' do, but the objects of contemplation are not meant to be (merely) entertaining. They have to be more than amusements, child's play, sport or games. Aristotle places this activity at the culmination of intellectual endeavors to understand such things as earthly natures, the heavens and the divine principle that is ultimately responsible for the cyclical changes observed in the heavens and on Earth. It is not research into these matters (1177a27) but the appreciation of the results of research. *Theorein* in this sense cannot take place unless a great deal of discursive thought has been invested in assembling and articulating bodies of understanding (*epistēmai*), what we now call 'theories.' This is why it recommends itself as the best use we can make of our capacity for discursive thought; it is a most demanding exercise of our best capacities and is directed toward the highest objects (1177a20–1).[8] It is the sort of thing that we imagine is a suitable activity for a god (1178b20–3).

Theoreticians – our custom of calling people this ultimately goes back to this Aristotelian doctrine – commonly speak of the beauty of their theories and the pleasure they derive from them. Aristotle is familiar with this phenomenon: 'We think *eudaimonia* has pleasure mingled with it, but the activity of wisdom is admittedly the pleasantest of excellent activities; at all events philosophy is thought to offer pleasures marvelous for their purity and their enduringness' (1177a23–7). We can engage in this activity, Aristotle claims (a22), more continuously than anything else. Moreover, it is a self-sufficient activity; when everyone is provided with the necessities of life, the just man still needs people toward whom and with whom he can act justly. Likewise for the temperate, the courageous, etc., but 'the wise man, even when by himself, can contemplate and the more so the wiser he is' (a32). Here the final book of the *Nicomachean Ethics* adopts the sense of 'self-sufficient' explicitly laid aside when using the word to characterize *eudaimonia* in the first book.

Moreover, there is a tension between the claim made for the self-sufficiency in Aristotle's defense of contemplation and the attempt he makes in his discussion of friendship to argue that friends are constituents of *eudaimonia*, not merely indispensable conditions. This argument for friends as a constituent of *eudaimonia* is somewhat lame, but the direction in which it limps seems to lie directly opposite to the argument mounted here. Even an excellent individual intent on contemplation needs other people, Aristotle argues, particularly to appreciate his or her own excellence, for 'we can contemplate our neighbors better than ourselves and their actions better than our own' (1169b33–4); 'and this will be realized in living together and sharing in discussion and thought; for this is what living together would seem to mean in the case of man, and not, as in the case of cattle, [merely] feeding in the same place' (1170b11–12).

9.3 *Eudaimonia* and the ethical excellences

Contemplation and public service

There are even more troublesome questions about how the exercise of the intellectual excellence of theoretical wisdom relates to the exercise of the ethical excellences. These can be most directly brought to light by returning to the criminals who used discursive thought successfully to extort money but could not claim that this exercise of discursive thought contributed to *eudaimonia* so long as it was directed toward pleasure or honor. Now what if they sought, however unlikely this might be, the material means of having the opportunity (the leisure) to engage in the contemplation of the highest and most noble things?[9] It is clear that insofar as their thinking was directed toward a(n external, instrumental) means to this goal, it contributes no more to their *eudaimonia* than does engaging in public affairs. But with money to purchase the leisure to contemplate, will they not be *eudaimones*?

What is troubling is that this group of people, singularly deficient in the ethical excellence of justice, if in no other, should have any claim at all to be the successful, admirable human beings that being *eudaimones* implies. Whatever happened to the claim that *eudaimonia* consisted of the actualization of the ethical excellences? What happened to the idea that to be just or temperate or courageous, one has to choose to do just or temperate or courageous deeds for their own sake, and to the implication that for a person with the excellence in question, these deeds are worth doing for their own sake and are part of what it is to live well (see Section 8.4)? What happened is that it was allowed that there might be one excellence that would have to be cultivated and exercised above all the rest (the 'dominant view'). Once an excellence – in this case the intellectual excellence of theoretical wisdom – is accorded that role, the only role remaining to the ethical excellences seems to be that of instrumental means, of domestic servants, to the one thing that really fulfills the life of a human being.

The image of the ethical excellences functioning as maidservants (with *phronēsis* functioning as chief housekeeper) to something else valued for its own sake was applied by an opponent to the views of a philosopher, Epicurus, who established himself during the generation following Aristotle's death. We will look at the views of Epicurus and how they differ from Aristotle's in the following chapter. Aristotle, however, does not appear to have been as comfortable with leaving the exercise of the ethical excellences in this subservient role as Epicurus was. Having reached the conclusion at the end of the *Nicomachean Ethics* that the life of intellectual contemplation (the activity that realizes theoretical wisdom) is the best, the most pleasant and the most *eudaimōn*, a new chapter continues to add support for this conclusion but begins:

> Life in accordance with the other excellences [is *eudaimōn*] in a secondary way. For activities in accordance with these is human. Doing what is just (right) and courageous (manly) and in accordance with the other excellences toward one another in all our contracts and services and actions and in the passions (emotions) – all this seems to be human.
>
> (1178a9–13)

The stress here on 'human' follows Aristotle's argument that contemplation, although characteristic of divine, god-like beings, is also characteristic of the best in human beings.

On what basis can Aristotle claim that the ethical excellences contribute, even in a 'secondary' way, to *eudaimonia*? Actualizing them is a function of our mortality (gods do not engage in activity, *praxis*); it is unleisured, dependent on other people, uses (apparently) the capacity for discursive thought in a subservient way and is not directed toward the higher forms of reality. To have an excellence, X, we have to act for the sake of doing X things, but the picture of a life fulfilled by one supremely excellent intellectual activity raises the question, 'why do anything for the sake of anything other than this?'

It is important to bear in mind that, although the ethical excellences that Aristotle identifies, analyses and discusses would facilitate social interaction in general, they were selected as traits needed by those who undertake civic responsibilities, those who are to manage the foreign and domestic affairs of a Greek *polis*. However, much of what is involved in the (collective) management of a Greek *polis* does not appear to Aristotle as being undertaken for its own sake (making war, maintaining the public treasury, adjudicating disputes). Hence a life exercising the ethical excellences is assigned at most to the second rank, and we have no account that explains why, if a person were for some reason unable to undertake the most fulfilling human activity, there would be any fulfillment anywhere else.

However, if we took Aristotle's principle that *eudaimonia* is to be sought in doing well the things that humans characteristically do and made two adjustments in the way the *Nicomachean* version develops that principle, a very different conception of *eudaimonia* would emerge. One adjustment would accord equal dignity to the function of discursive thought to govern – as in the following passage from the *Eudemian* version, which does not move to treat discursive thought in isolation from other general functions of the soul. The vegetative part (the respect in which we are alive in the same way that plants and animals are alive) is not relevant to our inquiry (1219b38 – 'for no horse, bird, or fish is *eudaimōn*,' 1217a26), but

> considering human beings as human, they must have the power of reasoning (*logismos*), as a determinant of action; now reasoning does not govern reasoning but desire and affections, so humans [considered as humans] must have these parts [i.e. capacities]. And as physical well-being is made up of the excellences of the several parts, so also is the soul considered as an end [or whole].
>
> (1219b39–1220a4)

This passage assumes that discursive thought in the guise of *logismos* has the task of governing, and to the extent that it is suggested that *eudaimonia* depends on excellences, the drift here seems to be toward a more inclusive view. Assigning to the activity of governing by thought this role in *eudaimonia* could qualify a number of lives for the dignity of *eudaimōn* – artists, athletes, agriculturalists, engineers and many more who invest discursive thought in what they do.

A second adjustment would be to place as much emphasis on the claim[10] that humans are by nature city-dwelling creatures as on the claim that they think discursively. In other words, acknowledge that human fulfillment consists not merely of what is done by people when they have leisure but also in what is done by them to sustain a common life (a 'commonwealth') in a public space. If that involves defense, finance, adjudication, arranging festivities, regulating markets, maintaining sewers, then doing these things well (under the guidance of discursive thought, of course) will be what it is for a human to do well as a human being. (And the other activities mentioned at the end of the previous paragraph are all richer for their involvement both in narrowly professional and in wider public spheres.)

Here a life exercising ethical excellences of the sort that Aristotle picked out and discussed at length in both versions of the *Ethics* will be assigned first – although not necessarily an exclusively first – rank. But to develop this requires firmly setting aside the dominant view of *eudaimonia* and embracing the inclusive view. It is interesting, therefore, that the Aristotle of the *Eudemian* version appears far less ambivalent between the inclusive and dominant views in his initial exploration of *eudaimonia*, and he makes no effort to mount a case for *theorein* as the highest of human activities. A passage in the *Eudemian* version that corresponds to those cited at the end of Section 9.1, uses the word *teleion* not in the sense of 'final' but in the sense of 'complete'.[11] This is clear from what is said in the following passage:

> But since *eudaimonia* is something complete, and living is either complete or incomplete and so also excellence – one excellence being a whole, the other a part – and the activity of what is incomplete is itself incomplete, therefore *eudaimonia* would be the activity of a complete life in accordance with complete excellence.
>
> (1219a35–9)

With the stress on completeness, we are directed toward the inclusive view, and the interpretation is confirmed by a remark a few lines later: 'nothing incomplete (*atelēs*) is *eudaimōn*, not being a whole' (1219b7). There is no echo in the *Eudemian* version of the cagey formula 'and if there is more than one (end or excellence), then the best and most final.'

The final book of the *Eudemian* version, however, presents something of a puzzle. It concludes with the passage quoted at the head of this chapter, which contains what appears to be a ringing endorsement of the position reached in the *Nicomachean* version. We must measure all goods (or the good of all things) by the standard of what 'will produce the contemplation of god'; what is bad is what 'hinders one from the contemplation and service of god.' The involvement of 'contemplation' and 'god' in this conclusion comes as something of a surprise; these notions are introduced without proper preparation or motivation, and the reference to 'service of god' is doubly puzzling because of an immediately preceding remark (1249b15) that 'god needs nothing.' The chapter, indeed the whole of the *Eudemian* version, contains no extended case for thinking that *theorein* is an especially worthwhile activity. If the *Nicomachean* version does represent Aristotle's more mature thinking, this passage might reflect a later addition (by Aristotle and/or by an editor) in an attempt to bring the two versions into line. It may also be the case that the notion of 'contemplation and service of god' has a different interpretation, one unlike that suggested by the argument at the end of the *Nicomachean* version. The general drift of the argument up to this puzzling passage is certainly very unlike that found in the *Nicomachean* version.

As we noted in Section 9.2, the shortlist of candidates for *eudaimonia* in the *Eudemian* version differs in significant respects from the list in the *Nicomachean* version: instead of recognizing the candidacy of the lives devoted to pleasure, honor and contemplation, the *Eudemian* version shortlists pleasure, excellence and *phronēsis*. The last chapter of the *Eudemian Ethics* contains an evaluation of these candidates, but by far the most attention there is devoted to excellence, and consistent with the earlier emphasis on complete excellence Aristotle sets out to describe the excellence that arises from the combination of the various excellences (1248b10).

Aristotle appropriates the Greek word *kalos* for 'the excellences and the works that proceed from excellence' (b37). *Kalos* is rendered as 'noble,' 'fine,' 'admirable' or 'beautiful' by various translators. One good reason for adopting 'admirable,' which incorporates the concept of people drawn to look up to something with approval, is that this is the closest English antonym to 'shameful,' 'disgraceful,' the meaning of the Greek antonym, *aischros*. Another is the assumed connection between excellence and what merits admiration and commendation ('For all goods have ends which are chosen for their own sake. Of these, we call *kalos* all those which are commended for their own sake' (b20)). To merit admiration, to be admirable, does not mean actually being admired or honored by other people. The excellent and the admirable are what people ought to look up to, admire and try to emulate. Honor and admiration depend on other people; being excellent or admirable can be achieved without recognition by other people. This is the significance of the *Eudemian* selection of 'excellence' rather than 'honor' for the shortlist of candidates.

Kalos does not label complete excellence, the excellence that arises from the combination of excellences. Aristotle adopts a portmanteau expression, *kalos kagathos*, 'admirable and good,'[12] and he labors to explain the difference between a merely good person and an admirable and good person. With a fairly shrewd grasp of the class interest that lay behind the admirable Spartan civic discipline (Section 3.1), Aristotle cites the Spartans to distinguish between people who possess admirable goods and do admirable deeds and those who possess admirable qualities and do admirable things *for their own sake*. The Spartan elite possess admirable qualities and do admirable deeds for the sake of holding on to their position of power and wealth. (Spartan aristocrats accumulated considerable wealth and were noted for their lack of decorum under the influence of wine when visiting foreign parts.) Complete virtue, like any partial virtue, must, to be present in the full and proper sense, be sought for its own sake. There is here no excellence, ethical or intellectual, that stands to usurp the claims of the other excellences taken together and to turn them into its servants. *Eudaimonia* is action in accordance with complete excellence.

Having concluded his summary discussion of complete excellence, Aristotle takes up pleasure briefly, stressing that what is pleasant without qualification is also admirable and that as pleasure is derived only from action, people who are truly *eudaimōn* (acting as they do with complete excellence) will live most pleasantly. The doctrine here is familiar from both versions of the *Ethics* and may be reduced to these claims (some of which will be treated in more detail in the next chapter): pleasure is specific to activities (we cannot obtain the same pleasures from different activities) and is not something separable from the activities that give rise to it. The pleasure that appears as an alternative to excellence is not pleasure without qualification, it is merely a mistaken appearance of what is really good (1113a15–b1). The exercise of excellence has its own specific pleasures (1104b4–28), and the aim in life is not to avoid pleasure but to take pleasure in genuinely good things. Doing so is experiencing pleasure without qualification (the really pleasant is good.) So in the *Eudemian* version, instead of setting up pleasure as an alternative way of life (one that perhaps only the immature and the children that never grow up will want to pursue), pleasure is treated as a necessary constituent of *eudaimonia*.

Aristotle then turns to *phronēsis*. Thirty-five lines from the end of the book and the end of the *Eudemian* version, the discussion picks up a thread left dangling from the last two sentences (1145a7–11) of the earlier book (common to both versions) that discussed *phronēsis*. There it was said that *phronēsis* looks after theoretical wisdom, just as medicine looks after our health or as politics (the management of civic affairs) looks after (the communal religious observances honoring) the gods. In the context of the *Nicomachean* version, this appears to foreshadow the service that *phronēsis* and the other ethical excellences will render to the possibility of a life devoted to contemplation, but the *Eudemian* version offers no *apologia* for contemplation.

It begins with the image of medicine giving orders by reference to a standard, namely the health of the body. So, when it comes to choosing things that relate to wealth and good fortune (the things that are naturally good, but only if carefully and intelligently managed), the good man needs a standard. To specify the standard, Aristotle reminds his audience that humans have a ruling element (thought) and a subject element (feeling), and that one should live according to the former. And here *phronēsis* is once again portrayed as issuing commands (like a physician) on behalf of our ability to contemplate, as though that ability were our health. The passage that appears at the head of this chapter is worth repeating here:

> What choice, then, or possession of the natural goods – whether bodily goods, wealth, friends, or other things – will most produce the contemplation of god, that choice or possession is best; this is the most admirable standard, but any that through deficiency or excess hinders one from the contemplation and service of god is bad; this a man possesses in his soul, and this is the best standard for the soul – to perceive the irrational part of the soul, as such, as little as possible.
>
> (1249b16–23)

Is 'contemplation' (observing, watching over?) simply the activity of an alert 'ruling element?' Then why is its object 'god?' If its activity is to govern, why should it perceive the irrational part of the soul as little as possible? Because of the misleading appearances of what is good that this part is likely to generate?

The drift up to this point has been that the three candidate lives of the *Eudemian* version do not represent exclusive alternatives, but that *eudaimonia* consists of all three, if properly related to one another. The end of this version may well point to the same line taken at the end of the *Nicomachean* version, but from within its own development it appears rather to be an attempt to hold the ethical and intellectual excellences together in a tight package and to offer their collective exercise as true human fulfillment. *Phronēsis*, we learned earlier (from the common book devoted to it; see Section 8.4, under (4)), is related to the rest of the excellences as an eye that helps them to see where true excellence lies, that is to see what is truly admirable. The ability to contemplate, see clearly and accurately, the highest things would have to be the health of that eye; it cannot, the earlier discussion of *phronēsis* made clear, exist without the ethical excellences. 'God' would then have to be identified in some way with those 'highest things,' which may in themselves need nothing from us, but nevertheless realizing them in the particular circumstances that make up our lives is a kind of service to them. Kenny speculates that,

> the service of God could well include acts of moral virtue. These are the *kalai praxeis* [admirable deeds] of the *kalos kagathos* [admirable and good person] which are the subject of the early part of the chapter; they could well be regarded as the many noble things which we, under the *arkhē* [leading principle] of God, find our fulfillment in performing and by which we make our contribution to the splendour of the universe.
>
> (1992: 102)

Regrettably, the *Eudemian* version seems to have left us needing to speculate.

The question 'Which of these versions represents the considered opinion of their reputed author?' will continue to be disputed by scholars. Regardless of whether and how that question is to be settled, the two versions examined here represent interesting alternative outcomes of the attempt to deliberate about what for humans is living well, or what human flourishing is. The *Nicomachean* version offers a view from the perspective of human beings regarded as individuals. In the next chapter, we will see just how close it comes to the most self-consciously anti-public, anti-political of the ancient Hellenistic schools, that of Epicurus. The *Eudemian* version offers a view from the perspective of human beings as essentially social creatures. To wind up this chapter, it will be useful to compare its vision with that of a radically different culture and philosophical tradition. Confucianism did not pose its questions in anything like the form 'What is it for human beings to live well, to flourish?' but, as we will see, it contains sufficient material for an answer to be constructed.

9.4 A Confucian take on *eudaimonia*

Blending reason and ritual

Aristotle believed both that humans naturally form associations wider than families and close friendships and that the second of these contribute in important ways to the health of the wider associations (cities; *poleis*): 'For friendship we believe to be the greatest good of cities and what best preserves them against civil strife' (1262b7–8). Having allowed that the *eudaimonia* of a friend (of 'another self,' see Section 10.2) can contribute to one's own *eudaimonia*, Aristotle is certainly open to the claim that seeing one's city collectively do admirable things and contributing to the collective effort can be a constituent of one's own *eudaimonia*. In his *Politics*, Aristotle considers what it is for a city to qualify as *eudaimōn*, but apart from insisting that a *eudaimōn* city is one that is best and acts well (1323b30), we are not given much idea of what Aristotle would count as 'the good society.' We are told unequivocally that conquering and tyrannizing one's neighbors is no part of doing well (1324b23–41), but we are given no guidance regarding the extent to which erecting public buildings, staging festivals, providing amenities, is part of what it is for a city to do well. The picture of the texture of social life in what Aristotle would regard as an admirable city seems to consist of citizens deliberating as among friends about how their *polis* can achieve what is admirable and good. Perhaps this vagueness is the result of the room that these citizens need to determine through deliberating for themselves what that is.

The stress on ritual interaction in the Confucian tradition produces an interesting contrast. To draw it out requires addressing an Aristotelian question to the Confucian sources: what for a Confucian counts as *eudaimonia*?

Confucians would certainly be comfortable with Aristotle's ('humanist') assumption that the best that could be achieved by human action does not answer to any higher goal. Confucians do not look beyond human beings and their natural environment for sources of moral authority any more than did Aristotle.[13] Aristotle's chief device for clarifying human good is in terms of an account of human nature. This move is likewise accessible to Confucians. Hsün Tzu offers a sketch of a hierarchy of being – inanimate, plant, animal, human – that would be instantly recognizable to Aristotle (as well as to Hellenistic philosophers who came after him), even if accounts of how to characterize the stages would differ.

> Fire and water possess energy but are without life. Grass and trees have life but no intelligence. Birds and beasts have intelligence but no (sense of) righteousness (*yi*). Man possesses energy, life, intelligence, and in addition (a sense of) righteousness. Therefore he is the noblest being on earth.
>
> (Watson 1963–4: 45)

The crucial difference between animal and human, according to Aristotle, is *logos*, discursive thought. The crucial difference between animal and man, according to Hsün Tzu, is the possession of *yi*, (a sense of) what is right or righteous.

Logos is what Aristotle sees as the key to the sort of social formations characteristic of the human species. Hsün Tzu goes on from the lines quoted above to explain why humans are organized in a manner superior to other creatures. With *yi*, humans set up hierarchical divisions (accept lines of authority), which in turn create harmony and ensure (social) unity. In unity is strength; in strength lies the power to conquer all things. 'Thus men can dwell in security in their houses and halls. The reason that men are able to harmonize their actions with the order of the seasons, utilize all things, and bring universal profit to the world is simply this: they have established hierarchical divisions and possess *yi*.' The absence of *yi* leads to quarreling, chaos, fragmentation and weakness – Hsün Tzu moves immediately to link *yi* to *li* (ritual propriety), a pair (translated 'ritual principles' by Watson) that occurs frequently in the texts attributed to Hsün Tzu[14] – 'This is why I say that ritual principles must not be neglected even for a moment' (46).

Although Aristotle emphasizes *logos*, he sees this as linked to the very feature of human beings that for Hsün Tzu distinguishes them from animals. To quote again (see Section 8.4 under (3)) from the *Politics*, 'For what distinguishes human beings from the other animals is their having a perception of good and bad, right and wrong and the other [things of this sort], and the sharing of these makes a household and a city' (1253a16–18). However, Aristotle does not immediately go on to stress the importance of a hierarchy of authority or of any recognized forms of conduct that would keep a hierarchy firmly in place. Social unity is based on common conceptions of how to judge things and on the practice of deliberation in which those common conceptions are used to govern collaborative activity. Social unity in Hsün Tzu's Confucian conception of society is based on everyone knowing his or her place in a hierarchy and employing a grammar of conduct, referred to as *li–yi*, that facilitates interaction between levels.

> He who can follow them (*li–yi*) in serving his parents is called filial; he who can follow them in serving his elder brothers is called brotherly. He who can follow them in serving his superiors is called obedient; he who can follow them in employing his inferiors is called a ruler.
>
> (*ibid.*)

But what is the point of following *li–yi*? Does doing so serve some further purpose?

One might, from reading more of the passage from Hsün Tzu, take away the impression that sustaining the material conditions for a comfortable existence was the ultimate point of observing *li–yi* and being hierarchically organized. Planting and cutting, breeding the six domestic animals, exploiting forests and fish stocks, cannot be properly co-ordinated except by 'one who is good at organizing men in society.' Prosperity (the argument appears to be) cannot be sustained for very long without careful governance of wider society; individuals or groups who cannot see how their conceptions of their material interests need to be subordinated within a wider framework are showing their inability to function above the level of animals.

This expectation that a ruler should promote the conditions for the material prosperity of his subjects is thoroughly Confucian, although Confucius also expressed a 'man does not live by bread alone' sentiment:

> Tzu-kung asked about government. Confucius said, 'Sufficient food, sufficient armament, and sufficient confidence of the people.' Tzu-kung said, 'forced to give up one of these, which would you abandon first?' Confucius said, 'I would abandon the armament.' Tzu-kung said, 'Forced to give up one of the remaining two, which would you abandon first?' Confucius said, 'I would abandon food. There have been deaths from time immemorial, but no state can exist without the confidence of the people.'
>
> (Chan 1963: XII.7)

The order of priorities that this reflects is important, and the concept translated as 'confidence' (Lau: 'trust') needs to be understood as more than a *feeling* that subjects should have for their ruler. Throughout the *Analects*, would-be rulers and superior men are advised to adhere to *li*: observe propriety, set a good example and the people will be easy to govern (e.g. XIV.41) and will flourish (e.g. I.9). The confidence or trust that people need is in their whole social environment. Confucius makes it sound (as in XII.7) like this confidence relates only to the ruler, because he is answering a question about governing, but he also believes that the ruler is principally responsible for general social well-being.

Does it follow that if almost everything people do is a manifestation of (ritual) patterns recognizable to other people, there will be throughout society a feeling of trust or confidence? Obviously not; knowing what to expect is not the same thing as being confident in the sense used to translate the Chinese. Does it follow that if such patterns keep people mindful of their position in a social hierarchy at all times, they will have confidence or trust? Obviously not; knowing one's place may only initiate profound mistrust. Somehow, the ritual forms must express and continually reinforce a message of mutual trust, particularly between those who stand as governor and governed.

Asked (XV.24) to provide a single word to guide conduct, Confucius offered *shu*, which Chan translates as 'altruism' and Lau leaves untranslated but with the gloss 'using oneself as a measure in gauging the wishes of others.'[15] Confucius' own gloss on *shu* in this passage comes out as what is sometimes called 'the negative formulation of the golden rule,' *viz.* 'Do not impose on others what you yourself do not desire.' Similar advice appears as part of what it takes to be a humane person (*jen*, XII.2). Asked (VI.30) whether someone who benefited the common people on a grand scale would be regarded as a humane person, Confucius was prepared to go one better and call such a person a sage. What the humane person (*jen*) can aim for, if not philanthropy on a grand scale, is this: 'wishing to establish his own character, [he] also establishes the character of others, and wishing to be prominent himself, [he] also helps others to be prominent. To be able to judge others by what is near to ourselves may be called the method of realizing humanity (*jen*)' (Chan 1963). Lau (1979) translates without the connotations of social advancement: 'helps others to take a stand in so far as he himself wishes to take a stand, and gets others there in so far as he himself wishes to get there,' and he translates the 'method' of the second sentence just quoted as 'the ability to take as analogy what is near at hand,' which he glosses in a note: '*viz.* oneself.' Waley (1938) translates 'you yourself desire rank and standing, then help others to get rank and standing. You want to turn your own merits to account; then help others to turn theirs to account – in fact the ability to take one's own feelings as a guide – that is the sort of thing that lies in the direction of Goodness [= *jen*].' This is close to a positive formulation of the golden rule: 'as ye would that men should do to you, do ye also to them likewise' (Luke 6: 31).

237

From this we might plausibly infer that what a Confucian would offer, as an analysis of what (in Greek) should be meant by a life that is *eudaimōn*, is this: living in a secure social environment in which people's confidence is constantly reinforced by the message communicated from others that those who are established (have a place to stand) wish them to be established (have a place to stand) and that those who are improving their own lot wish them to improve their own lot. Confucius and his followers believed that this could not be achieved without thoroughly structuring social interaction by means of a ritualized sense of propriety. The expression 'establish [oneself]' ('take a stand') is twice connected essentially to the *li* (VIII.8, XVI.13).

The image of *li* as a kind of grammar of action can be usefully unpacked at this point. When a language forms its sentences in different ways depending on whether one, two or more items of a kind are being discussed, when a language marks whether an action is to be viewed as ongoing or as a point in time, when a language distinguishes whether men or women are being discussed (and treats indeterminate or mixed groups as consisting entirely of men), the awareness of its speakers is shaped accordingly. A culture that expects people to quicken their step when passing those to whom respect should be shown, that requires large investments of resources to mark certain transitions (of life, of seasons), that requires certain postures, kinds of dress, facial expressions to match occasions, will likewise shape the awareness of its people.[16]

In response to the sort of question that would naturally occur to a Greek philosopher, 'what is *li* the means of achieving?' one very plausible Confucian answer is 'to achieve that climate of confidence or trust that is perhaps even more important to people (in so far as they are human beings) than being well fed.' Is *li* an instrumental or a constitutive means to this end? If the former, then one might imagine achieving this trust or confidence without *li* or with a radically different emphasis on *li*. But if ritualized forms are distinctively characteristic of human life, any other way of achieving this trust or confidence might well be argued by Confucians to amount to a failure to promote our humanity.

Animal ethologists do speak of rituals (of courtship, etc.); these, however, are instinctive (pre-programmed or 'hard-wired'). Humans have to rely on representing to themselves how ritual is to be conducted. Here the well-known aphorism by Kant quoted in Section 7.4 is applicable, provided that the second occurrence of 'law' is interpreted broadly enough to cover representations of how ritual should be carried out. 'Everything in nature works in accordance with laws. Only a rational being has the power to act *in accordance with his ideas* (*nach der Vorstellung*, literally: in accordance with the representation) of laws.' It then becomes clear that distinctively human rituals, depending as they do on representation, depend essentially on the human capacity for what the Greeks

238

called *logos*, even if the discursive practices of classical Greece and China were very different.

Could humans engage both in the practices of discursive thought that generate a sense of rational appropriateness and in ritual practices that sustain a sense of social propriety? Is there any reason why one of these accounts should be emphasized to the exclusion of the other? Could we deliberate fruitfully about adjustments needed in any prevailing sense of social propriety? Can we indeed deliberate fruitfully about anything unless our interactions with one another (especially when 'taking counsel' or consulting, i.e. considering together what is to be done) are governed by forms of social propriety? (Minimally, we rely on the rules of parliamentary procedure, Robert's Rules of Order, but doing so does not guarantee that any genuine deliberation takes place.) Might a *phronimos* who looked at the traditions of China have to acknowledge the importance of ritual forms? Might the true sage, having studied the philosophy of ancient Greece, have to acknowledge the importance of deliberation? Viewed at a very high level of abstraction, the two traditions seem merely to have emphasized different but equally important features of what it is to live a characteristically human life, and a synthesis of both accounts, one that improves on each, seems possible.

However, the possibility rests on a significant assumption shared by the two traditions about the value of community life – even if the forms of community in classical Greece and China were very different – as an indispensable part of what it is for humans to live well, to flourish. It might be argued that we would find it difficult to blend ritual and deliberation in this way because of the 'watershed' that our culture crossed in the seventeenth century. There certainly are critics, identified as 'communitarians,' who complain that we have lost the assumption of the value of community life (*communitas*) and live poorer lives because we understand our relations to one another strictly in terms of association (*societas*). People enter associations only to further their individual interests; collective goals have only instrumental value for the individuals involved, and only so long as their individual interests are served.

It is difficult to determine how much of the 'communitarian' critique is the result of exaggeration. Political theories can certainly be identified that have been based on the assumption of 'social atomism', *viz.* that humans enter society with their identities and interests already formed. Even if the implausibility of this assumption remains unacknowledged, it is hard to say how deeply our social practices have changed in the past three to four centuries. To be sure, we have come to rely increasingly on contractual relationships and rule-governed institutions instead of assessments of character and general trust in the social order. Whether that means we have no place in our lives for, and are incapable of, finding personal fulfillment in the success of a collective venture – whether that means (the question at the beginning of this section) that seeing our cities or states collectively do admirable things, and contributing to the collective effort cannot be a constituent of our *eudaimonia* – are not obviously rhetorical questions easily answered by 'of course not.'

Part of the difficulty is that unsophisticated 'communitarian' critics do not appreciate the extent to which conflicts in our society, although often framed in the rhetoric of the individual versus the state, are in fact conflicts between groups (or between the group identities of the individuals in conflict). There are, largely unremarked, rituals (the full range of social phenomena to which the Chinese word *li* would apply) that hold such groups together. If the social cohesiveness of some more comprehensive group needs to be improved, it needs its own rituals to be given an importance that overrides that of less comprehensive groups, as the emperor's rituals (and the corresponding loyalties) were to take precedence over those of families. On the whole, 'communitarian' critics do not address the relevant social mechanisms.

Two common assumptions further confuse the issues. The first is that the personal and the collective are mutually exclusive goals, that individuals cannot take a personal interest in the collective success of a collective enterprise. The second is that individuals entering collective enterprises (with private interests) cannot and do not modify their conceptions of their own interests and come to identify their personal interests with the success of the collective. When explicitly stated, these assumptions do not have a great deal of plausibility.

This is not to say that fairly narrow private interests cannot stand in sharp tension with more comprehensive collective interests. This tension, however, is not something that has arisen only in the wake of the seventeenth century. It is hard to say if any of Aristotle's contemporaries would have openly challenged the claim of the collective interests of their respective *poleis*, although within a generation of Aristotle's death there was a philosophical school in Athens ready to make this challenge. The founder of the school, Epicurus, whose views will be the subject of the first section of the next chapter, was also eager to claim a more dominant role for pleasure enjoyed privately (albeit with one's friends) in the account of what it is to live well. If there has come to be more tension between the private and public since the seventeenth century, the challenge of Epicurus may well prove to have more resonance with current attitudes than the views we have hitherto considered.

Further reading

For a strict deontological approach to ethics, see Fried (1978); and for a less strict approach see Scheffler (1982). Dancy (1993) also counts as a deontological approach. For a useful collection of articles on the dispute between consequentialist and deontological approaches, see Scheffler (1988). For Aristotle on *eudaimonia* and deliberative rationality, see Ackrill (1974), Wiggins (1978) and Nussbaum (1986: chapters 10 and 11); for Aristotle's use of the concept of the *ergon* of man, see Nagel (1972) and Wilkes (1978). For a sympathetic treatment of Aristotle on contemplation, see Rorty (1978). For a comprehensive treatment of the aspects of Aristotle's philosophy touched on in this chapter, see Cooper (1975) and for another, this one with attention paid to the differences between the two versions of the *Ethics*, see Kenny (1992). (For Hsün Tzu and Confucius, see on Confucians in the further reading for Chapter 8.) Mulhall and Swift (1992) collect what they identify as communitarian critics of John Rawls' liberal theory of justice (see Section 6.4). Avineri and de-Shalit (1992) is another useful collection of articles on communitarianism, its targets and its opponents, and Bell (1993) is a treatise on the same in dialogue form.

Notes

1 'Standard' translates '*horos*'; see Section 4.2.
2 Some crucial points in this chapter will turn on the differences between the two versions of Aristotle's *Ethics*. The two versions share three books, 'the common books' (*Nicomachean* V, VI, VII = *Eudemian* IV, V, VI). The *Nicomachean* has long been assumed to be the more mature and authoritative version, although this assumption has occasionally been challenged. A recent modest challenge to the preference given to the *Nicomachean* version was mounted by Anthony Kenny, who argued that the common books originated in and were more integral to the argument of the *Eudemian* version. For a retrospective look at how his challenge was received, see Kenny (1992: Appendix I).
3 According to Mautner (1996: respective entries), 'deontology' was coined by Jeremy Bentham (late eighteenth to early nineteenth centuries) to mean 'science of morality.' 'Teleology' was coined by the early eighteenth-century German philosopher Christian Wolff for any matter pertaining to purposiveness. 'Consequentialism' was coined by Elizabeth Anscombe in 1958 for the doctrine that people are responsible for the foreseen but unintended consequences of their actions and was subsequently applied where 'utilitarianism' had been common. Specific 'utilitarian' doctrines will be discussed in Chapter 10.
4 The etymology of *eudaimonia* is 'having a good *daimon*,' that is a good personal minor deity (not unlike a guardian angel or fairy godmother) to look after one. Aristotle sometimes (e.g. 1098a19) couples the adjective *eudaimōn* with another, *makarios*, which means 'blessed,' 'fortunate.' (Whether fortune has been kind to someone is another dimension of assessment that we treat as external or objective.) When *eudaimonia* and *makariotēs* are distinguished, it is in cases where, lacking in good fortune, an excellent person does as well as can be done with limited resources (e.g. 1100b35–1101a8), and hence is *eudaimōn* but not *makarios*.
5 This illustration is taken from Ackrill (1974: 15ff).
6 This terminology was introduced by Hardie (1965).
7 The *Nicomachean* version speaks of the *ergon* of a human being (1097b31), but it is clear from the discussion that Aristotle is considering the *ergon* of the human being *qua* living, hence of the human soul (*psuchē* = what makes a living thing alive). The *Eudemian* version speaks of the *ergon* of the soul (1219a24), specifically the human soul (1219b38).

8 It is, however, traditional to interpret the activity itself as non-discursive, as the intuitive appreciation of the splendor of the highest things from the clarity of the view afforded by our theories. Moreover, it is assumed to be as difficult to articulate and communicate as the grasp that a mathematician seeks of the whole of a proof once the sequence of steps has been followed one by one.

9 'Someone thinks he will do well if he spends his life in scientific research; to do this he must have leisure; to get the money for his living expenses he does a disgraceful but not time-consuming thing: one great fraud' (Anscombe 1965: 65).

10 See *Politics* 1253a2–18 (quoted in Section 8.4 under (3)) and *Nicomachean Ethics* 1097b8–11 (quoted in Section 9.1).

11 The interpretation here follows that of Kenny (1992: 16–19).

12 The word for 'and' merges with the word for 'good,' and the concept appears in the texts as a variety of fused words: *kalos kai agathos* becomes *kalos kagathos*, (adjective, 'admirable and -good') to *kalon kagathon*, (noun phrase, 'the admirable and -good') *hē kalokagathia* (substantive, 'admirable-and-good-ness'). These were common Greek expressions applied, sometimes with a touch of irony, to recognized worthies; compare the English expressions 'the great and the good' and 'the beautiful people'.

13 Although his use of 'humanism' is not spelled out directly in terms of the assumption attributed here to Aristotle, Chan Wing-tsit (1963) is able to title his chapter of selections from the *Analects* 'The Humanism of Confucius' partly because human good is in effect treated in Confucian thought as not answering to any wider constraint.

14 'In Hsün Tzu, for example, more than a third of the occurrences of *yi* are in the binomial expression of *li–yi*' (Hall and Ames 1987: 98).

15 In two passages of the *Analects*, Confucius claims that there is a single thread binding his thought together; in one, a trusted disciple explains in his absence that the thread consists of being conscientious (*chung*) and in *shu* (IV.15; cf. XV.3). See note 10 to Chapter 8 on *chung* as parallel to Kant's good will, and compare '*Chung* is the doing of one's best and it is through *chung* that one puts into effect what one has found out by the method of *shu*' (Lau 1979: 16).

16 *Cf.* the thesis of Jonathan Z. Smith that ritual is a 'mode of paying attention' and of 'having attention focused,' Section 2.2 and note 4 to Chapter 2.

10

PLEASURE AS THE MEASURE

> For we recognize pleasure as the good which is primary and congenital; from it we begin every choice and avoidance, and we come back to it, using the feeling as the yardstick (*kanōn*) for judging every good thing.
>
> (Epicurus (third century BCE): LS 21B2)[1]

> ... in the civil state [a man acquires] moral liberty, which alone makes man truly the master of himself. For to be driven by appetite alone is slavery, and obedience to the law one has prescribed for oneself is liberty.
>
> (Jean-Jacques Rousseau 1762: 27)

Recapitulation: To possess genuinely admirable qualities of character, according to Aristotle's account, a person's responses have to be able to be connected properly via deliberative reasoning to an adequate concept of what it is that constitutes living well for a human being. The word *eudaimonia* represents this concept in Greek, and Aristotle proposed to assess the claims of different ways of life to realize *eudaimonia* by reference to the unique role of discursive thought (*logos*) in human life. Aristotle's own texts, however, are ambivalent toward the question of whether *eudaimonia* should include scope for the exercise of many excellences or was to be achieved by maximizing the time spent on a single supremely valuable activity. The line of thought that proceeded through the second of these alternatives, which was developed in the *Nicomachean Ethics*, did not appear able to ensure anything more than an instrumental role for ethical excellences and opened up the possibility that the supremely valuable activity it identified, contemplation, might justify conduct and qualities of character that were arguably anything but admirable. To develop a more satisfactory account, it seemed, Aristotle should have given more attention to another feature that he explicitly associated with the nature of human beings (and with their capacity for discursive thought): their need to carry out part of their lives in public activities. The account developed in the other version of the *Ethics* generally made more room for ethical excellences and, in common

243

with classical Confucian thinkers, allowed for the importance of social relations in its account of human flourishing.

Prospectus: The Epicurean school of Athens (established not long after Aristotle's death) stood as a challenge – as much by the way of life its members followed as by the teachings of their founder – to the claim that humans are by nature animals that find (at least part of their) fulfillment in civic life. Epicurus advised against participation in public affairs as a consequence of applying the measure ('straightedge') that formed the centerpiece of his doctrines, *viz.* that humans could be counted as living well precisely to the extent that they experienced pleasure and avoided pain. These guiding experiences are personal, private and peculiar to individuals, and applied at the level of individuals they constitute a highly variable standard. Epicurus admitted that the experience of pleasure could be enhanced by sharing with others, and the possibility that people can enlarge their conceptions of their own personal fulfillments to include the well-being of others suggests that the difference between self-regarding concerns and other-regarding concerns is neither sharp nor difficult to bridge. How far we each ought to enlarge our personal concerns, however, is not easy to determine. Theorists who have insisted that we must extend them to everyone tend to overlook the values realized by partiality. Some have insisted that our moral concerns must extend beyond the human species to all sentient creatures.

10.1   The protean standard of hedonism

Whose pleasures? Which assessment of risk?

Sixteen years after Aristotle's death, a native of the island of Samos in his mid-thirties named Epicurus bought a house and garden in Athens and with a circle of friends embarked on a quiet, private life free from involvement in civic affairs. He offered a carefully articulated philosophical position in support of this way of life. This included a comprehensive theory of nature and of the gods, a theory which he believed removed much of the basis for the fears and superstitions that haunted the lives of ordinary people. But he offered this theory not as the object of the sort of contemplation that made for a fulfilled human life but as the instrument for removing psychological states that might detract from the true aim of life, which was the very ordinary pleasures that could be experienced in a tranquil life.[2]

When we say that pleasure is the end, we do not mean the pleasures of the dissipated and those that consist in having a good

244

time, as some out of ignorance and disagreement or refusal to understand suppose we do, but freedom from pain in the body and from disturbance in the soul. For what produces the pleasant life is not continuous drinking and parties or pederasty or womanizing or the enjoyment of fish and the other dishes of an expensive table, but sober reasoning which tracks down the causes of every choice and avoidance, and which banishes the opinions that beset souls with the greatest confusion.

(LS 21B5)

Pleasure was, as Epicurus put it, the straightedge (yardstick, *kanōn*; see first quotation at the head of this chapter), simultaneously the end for which we should (rationally) aim and the standard of value to be used in making our judgments about what to do.

Placed against this criterion, it was clear to him that one should be law-abiding, not because by itself being so gave one a better life but because breaking the law risked retaliation from people (LS 22A5), which in turn jeopardized, in a way that simply was not worth the risk, one's prospects for a life of pleasures enjoyed in tranquility. Such excellences of character as one needed to live this quiet, private life were, as one of his opponents, a Stoic named Cleanthes, put it (21O), mere handmaidens to pleasure. Indeed, Epicurus assigns a role to what he calls *phronēsis*, which like Aristotle he treats as the chief virtue and source of all other virtues. But instead of making *phronēsis* subservient to theoretical wisdom, or to the exercise of theoretical wisdom in contemplation, he makes it entirely subservient to living pleasurably as he understood it (21B6). In the *Nicomachean Ethics*, Aristotle recommended philosophical contemplation because it exercises the characteristic human capacity on the best possible object, making it the activity most worthy of human beings, but he also insisted that it is an enjoyable thing to do. Epicurus made no distinctions in terms of what is worthwhile; if it is enjoyable and will not reduce your prospects for further enjoyment, then it is a constituent of your *eudaimonia*.

Aristotle had dismissed the view of those who identified pleasure as the good that belongs to human beings, because pleasure is something that we share with other creatures. But Epicurus could easily reply that he was recommending a perspective on pleasure (the use of pleasure as a *kanōn*) that was possible only for a human being. All animate creatures make efforts to adjust their relations to the environment (heat loss, oxygen intake) and seek to undergo certain kinds of process (ingesting food, engaging in reproductive activities); they also exhibit aversions to undergoing certain processes. What an animal avoids is taken to be uncomfortable, distressing or painful for it; what an animal seeks is taken to be comfortable, enjoyable or pleasurable for it. For the most part, these responses are to fairly immediate stimuli. What makes this kind of seeking and avoiding distinctively human is that humans are able to represent to themselves the connections between events and to time their responses in order to secure and avoid what lies at some distance in the future. They are also able to represent their lives as a whole and to weigh the consequences of actions (pursuits and aversions) for the overall pattern of experiences, those that they prefer to undergo and those that they prefer to avoid.

The word 'weigh' in the last sentence involves the metaphor of standards and measurement, which we have been following through a variety of traditions. In this case, the metaphor is anchored to the fact that faced with alternative turns of events people can say of each considered in isolation which they prefer to undergo. With a further exercise of imagination, they can consider each as a package of consequences both short- and long-term and say which total package they would prefer to undergo. It often takes an effort of imagination to make the latter sort of comparison, as well as efforts to discipline one's habits of response and to endure some short-term discomforts in order to find and follow a course of action that will have better overall prospects of comfort and enjoyment and fewer of pain and distress. Thus one may invest time comparing retirement plans, resolve to give up smoking or steel oneself for a trip to the dentist.

Rational hedonism (from Greek *hēdonē*, pleasure) recommends the policy of making the effort to find and adopt the course of action with maximal prospects of comfort, enjoyment and pleasure and minimal prospects for pain, distress and discomfort. One can, of course, not trouble to make the effort of imagination and simply respond, as an animal does, to immediate prospects without giving thought to or having concern for long-term consequences. This might be called 'hedonism of the present moment.'

There are also those who find the effort involved in rational hedonism and its effects (e.g. the realization of the possibility that one may unavoidably find oneself in a no-win situation) to be an overwhelming source of distress. As a consequence, these people recommend 'living for today' as the best policy. They may envy, and recommend the life of, those who never develop much of their human capacity for appreciating long-term consequences and for controlling their current actions accordingly. The conclusion they reach is in effect that rational hedonism, if thought out carefully and consistently, reduces to hedonism of the present moment. From the standpoint of someone who believes that what is distinctive about human beings is their ability to use discursive thought to control their actions, to recommend hedonism of the present moment is to recommend abandoning an important part of one's humanity.

However, it is quite unfair to suggest that anyone who offers to explain what it is for a human to do or live well in terms of pleasure and the avoidance of distress is thinking only in terms of hedonism of the present moment. Epicurus held that in general mental distress (fear, apprehension) could well be worse than bodily distress (21**R**2) – the resulting insecurity is the reason Epicurus gave for not preying upon one's neighbors (22**A**5) – but he did not for that reason recommend living for today. His rational hedonism required constant mindfulness of the consequences of one's actions and habits. This is obviously not a life that could be sought without an investment of discursive thought.

Epicurus offered an image of this life as sober, frugal, restrained, aiming more at avoiding distress than seeking exhilaration or euphoria. Although his recommendation of this life was based on the idea that alternatives would yield more distress and less enjoyment overall, there is no attempt, the metaphors of standards notwithstanding, to quantify pleasure and justify his recommendations on the basis of anything like numerical calculation. Determining what to do or how to live on the basis of measuring and calculating the pleasures and pains that would result from different options is an idea that pre-dates Epicurus – it appears, for example, in a dialogue, the *Protagoras*, which Plato wrote before Epicurus was born – but the conceptions of measurement and calculation involved were probably no more sophisticated than what would have been used on a building site.

It may well have taken developments in commerce (double-entry book-keeping) and natural science (mathematical physics) before someone like Jeremy Bentham, who lived in the late eighteenth and early nineteenth centuries, could see and take seriously the possibility of the elaborate sort of reckoning that would deserve to be called 'a calculus of pleasure and pain.' The image of numerical assignments and computations of the sort that we make in engineering, however, encounters a number of conceptual difficulties. Bentham himself appreciated what is known as the 'law of diminishing returns,' which is illustrated by the familiar observation that twice as long of the same pleasurable activity or twice as much of the same pleasurable food is often not twice as pleasurable. The mathematics of measurement, however, commonly relies on the principle (known as the Archimedean axiom) that where one quantity is less than another, there is a finite number by which one can multiply the smaller so that it exceeds the latter. If 'returns' are diminishing, there may be no finite number of the lesser quantity that will as an aggregate exceed the greater.

'Quantity' is used here to refer to a measurable thing, an object with a length or weight – or a pleasurable or painful experience, if the notion of measuring pleasure and pain is to make sense – rather than a numerical value. (The term 'magnitude' may be used for the numerical value assigned to a quantity.) 'Multiplying' quantities by n means adding (aggregating) n things with the same magnitude. Mathematicians have acquired an interest in the consequences of suspending important axioms, e.g. in geometry, and doubtless find non-Archimedean measures interesting, but it is far from clear that any practice that might be built on such a concept of measure would provide a basis for the kind of adjudication that we are seeking. The problems raised in the next paragraph, however, render even this question otiose.

Familiar measuring practices also assume that any two (would-be) quantities are comparable, either greater than or less than or equal, and that equal quantities are for the purposes of the measuring practice indistinguishable and may be substituted one for another. Neither of these assumptions is secure when it comes to the things we undergo that we regard as pleasures, enjoyments, comforts, pains, distresses or discomforts. There are definitely circumstances in which we are clear which of two alternatives is going to yield more of what we want or do not want, but there are many circumstances in which the attempt to compare seems out of place and the fact that we would not rate one of them as offering more of what we want in no way warrants treating the two as interchangeable.

The reason for this was noted by Aristotle. Pleasure is not one thing; pleasures differ in kind depending on the kind of thing that is found to be enjoyable. This for Aristotle was a consequence of his theory that pleasure 'completed' an activity, and since in general different things are completed in different ways it is hardly surprising that the pleasures that are derived from different activities are very different (1175a21–b23). But the observation does not require the support of theory; the pleasure of tasting ripe raspberries is as unlike that of hiking in the mountains as the two activities are unlike one another. The idea that one could compare the pleasures involved and decide whether one is greater than the other reduces to whether people are able to say they have a preference for one over the other. Now when we talk about pleasure in the abstract, it is made to sound like something objective that can be measured; preferences, on the other hand, obviously depend on whose preferences are in question and often on the transient circumstances that people find themselves in. Someone feeling restless and overfed would prefer a hike in the mountains; someone physically exhausted and in need of refreshment would clearly prefer a serving of raspberries.

There are also differences in preferences that emerge if we factor out the effects of special circumstances. All things being equal, some people would prefer to eat more and some would prefer to be more active; the former are said to take more pleasure in eating, the latter to take more pleasure in activity. It depends on the sort of people they are. This is another point that Aristotle made. What people enjoy or find distressing is a sign of their states of character (*hexeis*). People who are self-controlled are more comfortable abstaining from excessive eating, drinking or sex and find it annoying if for some reason they are obliged to participate (to the same degree) in activities that self-indulgent people relish. Likewise, a brave man finds danger less distressing than a coward (1104b4–10). The reason for this is that preference, and consequently what people enjoy or find distressing, is a function of habituation. Many tastes are 'acquired'; many aversions are 'grown out of.'

Another aspect of Aristotle's theory, that pleasure is or arises in unimpeded activity (1153a15), explains this. The more people do something and become habituated to it, the easier they will find it (the less impeded they will be in doing it) and consequently there is a greater chance they will enjoy doing it. But again there is no need for theory to support the claim that what people enjoy or find distressing depends on the sort of people they are, or the sort of people they have become through habituation. This observation could provide a basis for Aristotle to raise a much more telling objection against Epicurus. Pleasure is not in fact a stable *kanōn*; if taken as a *kanōn* it will have one shape when the preferences of some individuals are taken into account, other shapes when other people's preferences are taken into account. If this is to amount to more than the 'every man is the measure' doctrine attributed to Protagoras by Plato (see Section 5.1), the question that needs to be addressed is, '*whose* pleasures are to be the measure?'

Some people derive pleasure from robbing or intimidating their fellow human beings. Epicurus believed that individuals who gratify themselves in this way are very likely to be made so miserable by the people they prey upon that they will not count their earlier enjoyments as worth the cost. It is not clear that this will always be the case; some scoundrels will, after pleasures purchased at their neighbors' expense – and enjoyed in some considerable measure *because* they are at their neighbors' expense – derive enough enjoyment (however perverse) from defying their neighbors' best efforts to exact vengeance as to make the package seem worthwhile. Epicurus believed that no pleasures purchased through injustice could make up for the fear of what will be done to one by those who have cause to exact vengeance, but some people find that risk adds interest and increases the enjoyment, rather than the distress, that they derive from what they do.

Epicurus in effect held the measure to be not pleasure so much as the person who can enjoy sober conviviality, frugal comfort and private (rather than public) preoccupations. People who are not habituated to enjoy this kind of life would be told that they are confused; they are not getting as favorable a balance of pleasure over pain as life can afford. But the pleasures people derive and the distress they experience is in large measure a function of what they are habituated to do. On what basis can it be said that with different habituation they will experience less discomfort, distress or pain and have more comfort, enjoyment or pleasure? The Epicurean life involves suppressing impulses not only to overindulge in food, drink and sex but also to seek public recognition. There will be some discomfort, not to say distress, in reaching a point where living like this becomes easy and enjoyable; that is to say, most people are not content living as Epicurus recommended without first undergoing some form of discipline.

But if people can come to enjoy a lifestyle in which these otherwise natural impulses are severely curtailed, could they not habituate themselves to very different lifestyles and simply learn to live with whatever frustrations this entailed? People might choose a life (of sensual pleasure, fame, power) involving risks that Epicurus deemed to be too great. They could allow the risks involved to intensify whatever satisfactions such a career entailed and live with the frustrations in the same way that Epicurus is reported to have lived with great physical discomforts in old age – by concentrating on the memory of past pleasurable experiences (24**D**). Could we say that this attitude (toward sensual pleasure, fame, power) would lead to a less pleasurable life overall than one centered on simple meals and small talk with a circle of friends? If a person took more pleasure in working to benefit other people than in the security derived from staying out of the public gaze, more pleasure in playing a musical instrument extremely well than in a secure economic future, or more pleasure in reaching a profound level of understanding nature than in small talk, might we not raise questions about which were better things to enjoy? What humans *actually do* enjoy is, after all, in some measure a matter of choice. It is true that what we *are able to come to* enjoy is given to us as part of our (individual or species) nature, but in recommending his preferred lifestyle Epicurus tended to obscure this important difference by suggesting that what we do enjoy is what is given to us as part of our nature.

The claim that there are better and worse things to enjoy (or 'higher and lower pleasures') seemed to the nineteenth-century philosopher John Stuart Mill both obvious and the most effective way to defend his own hedonism-based ethics against the charge that it was 'a doctrine worthy only of swine' (1861: 282). Mill located himself (280) within an intellectual tradition stretching from Epicurus to Bentham (his father's close friend) and insisted that 'there is no known Epicurean theory of life which does not assign to the pleasures of the intellect, of the feelings and imagination, and of the moral sentiments, a much higher value as pleasure than to those of mere sensation' (282).[3] Mill based his claim on the preferences for what he regarded as 'higher pleasures' that he believed would be displayed by 'those who are competently acquainted with both' (283). For 'it is an unquestionable fact, that those who are equally acquainted with and equally capable of appreciating and enjoying both do give a most marked preference to the manner of existence which employs their higher faculties' (*ibid.*).

Not everyone 'equally acquainted' was 'equally capable,' however. Mill entertained an objection to the effect that 'infirmity of character' (284), specifically 'indolence' and 'selfishness' (285), might render one unfit to appreciate the higher pleasures. His defense was that no one ever chose thus to become incapable of enjoying the higher things, but he allowed that 'Capacity for the nobler feelings is in most natures a very tender plant, easily killed, not only by hostile influences but by mere want of sustenance' (*ibid.*). In other words, competence is a matter of habituation, not merely of trying two things and finding one more agreeable than the other. Indeed, the habituation required is one that, as Aristotle would have insisted, reflects one's character. Why does 'a being of higher faculties . . . never really wish to sink into what he feels to be a lower grade of existence' (283)? Mill entertained a variety of explanations based on character, 'pride,' 'love of liberty,' 'love of power,' 'love of excitement' and offered his own, 'a sense of dignity' (284). The measure in Mill, even more obviously than in Epicurus, is not pleasure but the person of good character.

10.2   Private pleasures and public responsibilities

Selves, friends and fellow citizens

Epicurean aspirations were for a life with as little discomfort and as much innocuous pleasure as could be managed. Excellences of character, in particular the chief excellence of *phronēsis*, were to be cultivated and exercised precisely to the extent that they contributed to the realization of that aspiration. Aristotle had in the *Nicomachean Ethics* a loftier aspiration. Although he believed that contemplation afforded the highest type of pleasure available to a human being, this was because it was pleasure in a far more worthwhile activity. But the consequences of his lofty aspiration were disturbing because it appeared that as a result of giving it the attention it deserved, the cultivation and exercise of the ethical excellences, including that of *phronēsis*, would be left only with the role of making sure that one's life would provide maximum opportunity for that activity.

It needs to be stressed that neither Aristotle nor Epicurus imagined that individuals seeking *eudaimonia* would try to do so on their own. However unconvincing Aristotle's argument for the status of friendships as necessary constituents of *eudaimonia* may appear (end of Section 9.2), it is clear (1169b33–4) that he regarded a life devoted to contemplation as involving close relationships with other human beings. But the social circle needed to sustain this appears rather similar to that which Epicurus assumed would be necessary to experience a maximum of the innocuous pleasures that life affords.

Epicurus is even more emphatic than Aristotle on the importance of having friends if one is to live well: 'Of the things wisdom acquires for the blessedness of life as a whole, by far the greatest is the possession of friendship' (22E1; see also 22F5, 7). And Aristotle's remark that living together for human beings means more than, as in the case of cattle, feeding in the same place (1170b11–12; quoted at the end of Section 9.2) should be considered alongside the remark attributed to Epicurus by Seneca: 'you should be more concerned at inspecting with whom you eat and drink, than what you eat and drink. For feeding without a friend is the life of a lion or a wolf' (LS 22I).[4]

Relationships with friends, along with family ties, constitute private life. 'Private' has its roots in the Latin word *privus*, meaning 'each single' (*cf.* Greek *idios*, from which we have 'idiosyncracy,' 'idiotic') and traditionally stood in opposition to the public. But the original conception of the private affairs of an individual involved a family (its economic survival and its ancestral cult) or any other people that an individual found it agreeable to pass the time among (friends).

The idea that social relations of all kinds are inessential to being human – that you can associate with others if you want, but you could as easily do without – would have struck ancient thinkers as bizarre. Aristotle's attitude to those who live without others is clear:

> And one who by nature and not through fortune is without a city is either better than a human being or (like the 'tribeless, lawless, homeless one' condemned by Homer, at the same time naturally outcast and belligerent) worthless, like an isolated piece on a board game.
>
> (1253a3–6)

It is only in recent centuries, with the rise of the 'partnership' (*societas*) concept of human relations (see Section 7.1), that it has become common to attempt to conceive human individuals in isolation from all social roles and relationships.[5]

For all his emphasis on the importance of friends, there are important questions to be raised about the status of friendship in Epicurus: for example, if pleasure is the sole end in life, can friendship have any status other than as instrumental means to pleasurable experiences? The implication would be that once people offer no prospect of affording you pleasure, there ceases to be any reason for treating them as friends. Aristotle's analysis of friendship affords a different view of the implications of Epicurus's position.

In his *Rhetoric*, Aristotle defines a friend (*philos*) as one 'who loves and is loved in return' and defines love (*philein*) as 'wishing for anyone the things which we believe to be good, for his sake, but not for our own, and obtaining those things for him as far as it lies in our power' (1380b36–81a2). In the *Nicomachean Ethics*, Aristotle indicates that there are three main reasons why people come to wish well of each other: they find each other pleasant, useful or good (1155b19). Friendships based on the first of these – on a mutual appreciation of each other as a source of pleasure, comfort or agreeable experiences – are common among young people and if based on nothing else are fairly transient. Friendships based on the second are the foundation of business partnerships. Aristotle regards those based on the third as final (complete, perfect, *teleia*; 1156b5) friend-ships. Insofar as all three relationships involve wishing friends to have what is good and trying to see that they get it, the *eudaimonia* of each person becomes a constituent of what that person's friend regards as the chief good in life. When people do well (fare well) or get what their friends regard as good, this becomes part of their friends' fulfillment. This is what lies behind the remark at 1170b7: 'a friend is another self.'

Whether or not other people and their welfare are necessary constituents of *eudaimonia*, the possibility that other people *may* function as constituents in a person's *eudaimonia* is itself extremely interesting and important. Whatever we may do to help our friends will be done as much for ourselves as for them; if we have stable conceptions of the good for our own lives, so we will have stable desires to help and see our friends do well, as they will be a part of that conception. Those who have this status in our lives (who are to us 'other selves') are not instrumental means to our *eudaimonia*; any effort or sacrifice that we make on their behalf will be in our own perceived interests. As it is not at all uncommon for parents to take the view that the prosperity or well-being of their children is a constituent of their own prosperity or well-being, this possibility should be familiar for at least some of the relationships to which Aristotle applied the term 'friendship' (*philia*) – 'parent seems by nature to feel it [*philia*] for offspring and offspring for parent' (1155a16).

It is argued (plausibly) that because one must be personally involved in all one's pursuits, every consciously framed desire that one has reflects an interest of one's self. (This is plausible, although a challenge to the claim that it is a necessary truth will be considered at the end of Section 11.2.) From this plausible position, a very questionable inference is sometimes made, *viz.* that a person's desires are all reflections of self-interest, self-love, selfishness. But it is not even plausible to hold that all our natural impulses to seek or obtain things are properly thought of as expressions of self-love. Writing early in the eighteenth century, Joseph Butler distin-guished between self-love and particular passions (1726: 167–8). The latter were directed toward external things, and did not necessarily involve the self, which Butler regarded as having an 'internal' object, our own happi-ness, enjoyment, satisfaction. Indeed particular passions were presupposed by the possibility of self love. The same point was made in an excep-tionally clear way by William James late in the nineteenth century:

> When I am moved by [what people call] self-love to keep my seat whilst ladies stand, or grab something first and cut out my neighbor, what I really love is the seat; it is the thing itself which I grab. I love them primarily, as the mother loves her babe, or a generous man a heroic deed. Whenever, as here, self seeking is the outcome of simple instinctive propensity, it is but a name for certain reflex

acts. Something rivets my attention and fatally provokes the 'selfish' response. . . . In fact the more thoroughly selfish I am in this primitive way, the more blindly absorbed my thought will be in the *objects* and impulses of my lust and the more devoid of any inward looking glance.

(1890: Vol. I, 320)

Self-love requires, Butler saw, 'sensible creatures who can reflect upon themselves and their own interest or happiness, so as to have that interest an object to their minds' (1726: 167). Egoistic self-regard, far from being a universal framework encompassing all animate action, is an achievement accessible only to sophisticated animals with cognitive capacities.

James suggested that what is criticized as self-love is (at least in some cases) better regarded as a lack of awareness: 'His so-called self-love is but a name for his insensibility to all but this one set of things' (321). What is needed is a greater awareness of himself, of the consequences of his actions for himself as well as other people. For such cases, Butler recommended a more thoroughgoing self-love:

Upon the whole, if the generality of mankind were to cultivate within themselves the principle of self-love; if they were to accustom themselves often to set down and consider, what was the greatest happiness they were capable of attaining for themselves in this life, and if self-love were so strong and prevalent, as that they would uniformly pursue this their supposed chief temporal good, without being diverted from it by any particular passion; it would manifestly prevent numberless follies and vices.

(1726: 25)

Butler here recommends a form of 'ethical egoism', the doctrine that all humans should pursue their self-interest as intelligently and consistently as possible.

The particular form of egoism that Butler recommended did not entail that people should not consider the welfare of others. For as Butler understood the motive of 'benevolence' – 'an affection to the good of our fellow creatures' (172), what is now commonly called 'altruism' – there was no incompatibility between the two, no reason why the interest of the self could not include the good of others. Indeed, it was both natural for people to find satisfaction in promoting the happiness of others and worth everyone's while considering whether this might not be the greatest source of personal happiness (176–8). The idea that self-regarding motives are incompatible with other-regarding motives is a consequence of taking too narrow a conception of self that is the object of self-regard – narrowed by the range of objects that it is assumed will gratify a human being.

Aristotle, as we have seen, recognized the possibility of making the *eudaimonia* of another person a part of one's own. He also recognized that 'selfish' (or 'lover of self', *philautos*; 1168a30) was a term of reproach, but he saw no need to conclude that we should direct our efforts exclusively to the good of others (i.e. in a way that excludes our own), let alone count as ethically excellent for doing so. Given that friends wish (to see) each other (do) well, for this to mean *true* friends and *really* do well, the desire must be for their friends to have and do what is genuinely admirable and best. Moreover, as Aristotle thought, people can intelligibly be regarded as their own friends – they do not, after all, live more closely or more continuously with anyone else – so they should desire the same for themselves.

In other words, as Aristotle saw it, the problem that is ordinarily labeled 'selfishness' does not arise because people act with self-regard but because they act with an inadequate conception of the admirable and good that they should seek for themselves (a point similar to that Butler found it necessary to stress more than 2,000 years later). Their conception is the product of not applying discursive thought (*logos*) to how things affect them (their 'affections,' *pathē*[6]) beyond working out what will be advantageous in obtaining what immediately allures, entices or fascinates them:

> From which it follows that the true lover of self is as different from the kind that merits reproach as living according to *logos* differs from living as feeling dictates, and desiring what is admirable differs from desiring what is advantageous. Everyone praises and approves those who work hard to do what is admirable, and if all were to strive for what is admirable and to do admirable deeds, the common good would be realized and everyone would enjoy the greatest good, since excellence is the greatest of goods.
>
> (1169a3–11)

Epicurus would insist that we cannot distinguish between pleasure and the good and consequently would reject Aristotle's distinction between friendships based on pleasure and those based on good (or on what is admirable), but it is open to him to make similar claims about friends not necessarily being instrumental means to our pleasures.

To do so, he will have to accept that pleasure is not separable from the activities we enjoy, so that eating, playing tennis or solving crossword puzzles are not instruments of or means to something else, the experience of pleasure, but simply are pleasures or enjoyments. Now it is entirely feasible that any of (1) sharing the company of others, (2) experiencing evidence of their enjoyment in what they are doing, or (3) sharing with them the enjoyment of an activity, are all themselves pleasures (enjoyments).

This may well be what Epicurus has in mind when he suggests that being with someone who is a friend is among the most important of the agreeable experiences available to a human being, and it is reasonable to read him as believing a community of friends to be a constituent of a *eudaimōn* (pleasant) life.

From this standpoint, the difference between Epicurus and Aristotle's *Nicomachean* doctrine now appears relatively slight. It is altogether too easy to imagine *eudaimonia* as contemplation being realized in what amounts to an Epicurean community with peculiarly refined tastes: a small circle of people who derive shared pleasure not so much from a simple diet and small talk but from sharing a vision of the most noble things in the universe.

However, some questions need to be raised about the relationship between any such self-contained quasi-family and the wider social world. Any family-sized group of people leads a difficult and time-consuming, not to say precarious, economic existence unless it can participate in a larger economy.

Epicurus recommended that we 'liberate ourselves from the prison of routine business and politics' (22D1), but Peter Green notes that 'the Epicurean commune ... remained parasitical upon – indeed, systematically invested in – the society it had rejected. ... It required a strong framework of law and political rule to guarantee security and freedom from anarchy' (1993: 626). It had, if nothing more, 'to pay its way' (627), and although the evidence leaves one able only to speculate, it would appear that Epicurus and enough of his friends had wealth to invest – 'the commune ... was a rentier foundation' (*ibid.*). The *Nicomachean* Aristotle seems to require very similar arrangements for realizing his conception of *eudaimonia* – the same 'Athenian upper-class establishment, its ideal the perpetuation of endowed leisure' (*ibid.*) – needed by Epicurus.

As far as one can tell from what survives of his writings, Epicurus never considered the question of whether those who are 'systematically invested' in a wider economy and political establishment have any kind of responsibility to participate in or help to sustain the wider framework. Asked whether it might not be at least prudent to do so, Epicurus apparently would reply 'no.' He recommended staying out of public life for the very good reason (from his standpoint) that in public life one runs the risks of incurring enmity and jealousy, giving rise to both the fear and the reality of ruination, misery and death. Public life was no less hazardous during previous generations, but Aristotle in the *Nicomachean Ethics* seemed less concerned with the risks to life and comfort and more with the risks of disappointment to those who seek public recognition, honor. Honor depends on other people. Living as a contemplative might seem preferable to risking frustration.

There remained, Aristotle recognized, a life exercising all the excellences that should earn honor – regardless of whether people are prepared to give honor where it is due – excellences that relate to interaction with other people ('contracts, services and actions,' 1178a12) in various social spheres, public and private. This way of life appeared to offer at least a second-rate kind of *eudaimonia*, but a life of contemplation had been recommended in such glowing terms (see Section 9.3) that it was difficult to see how a life lived in accordance with the other excellences rated at all, or why excellence in how one deals with other people should rate above excellence in architecture, music or acrobatics.

The position that Aristotle develops in the *Eudemian Ethics* does not have these problems. By taking an inclusive view of *eudaimonia*, Aristotle can insist that a *eudaimōn* person must exercise a complete set of excellences, not merely one – even if that one excellence be that of a human's highest and most characteristic activity. With exclusive dignity accorded to contemplation, the claim that man is a creature that naturally lives in cities competes with a vision of human fulfillment that does not involve participation in civic affairs. Aristotle, no more than Epicurus, raised questions about people's responsibilities to the wider economic and political framework or to what extent it might be prudent to participate in it. But taking an inclusive view of *eudaimonia* permits, indeed requires, a wider framework in which to manifest the full range of excellences. The exemplary person as conceived in the *Eudemian Ethics* will, like Confucian exemplary individuals, participate in public life (when and where it is appropriate to do so) as well as engage in the most worthwhile activities in private.

The Epicurean perspective, which confines the arena of human flourishing to the private sphere, not only prevents questions being raised about the conditions under which mankind as a whole can flourish but also it precludes the question whether some condition of the social sphere beyond the private is a necessary condition for individuals to flourish – from considering, that is, whether and under what conditions either a community, larger than an extended family but small enough for its members to interact face to face, or the wider public sphere consisting of people whose activities affect in some way the interests of one another, can be said to contribute to the *eudaimonia* of its members. To write these larger spheres off as inevitably corrupt or hostile is to discard without due consideration an important dimension of human life.

10.3   The universal standpoint

Concern for everyone, general happiness

We have seen that it is possible for an individual's conception of doing well and living well to include the doing well and living well of other people, and we have thus seen reason for rejecting the assumption that self-directed interests and other-directed interests are exclusive and must compete with one another. This is not to say that there will never be conflicts between interests that are more and less narrowly self-directed. It will on occasion take practical wisdom to determine how best to distribute resources of time, effort and personal possessions, resources that might be invested in one person's faring well rather than another but cannot be used for both. Not much can be said in general terms about how to do this well, except that with flexibility and imagination it is sometimes possible to reconcile conflicting demands and possible for several people to find ways of doing well where it seemed there were resources for only one to do so.

What does still need to be addressed is whether anything can be said about how inclusive of others should be one's conception of what it is for oneself to live and do well. In the previous section, we have seen Epicureans drawing the line narrowly, including at most a small private sphere of like-minded people, while at least one tendency in Aristotle's thought included the prosperity of the wider community to which a person belongs. Does anything stand in the way of narrowing the range of one's concern down to that single most intimate friend that everyone has (as Aristotle put it), oneself? And how widely might it be reasonable to expect a person to extend that circle?

Aristotle classified the individual who lives outside human society (outside a *polis* at any rate) as either god-like or worthless (see Section 10.2). Those who live within society but are without friends (without people whom they wish to see do well and who reciprocate this) live impoverished lives; no one would regard it as more worthy of choice (*prohaireteron*) to live in this way. Kant (Section 8.1) approached this from the standpoint of duty rather than living well and took it that to live maximally in accord with duty (to perfect ourselves) we would need others to help us, and we need to accept the benefits of our relationships with others (friends, fellow citizens), and so if we do not do anything to reciprocate appropriately this would, however one formulated the maxims involved, violate the requirement of universalizability. Narrowing the range of one's concern to oneself is, from either the standpoint of classical virtue or the standpoint of duty, self-defeating.

But how widely should one's concern extend? Aristotle gives no hint that it need extend further than the city limits. Kant leaves us with negative duties (not to harm, enslave, dispossess or break promises) toward every rational creature but a great deal of choice, and little advance guidance, as to how much we should do to help others, especially those beyond the limits of our community or nation-state. Confucians, as we have seen, insisted that people's concern must be directed in the first instance toward the members of their families, although where appropriate this concern should be extended by those with the necessary talents to carry out civic responsibilities with humanity (*jen*). In the fluid intellectual world of the fifth to the third centuries BCE in China, it was possible for the Confucian Mencius to identify representatives at extremes on both sides of his position:

> Yang Chu's choice was 'everyone for himself'. Though he might benefit the entire world by plucking out a single hair, he would not do it. Mo Ti [Mo Tzu] advocated universal love [concern for everyone]. If by rubbing smooth his whole body from head to foot he could benefit the world, he would do it.
>
> (Chan 1963: 80 [7A:26])

Unlike Mo Tzu, there are no surviving texts attributable to Yang Chu (Tzu), but his name became emblematic of narrowly conceived self-interest. A chapter of a third-century CE Taoist 'book', the *Leih-tzu*, bears his name,[7] and the point of the narratives and anecdotes it contains (which are not in character with the remainder of the text) are that a person should not seek public office but enjoy what people naturally enjoy: 'Yang Chu said: "A grand house, fine clothes, good food, beautiful women – if you have these four, what more do you need from outside yourself?"' (Graham 1960: 156: *cf.* 142). Behind the hedonism that was later identified as 'Yangist,' however, there appears to have been an original concern less with pleasure than with a preference for the integrity of one's physical nature (the body, its health and survival) over external possessions, honor and power.

One portion of the Yang Chu chapter of the *Leih-tzu*, which appears to have a source much older than the rest of the chapter (perhaps fourth century BCE), begins with a exchange between Yang Chu and a Mohist named Ch'in Ku-li. The latter listens to Yang Chu's claim that if no one were willing to sacrifice even a hair to benefit the empire, the empire would be in good order – evidently blaming social evils on the drive for personal aggrandizement and recommending a form of egoism more narrowly construed than that of Butler (see Section 10.2). Ch'in Ku-li then asks Yang Chu whether he would refuse to sacrifice one hair from his body if he could help the whole world. Yang Chu replies that this is very unlikely to help anyone, but when Ch'in Ku-li persists he falls silent. Later, one of Yang's disciples defends his master by asking Ch'in Ku-li whether he would be willing to lose an arm or a leg to gain a kingdom. Now it is Ch'in's turn to fall silent, and Yang's disciple broadens his riposte by adding that although a single hair is trifling compared with skin and flesh, 'enough hairs are worth as much as skin and flesh, enough skin and flesh as much as one joint. You cannot deny that one hair has its place among the myriad parts of the body; how can one treat it lightly?' (149). Mencius and this text appear to have a common source in the historical Yang, but this text suggests that Yang's self-concern is not unprincipled (Graham 1989: 60–1).

259

The riposte of Yang's disciple is effective because the Mohist automatically conceives 'helping the world' as shouldering the responsibilities of office, but from the standpoint of the Yangist, this is the acquisition of an external thing, e.g. a kingdom, and the challenge proceeds on the assumption that in the scale of everyone's preferences bodily integrity is more important than any external thing. The Yangist spirit is that of 'what profit is there in gaining the whole world if you lose your soul in the process?' where we are to read 'self' for 'soul' and identify the self very strongly with the body. (It is all folly on a level with exchanging a foot for a shoe.) With the self so closely identified with the body, and the world categorized exclusively into body and potential possessions, it is hard to see how the original (let alone the latter-day hedonist variety of) Yangists can have friends who are 'other selves,' or see themselves in effect, as the Confucians urged, as integral parts of a family organism.

Mo Tzu appeared to Mencius at the opposite extreme to that occupied by Yang, as Mo argued that the identification with only few (family, friends) of the people around one and the willingness to exert effort only on their behalf was the root cause of the world's troubles. It was not that Confucians allowed people to follow their subjective feelings in forming close personal relationships. The different ritual signs of respect that were due to different people in different roles were constantly to remind all of where objectively they belonged. For example, one was not to mourn the death of a relative in proportion to the personal feelings one had for that relative but strictly according to whether that person was a parent, a sibling or a spouse, male or female, etc. The idea of 'concern for everyone' (*chien ai*),[8] which Mo and his followers advocated, was as much the antithesis of what Confucians believed was needed for healthy social relations as it would be to cultures such as ours that expect individuals to follow their subjective preferences in their personal relationships.

Mo held that our natural partiality (the unevenness of the concern we show) for family, friends and countrymen is the single most significant source of disharmony, oppression and conflict in the world, and that if we could just flatten out differences in the degrees of our concern for other people, we would all benefit. Mo, as we will see, was very materialistic in his conception of benefit, while harm consisted for him of the strong oppressing the weak, the many misusing the few, the cunning deceiving the simple-minded, the high and mighty lording it over the humble, and violence together with lack of generosity, loyalty, kindness and filial piety (Mei 1929: 87). All this arises from 'partiality,' a concern only for a part of humanity rather than 'impartiality,' concern for everyone. In response to the objection that learning concern for everyone is difficult, Mo cites examples of how with good leadership, ordinary people acquire dispositions that enable them to take all manner of hardships for granted (95–7). So why not invest effort in developing the disposition of concern for everyone in people, given its evident power to cure the ills from which we all suffer?

Quite how concern for everyone is to be understood is not entirely clear. One version of Mo's argument includes a parable of a man about to go off to war and needing to entrust the care of his family to someone. Mo claims that the choice between a partial man, who would presumably look after his own family first, and one who has concern for everyone, was obvious. 'It seems to me, on occasions like these, there are no fools in the world. Even if he is a person who objects to concern for everyone, he will lay the trust upon the man with concern for everyone' (90). But if Mo is thinking of a man who literally and strictly has (equal) concern for everyone, will this man not invest as much effort in people very remote from him (in, say, relief efforts in any distant part of the world that comes to his attention) as he will for his own family or the family members of the man who has gone to war? Surely the shrewd warrior will try to find a trustee who has some connection to his family (a brother or cousin), so that even if the warrior's family comes second in the trustee's concerns, at least the warrior's family will take precedence over people remotely connected to the trustee.

There is a further problem related to this. Mo recommends concern for everyone as a way of producing benefit as well as ameliorating harm. Benefits, as was suggested above, are conceived in fairly materialistic terms: 'There are three things that the people worry about, namely that the hungry cannot be fed, that the cold cannot be clothed, and that the tired cannot get rest' (176). But if everyone acts from concern for everyone, no matter how remote, will that not in the end feed, house and clothe fewer people than if people divide into circles of family or friends and concentrate their efforts locally where they will do the most good? Was that not Yang's point, that if people plowed their own fields instead of plotting to take over the empire, the empire would prosper?

Mo can certainly accept that society is more likely to prosper materially if local efforts are directed to local needs, but he insists that these efforts should always be subordinated to a wider perspective ('a distant view,' see Section 5.4), and if from that perspective it is seen that some people would suffer from a relentless concentration on local needs, the local efforts should be redirected in part to non-local needs. The point is not to decide whether local efforts or efforts directed from the standpoint of everyone will benefit everyone; what concern for everyone means is that we choose that mix of locally and more distantly directed effort that will maximize what can be done to meet everyone's needs.

But why extend that concern to everyone? In what survives of Mo and his followers, it is simply assumed that the goal is to meet everyone's needs as best we can. We must view our efforts from the perspective of everyone's material prosperity, rather than that of our nation, our city, our family, our own individual bodies. Confronted with Wu Ma-tzu, who claims to be incapable of concern for everyone, who admits to more concern for his compatriots than for foreigners, more for the people of his district than for his compatriots, more for his family than for the people of his district, and more for himself than for his family, Mo offers the following variant on the 'self-defeating' argument: if Wu's doctrine becomes widely known and accepted, Wu will suffer at the hands of those with concern only for themselves, and if it is widely known and rejected he will suffer at the hands of those who think it a wicked doctrine (219–20). (Nothing is said about the consequences of Wu keeping his attitude to himself.)

Mo and his followers are nowadays commonly said to have advanced a form of 'utilitarianism.' This is a kind of consequentialism that, if one follows the literal sense of the word, assesses the value of everything in terms of what it may be used for. Mohists seem not to have worried about whether the chain of 'what can this be used for?' questions ever came to an end. As we saw (Section 8.3), Mohists challenged the Confucians over the waste of time and resources that went into rituals that included music and cultural activities (dance, costume, drama) in general. Making musical instruments, playing musical instruments, sitting and listening to performances, Mo argued, all take time and effort away from providing the people with what they need: food, clothing and shelter (175–6). In one passage, Mo asks a Confucian why he pursues music and is told that it is because it is a joy. The characters for music and for joy are identical, although pronounced differently, so the reply has the flavor of a tautology (Graham 1989: 40–1), and Mo rejects this as tantamount to answering the question 'Why build houses?' with 'houses are built for houses' sake' (Mei 1929: 237). If the Confucian cannot give an answer for music like that for 'why build houses?' (i.e. 'to keep off the cold in winter, to keep off the heat in summer and to separate the men from the women') his efforts to make music are in Mo's eyes a waste of time and resources. But if it is obvious that food, shelter and clothing are for maintaining life, can one not ask if there is any use in living, especially if life is nothing more than constant effort to sustain itself?

When the 'principle of utility' was advanced by Bentham late in the eighteenth century, it was assumed that there needed to be something that could be treated as worth having for its own sake – an end in the unqualified sense (see Section 9.1) – so that there would not be an infinite regress of questions of the form 'what is this to be used for?' Bentham's answer was that pleasure and avoiding pain are worth having for themselves, and all other calculations of usefulness or utility were to be made relative to the pain and pleasure produced. In the famous exposition of the utilitarian doctrine that Bentham's follower J.S. Mill provided, a criterion of right and wrong is advanced. It is based not on maximizing the pleasures and minimizing the pains that might be experienced by this or that individual, which Mill treated as defining a person's 'happiness' (1861: 281),[9] but on 'the Greatest-happiness': 'actions are right in proportion as they tend to promote happiness [pleasure and the absence of pain], wrong as they tend to produce the reverse of happiness [pain and the privation of pleasure]' (281), 'not the agent's own happiness but that of all concerned' (291), with 'everybody to count for one and no more than one' (336). Mill clearly meant not a small circle of friends whose enjoyments might become a source of pleasure for one another; he meant to involve people who were unknown to one another except as potentially affected by each other's actions.

This criterion directs our 'concern' to 'everyone,' not the flourishing of the whole over and above its individuals parts, but to the sum of the pleasures and pains of the parts. Again, what is the basis of the claim that our 'concern' be for 'everyone'? Mill offered a notorious argument that took for granted that people could see the need to have special regard for themselves and tried to show why it would be reasonable to move from this self-regarding stance to judging matters of conduct from the standpoint of the good of the human race in general, 'the general happiness.'

No reason can be given why the general happiness is desirable, except that each person, so far as he believes it to be attainable, desires his own happiness. This, however, being a fact, we have not only all the proof which the case admits of, but all which it is possible to require, that happiness is a good, that each person's happiness is a good to that person, and the general happiness, therefore, a good to the aggregate of all persons.

(309)

Mill later clarified what he thought he had proved:

I did not mean that every human being's happiness is a good to every other human being, though I think in a good state of society and education it would be so. I merely meant in this particular sentence to argue that since A's happiness is a good, B's a good, C's a good, etc. the sum of all these goods must be a good.

(309 n2 on 339)

This may be all the proof the case admits, all it is possible to require, but as it involves a serious fallacy, it is hardly all we might have hoped to see.

The premise in the original argument is that individuals regard their own happiness as desirable, and the conclusion is that the general happiness is a good to the aggregate of all persons. (The premise in Mill's subsequent gloss drops the qualification 'to that person.') This claim could be challenged by asking 'what if the happiness of the person in question involved taking pleasure in inflicting gratuitous pain on other people?' If we leave the qualification 'to that person' in place, are we then to take it that 'general happiness' includes the perverted pleasures of sadists? Why should the result necessarily be good, either without qualification or to anyone or to the aggregate of all persons?

A's happiness is a good to A, and the sum of these individuals' happiness may be a good to the aggregate of all persons (whatever that may mean), but why should A care about any part of the aggregate other than A's own? If the aggregate were a condition of the part that is A's happiness, then for A to desire A's part and regard it as desirable, it might be argued that A would have to desire the aggregate and regard it as desirable. Quite possibly this is how things appeared to Mo Tzu: none of us will prosper unless all of us prosper together. But there are many imaginable circumstances in which this will not be true. In some circumstances, a few will be able to prosper, experience pleasure and happiness, while the rest of mankind lives in misery. Nor in general does it follow that if people regard something that is a part of a larger thing as desirable, they will regard the rest of that thing as desirable or feel they should work to preserve or enhance anything other than the part that they think desirable. If they regard a rhinoceros horn as desirable, they do not necessarily regard a rhinoceros as desirable; they must at most regard it as desirable that a rhinoceros has grown a horn, which can be detached and possessed while the rhinoceros is left to perish.

10.4   The golden rule and the expanding circle

Respect for sentience and the throne of pleasure and pain

Mill's argument sidesteps questions about whether an increase in general happiness might entail a decrease in personal happiness (balance of pleasure over pain) for some. 'Each is to count for one and no more than one' ensures only that the happiness of some will not be treated as *a priori* more important to realize than the happiness of others, but it does not ensure that some will not be called on to make sacrifices. At least it is possible in an ideal world, Mill believed, to reconcile people to the loss of opportunities for purely personal gratification. He goes on to acknowledge the phenomenon, which impressed Aristotle, that as people develop what their pleasure or happiness consists in may change (1861: 309–12). A miser may come to find pleasure or happiness in the mere possession of money; it is possible to find pleasure or happiness in possessing and exercising a particular excellence or virtue. Finding personal happiness in the general happiness is what Mill understood by 'virtue.'

Should we not then, if we subscribe to the 'greatest happiness principle,' encourage people to take as much personal pleasure as they can in maximizing general happiness? So if some people should suffer a decrease in personal happiness as a consequence of some measure taken to increase general happiness, could this not be taken as a sign that these people are not sufficiently virtuous (or socially well adjusted) to rejoice where rejoicing is called for and enjoy what people really should enjoy, i.e. seeing general happiness increase instead of the maintenance of opportunities for their own private gratifications?

Although Mill's notion of happiness is much closer to Kant's *Glückseligkeit* (see Sections 8.1, 9.1) – it is what individuals take subjective satisfaction in experiencing – Mill at this point has in effect introduced a distinction that brings him close to Aristotle's position. In both of these teleological theories, there is a difference between what people initially and actually take their happiness or *eudaimonia* to consist in and what on reflection they ought, ideally, to take their happiness or eudaimonia to consist in. What we are to work for thus turns out to be a much more complex target than simply the sum of what people would prefer or would enjoy. At least some, the virtuous (ideally this would be everyone), should prefer and find more enjoyable a world in which general happiness is maximized. The goal of achieving general happiness where general happiness is itself a cause of happiness or an object of satisfaction will not at all be something that is straightforward to determine.

This respect in which Mill's consequentialism becomes, like Aristotle's – non-rigid (see Section 9.1) and in need of work to specify its ideal goal – makes it all the more urgent that we understand why unrestricted general happiness or a 'concern for everyone' should operate as a constraint on how we assess conduct and policies. Mill suggested (291) that his requirements, that an agent take the happiness of all as a standard and be 'as strictly impartial as a disinterested and benevolent spectator,' could be reduced to the 'golden rule of Jesus of Nazareth' (see Section 10.2) in which 'we read the complete spirit of the ethics of utility.' But the maxim (attributed to Yang Chu by Mencius) 'everyone for himself' allows people to do to each as they would be done by and to ignore the size of the sum of satisfactions that results. Kant for his part took a dismissive attitude toward the golden rule. In a footnote, he called it 'trivial,' derivable from his principle of universalizability, but only with qualifications, for

> it cannot be a universal law since it contains the ground neither of duties to oneself nor of duties of kindness to others (for many a man would readily agree that others should not help him if only he could be dispensed from affording help to them), nor finally of strict duties towards others.
>
> (1785: 430n)

If wide duties cannot be derived from the golden rule, how could it entail a concern for whether the overall sum of people's satisfaction is greater or less? If one were to acknowledge Kant's two ends that are also duties, to perfect oneself and to contribute to the happiness of some others (see Section 8.1), what might require one to consider the happiness of anyone beyond immediate associates, let alone the general happiness? Kant was not interested in happiness (the satisfaction of people's wants) except as a means to a higher end. If one rejects the first of Kant's high-minded 'ends that are also duties' (*viz.* to perfect oneself) and simply adopts personal happiness as a goal, what might lead one to Mill's position?

R.M. Hare (1981) tried to use Kantian resources to reach Mill's position by drawing out the consequences of his own claim (see Section 5.4) that universality is what distinguishes moral or ethical prescriptions from ordinary imperatives. Anyone who professes commitment to a prescription (including uttering it with the intention that it be followed) cannot claim this commitment to be 'moral' unless the same commitment applies to all situations with the same general properties. A consequence of this is that one will not prescribe something that frustrates another's preferences unless one is prepared to see one's own (relevantly similar) preferences frustrated in similar ways. Questions about how 'relevantly similar' is to be determined will reveal once again the need for the judgment of virtuous people (see Chapter 8), but for present purposes, these questions can be left to one side.

Hare's principle will work like the golden rule and will therefore be susceptible to people prepared to sacrifice their own preferences if they find greater satisfaction in seeing another's frustrated. Nevertheless, assuming that people will not derive that much pleasure from being malicious or perverse and will maintain a normal level of their initial preferences, it is plausible to argue that under Hare's constraints (his definition of what it is to prescribe morally and his assumption that people will engage in the practice), this will entail individuals wanting to see preferences maximized. That is, they will want to promote general happiness among the people they have to deal with every day, their corporations or professional communities, their local communities or nations. However, it is not clear how such a normal level of preferences will entail maximizing satisfaction for the whole of humanity, an unrestricted concern for everyone.

Mill gives no hint that the impartiality that he calls for ('of the disinterested and benevolent spectator') is relative to any local community to which one might belong. It is common, therefore, to treat the demands of utilitarian impartiality as entailing that individuals weigh the consequences of spending their personal resources on bringing up their own children (enriching their children's lives with piano lessons, say) and spending them on famine relief efforts in remote parts of the world. It is open to Mill to adopt the same general strategy that was available to Mo Tzu (see

Section 10.3) and allow that to the extent that general happiness will be promoted if people put more effort into promoting the welfare of those close to them, their family, friends and local community, and less into the welfare of those remote from them, this policy is justified on utilitarian principles. It is only when we see that the efforts we put into enriching the lives of those near to us do not result in general happiness worldwide that we have to adjust the distribution of our efforts.

A similar strategy has been offered for dealing with the apparent implications of utilitarian principles for the practices of justice. If it would promote the general happiness to make someone suffer undeservedly, it would seem that a utilitarian should advocate this. In reply, it is argued that as the general happiness will be promoted by a general policy of conforming to principles of justice, we should never make anyone suffer undeservedly. The strategy applied to this problem is known as 'rule utilitarianism' – it is in effect another Kant/Mill hybrid in which the test of a universal law is not its consistency but its efficacy in promoting general happiness.

The problem is that utilitarianism by itself does not seem able to sustain support for more than one exceptionless rule. For if it is clear that making an exception to the rules of justice, say by punishing an innocent person because it is clear that this will increase general happiness, then it is contrary to the values that structure the theory not to make the exception. Thus what is commonly called 'act utilitarianism,' which allows no exceptionless rules (except the rule to promote the general happiness), is taken to be the most consistent and stable form of utilitarianism. So utilitarianism remains exposed to the allegation that it would sanction the undeserved suffering of a few to promote the general happiness. The same weakness in the 'rule utilitarian' strategy will appear if one looks beyond the rule that would have one promote the welfare of those close to one and compares $40 spent on piano lessons and $40 spent to relieve famine on another continent. Whose needs are most pressing? Where will the $40 pay for more marginal utility?

The utilitarian demand for impartiality seems, therefore, to threaten the special relationships that we have to those near to us. These are sources of pleasure – a point that Mill must surely accept from Epicurus (see Section 10.2) – and therefore an integral part of human happiness. If we think and act only globally and deny our locality, does general happiness not suffer grievously?

Moreover, while we worry about human beings in distant places, we may find ourselves accused of neglecting beings close at hand, who belong within our circle of concern. Mo Tzu and Mill have, it appears, urged us to widen the circle of our concerns so as not to omit any member of the human race, but is this not still to draw the circle too narrowly? Must we not take the next step and recognize that non-rational sentient creatures, at least the larger and more complex of these, belong in our moral community? Until we have extended the circle of our concerns to include them, do we not remain as partial in a blameworthy sense as slave owners?

One might infer from the way Mill invoked the distinction between higher and lower pleasures to exonerate his doctrine of the charge that it was 'worthy of swine' (see Section 10.1) that it is unlikely that he will favor treating the pleasures and pains of non-human animals as having the same moral standing as those of human beings. Bentham, who made no attempt to distinguish between better- and worse-quality pleasures, was able to follow the hedonist element of his position more consistently than his *soi disant* disciple, John Stuart Mill:

> The day may come when the rest of the animal creation may acquire those rights which never could have been withholden from them but by the hand of tyranny. The French have already discovered that the blackness of the skin is no reason why a human being should be abandoned without redress to the caprice of a tormentor. It may one day come to be recognized that the number of legs, the villosity of the skin, or the termination of the os sacrum are reasons equally insufficient for abandoning a sensitive being to the same fate. What else is it that should trace the insuperable line? Is it the faculty of reason, or perhaps the faculty of discourse? But a full-grown horse or dog is beyond comparison a more rational, as well as a more conversable animal, than an infant of a day or a week or even a month old. But suppose they were otherwise, what would it avail? The question is not, Can they reason? Nor Can they talk? But, Can they suffer?
>
> (1789: 311n)

What is special, Kant will reply, is that the capacity for reason is the capacity for a kind of freedom that is not available to creatures who can only 'work in accordance with laws,' that is respond mechanically through predetermined patterns (instincts and acquired habits) to the influences from the environment around them. Our capacity to act in accordance with our ideas of laws gives us a special standing in the world, because with that capacity we become capable of freeing ourselves from the bondage imposed on all animals by their inclinations, and become answerable for our conduct ('morally responsible') in a way that non-rational creatures are not.

Bentham, however, did not accept that humans had this special power to free themselves from their inclinations and thus was not prepared to acknowledge that they were capable of higher and intrinsically more valuable achievements than anything a non-rational creature can manage:

> Nature has placed mankind under the governance of two sovereign masters, *pain* and *pleasure*. It is for them alone to point out

what we ought to do, as well as to determine what we shall do. On the one hand the standard of right and wrong, on the other the chain of causes and effects, are fastened to their throne. They govern us in all we do, in all we say, in all we think: every effort we can make to throw off our subjection, will serve but to demonstrate and confirm it.

(ibid.: 1)

Humans no more than animals can free themselves from the 'chain of causes and effects . . . fastened to' the throne of pleasure and pain; we too are inescapably in thrall to our inclinations.

If one bears in mind that Bentham and Kant represent two common theoretical frameworks still used today to articulate the basis of our assessments of conduct and institutions, it should be clear why philosophers continually return to the issues of free will and natural determinism. Belief in determinism is the basis for thinking that causes and effects chain us to the throne of pleasure and pain; rational thought may lengthen or shorten the chain, but it does not free us from our true sovereign masters. The most pressing objection that has to be answered by those who subscribe to this belief is that the conduct of individuals would appear, as a result, not to be something they do but the product of something that happens to them; it is therefore incoherent to hold them responsible for what they do. Likewise, the practices of judgment about people's conduct and attitudes are the simple products of natural forces and questions about the validity of these judgments and make no sense. For this reason, perhaps more effort is invested by philosophers nowadays in the subsidiary issue of whether determinism is compatible with our practices of moral assessment and of holding people accountable for what they do. (The claim that it is is known as 'compatibilism.')

Kant was in no doubt that moral assessment and accountability required that we believe that some of what we do is not determined entirely by natural causes. However, he did not claim to be able to show that we are capable of the freedom required to rise above the bondage to natural causes, to which non-rational creatures are condemned. It was one of the objectives of his 'critique' of pure reason to show that reason could not pretend to prove either that all our actions are determined by natural causes or that some of them are not (1781/1787: A532–58/B560–86). That we cannot prove the former – that it remains possible to think of ourselves as capable of freedom – was enough to satisfy Kant. Without that possibility, there would be no notion of duty or objective imperatives, no coherent idea of a good will, no canon of moral judgment. With that possibility, even if there is no proof that it is an actuality, we have a clear idea of what morality requires of us. What it requires is that we recognize the supreme value of any creature capable of formulating a law for itself and conforming to that law. To formulate a law is to formulate an objective principle that is valid for every rational being; to conform to a law that one has prescribed for oneself is freedom. (See the quotation at the head of this chapter from Rousseau, a writer whom Kant much admired.) Freedom for Kant means literally 'autonomy' (auto = self + nomos = law).

It needs to be emphasized that even if rationality is the only source of respect in Kant, we are not thereby entitled to abuse the non-rational components of the natural world. To abuse (misuse) anything is by definition irrational; for abuse is using a thing in ways that one has good reason not to use it. Moreover, if we adopt Kant's view of our inclinations as what our rational faculties are to help us to rise above,[10] it will appear that as most of our (mis)treatment of sentient creatures arises from inclination, man's alleged inhumanity to animals is largely based on motives that Kant would not view as morally worthy. That is to say, much of what is objectionable in what we do daily and on a vast scale to sentient creatures is a consequence of efforts to gratify capricious tastes, to enhance a sense of power, to satisfy vanity, to escape boredom, etc., and is not licensed by any principles that Kant attributes to reason alone.

The objection to Kant from the Benthamites, however, is that under his theory a living but non-rational creature remains a *thing*, which may be used for whatever rationally legitimated ends humans may set for themselves. Humans have under Kant's canon the right not to be interfered with, neither killed, nor confined, nor injured, because all rational creatures have a duty not to interfere with them.[11] Non-rational animals, however, have no such rights; they may be killed for food or simply because they are a nuisance; they may be captured and held prisoner for study or amusement; they may be subjected to painful injury in the interests of promoting human health and well-being.

For a rational creature to use another rational creature in this way (treat as a means, not as an end) is to abuse that creature; for we have, according to Kant, an overriding reason (a duty based on the supreme principle of practical reason) not to do this. We can make use of other rational creatures with their permission (hence not only as a means), if they can recognize their service to us as falling under a principle that could function as a universal law of nature. Sentient but non-rational creatures cannot render us service (be used) in this way, because we cannot communicate with them sufficiently well to establish the necessary common understanding. Nevertheless, the premise behind the objection to Kant is that sentience rather than rationality ought be the basis of the duty not to take the life, interfere with the liberty or cause distress to a creature, and of the right that such a creature has not to be subjected to any such interference.

There are in play here two quite different attitudes to pleasure and pain: one that they are all that matter and the other that they are for human beings obstacles to be overcome. Also, two different notions of freedom are involved: the one views freedom as the absence of discomfort, annoyance and frustration, the other as scope to construct or reconstruct what impulses and inclinations nature has given us. Indeed, there are here two different ways of conceiving human beings, the one as creatures who accept the inclinations they have and use their minds to follow them, the other as creatures who are able to use their minds to examine their inclinations and decide which they should follow. Numerous traditions have viewed the outlook of self-professed hedonists and their attachment to what they called 'pleasure' as symptomatic of a failure to free themselves from what Bentham acknowledged as our sovereign masters, pain and pleasure – masters that anti-hedonists regard as tyrannical despots. Many who despise what they see as their own enslavement to physical pleasures and pains, or psychological comforts and distress, want nothing of them at all in their lives. Many who conceive their natural selves as nothing more than so many places where chains can be attached to the thrones of their sovereign masters do what they can to flee those selves. The next chapter will examine some of the efforts by the slaves to revolt.

Further reading

Long and Sedley (1987) (= LS) provide a valuable commentary with each chapter of selections. The chapters on Epicurean ethics are 20–5. See also Nussbaum (1994): chapters 4 are on Epicurus and 5–7 are on Lucretius. On the history of the Epicurean movement through to its influence on seventeenth-century European thought, see Jones (1989). On Aristotle on pleasure, see Urmson (1968), and on pleasure and happiness in Mill, see Austin (1968). Badhwar (1993) is a useful collection of recent work on friendship (including discussions of Aristotle and Kant). On the idea that we may conceive our 'selves' as more and less inclusive, see Dewey and Tufts (1932: chapter 15). On Mencius and Mo Tzu, see Hansen (1992: chapter 5) and on Yang Chu-tzu and Mo Tzu, see Graham (1989: I.2–3, II.2–3; 1985). For an author advocating an egalitarian impartiality, see Singer (1979: chapters 2 and 8); for an author who finds this extremely problematic, see Nagel (1991). On Mill's moral philosophy, see Skorupski (1989: chapter 9) and Berger (1984: chapters 2 and 3). For the role of virtue in Mill's moral philosophy, see Semmel (1984). Hare's attempt to reach utilitarian principles from his universal prescriptivism will be found in Hare (1981). Lyons (1965) is a thorough treatment of rule versus act utilitarianism. Three authors who support the claims of animals to be included in our moral community are Singer (1975; 1979: chapters 3 and 5), Regan (1983) and Clark (1997). For two of many sources on the bearing that the truth of determinism would have on our moral practice, see Trusted (1984) and Honderich (1993).

271

Notes

1 This is translated (from a letter purportedly written by Epicurus to his friend Menoeceus and preserved by Diogenes Laertius) in Long and Sedley (1987). It is selection 21B2 (chapter 21, selection **B**, second sentence). References to Epicurean and Stoic sources will cite Long and Sedley in the form: LS + selection number.

2 His view of the natural world, which owned much to Democritus, a contemporary and compatriot of Protagoras, was that its ultimate constituents were indivisible material particles ('atoms') moving in a void. Epicurus offered reasons for accepting this view and it was not held to be true merely because it provided grounds for removing fears of death, of an afterlife and of malevolent deities. Nevertheless, it was held to be worthwhile to study and dwell upon because it offered this solace. On the solace offered by Epicurean doctrines of nature, see LS 25A, **B**.

3 The claim is somewhat disingenuous. Bentham is remembered for this remark expressing a more egalitarian attitude to pleasures: 'Prejudice apart, the game of push-pin is of equal value with the arts and sciences of music and poetry. If the game of push-pin furnish more pleasure, it is more valuable than either' (1843: Vol. II, 253). Three representative fragments of Epicurus, 21L–N, likewise count against Mill's claim, e.g. **N**: 'The comfortable state of the flesh, and the confident expectation of this, contain the highest and most secure joy for those who are capable of reasoning.'

4 Apropos Aristotle's assumption that contemplation would not be satisfactory if engaged in entirely on one's own is a saying that Cicero reports as traditional: 'If a man should ascend alone into heaven and behold clearly the structure of the universe and the beauty of the stars, he would take no pleasure in the awe-inspiring sight that ought to fill him with delight, unless he had had someone to whom he could describe what he had seen' (Falconer 1923: 88).

5 The interest taken in recent decades in the possibility of individuals inventing a language for themselves ('a private language') has arisen because, if this notion is incoherent, so is the idea of a human conceived independently of human society.

6 Aristotle uses in a neutral sense the word *pathos*, plural, *pathē*, which the Stoics later applied only to what they regarded as bad (pathological in the sense of 'diseased') affections, feelings or passions (see Section 11.3).

7 Two other 'books' contain substantial portions that scholars identify as 'Yangist,' *viz.* chapters 28–31 of the *Chuang Tzu* (Watson 1958: 309–52) and portions of the *Lü-shih ch'un-ch'iu*, on which see Graham (1985: 74).

8 Graham (1989: 41–2) argues persuasively against the traditional translation of this concept as 'universal love'. Many Mohist texts survive in three distinct versions, which Graham (36) conjectures are different written versions of a common oral tradition set down (or made up) by different groups of followers of Mo.

9 'By happiness is intended pleasure and the absence of pain, by unhappiness, pain and the privation of pleasure' (*ibid.*). Compare the 'happiness of the philosophers,' 'not a life of rapture, but moments of such, in an existence made up of few and transitory pains, many and various pleasures, with a decided predominance of the active over the passive, and having as the foundation of the whole not to expect more from life than it is capable of bestowing' (287).

10 'Inclinations themselves, as sources of needs, are so far from having an absolute value to make them desirable for their own sake that it must rather be the universal wish of every rational being to be wholly free from them' (Kant 1785: 428).

11 And insofar as the experience of pain interferes with a person's freedom to think and act, this right extends arguably to not being made subject to gratuitous pain, even that which does not accompany harm in the sense of long-term impairment of faculties.

11

THE SELF AS A PROBLEM

Contacts with material things, O son of Kuntī, give rise to cold and heat, pleasure and pain. They come and go, they do not last forever; endure them, O Bhārata. The man who is not troubled by these, O bull among men, who remains the same in [treats alike] pleasure and pain, who is wise; he is fit for eternal life.

(Bhagavad Gītā (fourth century BCE?) II. 14–15;
Radhakrishnan and Moore 1957: 107)

O Lord, I am working hard in this field, and the field of my labors is my own self. I have become a problem to myself, like land which a farmer works only with difficulty and at the cost of much sweat.

(St Augustine, *Confessions*, X.16 (fourth century CE);
Pine-Coffin 1961: 222–3)

Recapitulation: Epicurus offered pleasure and the absence of pain as the straightedge by which to draft a picture of a life fit for a human being. Epicurus' straightedge was not, however, indifferent to the kind of pleasures sought and the pains avoided; rather, it was fashioned with a particular conception of a flourishing person in mind, one who could do with the modest pleasures of private life and eschew both the risks and rewards of public life. That people can take pleasure in witnessing (sharing) the pleasures of others (as well as regard the flourishing of other people as constituents of their own flourishing) means that humans are not essentially self-regarding, even those who choose exclusively by reference to Epicurus' straightedge. Epicureans, however, have no reason to listen to calls to expand the circle of their concerns to include the public sphere of their wider community or of humanity in general; their *kanōn* assigns no validity to the universal standpoint (concern for everyone). Combining the belief that suffering and enjoyment are the only morally significant capacities with the universal standpoint, however, yields a challenge to the belief that our moral concerns need extend no further than humans beings. Traditions that assign special moral standing to humans have commonly regarded the capacities to enjoy and suffer as needing to be transcended and the Epicurean *kanōn* as not worthy of our humanity.

Prospectus: The discussion of the conception of what it is to live well has so far been preoccupied with ensuring that we realize our full potential as human beings and that nothing important is omitted from our natural development. Other traditions have been preoccupied by the belief that our own nature poses a variety of threats to our proper development, threats that we need to work against constantly and vigilantly if we are to live well. In some cases, these threats are seen in terms of the temptations of pleasure, in other cases the threats arise from our susceptibility to suffering – the remedy in either case is the discipline of desire and the remaking of the individual self. Some traditions view this as best carried out entirely outside the realm of ordinary human life, either alone or in communities that refrain from the demands of economic production and biological reproduction. Others accept the challenge posed by the task of living well in the midst of the influences – even engaged in the very activities – that threaten to enslave us.

11.1   Asceticism and salvation

Dependencies, holy virginity and soteriology

Aristotle's analysis of the concept of pleasure allowed him to assign it a place not only in the lives of the self-indulgent and the ambitious seekers of power and fame but also in ways of life that he regarded as the best for a human to live, whether that life be devoted to genuinely admirable accomplishments or to contemplating the universal and necessary principles governing the world. Pleasure, however, is often assumed to be a hazard that people with high-minded objectives, whatever these may be, must avoid or overcome. This is because 'pleasure' (and the same is true of Aristotle's word *hēdonē*) is closely associated in the minds of people with satisfactions derived from such activities as eating, drinking and sex. Sometimes 'pleasure seekers' are taken to include those whose excessive passivity amounts to sloth or whose fondness for trivial (non-edifying) entertainment amounts to indolence. Pleasure seekers, in other words, have some of the character traits that according to Mill (see Section 10.1) affect the competence of people to judge what are the better (higher) pleasures.

Viewed in this light, 'pleasure' is at best a word for distraction, something that interferes with more important activities; at its worst, it is a form of servitude that leaves no time or energy for other, better, things.

'Pleasure' in this narrower sense represents a path down which it is alto-gether too easy to travel, a force that requires strength (of character) to resist. Those addicted to this drug (as it is portrayed) will neglect their responsibilities and use other people unfairly in order to have the resources to 'feed their habits.'

'Pleasure' is associated with the senses, because the most common distracting and destructive of these proclivities and inertias are referred to the senses, specifically that of touch. This at any rate was the sense modality that Aristotle identified (1118a26) as the domain of application of the concepts of *sōphrosunē* (intelligent self-control, moderation, temperance) and self-indulgence (*akolasia*, intemperance, lack of chastisement, lack of discipline).

However, distractions are not intrinsically related to touch or even to the passive exercise of the senses; various people are fond enough of sports, gossip, even mathematics to produce a neglect of more important things or a tendency to use others unfairly. More discerning movements of moral reform, from ancient Buddhism to seventeenth-century Puritanism, have recognized the power of what might be called 'cultural sources of distraction' – festivals, sports and theater – as well as the more widely condemned temptations of the flesh. But the recognition that the attractions and distractions of sex, food and intoxicating drink are both powerful and based in the biological nature that we share with other animals has contributed to a long-standing mythology centered on 'the senses' and 'the body.'

An example of this can be found at the beginning of Plato's *Phaedo*, his dramatic portrayal of Socrates' execution. Socrates expresses no regrets at having to die. As those who have practised philosophy correctly have been preparing themselves for dying and death, it would be absurd for them to be troubled by something they have so long looked forward to and prepared for (64a). Death is simply the separation of the soul from the body; the philosopher, the better to think and grasp the truth (65b–c), has already had to effect something of a separation of the soul from the body by giving as little attention as possible to the pleasures connected with food and drink, sex, clothes, and bodily ornament (64d). This avoiding and despising the body (65c–d), endeavoring to release the soul from its innumerable distractions (66b), is to train oneself to live in a state as close as possible to death (67c). That Socrates has any basis for thinking that the clear view of the truth will at last be his once he has died depends, of course, on whether the soul is released rather than destroyed by being separated from the body. (Much of the discussion of the *Phaedo*, not surprisingly, centers on Socrates' attempts to provide this basis.)

If we accept this picture and identify ourselves with a life principle (our 'soul' or *psuchē*), the nature of which is thought rather than any activity more obviously dependent on the body, then pleasures associated with the body represent a threat rather than any part of what makes life worth-while or fulfilling. Plato gives us a picture of our nature as burdened by the body and needing release from it. This focus of attention differs from that found in Aristotle and Confucianism. The latter two tend to be concerned to include in life what it should have; if we have to practise, put forth effort to cultivate ourselves, it is to complete a natural course of development, to fill in something that would otherwise be lacking. Thus it was natural to use the word 'fulfillment' when discussing the lives recom-mended by Aristotle and the classical Confucians. In Plato's case, the concern is with a threat to our nature from something alien to it. We need to make efforts to drive out this alien influence, to purify what is really us and ours. Plato suggested that it would be entirely up to our efforts to achieve this purification; those who believe that individuals cannot achieve this entirely by their own efforts look for (or offer themselves as) saviours. Often salvation requires a measure of self-help as well as assistance from another.

Greeks who practised or trained for athletic competitions, or for a profes-sion, were said to undertake *askēsis*; an *askētēs* was an athlete or the practitioner of a trade or profession; the adjective *askētikos* meant 'indus-trious' or 'athletic'. From this we get the notion of asceticism – an ascetic being one who practises self-denial in the interests of self-improvement. The efforts we need to make, according to Plato, to purify our souls ('culti-vate death in this life') would constitute a form of asceticism. Asceticism has taken a wide variety of forms, depending on the conception of the nature of the human beings who have to ward off or extricate themselves from whatever threatens – as well as on the conception of that threat.

Radical Christians in the early centuries of their movement, in many cases drawing on Plato to help to articulate their attitudes, came to place a great deal of emphasis on sexual desire as a threat to the purity that they were called on by Christ to preserve against the corrupting influence of 'the world.' Christian asceticism focused on the disciplining of sexual desire. One transmogrification of the hope for Christ's second coming, the establishment of His kingdom on Earth and the end to the current age (the *saeculum*), was that by spreading the practice of continence, Christians themselves would bring sinful human life to an end (Brown 1988: 32). Married couples were encouraged to live continently, and living a life entirely without sexual experience, 'virginity,' became a Christian ideal for both men and women. Origen, a Christian neo-Platonist of the early third century CE in Alexandria, held a view of human nature in which, according to Brown:

> Virginity stood for the original state in which every body and soul had joined. It was a physical concretization, through the untouched body, of the pre-existing purity of the soul. . . . The continent body

was a waxen soul that bore the exact 'imprint' of the untarnished soul. Identified in this intimate manner with the pristine soul, the intact flesh of a virgin of either sex stood out also as a fragile oasis of human freedom. Refusal to marry mirrored the right of a human being, the possessor of a pre-existent utterly free soul, not to surrender its liberty to the pressures placed upon the person by society.

(*ibid.*: 170)

Non-Christians had fewer anxieties about sex but on occasion developed other ideas of what could defile the soul. The locus of concern with purity for Origen's younger contemporary, Porphyry, a pagan neo-Platonist, was food rather than sex. By a sparse diet that completely excluded meat, Porphyry believed he could help his eternal mind to free itself from entanglements with the 'cloying materiality,' 'the "blood drenched surge" of the body' (182, 183).

Not all Christian ascetics conceived their enterprise as freeing the soul from the corruptions of the body. Christian renouncers in Egypt at this time took to living as holy hermits in the desert. Brown notes that some of the 'Desert Fathers,' recognizing the sinful proclivities of their souls, used the mortification of the body as a way of bringing humility to the soul.

In the desert tradition, the body was allowed to become the discreet mentor of the proud soul. . . . The material conditions of the monk's life were held capable of altering the consciousness itself. Of all the lessons of the desert to a late antique thinker, what was most 'truly astonishing' was that the immortal spirit can be purified and refined by clay.

(237, citing John Climacus, *The Ladder of Divine Ascent*)

Christian celibacy was not entirely an unprecedented phenomenon. The Jewish sect of the first century CE represented by the Dead Sea Scrolls, the Essenes, required a group of its male members to 'live under a vow of celibacy for an indefinite period.' They conceived of themselves as soldiers engaged in a holy war on behalf a beleaguered community. The ideal that this practice served was known as 'singleness of heart,' the basis of male solidarity, an ungrudging loyalty to the community; women were regarded as causes of lusts and jealousies that pitted males against each other (36–9). Here the conception of humanity served, and the threat to purity warded off, by ascetic discipline is socio-psychological rather than based on the metaphysics of the mind's relation to the body.

Asceticism is normally taken to involve the permanent or long-term suppression of some naturally occurring desire. The mere postponement

277

of response to, or other modification of, an impulse is treated as a matter of prudent self-control rather than ascetic self-denial. Epicurus would appear from this perspective as a representative of the former rather than the latter, but his position is complex, a rational hedonism that views pleasure with many of the same suspicions that motivate the avowed opponents of pleasure such as Plato. Epicurus adopts this curious posture because although he claims pleasure is the good, he is actually preoccupied not with achieving pleasure but with avoiding suffering. The life that he recommends is free from bodily suffering and mental disturbance, and it is freedom from disturbance (*ataraxia*) rather than maximization of pleasure that best characterizes the Epicurean goal in life.

Epicurus' claim that pleasure consists of the absence of pain reflects this:

> The pleasure in the flesh does not increase when once the pain of need has been removed, but it is only varied. And the limit of pleasure in the mind is produced by rationalizing those very things and their congeners which used to present the mind with its greatest fears.
>
> (LS 21E1)

Removing sources of unnecessary fear was thus extremely important to Epicurus, and on this basis in particular he recommended his theology, which insisted that the gods had no reason to trouble human beings, and his theories of nature, which implied that human experience could not occur once the body had disintegrated. If people understood these truths, they would not be plagued by fears based on superstitions (for which the Roman Epicurean Lucretius used the Latin word *religio*) and above all would not fear death. 'Accustom yourself to the belief that death is nothing to us. For all good and evil lie in sensation, whereas death is the absence of sensation' (LS 24A1).

Epicurus' preoccupation with a life that avoids distress and disturbance leads to an effort to purge impulses that have unwelcome consequences, just as Plato's preoccupation with the unhindered use of the mind leads to an effort to purge impulses that interfere with that goal, or as the Christian preoccupation with purity of spirit leads to an effort to purge impulses of the flesh. Each is more concerned with trying to exclude from life what it should not have than with what would complete or fulfill life. The human condition threatens the Epicurean as much as the Platonist or the Christian. It should come as no surprise that Epicurus was represented by his followers as a saviour. Two centuries after Epicurus' death, Lucretius offered this encomium:

> Dead though he is, his godlike discoveries spread his fame of old and now it reaches to heaven. When he saw that mortals were

already supplied with almost everything that need demands for
their livelihood ... yet that at home no one's heart was any less
troubled and that people were constantly wrecking their lives,
despite their intentions, under a compulsion to rage with aggres-
sive complaints, he recognized that the flaw was *there*, caused by
the vessel itself, and that by its flaw everything within was being
befouled ... so he purged people's hearts with his truthful words,
and established the limit of desire and fear, and laid out the nature
of the highest good to which we all strive, and indicated the way
by whose narrow path we may press on towards it on a straight
course.

(LS 21**X**)

Epicurus offers to save us from the distress caused by our flaws, by the
unnecessary desires and fears that result from our failure to see and know
things as they are.

11.2 Suffering as the problem

Four noble truths and an eightfold noble path

Guidance (with or without the image of standards and measurement) as
to how humans should conduct their lives will in general face in one or
both of these directions – either taking for granted that something threatens
to ruin our lives or that something is needed to complete our lives (or
some combination of the two). For example, an older contemporary of
Confucius (by about fifteen years), Siddhārtha Gautama, born on the
northern borders of India in what is now Nepal, saw suffering as the
problem that humans face, and he is recognized as the Enlightened One,
the Buddha, as a consequence of realizing what mankind must do to avoid
suffering. The first of the four noble truths that constitute his central
message identifies the pervasiveness of suffering in human life:

The Noble Truth of suffering (*dukkha*) is this: Birth is suffering;
aging is suffering; sickness is suffering; death is suffering; sorrow
and lamentation, pain, grief and despair are suffering; association
with the unpleasant is suffering; dissociation from the pleasant is
suffering; not to get what one wants is suffering – in brief, the
five aggregates of attachment are suffering.

(Rahula 1974: 93)[1]

Because Buddhist doctrine takes as its starting point something that
threatens humans, it has a 'soteriological' dimension which is present in
Plato, Epicurus and Christianity but missing in Aristotle and Confucianism.

In particular, Epicurus and the Buddha offered to individuals, whom they took to be dissatisfied with their situations, a way of avoiding the sources of distress in human life.

The Buddha's diagnosis and prescription, however, are a good deal more radical than that of Epicurus. The Second Noble Truth identifies the cause of suffering not in the concomitant effects of having certain desires fulfilled but in a kind of desire that people universally have. They are afflicted by craving (*taṇhā*, 'thirst') – which is a mixture of attraction (greed), revulsion (hatred) and ignorance – that will not be satisfied by being gratified even if the gratification brings no concomitant ill-effects. To cease suffering, people have to bring about the cessation of this kind of desire. This is the Third Noble Truth. The Fourth outlines the way to bring this cessation about; it requires rectifying eight aspects of one's life – 'the Eightfold Noble Path' – that is, one must practise right views (understanding), right resolve (thought), right speech, right action, right livelihood, right effort, right mindfulness and right meditation (concentration).

For Epicurus, it was enough to think through the effects of gratifying a desire, i.e. to see whether these effects would bring more distress than would result from leaving the desire ungratified. The Buddha recommended comprehensively reshaping one's life to extinguish all 'attachment' (*upādāna*) that arises from craving – indeed, the notion of being extinguished or 'blown out' like the flame of a candle is preserved in the etymology of the word for the goal of Buddhist efforts, *nirvana* (Pali: *nibbāna*). The difference between the two approaches can be seen by contrasting their respective attitudes to human sexuality. The Epicurean attitude to sexual intercourse is well illustrated in advice given by one of Epicurus' close associates, Metrodorus, to a younger Epicurean, Pythocles:

> You tell me that the movement of your flesh is too inclined towards sexual intercourse. So long as you do not break the laws or disturb proper and established conventions or distress any of your neighbors or ravage your body or squander the necessities of life, act upon your inclination in any way you like. Yet it is impossible not to be constrained by at least one of these. For sex is never advantageous, and one should be content if it does no harm.
>
> (LS 21**G**3)

Sex like any other pleasure is in itself good, but it is hazardous and probably unwise to indulge. This stands in contrast to the attitude expected of those most firmly committed to following the Buddha's Eightfold Noble Path, where sexual desire appears as a paradigm of the craving that lies at the root of all suffering.

Buddhism arose within an antecedently existing subculture in which asceticism played an important role. According to traditions concerning his

280

life prior to his enlightenment, the Buddha had abandoned wealth and privilege to live as one of a number of itinerant teachers of philosophy and practitioners of religion, dependent on the charitable support of people who saw their alms as gaining them a better prospect in the next life. Collectively, these mendicants were known as *śramaṇas*;[2] many of them practised extreme ascetic techniques, for it had long been a tradition in India that ascetic discipline was a way of increasing one's power not only over oneself but also over nature and the gods.[3] Many recommended mental disciplines involving concentration 'on a single point'; this could be a physical object, some part of the person's body, a thought or God. This is the basis of the yogic meditation found in a variety of Indian traditions (Eliade 1958: 47).[4] Those who aspired to the power or wisdom believed to be obtainable through a combination of ascetic and meditative practice went alone for extended periods into the forest, which in India served the same function as the Egyptian desert for Christian renouncers 800 years later.

Gautama tried the doctrines and techniques of a number of *śramaṇas* without finding the spiritual satisfaction he sought: 'an unsurpassed excellent state of calm.' Part of the enlightenment that he subsequently achieved was a doctrine known as the middle way, *viz.* that extreme self-mortification is no more the route to salvation than is self-indulgence. The 'first sermon of the Buddha' following his enlightenment (Rahula 1974: 92–4) was addressed to five ascetics (his former companions). It begins by insisting that both 'self-indulgence of sense pleasures' and self-mortification are 'unworthy and unprofitable' and that both extremes must be avoided.

From the standpoint of the ordinary person, however, the Eightfold Noble Path contains significant ascetic features. According to tradition, the Buddha formed a community (the *Sangha*) of those who were most intent on following the path that he had prescribed for bringing about the cessation of craving and suffering. For the *Sangha*, a code of discipline (*Vinaya*) was laid down, and the four most strictly proscribed acts or 'offenses of defeat' (Keown 1992: 32) were manslaughter, theft, sexual intercourse and lying (specifically about spiritual accomplishments). In other words, the Buddha regarded sexual activity as incompatible with the aspiration to extinguish the craving that gives rise to suffering; and sexual desire, by implication, was regarded as a cardinal instance of attachment. Other cardinal instances represented in the 'offenses of defeat' are greed, which might tempt one to steal; a yearning for admiration, which might lead one to exaggerate one's accomplishments; and fear or anger, which might lead to spilling blood. The resulting acts are not forbidden because they have potentially distressing consequences but because they are the most obvious and serious manifestations of what needs to be extinguished if suffering is to be tackled at its source.

The *Sangha* was comprised of mendicants (*bhikkhus*[5]) – monks whose minimal material needs were met by alms from the surrounding community

– and like the Epicurean community was thus economically dependent (parasitic) on the wider social sphere. But unlike Epicureans, who took themselves to have no responsibilities to the world outside their communities, the *Sangha* taught the Buddha's message when receiving food and other necessities. Non-ordained individuals (the 'laity,' 'householders') were offered 'the three refuges' – the Buddha, his teaching and his *Sangha* – and they would associate themselves with specific groups of *bhikkhus* and would worship with them in buildings and parks set aside for the *Sangha*.[6]

For the laity, 'four vices in conduct' correspond to the 'four offenses of defeat,' except that 'sexual misconduct' ('unchastity' or 'adultery') replaces 'sexual intercourse.' These vices give rise to 'five precepts,' which proscribe intoxication along with the four vices (80), each of which has a positive counterpart, e.g. with the first precept not to kill or injure goes the practice of loving kindness (*metta*) to all (Saddhatissa 1970: 76ff). Where *bhikkhus* are also forbidden from receiving gold and silver and adornment (along with personal possessions other than their robes and a bowl out of which to eat), householders are encouraged to protect their wealth, make their businesses prosper and provide adornment for their wives. Where *bhikkhus* are forbidden dancing, singing and shows, householders were merely advised that these are among the 'six doors of dissipating wealth.'[7]

Buddhist beliefs about death and reincarnation (Buddhist eschatology) provide a natural motivation for the dual structure of the Buddhist community – the stricter subculture of the *Sangha* within the wider, less rigorous, lay culture. According to these doctrines, humans are caught in the cycle of rebirth (*samsara*), and the only way to break free and ensure that one will not be born into yet another life is to extinguish totally the craving and attachment that lies at the foundation of all suffering and at the foundation of what people normally think of as their selves – this is regarded by many as involving the total dismantling of the self. Being moved to join the *Sangha* is a sign that one hopes to make definite progress toward this goal; hence a *bhikkhu* is expected to put aside interest in possessions, comforts and sex. The laity are left to work (through good deeds, e.g. supporting the *Sangha* materially) for a more favorable birth in the next life. Pious laymen aspire to enter the *Sangha* in a future life, when they will begin more thoroughly and comprehensively to detach themselves.

Viewed from the perspective of its eschatology, Buddhism hardly appears to be a 'life-affirming' outlook. Humans are portrayed as beings normally condemned to live, and thus to suffer, over and over again. Suicide is no way out; not only is one ushered back into (yet another) life, but the doctrine of *karma* (see Section 3.2) entails that one's new situation will only be worse. Acts committed in previous lives create an ongoing burden that makes attachment and suffering worse. Suicide, after all, in violating the precept against taking life, manifests a negative form of the 'craving' (*viz.* self-hatred) that leads to rebirth and suffering. Such *karma* must be purged by meritorious actions before a person can hope for rebirth in a more comfortable situation, let alone achieve sufficient detachment to bring about the cessation of his or her own cycle of rebirth. The Buddha taught that whatever gives life to a succession of bodies is not indestructible, but *karma* ensures that it will be difficult to terminate. The ultimate goal of the Eightfold Noble Path is thus not merely to achieve a degree of non-attachment but a complete and comprehensive non-attachment sufficient to bring that termination about.

Buddhist eschatology stands in stark contrast to Western traditions, which consign the dead to a permanent shadow world, either divided into regions of torment and bliss or as in the case of the Jewish *sheol* 'a sad, disturbing place but one devoid of punishments' (Le Goff 1984: 7). Buddhists believe that heavens and hells exist, but residence in such realms is not permanent. The highest Western eschatological aspiration is everlasting bliss; the most pressing need for salvation is from everlasting torment. Epicurus saw mankind as needing salvation above all from such beliefs and taught a view of human life and experience as dependent on the body in such a way that neither experience nor the effects of one's actions were capable of surviving the disintegration of the body:

> For all good and evil lie in sensations, whereas death is the absence of sensation. Hence a correct understanding that death is nothing to us makes the mortality of life enjoyable, not by adding infinite time, but by ridding us of the desire for immortality.
>
> (LS 24A1–2)

To the Buddha, the solution to the problem of suffering could hardly be a matter simply of adjusting one's beliefs about the hereafter. To an Epicurean, the Buddha's message would appear to be based on yet another superstition – another of what Lucretius called *religio* – that unnecessarily torments the minds of human beings and adds misery to what little time they have to live. To a Buddhist, however, Epicurus' doctrines, which entail that actions in one life have no effects on future lives and indeed that there is no rebirth, are the sort of wrong views that constitute one of the four principal objects of attachment, clinging to which ensures the perpetuation of suffering. This represents not only a challenge to the truth of Epicurus' doctrines regarding nature but also raises the possibility that what we believe about the world around us is dependent in crucial ways on our dispositions to desire certain things.

The eschatological issues are impossible to settle, but the relationship between belief and desire needs further consideration. On this turn the questions of whether it is correct to conclude that Buddhism is not a 'life-affirming outlook,' that the Buddha ultimately only offered salvation from life itself, and that the most important thing to be 'extinguished' or 'blown out' is an individual's continuity. A number of modern scholars and apologists have insisted that this last would be a distorted understanding of *nirvana*. The goal is the extinction or the blowing out of the fire of 'craving,'[8] the dissolving of attachment and the dismantling of the self. The result is not merely salvation (present and permanent) from suffering, but human fulfillment, a way of living the rest of one's natural life that is both worthy and satisfying. This the Buddha and numerous *arahants*[9] managed to achieve before their final bodily death, when the cycle of their rebirths terminated, and their achievement should be intelligible and appealing even to those who do not believe in the cycle of rebirth. *Nirvana*, understood as the extinguishing of the craving that leads to suffering, and the immediate consequences of its achievement for the remainder of a person's natural life thus require closer examination.

To understand what this might involve, recall that as humans mature (see Section 10.2 on James and Butler), they acquire a conception of their own individual prosperity (which may, but need not, be broadly conceived to include the good of other individuals and/or the good of some collective body) and also develop an awareness of how their particular passions bear on that conception. It might then be claimed that all mature human behavior − when 'behavior' qualifies as 'conduct' − is in this sense self-regarding. Even what appears to be self-sacrifice and not merely benevolent action is really self-regarding, because the self in such cases is broadly conceived and we must take that person to be acting in furtherance of that broad conception or we will not be able to understand that person's actions. Given that we are defining conduct as behavior that involves a concept of the self and given the strategy for finding a broad enough notion of the self to disallow any exception to the claim that conduct is always self-regarding, this claim appears to be true either by definition or by the analysis of the meanings of our terms (is an 'analytic truth').

But if this claim that all human conduct is self-regarding is necessarily true, what sense can be made of the Buddhist aspiration to extinguish altogether the self conceived as a complex of attachments? What is the meaning of the advice in the *Dhammapada* 285 (Radhaknishnan and Moore 1957: 314): 'Cut out the love of the self as you would an autumn-lily with the hand?' This is usually taken to involve more than merely rooting out the desire for natural gratifications and for the high opinion of other people. But is it not incoherent to try to live and act without any self-regard?

If James and Butler are right (Section 10.2), there is a primitive condition in which action is totally absorbed in its object without any regard for the self, that is for anything conceived as the agent of the action. Clearly, Buddhism does not call for a return to this primitive condition, but the condition points to the possibility of acting without regard for self, a possibility that might be realized in other ways. Mature individuals occasionally experience what they describe as 'loss of self' when they become engrossed in watching a drama, reading a novel, making something or managing some undertaking. When they have finished, they sometimes feel a mild shock as they reconnect to their ordinary concerns, concerns structured by their awareness of how their experiences bear on their self-image, their self-esteem, their personal projects and personal property.

Now if the mind can be drawn into something as complex as solving a mathematical problem or managing a crisis without connecting itself to preoccupations with the self, could one not seek a way of life in which this loss of self was permanent? Puzzle solving and crisis management may well not be the best activities to try if one hopes to sustain the loss of self. Governing, creating or being entertained may also be insufficiently stable, because they cannot be prolonged and hence the loss of self cannot be sustained indefinitely. But if one could establish a routine removed from everyday life in which long periods are spent developing and disciplining the mind's ability to concentrate on objects, in which social interactions reinforce or at any rate do not distract from that discipline and in which the manner of meeting the necessities of existence (food, shelter, etc.) is wholly uncluttered by opportunities for self-concern, might one not bring about a permanent loss of self? All activities would be done because they are to be done, not because I, this person, need or want or should do them. Everything would be done with as little self-regard as breathing is normally done. All humans would draw the same response of concern and compassion from me, not merely those who mean something *to me*.

The project begins with a measure of egoistic concern. For reasons more readily accessible to those who accept the framework of *karma* and rebirth but not inaccessible to those who do not, egoistic concern turns on itself, and the terminus of the process of trying to think out what is best for me ends with the thought that what is best for me is that I lose all concern with what is best *for me*. If the claim that all human conduct is self-regarding is a necessary truth, this conclusion (terminus) is incoherent and the project it suggests is unattainable. To the extent that some Buddhists do appear to exhibit the external signs of a total lack of self-regard and thus appear to have achieved the goal of becoming *arahants*, it seems that even this minimal self-regard is not a necessary condition of human action.

11.3 Apathy (*apatheia*) and non-attachment (*anupādisesa*)

The pathology of the passions

Buddhists and Epicureans, as we have seen, both address the problem of suffering, but whereas the latter outline a policy of avoidance, the former prescribe rooting out the cause. The approach recommended by the Buddha has some important similarities to that of the Epicureans' rivals, the Stoics. Stoics did not begin with the problem of suffering or the avoidance of distress. They began with the same problem that provided Aristotle's starting-point, which was to articulate the goal toward which people should direct their lives.[10]

Like Aristotle, they saw fulfillment as lying in excellence (virtue, *aretē*) that is in the best life that a human being could live, and they regarded the sort of emphasis placed on pleasure and pain by Epicurus as seriously misguided. Pleasure and pain are not merely objects about which we make judgments and reason our way to obtaining or avoiding. It is through our desires and aversions that pleasures and pains commonly infect our discursive thought in ways that distort our judgments and reasoning. Pleasures and pains were among the states of a person which the Stoics called *pathē* and which they classified as 'opinions' (*doxai*, defined as weak and false assents or judgments, 41C3), just as Buddhists treat ignorance as a crucial component of craving (*tanhā*, 'thirst'). Indeed, both traditions stress the difficulty of disentangling the cognitive and affective states of a person.

Epicureans held that pleasure is the natural object of an animal's impulse. Stoics denied this, insisting that if pleasure and pain occur in animals this would be as a by-product of the activities that they engaged in naturally as a means of sustaining their lives and continuing their species (LS 57A3). The activities rather than the by-product should be thought of as the natural object of their impulses. Human infants behave in this respect like non-linguistic animals (even if they do so much less effectively than do even the young of other animals, and thus need constant care and supervision). In human animals, there is a further natural development, which is the capacity to govern responses to impulses of desire and aversion by means of discursive thought. It is this that qualifies appetites and aversions as the kind of opinion that the Stoics called *pathē*.

According to the Stoics, 'pleasure' is for the most part a name for what we get when an appetite (shaped by discursive thought) is satisfied or we avoid something for which we have a (discursively shaped) aversion; 'distress' is a name for what we get when such an appetite is frustrated or we experience an object we want (in this cognitive fashion) to avoid (LS 65A4). In addition, experiences such as that of fulfilling a desire shaped by discursive thought will be infused with and in part constituted by beliefs about what one is undergoing. Pleasure in this sense is undergone by the body–mind as 'an irrational swelling' or 'elation,' which can be described from a slightly different perspective as 'a fresh opinion that something good is present' (LS 65B). In a similar fashion, pain or distress is also treated as a *pathos* and hence as a kind of opinion.

As the capacity for discursive thought does not normally perfect itself in adult humans without a great deal of personal investment and guidance from others, most human desires and aversions, satisfactions and dis-comforts, are 'disobedient to reason.' This is not merely because they are formed as a result of ignorance or of inadequate reasoning; the desires and aversions as well as the satisfaction and distress that are said to moti-vate humans do not always respond to improved information or reasoning (LS 65A6–8). Insofar as these *pathē* involve false beliefs about what is good for a person, they will tend to damage that person's interests. Inadequate beliefs do not always result in choices that damage one's inter-ests, but insofar as such beliefs are not secured by thorough understanding, one's choices can easily be turned in other directions. Indeed, the Stoics regarded *pathos* as co-extensive with 'fluttering' (LS 65A2), a state of mind that might be translated as 'liable to dithering.' The exemplary person, the Stoic 'wise man,' will have freed himself of all *pathē*: he will have achieved a state of *apatheia*.

Whereas Stoics develop their analyses of these notions by contrasting the capacities of humans and animals to secure what will contribute to their welfare, the corresponding Buddhist analyses attempt to spell out the meaning of a doctrine, that of 'dependent arising' (*paṭiccasamuppāda*), which opens up the possibility of identifying and rooting out the source of suffering. The doctrine is that everything that is depends for its being on certain conditions; that is to say, there is nothing that does not depend on something else for its being what it is, the way it is and its continuing to be at all. This applies to human individuals, for example, and has the consequence that we do not have permanent, indestructible 'souls,' although, as we have seen, we have a highly resilient tendency to sustain through our actions a continuum of suffering associated with a series of living bodies. This continuum the Buddha saw as dependent on what he called attachment, which in turn is dependent on the sort of desire char-acterized as 'craving,' which in turn is dependent on feeling (including pleasure and pain), which in turn is dependent on the sort of contact that a biologist or psychologist would characterize as stimulus, which in turn depends on a sentient body.[11]

Buddhism and Stoicism, like Epicureanism, are materialist philosophies in the sense that each insists that there is no mind or consciousness without a (sentient) material body. The chain of dependence traced in the previous paragraph is extended by two steps in which the Buddha insists that a sentient body is dependent on consciousness and consciousness on a sentient body. Now if we trace the chain of dependency from the inter-dependent pair, consciousness and sentient body, through stimulus as far as feeling, we will locate the sort of pleasures and pains that the Stoics allowed as a by-product of animal activity. If, however, these activities become objects of craving, we have something closely analogous to Stoic *pathē*. This is particularly so as craving is not possible without a cogni-tive component.

287

This is clear from an excursus in the text,[12] which traces an upward chain of dependency on craving through searching ('upward': that is searching depends on craving, etc.), [for] gain, [resulting in] decision making, [expressing] passionate desire or greed, [giving rise to] coveting, [for] acquisition, [which generates] avarice and [a posture of] guarding. This last appears to be something like a 'dog in the manger' attitude, as it is said to produce quarrelling, strife, dispute, malice, calumny, falsehood and a tendency to resort to deadly force ('taking up stick,' 'taking up sword'). One does not have to believe in rebirth to see the plausibility of this diagnosis of the sources of human misery.

This excursus is doubtless one of many possible ways to elaborate on the link between desire and attachment. Another text lists four general kinds of attachment, viz. to sensual pleasure, to opinions (or 'wayward beliefs,' cf. Stoic doxai), to fanatical conduct (in pursuit of virtue) and to the theory (or assertion) that there is a (permanent) self or soul (Warren 1896: 190). The second of these makes the point that enlightenment cannot be merely a matter of receiving better information about the true nature of things. Attachments to beliefs are as much appetitive and affective as they are cognitive. The third reveals that without enlightenment (or the guidance of an enlightened person), efforts toward excellence can be as damaging as a life of sensual indulgence. The fourth is not merely an important instance of the second; it is a misconception about oneself reflecting a complex of concerns that stand in the way of nirvana.

These attachments eventually exert influence on the sentient-body-cum-consciousness of an individual born after an agent's death. Another text traces the dependency of consciousness on two factors, ignorance and saṅkhārs,[13] and it is here that the effects of previous lives are supposed to be felt. As people are predisposed to react in dysfunctional ways to the feelings that arise when their capacities to be affected are stimulated, their ignorance (like Stoic undeveloped rational capacities) will initially handicap them with tunnel vision, which focuses their efforts so that they form attachments. The idea that the attachments of an individual human being of one generation will have identifiable effects on the life of an individual of a future generation may well be specific to traditions that originated in India. But if saṅkhārs were viewed as culturally transmitted, and if the idea were to be modified to the claim that the actions of a group of people have identifiable effects on the generations that inherit their culture, the doctrine would be a truism.

In any case, Buddhists would join the Stoics in rejecting Epicureanism for taking our desires and aversions as given and focusing concern only on the external effects of allowing them to determine what we do. To achieve real freedom from disturbance, real peace of mind, one has to take control of, and reshape, one's desires and aversions. Both Buddhists and Stoics insist that something like the ataraxia sought by Epicureans is a concomitant of achieving their respective goals. From the *Dhammapda* (94–5):

> He whose senses are mastered like horses well under the chario-
> teer's control, he who is purged of pride, free from passions, such
> a steadfast one even the gods envy (hold dear). Calm in the thought,
> calm the word and deed of him who, rightly knowing, is wholly
> freed, perfectly peaceful and equipoised.
>
> (Rahula 1974: 128)

From Seneca:

> What is a happy (*beata*) life? Peacefulness and constant tranquil-
> lity. Loftiness of mind will bestow this, and consistency which
> holds fast to good judgement. How are these things reached? If
> all of truth has been seen, if orderliness, moderation, and seem-
> liness are preserved in action, and [there is] a will which is guiltless
> and kindly, focussed upon reason and never departing from it, as
> lovable as it is admirable. To put it in a nutshell for you, the wise
> man's mind should be as befits god.
>
> (LS 63F)

Both insist that only by mastering oneself in this way can one have freedom worthy of the name. The *arahant* is free of the prospect of rebirth, free of the fires of craving and hatred, free of ignorance (Rahula 1974: 38). The Stoics claimed that a wise man is the only person who is free in the sense of having the power of autonomous action; everyone else is a slave (LS 67M1).

Both Buddhists and Stoics are accused of having to give up too much to achieve peace and freedom. But a Stoic wise man is supposed to rid his soul only of pathological states; he is not supposed to live altogether without feelings or emotions. His *apatheia* achieved, his *pathē* removed, he is left with three categories of good feeling (*eupatheia*): cheerfulness instead of pleasure, circumspection instead of fear, aspirations instead of desires (LS 65F); there is no good feeling that corresponds to pain. *Arahants* are sometimes thought to have no motives to act because they are supposed to have freed themselves from all desires (as those who have achieved what the Stoics called wisdom are thought to have no emotions because they have freed themselves from all 'passions'). But unless we apply a similar distinction to desires, between bad, unhealthy cravings and benign, healthy aspiration, it will be impossible to make sense of the Buddha's mission, that is of the tradition that after his enlightenment he was moved by compassion for human beings to teach others the Four Noble Truths and the Noble Eightfold Path.

Because compassion or pity in ordinary mortals can influence them to act improperly, Stoics classified this affection (what they called *eleos*) as one of the *pathē* (LS 65E4). Taken in isolation, the claim that a good and wise man should not feel pity or compassion makes the Stoic ideal sound inhuman. Again, the doctrine that there are healthy affective and motivational states of mind has to be applied. The healthy aspirations of the Stoic wise man were clearly intended to include the welfare of other people. The Stoic is concerned on all occasions to do the appropriate thing, while recognizing that humans are sometimes naturally moved by the plight of their fellows to do the wrong thing. Offering aid instead of encouraging self-reliance because one feels sorry for someone else, for example, may ultimately be unhelpful to that person. To the extent that the Buddha (because of his enlightenment) was 'accurately motivated' by concern for the plight of other human beings – meaning that he understood their problem and could offer a real solution – he was not moved by what the Stoics call *eleos*. The Pali word that is translated as 'compassion,' *karuṇā*, could be added to the Stoic vocabulary to provide a word (which Greek appears to lack) for a necessary aspect of a wise man's excellence.

The two outlooks differ profoundly in their conceptions of nature, of the place of humans in nature and hence of the self, as well as of the goal of human life and of the appropriate means of achieving it. Stoics believed that the universe is a single living organism, whose soul is God (in other words, they were pantheists, LS 54A–I), and that human beings are organs of that organism who have functions to perform just as do organs of any living body. To perform their functions correctly, moreover, they have to use their minds to understand their place in the world (LS 63E5–6). It is this function (necessarily involving its own proper conception) that determines what excellence involves for individual people and thereby what their particular happiness consists of. A person with sufficient insight to determine that role (what the Stoics called one's 'fate') will be content to fulfill it – lack of contentment with one's fate would be a sign of having failed to understand oneself, indeed of being attached to an inadequate conception of oneself. (The word 'attachment' here would have many, although not all, of the connotations of the Buddhists' word *upādāna*.)

Buddhists, on the other hand, do not see themselves as answering to any higher purpose than to end their own and others' attachments. Enlightenment does not show people their place in a larger project. Such a notion would strike a Buddhist as an attachment to wrong views, especially as a Stoic accepted that his fate might dictate that he should do away with himself (LS 66G, H). In general, it would be fair to say that the account of how to live prescribed in Buddhist precepts would be treated as a measure of 'right view.' People who claimed to be right in departing from the precepts would be judged to have attached themselves to wrong views.

On the whole, Stoics expected to conform to standards of propriety prevailing in society around them (LS 59E2–4 on 'proper functions,' *kathēkonta*). Such standards were natural means of achieving a natural end (human sociability) in the same way that an animal's impulses are natural means of maintaining (for its normal life span) the natural end of its own existence (LS 59**B**). And just as an animal's impulses may sometimes lead it astray, proper functions have similar limitations in that in some circumstances they are not the right things (LS 69**F–K**, *katorthōmata*) to do. (Stoics, who were committed to excellence and the admirable, scandalized their contemporaries by insisting that incest or cannibalism were not in all circumstances wrong actions.) The only thing that it was always right to do was to act virtuously in accordance with right reason (LS 59**M**). On whether we have a similar cognitive capacity with the authority to do what the precepts say should not be done or fail to do what the precepts encourage, the two main Buddhist traditions (see note 9) differ:

> The Mahāyāna emphasis on 'skilful means' entails that this tradition has a greater tendency than Theravāda to flexibly adapt the precepts to circumstances. A sanga's *Bodhisattva-bhūmi* says that a *Bodhisattva* may kill a person about to murder his parents or a monk, so that the assailant avoids the evil karma of killing, which is experienced by himself instead. He may also lie to save others, and steal the booty of thieves and unjust rulers, so that they are hindered in their evil ways.
>
> (Harvey 1990: 201–2)

In Buddhism, as in some Western traditions, the ability to exercise judgment is assigned different degrees of responsibility by different parts of the tradition.

The development of right reason (the excellence of the capacity for discursive thought) is evidently crucial for Stoic fulfillment, although this is not an excellence that one can develop without moral excellences. As in Aristotle, *phronēsis* was the chief virtue, but in a fashion more Socratic than Aristotelian, the moral virtues were defined as kinds of understanding ('sciences,' *epistēmai*, LS 61**H**). Buddhist enlightenment is likewise simultaneously a cognitive and a motivational/affective state. Where one of the three main subjects of the Stoics' curriculum,[14] logic, encouraged the development of discursive thought, one form of Buddhist 'mental culture' ('meditation') employed discursive thought, and some Buddhist schools have developed logical techniques every bit as sophisticated as those developed by the Stoics.

But the Buddha incorporated into his way a further kind of mental culture or meditation, which through increasing the control of concentration and mindfulness helps directly to achieve non-attachment. For example, one is taught first of all to narrow the focus of one's attention on a very basic bodily activity like breathing.[15] Achieving this for any length of time is by no means easy, but it has the effect of taking one temporarily out of the nexus of attachment, and the effect is one of helping to loosen those attachments when engaging in ordinary activities. It may well be that Stoics who made some progress in controlling the effects of the *pathē* on their thoughts and action did so by stumbling on techniques similar to that taught by the Buddha but no record survives of their using any such techniques or of their being incorporated into Stoic doctrines.

11.4   In the world but not of it

Hermits, monks and early capitalists

One further contrast between Buddhists and Stoics deserves to be explored, as it appears elsewhere and represents an important fork in the road for ascetics. Buddhists intent on *nirvana* saw the need to remove themselves from ordinary society and create for themselves a special social environment where they could pursue their objectives; Stoics (unlike Epicureans) did not form anything like a monastic movement. There are a variety of possible sources of the idea that an individual may (or even can only) live a satisfactory (or fulfilled or exemplary) life if free of certain forms of involvement with other people. Some of these give rise to extreme forms of renunciation. The act of removing oneself to live alone in the deserts of Egypt or the forests of India clearly draws a line between the individual 'renouncer' and the entire sphere of human relations. Any involvement with other people may be regarded as insignificant (if not detrimental) when considered in the light of goals such as maximizing time spent in prayer or meditation, purifying a soul polluted by its association with the flesh, emptying the vessel of the self so that it may be filled with the holy spirit, mastering the desires of a recalcitrant body or the thoughts of a haughty spirit, or charging a psychic battery with supernatural power.

There are also individuals who without any particularly lofty motives deliberately situate themselves on the margins of society and cultivate a sense of personal satisfaction through standing apart from ordinary human affairs. A loose collection of such drop-outs, who had, to be sure, their own lofty aspirations, was first constituted as a recognized 'school' of philosophy in Athens during the lifetime of Plato. They were known as 'Cynics,' from the Greek word for 'dog,' because they lived rough like stray dogs, feeding themselves by begging. Instead of devoting themselves to prayer or meditation as would mendicant monks, they engaged in conversation with one another and professed a philosophy that rejected social conventions, claiming that, through the ascetic disciplines that their lives required, they had secured freedom and self-mastery. Ancient Cynicism, however, does not appear to have explicitly claimed that human fulfill-ment is possible without any human relationships; an isolated Cynic would, at the very least, not have had the benefits of conversations with like-minded individuals. Ancient Cynicism was Epicureanism taken out of 'the garden' (or out of 'the commune') and practised in public with the Epicurean pursuit of pleasure converted into pride in personal austerity and the Epicurean desire to live unnoticed converted into open contempt for those who lived in thrall to the comforts of civilization.

Hermits, on the other hand, bent on one or another form of strictly personal fulfillment, can act, even live, co-operatively so long as their association with one another is based on the premise that fulfillment or salvation is an individual affair. This was the case with many of the so-called 'Desert Fathers' (Brown 1988: chapters 11 and 12). Nor does every effort to cultivate oneself require withdrawing from society. Confucians pursued 'learning' with the intent of becoming more accomplished social creatures. Ascetic disciplines by themselves need not set the self against the rest of society. Spartan discipline (see Section 3.1) and the vows of chastity on the part of the community of males that appears in the Dead Sea Scrolls (see Section 11.1) helped to maintain group solidarity.

Monastic movements, which are not founded on the premise that fulfill-ment or salvation is entirely an individual matter (best pursued by hermits), may nevertheless foster this attitude by encouraging their adherents to focus their commitment on a super-social reality such as God, or a goal such as *nirvana*, in a way that involves other individuals only incidentally. Practices of rigorous self-mortification and self-examination ('soul searching') direct individuals to roles and projects that may not be seen as integral to any wider social framework. People for whom a personal relationship to God or their achievement of a certain state of mind is para-mount will readily conceptualize themselves as standing apart from other human beings.

Although St Augustine spent much of his life in conversation with friends, and a fair proportion of his surviving works are letters written or dictated to friends, his literary output includes examples of very intense self-examination. The *Confessions* takes the form of an extended prayer[16] to God in which Augustine reviews his life trying to comprehend his personal history and his own nature. The problem that Augustine's self presents to him is the recalcitrance of his own motivational impulses. As a young adult he had been torn between his desire to be baptized into the Church and his reluctance to break with his dependency on sexual grati-fication: 'my state of bondage ... I was a prisoner of habit' (Pine-Coffin 1961: 129). He is still, more than a decade after a decisive conversion experience, facing the temptations presented to him through each of the sensory modes or by the mind's own self-indulgences – the satisfaction of its inquisitiveness, indulgence in idle speculation, the gratifications of praise, the vanity of self-complacency (see concluding chapters of Book X). Augustine's *Confessions* model a practice of self-scrutiny that searches beyond what any person could possibly find peering into murky depths that only an omniscient God can fathom: 'I cannot understand all that I am . . . the mind is too narrow to contain itself entirely' (X.8, 216).

Close scrutiny of the self is also recommended in an important Buddhist text, 'Discourse on Measuring in Accordance with' (*Anumānasutta*), in which *bhikkhus* are given sixteen 'qualities' that are to be used as 'measures of the self against the self' (Horner 1959: 124–31). The qualities are those that would determine whether a monk was 'easy to speak to, tractable, capable of being instructed.' The *bhikkhu* must examine himself for evil desires, a tendency to exalt himself and disparage others, a tendency to anger (and as a consequence find fault, take offense, utter angry words), to resent reproof (and as a consequence disparage the reprover, answer back, sulk and decline to explain his actions), become harsh and spiteful, envious and grudging, treacherous and deceitful, stubborn and proud, and finally to seize, grasp tightly and not easily let go of temporal things.[17]

Mainstream Buddhist thought assumes that this kind of tractable, non-attached self is best developed in a special social environment into which a *bhikkhu* withdraws from the everyday social world, leaving behind as much as possible the concerns with economic production and biological reproduction that structure that world. Buddhism, like Christian monasticism, views ordinary social roles as more often than not obstacles to fulfillment or to salvation. This view is open to the challenge that it would be a greater achievement to maintain the discipline required for fulfillment without the crutch of a special social environment. The *Bhagavad Gītā*, indeed, can be read as presenting this sort of challenge to Buddhism, although it is interesting how much of Buddhist doctrine is left behind as the project is outlined.

In Section 4.1, we considered the arguments by which Arjuna's charioteer, Krishna, an incarnation of the god Vishnu, tried to persuade Arjuna to participate in the battle about to commence, and we found Krishna's arguments to be at best inconclusive. The fuller treatment of the framework of Indian thought (*karma* and rebirth) that was provided in Section 11.2 with the discussion of Buddhism offers a more adequate appreciation of how Krishna views the source of Arjuna's anguish and how he tries to remove Arjuna's misgivings.[18] The wisdom that Krishna offers to Arjuna involves more than simply appreciating the indestructibility of 'the eternal embodied [souls]' – his own as well as those of the people he is about to try to kill. Arjuna, he assumes, is concerned with the effects of his actions (*karma*) on his place in the cycle of rebirth. The remedy he offers will absolve Arjuna from those effects: 'The wise [and by clear implication, the exemplary] discipline their intelligence and having abandoned the fruits of action are freed from the bondage of [re]birth and attain the sorrow-less state' (II.51).

According to Krishna, *karma* rebounds on agents because of their attachment to the fruits (the objectives) of their actions; the remedy is a form of non-attachment, especially to the outcome of one's actions. 'He who is not attached to (has no love for) anything, who is neither delighted nor is upset when he obtains good or evil, his mind is firmly established in wisdom' (II.57). 'If a person's desires flow into him like water into the sea, which though constantly being filled is unchanged, that person attains peace, but not if he clings to his desires' (II.70). The peace that this brings is characterized as the '*nirvana* of Brahman,' but the phrase is used in such a way as to make clear that this is not a state of extinction but a state of conscious well-being (V.24–6); thus translators commonly render *nirvana* in this context as 'bliss.' The path to this peace is said to lie through *yoga*, which suggests ascetic and meditative disciplines (see note 4). This not surprisingly leaves Arjuna puzzled (III.1, 2), since it seems that he should give up not only his worries about the consequences of the battle about to take place but also any thoughts of fighting to win, and should sit quietly meditating like a monk, unattached to anything about to happen.

Krishna, however, is recommending that Arjuna cultivate a kind of non-attachment even while hacking his way through the thick of mayhem. The secret is to act, to draw the bow, to swing the sword, without clinging with the mind (through desire or concern) to the intended outcome, death for one's enemies, victory for one's own side. Since we are dependent on our bodies, Krishna observes, we cannot in any case continue to exist without engaging in some kind of action all the time (III.5, 8). The attitude that the wise man takes toward what he does is the same as the attitude of a person offering food as a sacrifice to the gods; as a portion of the food ostensibly surrendered to the god may be eaten by the sacrificer (shared with the god), so that person simultaneously surrenders and shares in what he has surrendered (III.9–16). Thus a wise person is to carry out his caste *dharma* in a spirit of sacrifice, without attachment to the action. (Arjuna's, recall, is the *dharma* of a warrior, which requires him to fight in battles like that about to begin.) 'Better one's own *dharma*, though imperfectly carried out, than the *dharma* of another carried out perfectly. Better death in the fulfillment of one's own *dharma*, for another's is dangerous' (III.35).

So a higher level of understanding reveals that one can both act and do nothing because one has abandoned attachment to the fruits of action (IV.20). In response to Arjuna's question of whether it is better to renounce action or perform it, Krishna is unequivocal: 'Both renouncing actions and performing them ["as spiritual exercise," Zaehner] lead to the highest goal; but of the two, engaging in action is better than renouncing action' (V.2).

Being able to do this requires a special kind of discipline, *karma yoga* (III.7, V.6–12); its consequences are that the 'embodied [soul]' establishes sovereignty within the body ('the city of nine gates'), governing it without doing anything (V.13–14). The successful practitioner of this discipline, 'unattached to external contacts finds joy in [him]self' (V.21). Krishna repeatedly encourages the would-be practitioner of *karma yoga* to cultivate a sense of self hermetically insulated from a strenuously active body by focusing on Krishna as God, both as an example (III.22–4) and as an object of devotion (XII; XIV.26). The effort requires intense self-preoccupation (III.17) and induces a form of self-absorption.

The sixth book recommends (yogic) meditational practices like those central to Buddhism, but where Buddhism directs the focus of meditation toward the insubstantiality of self and onto the task of breaking its attachment to things in order to terminate its continuity, the *Bhagavad Gītā* offers reassurance of the substantiality of the self and works to break its attachment to worldly things, only to fasten it firmly on a divine being in order to realize a divine bliss. The call for a life of devotion to a god contrasts starkly with the Buddhist tradition, which makes provision for venerating only individuals who have lived exemplary lives. Equally stark is the contrast between calling on someone to strive to take human life in the fulfillment of a *dharma* (role) with a *dharma* (teaching) that forbids taking life.

Devotion to God, the *Bhagavad Gītā* suggests, is enough to sustain a life of non-attachment within the everyday world. One does not need to renounce acting in the world (except perhaps temporarily for the purposes of establishing yogic discipline) in order not to be *of* the world. Focusing on one's relationship to a transcendent (supernatural as well as supersocial) being provides a refuge but at the same time fosters within individuals a conception of themselves as independent of their relationships to other human beings. If one feels called by circumstances to act against family or friends – as Arjuna is expected to fight against both some of his blood relations and some who have taught him the skills and expectations of his *dharma* – this conception of one's own individual fulfillment or salvation may well help to ignore contrary voices.

The tradition is that Siddhārtha Gautama, the Buddha, distressed both his parents and his wife by leaving home to seek 'an unsurpassed excellent state of calm' among the *śramaṇas* (see Section 11.2); this hermit tradition sustained a conception of individual self-fulfillment to be sought outside ordinary society. In time, the movement that Gautama founded stood (as did Christian monasticism) within society but to one side of ordinary life as an important force reshaping ordinary life.[19] What Krishna offers Arjuna, however, is a way of reconciling himself to what society expects of a person with his *dharma* (role) and a way of not feeling misgivings that arise from personal attachments. The effect of accepting Krishna's

teaching will be to leave society – for all the upheavals that will be generated by the imminent armed conflict that frames the dialogue between the
warrior and the god – with its structure and concrete morality intact.

Max Weber recognized in the *Bhagavad Gītā* a form of what he called
'worldly asceticism,' that is ascetic discipline carried out in everyday life
(1958: 185).[20] This form of asceticism rests on the assumption that it is
possible to do what people ordinarily do – produce, reproduce, trade, fight
– without normal emotional attachments and without inappropriate estimates of the value of one's achievements. Another instance of worldly
asceticism that interested Weber intensely was that found in Protestantism
(see Section 2.1). In harmony with deep democratic and egalitarian tendencies, Protestants resisted the idea that it was possible to receive God's
grace in different degrees; individuals were either saved or damned.
Whereas the medieval Church had recognized a distinction between
precepts (*praecepta*), to which everyone was expected to conform, and
guidance given to those who wished to excel, known as counsels (*consilia*)
of perfection, Protestants collapsed this distinction. There was only one
standard of conduct appropriate for someone in a state of grace; all other
conduct was what one expected from sinners. Protestantism consequently
repudiated the monastic way of life as offering any special standing in the
eyes of God. (The first great reformer, Martin Luther, left a monastery
and eventually married a former nun and raised children.)

Both Protestantism and the Bhagavata religion require on the part of
the practitioner an intense devotion to a supreme deity and an attitude of
surrender (as sacrifice or stewardship) of the results of one's actions –
people are called on to act strenuously without claiming ownership of the
fruits of their efforts. The devotee of the Bhagavata religion, however, is
called upon to exhibit greater indifference to success or failure than the
Protestant, who must not merely perform a social role with diligence but
also apply good business sense and turn a profit – success being an indication of one's state of grace. Protestant thinking for its part operates
within a narrower range of social roles. Protestantism is a bourgeois movement; it despises the honor and glory valued by military aristocrats like
Arjuna (recall the sense of honor to which Krishna appeals when he begins
his exhortation); it rejects lives of renunciation and contemplation, which
Krishna allows are valid, if second-grade, forms of devotion. But both
encourage individuals to cultivate an awareness of and concern for their
selves by making them focus attention on *how* they are engaged in the
world. Individuals are to live for a super-social reality, not for their wives
and children, or their extended families, or their venerable teachers.[21]

Anxieties about pleasures and pains, whether their sources lie in animal
(food, sex), familial (companionship, filial affections) or wider social
(honor, spectacle) dimensions of human life, can no doubt sometimes
prevent people living full and flourishing human lives. But there is at the

root of these anxieties an important truth about us: human beings do not by and large automatically achieve the self-control that is necessary for the freedom and the special kind of agency that is distinctively human without some form of internal or external discipline. Passive responses to impulses and inclinations that are natural to human beings may well not amount to forms of activity that are characteristically human or to forms of life that can be described as anything other than impoverished.

At different periods in history in different cultural contexts, threats to personhood (see Section 7.1) may not come from individuals who seek to oppress or institutions that turn people into the equivalent of domestic appliances or industrial robots, but from individuals' own impulses and inclinations and the ways in which these are amplified, damped and channeled by the climates of attitude that prevail in their social environments. Achieving freedom, the opportunity to make something of one's own life, and to develop a full human personality, even to get what may be judged to be the maximum enjoyment out of life, may require efforts at forms of discipline and detachment.

Further reading

Brown (1988) provides an excellent survey of attitudes in the early centuries of Christianity toward the threats to salvation located in the body. Warder (1970) is a history of the development of Buddhism in India. For geographically more inclusive historical and doctrinal treatments, consult Harvey (1990: chapter 9 on ethics) and Kalupahana (1992: chapters VII–X on ethics). Rahula (1974) is a good brief introduction to Buddhist doctrine together with some translations of central texts. For surveys of Buddhist ethics, consult Saddhatissa (1970) and Kalupahana (1995). Keown (1992) is a comparative study of Buddhist and Aristotelian ethics. On Stoic ethics, see the commentaries to chapters 56–67 in Long and Sedley (1987), and for applications of (late) Stoic ethics to current issues, see Nussbaum (1994: chapters 9–12). On the *Bhagavad Gītā*, see the further reading for Chapter 4.

Notes

1 From the *Dhammacakkappavattana-sutta*, which represents the first words of the Buddha following his enlightenment. The five aggregates of attachment are intended to provide a comprehensive list of the bases of an individual's attachment to the world, viz. matter, sensation, perception, mental formation (including volition) and consciousness (*ibid.*: 20–3).

2 For a fuller description of the context of the *śramaṇa* movement in which Buddhism developed, see Warder (1970: 33–42).

3 'Technically, Indian asceticism was the most rationally developed in the world. There is hardly an ascetic method not practised with virtuosity in India and often rationalized into a theoretical technology' (Weber 1958: 148–9; *cf.* 163ff).

4 'The word *yoga* serves, in general, to designate any *ascetic technique* and any *method of meditation*' (4). *Yoga*, etymologically related to the English word 'yoke,' is derived from a word meaning 'to bind together.' 'The emphasis is laid on man's *effort* ("to yoke"), on his self-discipline, by virtue of which he can obtain concentration of spirit even before asking (as in the mystical varieties of Yoga) for the aid of the divinity' (5).

5 This is commonly translated as 'monks,' although the root means 'beggar' and the nearest Western parallels are 'friars,' members of mendicant orders (e.g. Franciscans, Dominicans) that were founded in the late Middle Ages in Europe. Women also appear to have formed (separate) groups of mendicants (*bhikkhuṇis*, 'nuns') at the outset of the movement, although the textual tradition has it that the Buddha was reluctant to permit this and did so only under pressure from his aunt, Mahāprajāpatī. For a translation of the relevant text, see Warren (1896: 441–7). This place of 'nuns' in (patriarchal) Buddhist societies has been precarious, and the female branch of the *Sangha* vanished altogether in Southeast Asia and Sri Lanka.

6 'Worship' in this case would be expressions of veneration, usually ritualized, for an exemplary individual who had attained the highest a human can aspire to achieve. The Buddha is not a god; divine beings are accepted as existing but play no significant role in Buddhist doctrine. Buddhism thus has the curious status of a religion without a central role for theology.

7 The Buddha's attitude to the laity is exemplified in 'Advice to Sigala' (Rahula 1974: 119–25). For the 'four vices' see (120); for the husband's responsibility to provide his wife with adornment (jewelry, etc.), see (123). For the Buddha's practical business advice ('investment philosophy'), see (83).

8 The 'Fire Sermon,' which is included in Rahula (1974: 95–7), is based on this image. The scholars and apologists alluded to in the previous sentence include Rahula (1974: chapter iv); Keown (1992: chapter 5) and Saddhatissa (1970: chapter 8).

9 An *arahant* has realized *nirvana* and will not be reborn. The enlightenment needed to achieve this may have to come from others who can find the way for themselves, buddhas. An *arahant* can induce enlightenment in others only by conveying the doctrine of a buddha. Buddhahood is thus regarded as a higher level of achievement. One important difference between Theravāda ('elder doctrine') Buddhism, which survives today in Sri Lanka and Southeast Asia, and Mahāyāna ('large vehicle') Buddhism, found today in Tibet, China and Japan, is that the latter encourages acolytes to aspire to the status of buddhas (to be what are known as *bodhisattvas*), rather than striving merely for *nirvana*.

10 This is not altogether surprising, as Stoicism was founded in Athens not long after Aristotle's death. As mentioned in note 6 to Chapter 4, the Stoics treated Socrates as one of their forebears. As Aristotle's school came to emphasize the study of nature and the Academy founded by Plato came to be dominated by skeptics (see Section 6.3), Stoics took up ethical and political questions in formulations given them by Plato and Aristotle. The reason they did not acknowledge the influence of Plato and Aristotle is probably that the schools founded by these two men continued to compete with them for pupils and for public standing.

11 The account here follows a dialogue, the *Mahānidāna Sutta*, translated in Warren (1896: 202–8) and discussed in Warder (1970: 107–17).

12 Omitted from Warren (1896), presumably the lacuna on (206); I am grateful to David Kalupahana for supplying a translation to compare with the discussion in Warder (1970: 111). The words in square brackets are conjectural and are intended to suggest a principle (foster an illusion) of coherence.

13 'Forces' (Warder), 'complexes' (Keown), 'volitional activities' (Saddhatissa), 'dispositions' (Kalupahana). The text is discussed in Warder (1970: 114).

14 The other two were ethics and physics (the study of nature); see LS 26A–D.

15 Buddhists commonly recommend beginning the development of mental concentration (*samādhi*, part of the eightfold noble path) through meditative practice by concentrating on one's breathing. See Rahula (1974: 69–71 and also 109–19) for a translation of a famous text, the *Satipaṭṭhāna-sutta*, in which the technique is described.

16 The *Confessions* is a self-consciously public prayer, written to be read by other people as well as heard by God: 'My confession [of faith as well as of past folly and sin] is made both silently in your sight, my God, and aloud as well' (X.2, Pine-Coffin 1961: 208).

17 '*Anumāna*,' according to footnotes to the translation, may also mean 'inference' or 'argument,' and the 'measures' may thus be read as the bases on which to infer whether the *bhikkhu* is tractable, etc. The notes also report that this text once had the status of a code of rules (*pātimokkha*) for *bhikkhus* and was intended to be reflected upon (chanted?) three times a day.

18 By almost any reckoning of dates, the *Bhagavad Gītā* was written after the advent of Buddhism in India. It is not, of course, a Buddhist text but a Hindu text, one that shows unmistakable signs of the influence of Buddhist thought (Zaehner 1972: 10–11, 158–9). Indian thought systems are divided into heterodox and orthodox, depending on whether they accept Hindu scripture (*Vedas*). Buddhism is unquestionably heterodox; the *Bhagavad Gītā* is treated as orthodox in spite of a few passages disparaging the Hindu scriptures. On the translations used here, see note 1 to Chapter 4.

19 Compare the expectations for Buddhist laypersons with the medieval Church's efforts to impose its conception of the proper conduct of sex and married life on the ruling laity of Latin Christendom. On the latter, see Gies and Gies (1989: chapters 4–6).

20 Talcott Parsons' term 'worldly asceticism' to render *innerweltliche Askese* is preferable to 'inner worldly asceticism'; see his note to his translation of Weber (1930: 193–4). The term of contrast, *ausserweltliche Askese*, is somewhat misleadingly translated 'other-worldly asceticism' (perhaps better, 'world-renouncing asceticism'). The difference is simply whether the (*ausserweltliche*) ascetic withdraws from everyday life, e.g. to a monastery, or practises (*innerweltliche*) ascetic discipline while otherwise living an ordinary life.

21 Taylor (1989: 226) cites the Puritan John Cotton's caution not to 'exceedingly delight in Husbands, Wives, Children' for it 'much benumbs and dims the Spirit.' Rather, 'such as have wives look at them not for their own ends, but to be better fitted for God's service, and bring them nearer to God.'

12

CONCLUSION: MEASURES THAT FALL SHORT?

> For each state of character has its own ideas of the noble
> and the pleasant, and perhaps the good man differs from
> others most by seeing the truth in each class of things, being
> as it were the norm and measure of them. In most things
> the error seems to be due to pleasure; for it appears a good
> when it is not. We therefore choose the pleasant as a good,
> and avoid pain as an evil.
>
> (Aristotle: *Nicomachean Ethics*, 1113a31–b1)

Recapitulation: Numerous concrete moralities and ethical traditions have been anchored in the belief that in one way or another our natural proclivities stand in the way of our living as we should. This belief has led to a variety of forms of renunciation of aspects of human life, ranging from basic biological and economic activities to intellectual and cultural pursuits and from emotional involvement in human relationships to any form of human association whatsoever. The goals of the ascetic impulse appear to be to avoid disturbance and find calm and to escape from what are perceived to be forms of bondage and achieve a release, perceived as a form of freedom.

Prospectus: This chapter will pull together the main threads of the previous chapters by examining a synthesis of the answers that Aristotle and Kant offer to the question, 'what basis, if any, have we for approving or condemning patterns of conduct?' This basis – in our natures as social creatures capable of discursive thought – for the measures of right, of virtue and of the good, is subject to challenges from three sources: from those who would assign higher priorities to the respect we owe to sentient creatures, from those who would assign value to a high degree of community solidarity and from those who would insist that not just our respect but also our concern should extend to everyone.

12.1 Challenging the sovereignty of reason

Slaves versus managers of the passions

Faced with conflicts and uncertainties over the attitudes that should be adopted toward patterns of conduct, people from different cultures and in different periods in history have frequently resorted to the image of a measuring device to describe what they felt was needed. Three general types of measure have been recognized, and in Section 4.4 these were (following tradition) labeled the measures of right, of virtue and of the good. Measures of right are made in terms of antecedently specified forms (commonly expressed as rules or general imperatives) against which acts can be assessed. Measures of virtue are made by reference to what we would expect exemplary (virtuous) individuals to do, given the qualities (virtues) that they possess which make them people worthy of admiration and emulation. Measures of good are made in terms of an account of what as a whole we are trying to do with our lives – what it is to do well, live well, flourish, achieve *eudaimonia*, etc. – and how a pattern of conduct contributes to or interferes with that objective.

Of course different rules can be formulated, different kinds of people can be admired and used as examples to be followed, different ways of living can be aimed at as best suited to human beings. The question 'what basis, if any, have we for approving or condemning attitudes and patterns of conduct?' becomes 'what basis, if any, have we for selecting measures of any of these three kinds?'

The most sophisticated of the answers applicable to measures of right is Kant's canon and the principle of right which he derived from that canon (Sections 7.3 and 7.4). Kant presented his canon in a number of forms; using one we measure what we propose to do by whether the maxims under which we act (the general imperatives that we as agents address to ourselves) can be made universal laws of nature. As it is not always straightforward to determine under what maxim an act is to be considered, it is easier to see the implications of another of the forms of the canon, that which has us measure what we propose to do by whether it involves treating rational creatures (human beings in particular) as persons or as things. If what we propose to do amounts to treating rational creatures merely as means and not also as ends in themselves, then the action does not 'measure up' and should not be carried out. The basis of all of the versions of the canon is an important distinction between different kinds of being in the world – between those beings, *viz.* persons, capable of a special kind of agency grounded in their ability to represent laws to themselves and those beings, *viz.* things, that can only respond to law-governed causal influences. From this canon comes the principle of right, that we may limit the freedom of persons to pursue their own ends only to prevent them interfering with the freedom of other persons.

Kant recognized that his canon did not (as it might have appeared from the way he presented it in some portions of his 1785 work) provide a procedure for determining what should be done in all circumstances. Some of the duties to which the canon gives rise, wide or imperfect duties, leave a great deal to the informed choice of each person, because how best to fulfill them depends on that person's particular circumstances. The upshot (see Section 8.1) was that even if Kant stressed the traits of strength or fortitude more than the traits of sound judgment, intelligence or wisdom, it would nevertheless take an ample measure of the latter to fulfill well the chief of the wide duties, *viz.* to perfect oneself and help others to achieve happiness. People cannot determine how resources of time, talent and effort should be distributed to achieve these 'ends that are also duties' without good use of their discursive capabilities. The measure in such matters would be a person with qualities like those of Aristotle's *phronimos*, a person with the ability to deliberate well about the ends we have that are unqualified (not qualified by some further end to which they are to be applied once achieved).

Kant, it seems, leaves us needing more than one measure. For some purposes his canon will do, for others we must use a measure of virtue. It was possible to anticipate this (at the end of Section 4.4) by elaborating a little the image of the measuring tool. Craftsmen do not get by with a single measuring tool. The thought that we might measure conduct with a single device, even a complex device like a system of law, may have been encouraged by a culture hungry for explicit guidance (end of Section 8.1), and this hunger may well be the root of the widespread attraction that theorists feel for one or another version of 'the morality system' (see Section 1.1), but hunger for totally explicit guidance is impossible to satisfy (see Section 6.2) and a diet consisting mainly of explicit guidance can sustain neither an individual life nor a culture.

Kant's virtuous person, moreover, cannot function on reason alone. The capacity to represent laws and rules and conform to them may be the basis of our freedom, but the truly excellent person needs an ability to recognize where laws and rules do and do not apply, the ability that Kant called 'judgment' and which he insisted cannot itself be reduced to rules (end of Section 7.4). Exemplary humans arguably need all of Kant's good will (beginning of Section 7.4), the full complement of Aristotle's ethical excellences (see Section 8.4) and that elusive quality of *jen* that Confucius sought to explain and instill (see Section 9.4), but the measure of virtue nevertheless turns crucially on the distinction between judging and judging well.

If in order to judge well an exemplary human being must, as Aristotle suggested, be able to deliberate well about the end in an unqualified sense (see Sections 8.4 and 9.1), the third type of measure will be required. For we cannot say whether a person is doing well or badly at fulfilling the

303

wide duty of perfecting self and promoting the happiness of others without some idea of what it is to live well. Kant would say that this is to live as far as possible in conformity with duty, but given that this includes wide duties, this is an unhelpful formula unless it is possible to fill out more fully what is involved in the duty to perfect oneself. Perfection, like harm (see Section 7.4) has to be determined relative to the thing being perfected or harmed, which cannot be done without an account of what it is for a human to do well over the span of a human life, in other words to live well as a human being. It is only with such a conception that individuals will be able to direct their efforts toward perfecting (or at least improving) themselves and also be able to select judiciously the help that they should give others to achieve happiness (in the sense of getting what they want). Without this conception, one might injudiciously help misguided people to get what they want – 'injudiciously' because what they want will in no way contribute to bettering their lives and may not even bring them satisfaction.

Now the reason that perfecting oneself is a wide duty is that there are multiple ways to go about it, multiple ways for an individual to live well as a human being, and how it is best for individuals to do so depends on their circumstances (their talents and the resources afforded by the societies in which they live). This should not be forgotten when considering Aristotle's suggestion that the basis for the measure of the good (life) lies in our capacity to use speech or discursive thought (*logos*). There are many possible ingredients in a human life, many roles, occupations and avocations, and many ways to combine those ingredients, but all of them can be pursued and their place in a person's life determined with a greater or lesser amount of discursive thought. The suggestion that activity in accordance with *logos* is what is characteristic of human beings, and the better we do it the more excellent we are, does not entail that there is only one thing that all successful human beings will devote their lives to pursuing – even if Aristotle does appear to have succumbed to the temptation to draw this inference (see Sections 9.2–3).

If we follow the implications of this synthesis of Kant and Aristotle, we will conclude that the basis of all three types of measure – of right, of virtue and of the good – lies in what is distinctive about us as creatures, not simply our capacity to reason (string together thoughts that provide reasons for one another), not merely in our capacity to represent rules, regularities and laws and to moderate our activities accordingly, but our capacity to combine these abilities with other functions built upon the sentient life (particular sensitivities and judgment) so that we are able to respond to features of our surroundings that are not accessible to creatures that lack our discursive capacities.

We must respect this complex capacity by not using creatures who possess it merely as means to our own ends, because it is what gives them the capability to determine their own ends. Those who exercise this capacity exceptionally well merit our admiration and deserve to be used as examples to be followed. The standard by which to assess harm and improvement (perfection) of humans *qua* human is the extent to which their lives have scope for, and exhibit, the realization of these capacities.

This is still far from sufficiently specific, and to air the questions that this synthesis leaves unresolved we can consider responses on its behalf to a number of challenges, the first of which is that which emerged at the end of Section 10.4. The relevant basis for our attitudes toward conduct should not, it was alleged, be the difference between persons and things but between sentient creatures and things. The possession of discursive thought (rationality broadly construed as in the previous paragraphs) is of no consequence. We are tied to the throne of pleasure and pain by causal chains, and our linguistic abilities give us at most the capacity to vary the length of those chains, not to break them. We are fooling ourselves if we imagine that by using our minds through our linguistic abilities we can achieve a level of freedom and dignity that places us on a level significantly different from, higher than, that of other sentient creatures with roughly our size and neural configuration. Reason remains, as Hume insisted (1739–40: 415), the slave of our passions and the servant of our desires, and we ought not to think of it in any other way.

But as Hume himself recognized (see Section 5.4), the capacity to represent the future to ourselves gives us a 'distant view or reflexion' and makes it possible for us to amplify a faint passion (of desire or aversion) for some future object into one strong enough to overcome the passions we feel for objects close at hand. If by using our rational capacities (along with our ability to imagine) we can place representations of two events – one bearing down on us, the other in the remote future – side by side and as a result we can bring about an adjustment of how strongly we feel about these respective events: 'reason' (broadly construed) is not merely serving our passions, it is managing them.

Hume's conception of 'reason' is as an ability to represent the way things are and is supposed therefore to be 'motivationally inert.' It follows from this conception, as he says in a passage that sounds reminiscent of Yang Chu (see Section 10.3), that ''Tis not contrary to reason to prefer the destruction of the whole world to the scratching of my finger' (416). But the ability to recognize that the destruction of the world may entail worse happening to one's finger than a mere scratch is part of that capacity that Hume labels 'reason,' and the desire framed on the basis of that modest 'distant view,' which is required to see the connection between such things, is not an original existence (see Section 5.4) that reason merely serves but one born of reason (the capacity for discursive thought). This is the difference between the claims of Yang and Hume: Yang would treat anything that amounted to 'cutting off one's nose to spite one's face' as folly and therefore contrary to any reasonable notion of reason.

If some individuals can, through looking 'dispassionately' at their bodily passions, bring about adjustments in the strength of their feelings, what prevents other individuals looking at the same passions and seeking to escape from all of them? In Chapter 11, we surveyed a variety of traditions that viewed our natural bodily (and in some cases social) desires as threats to human well-being. The reasoning that led to various efforts to repress bodily desires, and even eliminate totally the privilege normally given to the self, may not have been sound, but Hume's picture of human discursive capacities, as serving antecedently given desires, simply does not hold up in the face of these phenomena.

It should be acknowledged that however thoroughly human discursive capacities may restructure an individual's passions and desires, it is incoherent to imagine a person totally eliminating feeling or desire. Feeling is the general category of responsiveness to what is happening around one; desire is what, independent of immediate external circumstances, determines the character of one's response. If getting what one wants is pleasant and getting what one does not want is unpleasant, we are inescapably tied to the throne of pleasure and pain, for we will have wants in some form or other as long as we are agents.

But the capacity to represent our own feelings and desires is the condition of the possibility of making our feelings and desires the objects of (second-order) feelings and desires and thus to attempt, wisely or otherwise, successfully or otherwise, to alter them. We are not tied by causal chains to any particular pleasures or pains that may currently motivate us; we are tied only by habits, including those that give what strength there may be to our resolves. If we are tied to the throne of pleasure and pain by virtue of being agents, we can nevertheless reconstruct the throne to which we are tied by virtue of being creatures who represent to themselves the principles of their own agency. This is not something that appears to be true of animals without linguistic capacities.

If the basis of Kant's canon and the Aristotelian conceptions of virtue and human good are adopted, does that mean that we should regard ourselves as free to treat sentient creatures as things? For example, is smashing an old car to smithereens for 'emotional release' or to 'test its strength' no different from tormenting an animal to death for 'sport' or for 'science'? For those who believe that these are significantly different cases, the basis provided by Kant and Aristotle appears woefully inadequate. But what might be needed to support drawing a sharp moral distinction between things and non-rational sentient creatures cannot be seen clearly until we have considered how much regard, concern as well as respect, we should have for other creatures of our own (rational) kind.

12.2 Social animals

Associates, friends, communities

Humans do not acquire their distinctive form of agency without a social environment; they cannot make effective use of their characteristically human capacities without interacting with other human beings. Human relationships take a variety of general forms, one of which, 'an association,' is voluntarily entered into for the purposes of mutual benefit and is governed by tacit agreements, promises, contracts or formal partnerships. The give and take involved in reaching or maintaining agreement in these relationships involves each individual recognizing the others as persons and therefore as having their own ends, even though all have entered the relationship to further their own personal ends and would want to withdraw if those ends were to be frustrated rather than furthered.

We can assess the conduct of people in associations by Kant's measure of right (his canon) if we generalize his example of the perfect duty not to make lying promises (see Section 7.3). By this canon, people fail to 'measure up' who conduct themselves in co-operative endeavors (based on contracts, promises, tacit agreements) in ways that turn out to treat others merely as means. That is to say, each associate will have to maintain due consideration for the ends that the others had in entering the arrangement.

Thinking entirely in terms of relationships of association, however, is likely to distort the assessments that we make of how we relate to one another. An alternative to association, where individuals assess the value of their participation in terms of utility derived for themselves, is the general category of friendship (*philia*) found in Aristotle. The key to these relationships is that the personal goals of each 'friend' become integral to the personal goals of the others, which is what is implied by Aristotle's remark, 'a friend is another self' (see Section 10.2). Someone who lives only for personal pleasure, a 'subjective hedonist,' may well, given the variability of pleasure (see Section 10.1), find enjoyment in witnessing other people living pleasantly and may, if this enjoyment is mutual, have friends in this sense. Epicurus' warm endorsement of friendship makes sense if we understand him as appreciating what friends can contribute to a pleasant life, in a spirit similar to that which prompted Aristotle's recommendation of friendship as a vital component of a life devoted to contemplation (see Section 10.2).

Can this be generalized? Should anyone who appreciates what it is to be a human being – as a social creature as well as (in fact an essential ingredient of being) a creature with the capacity for discursive thought – recognize that friends in this sense are vital to living well as a human being? Kant, who thought mostly in terms of duties arising from the application of measures of right, insisted that along with our wide duty to perfect ourselves was a duty to benefit others without expectation of return (see Section 7.1). But this does not amount to a duty to have friends, a requirement that there be people whose goals are included in our goals and who include our goals in theirs. We can see the place of friendship in human life only if we apply measures of virtue and of the good. We have to be convinced that how ever well people may do individually, they will have done better if able to share in the successful application of their discursive capacities with others, that an exemplary person rendered unable by circumstances to share living well is to that extent unfortunate,[1] and that a person unable for psychological reasons to form friendships is not entirely exemplary (or 'fully virtuous').

To deny this, to reject what for Aristotle was a natural assumption about what is necessary for humans to live well, would be to embrace a weak form of (narrow) egoism (see Section 10.2) – not the doctrine that we would all be better off if we lived only for ourselves (in the narrow sense) but – the doctrine that there is no reason to prefer living for a narrow self to living for a more inclusive self. Kant's argument that we have duties to others appears to be addressed to this position, although its conclusion is a wide duty to benefit others rather than to expand what we think of as our self-interest.

In arguing that part of our wide duty to perfect ourselves includes duties of beneficence to others (1797: 450), Kant recognized that this interest in others might be very slight indeed compared with the interest we naturally took in ourselves:

> [In] making the well-being and happiness of others my *end* . . .
> I can, without violating the universality of the maxim, vary the
> degree greatly in accordance with the different objects of my love
> (one of whom concerns me more closely than another).
>
> (452)

Kant acknowledges that it is not obvious that the law that one should benefit some of those in need is to be found in reason: 'On the contrary, the maxim "Everyone for himself, God (fortune) for us all" seems to be the natural one' (*ibid.*). But if we recognize the duty to perfect ourselves and accept that we will not do this as well as we might if we must be able to make an equivalent return (must pay or reciprocate precisely) for everything that others do for us, we will see that the requirement that we universalize our maxims entails a duty to help others without the expectation of an immediate return (453). What does this duty entail? How far does it extend?

The opportunities that we have to benefit others in this way will be given shape by specific practices found in our social environment, which

will range from customs followed on an individual basis (alms for individual beggars) through private charitable institutions (to feed, house or
educate) to public tax-supported institutions (providing welfare, education
and general amenities). Kant's argument encourages us to think on the
level of the first of these, but it applies to all three levels. Even those who
are individually prosperous are afforded opportunities for a better quality
of life (to 'perfect themselves,' if we stay with Kant's idiom) by cultural
formations on all three of these levels. Everyone stands to benefit from
wisely following customs that govern interactions between needy individuals and those who can help, from the intelligently guided efforts of
voluntary collective activity and from sound policies carried out in the
comprehensive (government-managed) public sphere. The Epicurean isolation from and studied indifference toward anything that takes place outside
the private sphere came in for a species of moral condemnation from Peter
Green (see Section 10.2). Held against Kant's canon, the respect in which
Epicureans do not measure up is now commonly referred to by a term
that Green might have used, but did not: 'freeloaders.'

The importance of community, and of the cultural formations that sustain
it, is easily lost if we think only in terms of interactions and relationships
between individuals. As part of the trend in European thinking that has
extended from the seventeenth century to the present day (see Section
7.1), Kant tends to frame his discussion in individualist terms. But as we
have just seen, it is easier to use his principles to underwrite duties to
support social formations that benefit members of a community in general
than it is to explain the place of friendship in our lives.

There is, in addition to accepting responsibility for community life as
a means to the end of living well, a further function for the sense of
community, one with important similarities to friendship and which like
friendship seems to elude Kant's measure of right. There are people for
whom the welfare (the faring well) of a cultural formation is a significant
part of their idea of their own living well or faring well. For these people,
a cultural formation, which may be either their community as a whole or
some aspect of its shared life, serves as a 'quasi-other-self'; their notions
of their own *eudaimonia* are broadened in the way that the corresponding
notions of people who have friends are broadened. But instead of (or in
addition to) including the well-being of other individuals in their conception of what it is for them to do well, their ideas include the vitality and
effective presence of some aspect of their community's way of life.

The call for a renewed appreciation of the importance of community
(see Section 9.4) may be seen as coming from three directions, two of
which have just been mentioned. The first calls for an appreciation of the
resources for living well that are afforded to each of us by our willingness to work together for common purposes and the extent to which we
live impoverished lives if our existing attitudes and practices serve to

thwart efforts to do so. The second calls for an appreciation of the possibility of broadening people's conception of their own prosperity and welfare to include not only the faring well of friends but also the faring well of communal enterprises. The first involves a modification of the measure of right to yield a duty based on a better appreciation of how we should measure the good. The second suggests a measure of virtue that acknowledges that those who work for a better shared life not only deserve gratitude but also merit admiration and serve as exemplars. These two do not challenge the basis provided by Kant and Aristotle; they constitute a call for refinements of the measures founded on that basis.

From a third direction, however, does come a serious challenge. For the assumption in both Kant and Aristotle is that we live with one another for the sake of living well as individual human beings, and the forms of our relationships with one another need to be modified if they do not contribute to that end. The claim, contrary to this assumption, that individuals exist for the sake of the communities they constitute and for the cultural traditions they sustain and transmit, will lead to a devaluation of what individuals, even working co-operatively, take as their interests and set for themselves as the objectives for their lives.

It is certainly extremely common for societies to insist that some communal interests take precedence over those of individual members. Taxes are levied from the products of individuals' wealth or labor to support public institutions. Citizens may be called upon to risk their lives in defense of their communities or nations, and civilian populations may be called upon to make sacrifices 'for their father(or mother)lands' in time of crisis. Sometimes these expectations – especially those associated with social roles such as landed gentry and serf, parent and offspring, male and female – solidified in the distant past and operate at very deep levels in a culture. The practices that reinforce these expectations appear to be integral to the very structure of a society – 'built into the house in which we live . . . not to be removed without bringing it down' (see Section 2.4). But not all of these expectations help to sustain institutions that promote the well-being of the individuals concerned, or they provide advantages for only a few while serving as instruments of oppression for others.

It is far from clear that those who chafe under the burdens that a cultural form places on them, or who resent opportunities denied to them through the roles that they are required to fill, are asking for a 'free ride.' In many cases, they are asking for opportunities to shoulder important responsibilities as well as share in the associated rewards. If traditions that impose unequal burdens of pain, hardship and drudgery and limited opportunities on some sections of a society cannot be adapted to distribute the burdens more evenly or remove them all together, why should 'the house in which they live' not be 'brought down?' The (relativist) claim that there is no basis to prefer one way of life to another cannot, as we have seen (see Section 5.1), support the claim that any given way of life should be preserved. What must lie behind the claim that a way of life must be preserved regardless of the cost to certain individuals who are assigned burdensome roles, is the idea that cultures (societies and their ways of life) are more important than the individuals who constitute them.

Of course, individuals may decide that the continuance of a tradition (usually one into which they are born) is a part of their personal fulfillment, that contributing to the vitality of the way of life of their community is for them what it is to live and do well. This may involve accepting burdens of pain, hardship, drudgery and limited opportunity. What we are considering here, however, is the imposition of burdens even on those too young to choose them responsibly. The closing of minds and the modifications of bodies (see Section 1.4) may help to reproduce a way of life, but the solidarity sought by these means is, from the standpoint of Aristotle and Kant, not that of a human community but that of some other more tightly unified organic entity (see Section 7.1). Those who believe that there is an overriding value in forms of community solidarity that goes beyond what can be sustained by the commitment of 'free human beings' (adults with at least some grasp of alternative possibilities) have identified an end for which individual humans may be treated merely as the means.

12.3   Concern for everyone

Charity, compassion and contracting circles

We have identified two perspectives from which the basis for moral measures found in Kant and Aristotle will appear inadequate. From the standpoint of one, this basis does not sustain sufficient respect for sentience; from the standpoint of the other, it leaves us without sufficiently strong forms of community solidarity. A third perspective from which the basis appears inadequate is that which considers whether it encourages in people a sufficient regard, concern as well as respect, for human beings who do not belong to their own community. This perspective is becoming increasingly important as there are few people in the 'globalized' human world nowadays so isolated that they are not potentially able to affect or be affected by the activities of other people. We have acquired abilities to influence in a variety of ways people who do not share enough of our own language or culture to form with them a community in any sense. What basis is there to measure our responsiveness and responsibilities toward these other people?

Kant's canon ensures that we have some negative duties toward others by virtue of the respect they are owed as human beings. We are not to kill, injure, enslave or dispossess other peoples, where we have power to do so, even on the pretext of bringing them the benefits of civilization. Kant's own understanding of how his canon was to be applied entailed that most of the colonial activities that Europeans had been pursuing for more than two centuries were unjust (1797: 353). Arguably, prosperous industrialized nations have now turned to more subtle forms of economic exploitation. Dilemmas over whether to spend money on piano lessons for one's children or on famine relief (see Section 10.4) may as a result be premature if our participation in the global economic system has contributed substantially, even if indirectly, to the creation of famine conditions.

Such dilemmas are premised on 'concern for everyone' (see Section 10.3). Are we, in addition to making sure that we do not fail to respect the humanity of humans everywhere, called upon to feel any benevolence and carry out any acts that benefit anyone beyond our community? The argument that Kant offered against the maxim 'everyone for himself' depended on treating selfishness on the one hand and a duty of beneficence to members of one's community on the other as exhaustive alternatives. It did not suggest that there were duties beyond those toward one's 'fellowmen, that is, rational beings with needs, united by nature in one dwelling place' (453). It did not test the maxim 'everyone for his own most reliable support group.'

The idea that how well one's community (one's *polis*) does is either a necessary condition or a constituent part of that individual's *eudaimonia* was no doubt accessible to Aristotle, but neither entails an operative concern (a benevolence giving rise where possible to beneficence) for anyone beyond one's own community. Ethically excellent persons may well want to see their city flourish because they recognize that the environment provided by their city is a condition of their achieving *eudaimonia*, or, because being civic-minded they have identified the well-being of their city as a constituent of their own *eudaimonia*. But there is nothing in Aristotle to suggest that this should extend to a concern that even individuals in one's community who are not friends should do well, let alone those in other cities.

It is not altogether surprising not to find in Aristotle the generalized 'concern for everyone' advocated by such 'utilitarians' as Mo Tzu and J.S. Mill (see Section 10.3), as there is no recorded precedent for this in the West before the emergence of Stoicism some decades after Aristotle's death. Stoics were the first in the West to suggest that human beings had a responsibility to members of their species that transcended loyalties to their cities or nations, and it was they who introduced the idea of 'cosmopolitanism' or 'citizenship of the world' (LS 67**K, L**). A generalized 'concern for everyone' appears in the virtue of Christian charity, which includes loving your neighbor as yourself, where your neighbor may be a stranger from a group that your kind of people despises (Samaritans; Luke 10: 27–37) or who despises your kind of people. If this 'theological virtue,' as St Thomas

Aquinas classified it (IIaIIæ Qs23–46), does not play a prominent role in Kant's ethics, this only reflects a further respect in which Kant's general treatment of virtue is limited.

Kant not only assigned a less prominent role to wisdom than was traditional in framing a conception of an exemplary human being (see Section 8.1), he also worked to establish ethics on a purely rational basis. The concept of reason that Kant used was the 'practical' variety not the bare capacity to represent that Hume labeled 'reason.' Practical reason is goal-directed; it has ends. Having established limits on the means and ends that practical reason may adopt – they must not reduce other rational creatures to mere instruments – Kant, as we have seen, was far from clear about how inclusive our positive interests should be. Indeed, he went on from his argument against the maxim 'Everyone for himself, God (fortune) for us all' to raise the 'casuistical question' of whether it would not be better, as far as the happiness in the world is concerned, if we all concentrated on fulfilling our (narrow) duties of right and treated even benevolence (mere feeling), let alone beneficence (doing something positive), as morally indifferent. All he could suggest that might be 'missing from the world' if we did was 'a great moral adornment' (458). Aristotle would have had trouble understanding why concern extending beyond one's city should count even as an adornment.

While Kant insisted that we must wrest control of our decisions from the inclinations of the body, he was nevertheless far from advocating complete self-denial. The 'motivationally inert' conception of reason, as a mere power to represent, led Hume on the other hand to the further conclusions:

> 'Tis not contrary to reason for me to chuse my total ruin, to prevent the least uneasiness of an *Indian* or person wholly unknown to me. 'Tis as little contrary to reason to prefer even my own acknowledg'd lesser good to my greater, and have a more ardent affection for the former than the latter.
>
> (1739–40: 416)

Kant, along with philosophers ranging from Yang and Confucius to Aristotle and St Thomas Aquinas, would have rejected at least the second of these conclusions as contrary to (practical) reason. Practical reason begins with a presumption in favor of the interests of the person reasoning. It should moreover, Kant taught us, recognize limits to the pursuit of that interest in the persons of other rational creatures. It should furthermore, Aristotle taught us, recognize the need to make important adjustments to its initial conception of what its interests are. It may discover advantages to broadening its conception of its interest to include other people. But on a purely rational basis, which for Kant excluded any assurance (not founded on 'faith') of the existence of God or the truth of any particular religion, one important principle of Kant's own religious tradition, charity, is left without a basis.

Without a religious foundation the inclusion of 'concern for everyone' – even as a feature of a morally superior person, let alone as something that is a duty – appears to be without motivation. The arguments that Mo Tzu and J.S. Mill offered are evidently flawed (see Section 10.3). In a purely secular framework, the ultimate motivation can only be for individuals to work to be true to themselves. What need not be included in the self and its interests need not be a source of motivation. If there is reason to think that a self needs concern for *some* others, then exemplary people will make room for friends and possibly the prosperity of their communities, but what reason is there to think that a self needs 'concern for everyone?'

A transcendent God, who requires that charity (love in the first instance for Him) extend in appropriate degrees[2] to all mankind, provides a basis for a measure of virtue that is not exhausted in the goals that individuals choose to set for themselves. An immanent God, of whom all mankind is a part, as the pantheist Stoics believed in, provides a basis for a conception of living well that must extend to and include the well-being of the other parts of the whole of which one (one's self) is a part. Individuals, who accept the diagnosis that the attachments they form to things and to particular people will prove to be nothing but a source of suffering and who embrace a conception of living well that consists of systematically dismantling the self that is constituted by those attachments, are open to accepting the qualities of loving kindness and compassion as the excellences that should rule their lives. This diagnosis does not involve a theological basis, but it is characteristic, nevertheless, of a religious tradition whose founder, Siddhārtha Gautama, the Buddha (see Section 11.2), is taken to exemplify these virtues of universal compassion and loving kindness.

None of these traditions takes for granted the standpoint of universal concern; all recognize that this is something that needs to be worked toward, and doing so will face opposition from powerful forces that attach each of us, at least initially, to narrow concerns. A Stoic philosopher named Hierocles (first century CE) described each of us as the center of multiple concentric circles of interest. The closest was our body and its needs, the next our immediate families, the next after that our extended families (uncles and aunts, grandparents, cousins), then more remote relatives, then neighbors, fellow citizens and fellow countrymen; the outermost circle was the human race:

It is incumbent on us to respect people from the third circle as if they were those from the second, and again to respect our other relatives as if they were those from the third circle, for although the greater distance in blood will remove some affection, we must still try hard to assimilate them. The right point

314

will be reached if, through our own initiative, we reduce the distance of the relationship with each person.

(LS 57G6)

Hierocles did not regard it as an easy matter to 'intensify the indicated contraction of the circles' (LS 57G7), but doing so was part of achieving excellence and realizing *eudaimonia*.

Hierocles' ideal, like St Thomas Aquinas' conception of charity that admits of degrees, leaves the usual structure of human relations intact; we continue to distinguish people close to our concerns from those who are more remote. But the implication is that we are to draw more people into the groups for which we have greater concern in order to overcome the centrifugal forces that naturally arise when we operate with different degrees of concern for one another.

Hierocles takes the outermost circle to be the human race; Aquinas holds it to be inappropriate to extend charity to irrational creatures (IIaIIæ Q25 A3). Neither tradition, Stoic or Christian, extends the circle of concern to sentient creatures in general. Only Buddhism, the tradition that recommends the systematic dismantling of attachment, instead of a refocusing of attachment on a higher (transcendent or immanent) being, extends its precept not to kill or injure to animals, birds, fish and insects (Harvey 1990: 202).

Our nature as social creatures with the capacity for discursive thought provides a basis for a framework that can be synthesized from the work of Aristotle and Kant, one that includes universality of respect but does not necessarily include universality of concern. We may have this concern, we may admire (regard as virtuous) those who have it, but we are not equipped to say what makes this a worthy goal or an admirable trait of character. If it is held that systematic ethics should provide 'concern for everyone' with a basis, what seems to be required is a system of belief that reveals why an inferior role should be assigned to our natural tendency to value most highly what we as individual agents can achieve by interacting with persons as well as upon things that immediately surround us. Such a system of belief may not need a religious foundation to sustain it, but the relative lack of importance it will have us assign to our normal preoccupations is characteristic of attitudes that underlie the religious life.

Notes

1   Such a person is in terms of note 4 to Chapter 9 above, *eudaimōn* but not *makarios*.
2   On degrees of charity, see Aquinas IIaIIæ Q 26.

CHARACTER TABLE

Romanizations do not uniquely determine Chinese characters. As readers of my drafts who were fluent in Chinese expressed frustration at being uncertain about which character lay behind a given romanization, I have supplied the following table. (Wade–Giles romanization is used in the text; the following table also supplies Pinyin romanization.)

Wade–Giles	Pinyin	Meaning	Character(s)
cheng ming	*zhengming*	correction of names	正名
chien ai	*jian'ai*	concern for everyone	兼愛
ch'ih	*chi*	shame	恥
chung	*zhong*	conscientious	忠
chün tzu	*junzi*	superior man	君子
fa	*fa*	standard	法
hsiao	*xiao*	filiality	孝
hsiao jen	*xiaoren*	small man	小人
hsin	*xin*	heart–mind	心
hsing	*xing*	nature	性
hsüeh	*xue*	learning	學
en	*ren*	humane	仁
li	*li*	ritual (propriety)	禮
sheng jen	*shengren*	sage	聖人
shu	*shu*	altruism	恕
ssu	*si*	reflecting	思
tao	*dao*	way	道
te	*de*	virtue	德
t'ien	*tian*	heaven	天
yi	*yi*	righteousness	義
yung	*yong*	courage	勇
Names			
Chuang Tzu	Zhuangzi		莊子
Confucius	Kongzi		孔子
Han Fei Tzu	Hanfeizi		韓非子
Hsün Tzu	Xunzi		荀子
Hui (Shih) Tzu	Hui(shi)zi		惠施子
Mencius	Mengzi		孟子
Mo Tzu	Mozi		墨子
Yang Chu	Yang Zhu		楊朱

REFERENCES

Where possible, references are cited by means of the original date of publication; if a second date is given, it indicates that a later edition was used.

Ackah, C.A. (1988) *Akan Ethics*, Accra, Ghana: Universities Press.

Ackrill, J.L. (1974) 'Aristotle on *Eudaimonia*,' in Amélie Oksenberg Rorty (ed.) *Essays on Aristotle's Ethics*, Berkeley: University of California Press, 1980: 15–33.

Aiyar, P.S. Sivaswamy (1935) *The Evolution of Hindu Moral Ideals*, Calcutta: Calcutta University Press.

Allen, Reginald E. (1970) *Plato's 'Euthyphro' and the Early Theory of Forms*, London: Routledge & Kegan Paul.

Anscombe, Elizabeth (1965) 'Thought and Action in Aristotle,' in Jonathan Barnes, Malcolm Schofield and Richard Sorabji (eds) *Articles on Aristotle*, Vol. 2, London: Duckworth, 1977: 61–71.

Aquinas, St Thomas (1911) *Summa Theologica*, translated by the Fathers of the English Dominican Province, Allen, Texas: Christian Classics, 1981.

Arens, William (1979) *The Man-Eating Myth: Anthropology and Anthropophagy*, Oxford: Oxford University Press.

Aristotle (1984) *The Complete Works of Aristotle*, edited by Jonathan Barnes, Princeton, NJ: Princeton University Press.

Austin, Jean (1968) 'Pleasure and Happiness,' in J.B. Schneewind (ed.) *Mill: A Collection of Critical Essays*, London: MacMillan, 234–50.

Avineri, Schlomo and de-Shalit, Avner (eds) (1992) *Communitarianism and Individualism*, Oxford: Oxford University Press.

Ayer, A.J. (1936) *Language, Truth and Logic*, London: Victor Gollancz.

Badhwar, Neera Kapur (ed.) (1993) *Friendship: a Philosophical Reader*, Ithaca, NY: Cornell University Press.

Bales, Kevin (1999) *Disposable People: New Slavery in the Global Economy*, Berkeley: University of California Press.

Bell, Daniel (1993) *Communitarianism and its Critics*, Oxford: Clarendon Press.

Bellah, Robert N., *et al.* (1985) *Habits of the Heart*, Berkeley: University of California Press.

Benedict, Ruth (1946) *The Chrysanthemum and the Sword: Patterns of Japanese Culture*, Boston: Houghton Mifflin.

Bentham, Jeremy (1789) *An Introduction to the Principles of Morals and Legislation*, edited by Laurence J. LaFleur, New York: Hafner, 1948.

—— (1843) *Collected Works*, edited by Sir John Bowring, Edinburgh: William Tait.

Berger, Fred (1984) *Happiness, Justice and Freedom: The Moral and Political Philosophy of John Stuart Mill*, Berkeley: University of Calfornia Press.

317

REFERENCES

Bettenson, Henry (trans.) (1972) Augustine's *The City of God*, Harmondsworth, Middlesex: Penguin Books.

Blackburn, Simon (1984) *Spreading the Word*, Oxford: Clarendon Press.

Blake, C. Fred (1994) 'Foot-binding in Neo-Confucian China,' *Signs* 19: 676–712.

Bourdieu, Pierre (1980) *The Logic of Practice*, translated by Richard Nice, Stanford, Calif.: Stanford University Press, 1990.

Brandt, R.B. (1954) *Hopi Ethics: A Theoretical Analysis*, Chicago: University of Chicago Press.

Brink, David (1989) *Moral Realism and the Foundations of Ethics*, Cambridge: Cambridge University Press.

Brown, Peter (1988) *The Body and Society: Men, Women and Sexual Renunciation in Early Christianity*, New York: Columbia University Press.

Brunt, P.A. (1993) *Studies in Greek History and Thought*, Oxford: Clarendon Press.

Burkert, Walter (1985) *Greek Religion*, translated by John Raffan, Cambridge, Mass.: Harvard University Press.

Burnyeat, M.F. (1979) 'Conflicting appearances,' *Proceedings of the British Academy* LXV: 69–111.

Burnyeat, Myles and Frede, Michael (1997) *The Original Sceptics: A Controversy*, Indianapolis: Hackett.

Bury, R.G. (trans.) (1933) Sextus Empiricus, Vol. 1 *Outlines of Pyrrhonism*, Cambridge, Mass.: Loeb Classical Library.

Butler, Joseph (1726) *Butler's Fifteen Sermons and a Dissertation on the Nature of Virtue*, edited by W.R. Matthews, London: G. Bell, 1958.

Buxbaum, David (ed.) (1968) *Family Law and Customary Law in Asia*, The Hague: Martinus Nijhoff.

Carlyle, A.J. (1930) *A History of Medieval Political Theory in the West*, third edition, Vols 1 and 2, Edinburgh: William Blackwood.

Chan Wing-tsit (1963) *A Source Book of Chinese Philosophy*, Princeton, NJ: Princeton University Press.

Clark, Stephen R.L. (1997) *Animals and Their Moral Standing*, London: Routledge.

Cohen, David (1991) *Law, Sexuality and Society: The Enforcement of Morals in Classical Athens*, Cambridge: Cambridge University Press.

Cooper, John M. (1975) *Reason and Human Good in Aristotle*, Indianapolis: Hackett, 1986.

—— (ed.) (1997) *Plato: Complete Works*, Indianapolis: Hackett.

Dancy, Jonathan (1993) *Moral Reasons*, Oxford: Basil Blackwell.

Danquah, J.B. (1968) *The Akan Doctrine of God: A Fragment of Gold Coast Ethics and Religion*, London: Frank Cass.

Darnton, Robert (1985) *The Great Cat Massacre and Other Episodes in French Cultural History*, Harmondsworth, Middlesex: Penguin Books.

Davis, David Brion (1984) *Slavery and Human Progress*, New York: Oxford University Press.

Deutsch, Eliot (1968) *The Bhagavad Gītā*, translated with introduction and critical essay, New York: University Press of America.

Devlin, Patrick (1965) *The Enforcement of Morals*, Oxford: Oxford University Press.

Dewey, John (1939) 'The Theory of Valuation,' in *International Encyclopedia of Unified Science*, II, 4, Chicago: University of Chicago Press.

Dewey, John and Tufts, James Hayden (1932) *Ethics*, second edition, *John Dewey: The Later Works, 1925–53*, Vol. 7, Carbondale, Ill.: Southern Illinois University Press, 1989.

Dihle, Albrecht (1982) *The Theory of Will in Classical Antiquity*, Berkeley: University of California Press.

Dover, K.J. (1974) *Greek Popular Morality in the Time of Plato and Aristotle*, Oxford: Basil Blackwell.

Dumont, Louis (1980) *Homo Hierarchicus: The Caste System and Its Implications*, translated by Mark Sainsbury, Louis Dumont and Basia Bulati, second edition, Chicago: University of Chicago Press.

Dumont, Louis (1982) *Essays on Individualism*, Chicago: University of Chicago Press.

Durkheim, Emile (1897) *Suicide: A Study in Sociology*, translated by John A. Spaulding and George Simpson, London: Routledge & Kegan Paul, 1952.

Dworkin, Ronald (1967) 'Is Law a System of Rules?' in Ronald Dworkin (ed.) *The Philosophy of Law*, 1977, Oxford: Oxford University Press: 38–65.

El Dareer, Asthma (1982) *Woman Why do You Weep: Circumcision and Its Consequences*, London: Zed Books.

Eliade, Mircea (1958) *Yoga: Immortality and Freedom*, New York: Pantheon Books.

Ellerman, David P. (1995) *Intellectual Trespassing as a Way of Life: Essays in Philosophy, Economics and Mathematics*, Lanham, Md.: Rowman & Littlefield.

Eno, Robert (1990) *The Confucian Creation of Heaven: Philosophy and the Defense of Ritual Mastery*, Albany, NY: State University of New York Press.

d'Entrèves, A.P. (1951) *Natural Law: An Introduction to Legal Philosophy*, London: Hutchinson.

Evans-Pritchard, E.E. (1937) *Witchcraft, Oracles and Magic among the Azande*, Oxford: Clarendon Press.

Fakhry, Majid (1994) *Ethical Theories in Islam*, Leiden: E.J. Brill.

Falconer, William Armistead (trans.) (1923) Cicero *De Amicitia, De Senectute and De Divinatione*, Cambridge, Mass.: Loeb Classical Library.

Feinberg, Joel (1988) *Harmless Wrong-Doing*, New York: Oxford University Press.

Finley, Moses (1980) *Ancient Slavery and Modern Ideology*, New York: Viking Press.

Finnerty, Amy (1999) 'The Body Politic,' *New York Times Magazine*, May 9: 22.

Foot, Philippa (1978) *Virtues and Vices*, Oxford: Blackwell.

Fowler, Harold North (trans.) (1914) Plato *Euthyphro, Apology, Crito, Phaedo, Phaedrus*, Cambridge, Mass., Loeb Classical Library, 1990.

Frankena, William (1939) 'The Naturalistic Fallacy,' in Philippa Foot (ed.) *Theories of Ethics*, Oxford: Oxford University Press, 1967.

Freeman, Michael and Veerman, Philip (eds) (1992) *The Ideologies of Children's Rights*, Dordrecht, Netherlands: Martinus Nijhoff.

Garnsey, Peter (1970) *Social Status and Legal Privilege in the Roman Empire*, Oxford: Clarendon Press.

Gierke, Otto (1934) *Natural Law and the Theory of Society*, Vol. 1, translated by Ernest Barker, Cambridge: Cambridge University Press.

Gies, Frances and Gies, Joseph (1989) *Marriage and the Family in the Middle Ages*, New York: Harper & Row.

Gillis, John R. (1985) *For Better, For Worse: British Marriages 1600 to the Present*, New York: Oxford University Press.

—— (1996) *A World of Their Own Making: Myth, Ritual and the Quest for Family Values*, New York: Basic Books.

Godely, A.D. (trans.) (1922) Herodotus, *Histories*, Vol. III, Cambridge, Mass.: Loeb Classical Library.

Graham, A.C. (trans.) (1960) *The Book of Leih-tzu: A Classic of Tao*, New York: Columbia University Press Morningside Edition, 1990.

—— (1985) 'The Right to Selfishness: Yangism, Later Mohism, Chuang Tzu,' in Donald Munro (ed.) *Individualism and Holism*, Ann Arbor: University of Michigan Press, 73–83.

—— (1989) *Disputers of the Tao: Philosophical Argument in Ancient China*, La Salle, Ill.: Open Court.

Gray, John Henry (1878) *China: a History of the Laws, Manners and Customs of the People*, Vol. I, London: Macmillan.

Green, Peter (1993) *Alexander to Actium*, Berkeley: University of California Press.

Grönbech, Vilhelm (1931) *The Culture of the Teutons*, Vol. 1, translated by W. Worster, London: Humphrey Milford.

Grotius, Hugo (1625) *De Jure Belli ac Pacis*, (*On the Law of War and Peace*), Vol. 2, translated by Francis W. Kelsey, Oxford: Clarendon Press, 1925.

Guthrie, W.K.C. (1971) *The Sophists*, Cambridge: Cambridge University Press.

Habel, Norman C. (1975) *The Book of Job*, Cambridge: Cambridge University Press.

Hall, David L. and Ames, Roger T. (1987) *Thinking Through Confucius*, Albany, NY: State University of New York Press.

Hamilton, Edith and Cairns, Huntington (eds) (1961) *The Collected Dialogues of Plato*, Princeton, NJ: Princeton University Press,

Hansen, Chad (1992) *A Daoist Theory of Chinese Thought: A Philosophical Interpretation*, New York: Oxford University Press.

Hardie, W.F.R. (1965) 'The final good in Aristotle's ethics,' *Philosophy* 40: 277–95.

Hare, R.M. (1952) *The Language of Morals*, Oxford: Clarendon Press.

—— (1981) *Moral Thinking: Its Levels, Method, and Point*, Oxford: Clarendon Press.

Hart, H.L.A. (1958) 'Positivism and the separation of law and morals,' in Ronald Dworkin (ed.) *The Philosophy of Law*, Oxford: Oxford University Press: 17–37.

—— (1961) *The Concept of Law*, Oxford: Oxford University Press.

Harvey, Peter (1990) *An Introduction to Buddhism: Teachings, History and Practices*, Cambridge: Cambridge University Press.

Hawley, John Stratton (ed.) (1994) *Sati, the Blessing and the Curse*, New York: Oxford University Press.

Hegel, G.W. (1821) *Hegel's Philosophy of Right*, translated by T.W. Knox, Oxford: Clarendon Press, 1952.

Herman, Barbara (1993) *The Practice of Moral Judgment*, Cambridge, Mass.: Harvard University Press.

Hibino, Yutaka (1904) *Nippon Shindo Ron, or the National Ideals of the Japanese People*, translated by A.P. McKenzie, Cambridge: Cambridge University Press, 1928.

Hillers, Delbert (1969) *Covenant, the History of a Biblical Idea*, Baltimore: Johns Hopkins University Press.

Hobbes, Thomas (1658) *Man and Citizen*, translated by Charles T. Wood, T.S.K. Scott-Craig and Bernard Gert, Indianapolis: Hackett, 1991.

Hoebel, E. Adamson (1949) *Man in the Primitive World*, New York: McGraw Hill.

Hoffmann, Joseph (trans.) (1986) Celsus, *On the True Doctrine: A Discourse against the Christians*, New York: Oxford University Press.

Honderich, Ted (1993) *How Free Are You?* Oxford: Oxford University Press.

Hopkins, Keith (1980) 'Brother–sister marriage in Roman Egypt,' *Comparative Studies in Society and History* 22: 303–54.

Horner, I.B. (trans.) (1959) *The Middle Length Sayings*, Vol. III, London: Pali Text Society.

Hudson, W.D. (ed.) (1969) *The Is/Ought Question*, London: Macmillan.

Hume, David (1739–40) *A Treatise of Human Nature*, edited by L.A. Selby-Bigge, Oxford: Clarendon Press, 1975.

Hutton, J.H. (1963) *Caste in India*, fourth edition, Bombay: Oxford University Press.

Jackson, Beverley (1997) *Splendid Slippers: A Thousand Years of an Erotic Tradition*, Berkeley, Calif.: Ten Speed Press.

James, William (1890) *The Principles of Psychology*, in two volumes, New York: Dover Reprint, 1952.

Jones, Howard (1989) *The Epicurean Tradition*, London: Routledge.

Jonsen, Albert (1991) 'Casuistry as a methodology in clinical ethics,' *Theoretical Medicine* 12: 295–307.

Jonsen, Albert and Toulmin, Stephen (1988) *The Abuse of Casuistry*, Berkeley: University of California Press.

Kakar, Sudhir (1978) *The Inner World: A Psycho-Analytic Study of Childhood and Society in India*, Delhi: Oxford University Press.

Kalupahana, David (1992) *A History of Buddhist Philosophy: Continuities and Discontinuities*, Honolulu: University of Hawaii Press.

—— (1995) *Ethics in Early Buddhism*, Honolulu: University of Hawaii Press.

Kant, Immanuel (1781 = A/1787 = B) *Critique of Pure Reason*, translated by Norman Kemp Smith, second impression, London: Macmillan, 1933.

—— (1785) *The Moral Law: Kant's Groundwork of the Metaphysic of Morals*, translated by H.J. Paton, third edition, London: Hutchinson, 1956.

—— (1797) *The Metaphysics of Morals*, translated by Mary Gregor, Cambridge: Cambridge University Press, 1996.

Kelsen, Hans (1960) *What is Justice*, Berkeley: University of California Press.

Kenny, Anthony (1992) *Aristotle on the Perfect Life*, Oxford: Oxford University Press.

Keown, Damien (1992) *The Nature of Buddhist Ethics*, New York: St Martin's Press.

Keyes, Clinton Walker (trans.) (1938) Cicero, *The Republic and the Laws*, Cambridge, Mass.: Loeb Classical Library, 1938.

Khadduri, Majid (1984) *The Islamic Conception of Justice*, Baltimore: Johns Hopkins University Press.

Kipnis, Kenneth and Diamond, Milton (1998) 'Pediatric ethics and the surgical assignment of sex,' *The Journal of Clinical Ethics* 9(4): 398–410.

Kjellberg, Paul and Ivanhoe, Philip J. (eds) (1996) *Essays on Skepticism, Relativism and Ethics in the Zhuangzi*, Albany, NY: State University of New York Press.

Korsgaard, Christine M. (1996) *Creating the Kingdom of Ends*, Cambridge: Cambridge University Press.

Kosman, L.A., (1980) 'Being properly affected: virtues and feelings in Aristotle's ethics,' in Amélie Oksenberg Rorty (ed.) *Essays on Aristotle's Ethics*, Berkeley: University of California Press: 103–16.

Kunkel, Wolfgang (1973) *An Introduction to Roman Legal and Constitutional History*, translated by J.M. Kelly, Oxford: Clarendon Press.

Ladd, John (1957) *The Structure of a Moral Code, A Philosophical Analysis of Ethical Discourse Applied to the Ethics of the Navaho Indians*, Cambridge, Mass.: Harvard University Press.

Lau, D.C. (trans.) (1979) Confucius, *The Analects*, Harmondsworth, Middlesex: Penguin Books.

Lee, H.D.P. (trans.) (1974) *Plato's Republic*, Harmondsworth, Middlesex: Penguin Books.

Le Goff, Jacques (1984) *The Birth of Purgatory*, translated by Arthur Goldhammer, Chicago: University of Chicago Press.

Levi, Edward H. (1949) *An Introduction to Legal Reasoning*, Chicago: University of Chicago Press.

Lewis, David (1969) *Convention: a Philosophical Study*, Cambridge, Mass.: Harvard University Press.

REFERENCES

Llewellyn, K.N. (1930) *The Bramble Bush: On our Law and Its Study*, New York: Oceana, 1960.
Locke, John (1689) *Two Treatises of Government*, edited by Peter Laslett, Cambridge: Cambridge University Press, 1967.
—— (1690) *An Essay Concerning Human Understanding*, London: J.M. Dent, 1961.
Long, A.A. and Sedley, D.N. (= LS) (1987) *The Hellenistic Philosophers*, Vol. I, Cambridge: Cambridge University Press.
Longrigg, Claire (1997) *Mafia Women*, London: Chatto & Windus.
Luker, Kristen (1984) *Abortion and the Politics of Motherhood*, Berkeley: University of California Press.
—— (1996) *Dubious Conceptions: The Politics of Teenage Pregnancy*, Cambridge, Mass.: Harvard University Press.
Lukes, Steven (1973) *Individualism*, Oxford: Basil Blackwell.
Lutz, Cora E. (trans.) (1947) 'Musonius Rufus – The Roman Socrates,' *Yale Classical Studies* X: 3–147.
Lyons, David (1965) *Forms and Limits of Utilitarianism*, Oxford: Clarendon Press.
McCarthy, Richard Joseph, SJ (trans.) (1953) *The Theology of al-Ash'ari*, Beirut: Imprimerie Catholique.
—— (trans.) (1980) *Freedom and Fulfillment: Works by al-Ghazālī*, Boston: Twayne & G.K. Hall.
McDonald, Sister Mary Francis, OP (trans.) (1964) Lactantius, *The Divine Institutes*, Books I–VII, Washington, DC: Catholic University of American Press.
MacIntyre, Alisdair (1981) *After Virtue*, London: Duckworth.
Mackie, J.L. (1977) *Ethics: Inventing Right and Wrong*, Harmondsworth, Middlesex: Penguin Books.
Maitra, Sushil Kumar (1925) *The Ethics of the Hindus*, Calcutta: Calcutta University Press.
Makeham, John (1994) *Name and Actuality in Early Chinese Thought*, Albany, NY: State University of New York Press.
Margolis, Joseph (1991) *The Truth About Relativism*, Oxford: Basil Blackwell.
Marx, Karl and Engels, Friedrich (1847) *The German Ideology*, Part One, London: Lawrence & Wishart, 1970.
Mautner, Thomas (1996) *A Dictionary of Philosophy*, Oxford: Basil Blackwell.
Mbiti, John S. (1969) *African Religions and Philosophy*, second edition, London: Heinemann, 1990.
Mei Yi-Pao (1929) *The Ethical and Political Works of Motse*, London: Arthur Probsthain.
Mill, John Stuart (1859) *On Liberty* (with *Utilitarianism* and *Representative Government*), London: J.M. Dent, 1910.
—— (1861) *Utilitarianism*, in J.B. Schneewind (ed.) *Mill's Ethical Writings*, New York: Collier, 1965.
Miller, Fred D., Jr (1995) *Nature, Justice, and Rights in Aristotle's Politics*, Oxford: Clarendon Press.
Miller, Walter (trans.) (1913) Cicero, *De Officiis*, Cambridge, Mass.: Loeb Classical Library.
Mills, D.E. (1976) '*Kataki-uchi*: the practice of blood-revenge in pre-modern Japan,' *Modern Asian Studies* 10(4): 525–42.
Mishima, Yukio (1977) *On the Way of the Samurai*, translated by Kathryn Sparling, New York: Basic Books.
Moore, G.E. (1903) *Principia Ethica*, Cambridge: Cambridge University Press.
Morrow, Glenn R. (1960) *Plato's Cretan City*, Princeton, NJ: Princeton University Press.

REFERENCES

Mulhall, Stephen and Swift, Adam (eds) (1992) *Liberals and Communitarians*, Oxford: Basil Blackwell.
Mungello, D.E. (ed.) (1994) *The Chinese Rites Controversy*, Nettetal: Styler Verlag.
Nagel, Thomas (1972) 'Aristotle on *Eudaimonia*,' in Amélie Oksenberg Rorty (ed.) *Essays on Aristotle's Ethics*, Berkeley: University of California Press, 1980: 7–14.
—— (1991) *Equality and Partiality*, New York: Oxford University Press.
Noonan, John (ed.) (1970) *The Morality of Abortion: Legal and Historical Perspectives*, Cambridge, Mass.: Harvard University Press.
Nozick, Robert (1974) *Anarchy, State and Utopia*, Oxford: Basil Blackwell.
Nussbaum, Martha C. (1986) *The Fragility of Goodness*, Cambridge: Cambridge University Press.
—— (1994) *The Therapy of Desire: Theory and Practice in Hellenistic Ethics*, Princeton, NJ: Princeton University Press.
Obeyesekere, Ranjini (1991) *Dharmasēna Thera, Jewels of the Doctrine*, Albany, NY: State University of New York Press.
Oldenburg, Veena Talwar (1994) 'The Roop Kanwar Case: Feminist Responses,' in John Stratton Hawley (ed.) *Sati, the Blessing and the Curse*, New York: Oxford University Press: 101–30.
Oldfather, W.A. (trans.) (1925) *The Discourses of Epictetus*, in two volumes, Cambridge, Mass.: Loeb Classical Library.
O'Malley, L.S.S. (1932) *Indian Caste Customs*, Cambridge: Cambridge University Press.
O'Neill, Onora (1989) *Constructions of Reason: Explorations of Kant's Practical Philosophy*, Cambridge: Cambridge University Press.
Pascal, Blaise (1657) *The Provincial Letters*, translated by A.J. Krailsheimer, Harmondsworth, Middlesex: Penguin Books, 1967.
Pine-Coffin, R.S. (trans.) (1961) *St. Augustine – The Confessions*, Harmondsworth, Middlesex: Penguin Books.
Popkin, Richard (1964) *The History of Skepticism from Erasmus to Spinoza*, Berkeley: University of California Press, 1979.
Pound, Roscoe (1922) *The Spirit of the Common Law*, Boston: Marshall Jones.
Pukui, Mary Kawena, Haertig, E.W. and Lee, Catherine A. (1972) *Nānā I Ke Kumu (Look to the Source)*, in two volumes, Honolulu: Hui Hānai.
Quasem, Muhammad Abul (1978) *The Ethics of Al-Ghazali: A Composite Ethics in Islam*, Delmar, NY: Caravan Books.
Radhakrishnan, Sarvepali and Moore, Charles A. (eds) (1957) *A Source Book in Indian Philosophy*, Princeton, NJ: Princeton University Press.
Rahula, Walpola (1974) *What the Buddha Taught*, New York: Grove Weidenfeld.
Rawls, John (1971) *A Theory of Justice*, Cambridge, Mass.: Harvard University Press.
Regan, Tom (1983) *The Case for Animal Rights*, Berkeley: University of California Press.
Rhys Davids, Mrs [Caroline A.F.] and Woodward, F.H. (trans.) (1922) *The Book of the Kindred Sayings or Grouped Suttas, Part II, The Nidāna Book*, London: Pali Text Society.
Robb, Kevin (1994) *Literacy and Paideia in Ancient Greece*, New York: Oxford University Press.
Robinson, Richard (1953) *Plato's Earlier Dialectic*, second edition, Oxford: Clarendon Press.
Rorty, Amélie Oksenberg (1978) 'The place of contemplation in Aristotle's *Nicomachean Ethics*,' in Amélie Oksenberg Rorty (ed.) *Essays on Aristotle's Ethics*, Berkeley: University of California Press, 1980: 377–94.

Ross, David (1930) *The Right and the Good*, Oxford: Clarendon Press.
—— (1949) *Aristotle*, fifth edition, London: Methuen.
Rossiaud, Jacques (1985) 'Prostitution, sex and society in French towns in the fifteenth century,' in Philippe Ariès and André Béjin (eds) *Western Sexuality: Practice and Precept in Past and Present Times*, Oxford: Basil Blackwell: 76–94.
Rousseau, Jean-Jacques (1762) *The Social Contract* in *The Basic Political Writings*, translated by Donald A. Cress, Indianapolis: Hackett, 1987.
Saddhatissa, Hammalawa (1970) *Buddhist Ethics*, London: Wisdom Publications, 1987.
Sanday, Peggy Reeves (1986) *Divine Hunger: Cannibalism as a Cultural System*, Cambridge: Cambridge University Press.
Schacht, Joseph (1964) *An Introduction to Islamic Law*, Oxford: Clarendon Press.
Scheffler, Samuel (1982) *The Rejection of Consequentialism*, revised edition, Oxford: Clarendon Press, 1994.
—— (ed.) (1988) *Consequentialism and its Critics*, Oxford: Oxford University Press.
Schipper, Kristofer (1992) *Taoist Body*, Berkeley: University of California Press.
Schneewind, J.B. (1990) 'The Misfortunes of Virtue,' *Ethics* 101: 42–63.
Semmel, Bernard (1984) *John Stuart Mill and the Pursuit of Virtue*, New Haven, Conn.: Yale University Press.
Sharma, Arvind (1986)*The Hindu Gītā*, La Salle, Ill.: Open Court.
Sharma, I.C. (1965) *Ethical Philosophies of India*, Lincoln, Neb.: Johnsen Publishing.
Sherman, Nancy (1997) *Making a Necessity of Virtue: Aristotle and Kant on Virtue*, Cambridge: Cambridge University Press.
Singer, Peter (1975) *Animal Liberation*, New York: New York Review Books (Random House).
—— (1979) *Practical Ethics*, Cambridge: Cambridge University Press.
Sinha, Phulgenda (1986) *The Gita as it Was*, La Salle, Ill.: Open Court.
Skorupski, John (1989) *John Stuart Mill*, London: Routledge.
Sontag, Susan (1977) *Disease as Metaphor*, New York: Farrar, Straus and Giroux.
Sorabji, Richard (1974) 'Aristotle on the Role of Intellect in Virtue,' in Amélie Oksenberg Rorty (ed.) *Essays on Aristotle's Ethics*, Berkeley: University of California Press, 1980: 201–19.
Stein, Peter (1966) *Regulae Iuris: From Juristic Rules to Legal Maxims*, Edinburgh: Edinburgh University Press.
Stevenson, Charles (1944) *Ethics and Language*, New Haven, Conn.: Yale University Press.
Swearer, Donald (1995) 'Hypostatizing the Buddha: Buddha image consecration in northern Thailand,' *History of Religions* 34: 264–80.
Taylor, Charles (1975) *Hegel*, Cambridge: Cambridge University Press.
—— (1989), *Sources of the Self*, Cambridge, Mass.: Harvard University Press.
Taylor, Gabriele (1985) *Pride, Shame and Guilt: Emotions of Self-Assessment*, Oxford: Clarendon Press.
Tiles, J.E. (1992) 'Pleasure, passion and truth,' *Philosophy and Phenomenological Research*, LII, 4: 931–41.
—— (1996) 'The practical import of Aristotle's doctrine of the mean,' in Richard Bosley, Roger A. Shiner and Janet D. Sisson (eds) *Aristotle, Virtue and Mean*, Edmonton, Alberta: Academic Printing and Publishing: 1–14.
Trubek, David M. (1972) 'Max Weber on law and the rise of capitalism,' *Wisconsin Law Review*: 720–53.
Trusted, Jennifer (1984) *Free Will and Responsibility*, Oxford: Oxford University Press.

REFERENCES

Tuck, Richard (1979) *Natural Rights Theories: Their Origin and Development*, Cambridge: Cambridge University Press.

Urmson, J.O. (1968) 'Aristotle on Pleasure,' in J.M.E. Moravcsik (ed.) *Aristotle*, London: Macmillan.

—— (1973) 'Aristotle's doctrine of the mean,' in Amélie Oksenberg Rorty (ed.) *Essays on Aristotle's Ethics*, Berkeley: University of California Press, 1980: 157–70.

van der Linden, Harry (1988) *Kantian Ethics and Socialism*, Indianapolis: Hackett.

Waley, Arthur (trans.) (1938) *The Analects of Confucius*, New York: Random House, 1989.

Warder, A.K. (1970) *Indian Buddhism*, Delhi: Motilal Banarsidass.

Warren, Henry Clarke (1896) *Buddhism in Translation*, Delhi: Motilal Banarsidass, 1986.

Watson, Alan (1981) *The Making of the Civil Law*, Cambridge, Mass.: Harvard University Press.

—— (trans.) (1985) *Digest of Justinian*, edited by Theodor Mommsen and Paul Krueger, Philadelphia: University of Pennsylvania Press.

—— (1992) *The State, Law and Religion: Pagan Rome*, Athens, Ga.: University of Georgia Press.

—— (1995) *The Spirit of Roman Law*, Athens, Ga.: University of Georgia Press.

Watson, Burton (trans.) (1958) *The Complete Works of Chuang Tzu*, New York: Columbia University Press.

—— (trans.) (1963–4) *Basic Writings of Mo Tzu, Hsün Tzu, and Han Fei Tzu*, New York: Columbia University Press.

Watt, W. Montgomery (1962) *Islamic Philosophy and Theology, An Extended Survey*, Edinburgh: Edinburgh University Press, 1985.

—— (1968) *Islamic Political Thought*, Edinburgh: Edinburgh University Press.

Weber, Max (1930) *The Protestant Ethic and the Spirit of Capitalism*, translated by Talcott Parsons, London: Unwin.

—— (1952) *Ancient Judaism*, translated by Hans H. Gerth and Don Martindale, New York: Free Press.

—— (1954) *Max Weber on Law in Economy and Society*, translated by Edward Shils and Max Rheinstein, Cambridge, Mass.: Harvard University Press.

—— (1958) *The Religion of India*, translated by Hans H. Gerth and Don Martindale, New Delhi: Munshiram Manoharlal, 1992.

—— (1964) *The Theory of Social and Economic Organization*, translated by A.M. Henderson and Talcott Parsons, New York: Free Press.

—— (1978) *Economy and Society*, edited by Guenther Roth and Claus Wittich, Berkeley: University of California Press.

Westermarck, Edward (1906) *The Origin and Development of the Moral Ideas*, in two volumes London: Macmillan.

White, T.H. (1962) *The Age of Scandal*, Harmondsworth, Middlesex: Penguin Books.

Wiggins, David (1976) 'Deliberation and practical reason,' in Amélie Oksenberg Rorty (ed.) *Essays on Aristotle's Ethics*, Berkeley: University of California Press, 1980: 221–40.

Wilkes, Kathleen V. (1978) 'The good man and the good for man in Aristotle's ethics,' in Amélie Oksenberg Rorty (ed.) *Essays on Aristotle's Ethics*, Berkeley: University of California Press, 1980: 341–57.

Williams, Bernard (1972) *Morality*, Harmondsworth, Middlesex: Penguin Books.

—— (1985) *Ethics and the Limits of Philosophy*, London: Fontana/Collins.

Willis, Paul (1979), 'Masculinity and factory labor,' in John Clarke *et al.* (eds) *Working Class Culture*, London: Hutchinson.

Wood, Neal (1988) *Cicero's Social and Political Thought*, Berkeley: University of California Press.

Yack, B. (1993) *The Problems of a Political Animal: Community, Justice, and Conflict in Aristotelian Political Thought*, Berkeley: University of California Press.

Yamamoto, Tsunetomo (1716) *Hagakure*, translated by Minoru Tanaka, Albuquerque, NM, Sun Publishing, 1975.

Zaehner, R.C. (1972) *The Bhagavad-Gītā*, Oxford: Clarendon Press.

INDEX

a priori 170, 182, 186, 190
abortion 17–20, 22, 37, 117
abstract and general 91–3, 96–7,
    108–10, 112, 114, 135, 137, 168,
    216
Academy of Athens 113
act utilitarianism 267
admirable 2, 8–9, 147, 177, 180–1,
    191–3, 198, 231, 234, 240, 243,
    255, 291, 305, 310, 315; *see also*
    kalos
adultery 206, 212
aesthetic response 215, 239
aesthetic use of reason 68, 131
Aiyar, P.S. Sivaswamy 132
al Ash'arī and al Ghazālī 65–6
altruism 254
amusement 30, 225, 270
anarchism 107–112, 126
anomie 40, 49
apathy, *see pathos*
arahant 284–5, 289, 299
Archimedian axiom 247
Arens, William 13
Aristotle 2–3, 8, 9, 56, 97–8, 109,
    114–5, 131–2, 138–142, 146–8,
    157–61, 163, 180–2, 191–5,
    202–11, 213–36, 240, 243–5, 248,
    255–8, 264–5, 272, 274, 276, 279,
    286, 301, 303–4, 306–7, 311,
    315; *Nicomachean vs Eudemian
    Ethics* 2, 213–14, 230–4, 241,
    243, 256–7
Arjuna 76–9, 81, 294–6
asceticism 77, 276–8, 280–1, 293,
    301; worldly vs world renouncing
    297, 300
association (*societas*, partnership) 158,
    160, 239, 252, 307
ataraxia 278, 288; *see also* tranquility
atomism, social 239
attachment 280–4, 287–8, 292, 294
author (rational agent) 175–6

authority xi, 51–5, 61–71, 86–99,
    102–4, 107–12, 116, 126, 128,
    130–1, 139, 145, 148, 178; *see also*
    validity
autonomy 220; *see also* freedom
Azande 133
Aztecs 12–15

basis (grounds) x–xi, 1, 10, 14–15,
    26, 40, 47, 50, 56, 57, 60, 75, 87,
    80–1, 85, 93–5, 114, 118–19, 145,
    151, 174–5, 304–6, 310, 315
Baxter, Richard 29
belief 25, 57; *see also* opinion
Benedict, Ruth 5, 28, 72, 198
benevolence 197, 254, 312;
    beneficence vs benevolence 186
Bentham, Jeremy 241, 247, 250, 262,
    268–72
Bhagavad Gītā 76–9, 273, 294–7, 300
bhikkhu 281–2, 294, 301
Blake, C. Fred 16, 21
body, concern with 111, 260, 275–6
Bourdieu, Pierre 22, 28–9
Brown, Peter 276–7, 293
Bruner, Jerome 34
Buddha (Siddhārtha Gautama) 32, 36,
    59, 62, 183, 279–84, 286–7,
    289–91, 314
Buddhism 32, 33, 35, 59, 62, 275–92,
    294, 314–15
Burnyeat, M.F. 103, 125
bushido 63, 71, 72
Butler, Joseph 253–5, 259, 284

calculus of pleasure and pain 247
cannibalism 12–13, 34, 291
canon (*kanōn*) 82, 135, 171, 174–5,
    182, 183, 243, 245, 249, 269–70,
    273, 302–3, 306–7, 311
canon law 164
Carlyle, A.J. 163, 181
case law (recorded precedent) 135, 137

caste system 42, 57–8, 71, 72
casuistry 143–4
categorical imperative 171–3
Celsus 70, 94
Chan Wing-tsit 99, 197, 212, 237, 242
Chancery Court 141–2, 152
character 3, 86, 88–9, 91–2, 98, 116, 120, 131, 134, 190, 203–4, 239, 243, 248, 250–1
charisma xi, 51–4, 56, 57, 62, 70, 71, 73, 111, 201
charity, Christian 313–15
charivari 42
choice (preference) 204, 250
Christ (Jesus) 48, 60, 164, 296
Christianity, early 52, 70, 164, 168, 276–7, 279, 281; see also New Testament, St. Augustine
Chuang Tzu 110–111, 114, 116, 125
chün tzu (gentleman, superior person) 90, 109, 194
Cicero 153, 162–4, 166–8, 181–2, 272
city-dwelling creatures 207, 219, 229, 242, 257
civic (public) life 244, 256–7
civil law tradition 137
Cleanthes 245
cleverness, mere 209–10, 223–4
climate of attitude 27–30, 32–3, 37–42, 50, 95, 145; mechanisms for sustaining 33–7; moral vs non-moral 37–41; see also concrete morality
codification, legal 136–7
cognitive vs non cognitive ethical theories 119–121, 126
common law tradition 137
communitarianism 239–41, 301, 310–11
community (communitas, corporation) 158–160, 192, 239–40, 309
community, moral 268
compassion 77, 289–90
compatibilism 269
competence to judge 250, 274
complete, see final
concern for everyone 260–3, 265–7, 272–3, 285, 301, 312, 314–15
concrete morality x, 27, 32, 38, 41, 50, 61, 73–5, 105, 115, 153, 157,

170–1, 190, 301; illustrations of 28–30, 54–5, 63–4, 149–151; see also climate of attitude
conflicting appearances 103, 114
Confucian cultural traditions 39, 40, 62, 72, 92, 109, 207, 211, 235–40, 243, 257, 260, 276, 279
Confucius 80, 82–3, 90–3, 108–9, 191–203, 205, 236–7, 242, 279
consequentialism 215, 241, 262, 265; rigid vs non-rigid 215, 265
consistency 67–8, 74, 88, 131, 184–5, 187
constituents 216, 227, 238, 245, 253, 256, 265, 312; vs indispensable conditions 219
contemplation 219–220, 224, 226–7, 230, 232, 245, 251, 256–7
contempt 31–2, 78–9
contractual relationships 159, 166, 239
contradiction 67–8, 171, 173, 184, 187
convention (Weber) 25, 26, 37, 38, 40, 41–2, 104
conventionalism 104
Corpus juris civilis 137, 182
Cortés 17
courage 93, 97, 191–2, 203, 205, 208, 214, 227–8, 248
craving 280–2, 284, 286–7, 289
criteria 82, 87, 90, 93; externalized 85–6, 190
cultural reproduction 33
cultural variation 10, 39, 113
culture 1, 7–8, 21–2, 46–7, 61, 105
custom 1, 7, 23, 25, 26, 41, 51, 54, 56, 58, 68, 70, 73, 105, 127–8, 133, 159
cynicism, ancient 292–3

Dancy, Jonathan 99, 138, 151
Darnton, Robert 34–5
definition 82–92, 97, 101, 136
deliberation 3, 97, 138, 204, 207–1, 215–17, 303
Demaratus 50, 53–4
democracy, participatory 178
deon (needful, binding) 54, 216
deontological 215–16, 240–1
Descartes, René 169
Devlin, Patrick 45–6, 48

Dhammapada 284, 289
dharma 32, 59, 77–8, 80
dialectic 86–8, 97
diet 38–41, 57–58, 103
Dihle, Albrect 70, 157
discipline 77, 104, 112, 249, 274–6, 294, 296, 298; *see also* asceticism
discursive (articulate) thought 9, 108, 114–15, 160–1, 206, 208, 210, 222–4, 226–7, 229–30, 243, 246–7, 255, 286, 291, 303–4, 315; *see also* *logos*
disease 61
distant view (Hume) 122–5, 261, 305; *see also* wider perspective
dogmatic philosophy 113
drift in practice 199–201
Dumont, Louis 17, 71
duties 32, 52, 154–5, 160, 176, 180, 183–8, 258, 265, 269–70, 304; perfect vs imperfect 184–5, 190; wide (of virtue) vs narrow (of right) 185–8, 189, 214–16, 266, 302, 308–9, 313; *see also* obligation
Dworkin, Ronald 45–6, 48, 152, 180

egoism 254, 259, 285, 308
El Dareer, Astma 16–17
Eliade, Mircea 281
Ellerman, David 178, 182
emotive meaning, emotivism 117–19
empirical justice 135–7, 139
employment 178–181
ends, dominant vs inclusive 219–20, 223, 228–30, 243, 257
ends in itself (not to be treated merely as means) 172–3, 175; *see also* persons, respect for
ends in the unqualified sense 209–10, 213, 215, 217–18, 262, 303
ends that are also duties 185, 216, 266, 303
Epictetus 73, 82, 100
Epicurus, Epicureans 114, 228, 234, 240, 243–52, 256–7, 267, 271–3, 278–83, 286, 293, 307, 309
equality 162–3, 176–7, 291, 297
equity (*epieikeia*) 139–42
ergon (function) 221–3, 241
eschatology 278, 282–3

Essenes 277, 293
ethics as a social phenomenon 5, 21–2
ethics, intellectual vs motivational, problem in 9, 190, 195, 303
ethics, medical (clinical) 143–4
ethics, systematic study of 3–5, 13–15
etiquette 38–41, 93, 101, 104, 130
eudaimonia 218–34, 238, 241, 243, 251, 253, 255–7, 265, 302, 309, 312, 315; candidates for 219–220, 224–7, 231
eupatheia 289–90
Euthyphro, *see* Plato, *Euthyphro*
Evans-Pritchard 133
excellence, ethical (moral virtue) xi, 2, 3, 9, 32, 89, 92, 180, 264–5, 312, 314–15; in antiquity 189–211, 213, 222, 225, 227–33, 234, 245, 251, 290–1, 315; Kant on 181, 184–91, 303, 312–13; Mill on 264, 271
excellence, intellectual 203–4, 208, 223, 228, 233; *see also* *phronēsis*
exemplary, xi 32, 89–90, 98, 101, 131, 191–7, 202, 204, 213, 257, 296, 310
ex post facto laws 46

fa (standard) 198, 200–1
fact vs value 119, 125
fair, *see* just, justice
family 252–3, 258, 260–1, 267; *see also* parental authority
fashion 25, 38–41, 93, 101–4, 130
final (complete, *teleion*) 219–220, 230, 253
Finley, Moses 155, 158, 161, 181
Florentius 163
foot-binding 16, 21, 47
Franklin, Benjamin 29
freedom, xi, 162, 165, 167, 174, 177–9, 183, 243, 268–72, 277, 289, 293, 298, 301, 305–6
freeloaders, free riders 309–10
friends, friendship 227, 234, 251–3, 258, 263, 267, 307; another self 234, 253, 260, 307
fulfillment, human 53, 228–9, 239, 244, 278, 284, 293, 296; vs salvation 276, 279
function, *see* *ergon*

Gaius 128, 182
Galen 70, 94
general 88, 138–9 *see also* abstract
   and general
general happiness 263, 265, 267
generosity 203, 214
genital mutilation 16, 21, 22
genitalia, ambiguous 17, 22
gimu 198
giri 5, 28, 72
Gītā see Bhagavad Gītā
golden rule 237, 265–6
good, common 131, 165
good, measure of xi, 98, 101, 131,
   302, 304–5, 308, 310
Good, Plato's 87–8, 98
good will 174, 188, 210, 242
Graham, Angus 200, 211, 259, 262,
   272
Gray, Jonn Henry 150
Green, Peter, 256, 309
Grönbech, Vilhelm 28, 48, 149
Grotius, Hugo 165–9, 184, 190, 206
grounds, *see* basis
guilt 31–2, 48

habit, habituation 1, 2, 5–7, 50, 89,
   91, 105, 199, 203, 246, 249, 251,
   275, 293, 306
ḥakam 128, 134
Hall, David and Roger Ames 90, 211,
   242
Han Fei-tzu 200–1
Hansen, Chad 200, 211
happiness 186, 218, 254, 263–6, 272,
   289, 303, 313; *see also eudaimonia*
Hare, R.M. 118, 124, 138, 266
harm, principle of 179–180, 304
Hart, H.L.A. 43–5, 48
Hawaiian culture 53, 72, 128
hedonism 242, 246, 250, 259, 268,
   271, 278, 307
Hegel, G.W. 24, 27
Herodotus 50, 53–4
Hierocles 314
Hindu culture 34, 39, 42, *see also*
   Bhagavad Gītā
history, tradition and taste 91–2,
   108–110, 134, 215
Hobbes, Thomas 156
holism 138
homosexuality 46–7

honor 219–20, 224–7
Hopkins, Keith 60, 72, 75
horos 82, 241
hsüeh (learning) 92, 109, 207, 293
Hsün Tzu 109, 196, 198, 211, 235–6,
   242
Hui Tzu 111, 114, 125
human good 98, 221–3, 228
human nature 153, 172, 183, 211,
   220–3, 238, 274, 304–6, 310, 315
humanism 218, 235, 241
Hume, David 121–5, 305
Hutton, J.H. 42, 58

impartial, *see* concern for everyone
imputation 156, 175
incest 34, 49, 60, 72, 75, 103, 291
internalized attitudes 31–3
intuitive thought 108, 139
Isadore of Seville 131
Islamic law, custom, belief 39, 57,
   65–7, 72, 75, 128, 131, 134–5
ius (iuris) 128–130, 134, 145, 162,
   166; *civile, gentium* 163; *naturale*
   163, 166

James, Henry (Jr) 91–2, 100, 108
James, William 6, 253–4, 284
jen 196–8, 211, 237, 259, 303; *vs jin*
   198
Jewish law, culture 38, 40, 57, 70,
   166, 277; *see also* Old Testament
Job 63–5, 67–8, 77, 154
Jonsen, Albert 142–5, 151–2, 154,
   178, 180
judgment 180, 188–90, 291, 303
just, justice 68, 84–5, 87–9, 97,
   127–133, 139–142, 145–151, 160,
   164, 169, 192, 203, 227–8, 249,
   267
justice, culturally dependent
   conceptions of 147–9
justice, distributive vs corrective 146
justice, universal vs particular 146

kadi 134–5, 139, 142–5, 152, 215
Kakar, Sudhir 34
kalos (kagathos) 231, 242; *see also*
   admirable
Kant, Immanuel xi, 4, 10, 169, 191,
   195, 206, 214–16, 221, 223, 242,
   258, 266, 268–70, 302–4, 305–10,

311, 315, *Critique of Pure Reason* 170, 180, 269; *Foundations of Morals* 170–1, 180, 183, 184, 186, 188, 221–2, 238–9, 265; *Metaphysics of Morals* 9, 25, 138, 140–2, 154–6, 184–90, 218, 312
karma 59, 60, 71, 282–3, 285, 294–6
Kelsen, Hans 206
Kenny, Anthony 233, 244
Khadduri, Majid 128, 131, 135, 148

laity 282
Lamech 68–9
Lau, D.C. 99–100, 197, 211–12, 237
laughter 36
law xi, 25, 26, 38, 41–7, 105, 126–142; civil vs criminal 146; *see also* natural law
law of diminishing returns 247
law-finding vs law making 43, 46, 129, 152
law-giver (*nomothetēs*) 86–8, 139
leaders, rulers, as examplars 89, 193–5, 200–1, 225, 237
legitimacy, *see* validity
Leih-tzu 259, 272
leisure 226–9
lesbian rule 140–1
lex (pl. *leges*) 129–130, 145, 153, 162; *see also* law, natural law
lex rogata 129
lex talionis 68–70, 132, 149
li, see ritual practice/propriety
local vs global concerns 261–2, 267
Locke, John, 166–7, 169
Longrigg, Claire 28
logic 10
logos 9, 67, 132, 192, 204, 206–7, 222, 235, 238, 243, 255, 304; *see also* discursive thought
Lucretius 271, 278
Luker, Kristen 17–20, 37
Lukes, Steven 176–7, 180

Mackie, J.L. 116, 118, 125
manus 157, 163
materialist philosophy 287
mathematics 132, 168–170, 205
maxim: Jonsen 144–5, 154, 170, 180; Kant 170–1, 180, 187, 189, 216, 302
mean, doctrine of 190, 204–6, 214–15

meaningful vs meaningless discourse 116–17
measurement 247–8
Measures, *see* of good, virtue & right
measuring tool image x-xi, 73–4, 82–4, 92–3, 98–9, 101, 126, 130, 135, 144, 191, 198–201, 237, 244, 246, 302–3; *see also* canon, standard
meditation 111, 281
Mencius 109, 183, 200, 211, 259–60, 265, 271
middle way 281
Mill, John Stuart 179–80, 250–1, 262–8, 271–2, 312, 314
Mo Tzu 1, 73, 82, 199, 201, 259–62, 264, 266–7, 271–2, 312, 314
modes, skeptical 114
Molina, Luis de 160
monastic & mendicant movements 277, 292–4, 296–7; *see also Sangha*
Moore, G.E. 122, 125
moral strength 9, 188, 190, 275
morality system 4, 5, 32, 38, 40, 96, 188, 303
motivational inertness 119–20, 305, 313
Muhammad, the Prophet 70
music 196–7, 199, 262
Musonius, Rufus 80

names, rectification of (*cheng ming*) 90–2
nativism 108–9, 112, 139, 148, 215
natural law 164–8, 176, 181–4
natural moral excellences (virtues) 208–9
naturalistic fallacy 120–2
naturalize 56, 160
nature 56–61, 71, 153, 160, 221, 290
nirvana 280, 284, 292–3; of Brahman 295
New Testament 29, 48, 60–1, 69, 164, 168, 237, 312
noble truths, noble path 279–85, 289
nomos (pl. *nomoi*) 43, 49, 54–6, 71, 86, 89, 160
non-cogntivie theories, *see* cognitive theories

obedience 63–6
Obeyesekere, Ranjini 33, 36

objective 94, 116, 130, 260
objective pull 94–5
objectivity 95, 118–9, 123–4, 170; *see also* basis
obligation 4, 32, 96, 157
Old Testament 60, 62–5, 68–70, 85–6, 128, 150
O'Malley, L.S.S. 42, 58
opinions 286–8
oracles 133–4
Origen 276
original sin 60

parental authority 55, 78–81, 150
partial concern 244, 260, 268
particularism 138–8, 142, 180, 209
partnership, *see* association
Pascal, Blaise 143
paterfamilias 129, 156–7
pathos 255, 272, 286–7, 289
paṭiccasamuppāda 287
Paulus 182
peculiar institution, *see* morality system
Pelikan, Jaroslav 52
person, personality (moral, legal) 154, 156–7, 270, 298, 302, 305
person, respect for 174, 176, 178, 183–4, 215, 270, 304
person vs thing 173, 175, 270, 304
phronēsis, phronimos 97–8, 204, 208–11, 213–14, 217, 223–4, 228, 232–3, 239, 245, 251, 303
pity, *see* compassion
Plato 96–7, 109, 114, 135, 137, 180, 218, 279; *Charmides* 208; *Crito* 54–5; *Cratylus* 86; *Euthyphro* 78–9, 81–2, 84–6, 93–4, 136; *Phaedo* 275–6; *Protagoras* 23, 102, 192–3, 247; *Republic* 38, 70, 84–8, 146, 159, 196, 202; *Statesman* 87; *Symposium* 43; *Theaetetus* 86, 101–4, 114
pleasure and pain 3, 9, 191–2, 219–220, 224–7, 232, 240, 243–52, 255, 259, 262–4, 268, 273–5, 286, 305–6
pleasures, higher and lower 250–1, 268, 297
polis 159, 207, 229–34, 240, 258, 312
pontiffs, college of 127–9
Popkin, Richard 115

Porphyry 277
Pound, Roscoe 142, 151
precepts 282, 290–1; vs counsels 297
prescription vs description 119, 136
prescriptivism 118–9, 138
principles (Dworkin) 45–6, 152, 180
principles, tyranny of 142–3
private 240, 249, 252, 258
projectivism 120–1, 125
pro-life vs pro-choice 18–20
promises, lying 171, 173, 175, 187
property 160, 165, 177; bourgeois notion of 148–9, 152; slaves as 155–6
Protagoras, *see* Plato, *Protagoras* and relativism, Protagorean
Protestant ethic 29–30, 151, 275, 297
punishment 155–6, 195

Quakers 151, 176
quantity 83, 247
queer objects 116, 118, 121
Qur'ān 65–6, 127, 134

ratio 67, 132, 153, 162–3, 168
rational authority 57, 66, 70, 88–9, 92, 135
rational justice (Weber) 135, 137
rational want 172
rationalism 109, 216
Rawls, John 148, 151
realism, moral 96–7, 116
reason, Hume's use of the term 121–4, 305, 313
reason, rationality, xi, 67–71, 91–3, 95–7, 112, 114, 134, 162, 167–75, 216–17, 221–3, 238, 270, 287, 313
Recht 25, 42, 140–1, 174
reciprocity 68, 131, 159
rectification of names, *see* definition
relative to us (Aristotle) 205–6
relativism, cultural 104–7, 126, 310
relativism, Protagorean 102–7, 112, 114, 118–9, 125–6, 249
religion 5, 14–15, 61–2, 111–2, 115
religious propriety (*to hosion*) 78, 81–2, 93–4
revenge ethic 28–9, 68–72
right, Kant's principle of 174, 177, 180, 302
right, measure of xi, 98, 101, 130–1, 136, 302, 307–8, 310

right to life 14–15
rights, animal 14
rights, inalienable 167
rights, rightful claims 154, 157, 160–1, 165, 176, 178, 181
ritual 35–6, 49, 207, 238, 242
ritual pollution, purity 57, 71, 78–9, 81
ritual practice/propriety (Chinese *li*) 92, 109, 195–202, 213, 234–8, 240, 260
roles, social 41, 50, 59, 76, 80, 81, 157, 159, 161–2, 164–5, 195–6, 260, 297, 310; *see also dharma*
Rome, Roman law, custom, belief 127–9, 134, 137, 140, 143, 146, 152, 156–7, 162, 166
Ross, W.D. 206
rough music 42
Rousseau, Jean-Jacques 167
rule utilitarianism 267
rules 135–9, 190, 239, 303

Saddhatissa, Hammalawa 32, 282
sage, Chinese 200–2, 237, 239
Sahagún, Bernardino de 12–13
St Ambrose 168
St Augustine of Hippo 60, 164, 168, 273, 293–4
St Paul 164, 168
St Thomas Aquinas 126, 129, 131, 140, 152, 161, 164–5, 312–13, 315
salvation 62, 274–83, 296–8
saṃsāra 59, 77, 282, 284, 294
Sanday, Peggy 12–13
Sangha 281–2
satī 15, 17, 21, 22
Schacht, Joseph 75, 128, 134
Schipper, Kristofer 11
Schneewind, J.B. 184, 190
self, extinguishing of 282, 284–5
self-control 191–2, 198, 205, 208, 248, 275, 278, 293
selfishness, self-love 250, 253–5, 312
self-regarding 254, 258–67, 271–3, 284–5
self-sufficient (*autarkēs*) 219–220, 225, 227
Seneca 166, 251, 289
servant, servitude 155, 166, 177, 194, 274; vs manager 305
Sextus Empiricus 114

sexual activity, desire 18–20, 37, 57, 276, 280–2, 293–4
sexual exploitation 155, 162, 175
shame 31–2, 41, 48, 54, 192–3
shāriᶜa 131, 134
shu (altruism) 237, 242
Sita 34
skepticism 95, 110; ancient 112–4; modern moral 115–6, 118, 124; in Reformation 115
slavery 55–6, 154–67, 174, 181–2, 193, 268; voluntary 160, 165–6
social sanctions 7–8, 30–2, 42–3
social science, value neutrality of 10–15
Socrates 9, 54–5, 78–9, 81, 84–6
Sontag, Susan 61
sōphrosunē 208; *see also* self-control
soul as life principle 222, 241
sovereignty 140–1, 166
Sparta, Spartan culture 54, 56, 71–2, 89, 231, 293
standards, 82–3, 90, 232, 241, 265, 291, 297; *see also* measuring tool image, canon
standing 237–8
Stein, Peter 127, 129–30, 134–6, 152
Stevenson, C.L. 118, 125
Stoics, Stoicism 70, 80, 100, 114, 167, 245, 286–92, 299, 312, 314
stoic wise man 287, 289–90
Straight-body 80, 83–4
subjective end 172
subjective feelings 260, 265
subjective principle 171, 205
subjectivism 118, 205
suffering 278–80, 282
suicide 5, 17, 171, 173, 189, 282, 290

taboo 36, 38, 49, 60, 72
Tacitus 165
Taoism 11, 109–112, 259
Taylor, Charles 4
te 202–3, 205
teleological 215, 241, 265
theodicy 66
tolerance 105–6, 114–15
Toulmin, Stephen, *see* Jonsen, Albert
tradition, xi 51–3, 56, 62, 73–4, 106–7, 112, 133, 134, 210
training 35–6; training vs instruction 2

tranquility 114, 244–5, 296, 301; *see also ataraxia*
Twelve Tables (Rome) 69, 129, 132

Ulpian 163, 182
universal laws 170–4, 183, 189, 265, 267, 270
universal prescription 138, 266
universality 138–41, 144–5, 162, 170, 266
universalization 170–1, 173, 180, 184, 187, 308
utilitarianism 262–8
utility, principle of 262–3, 265

validity 13–14, 25, 26, 37, 39–51, 44, 50–72, 74, 93, 96–7, 101, 104, 128, 133, 154–5, 168, 201
virginity 276
virtue, *see* excellence
virtue, measure of xi, 98, 101, 131, 302–4, 308, 310
Vorstellung 25, 238

watershed in European thought 158, 160, 162, 164, 190, 239, 309
Watson, Alan 147, 151
Watt, Montgomery 65, 70
weapons, returning to a mad friend 85, 136, 138, 140, 147
Weber, Max 25, 26, 29, 32, 38, 41, 42, 48, 51, 52, 54, 66–7, 71, 88, 93, 127, 129, 133–7, 141–2, 144, 151, 297
wergild 69, 148
White, T.H. 113
wider perspective 260–2
Williams, Bernard 4, 22, 32, 118
Willis, Paul 8
Wu Ma-tzu 262

Xerxes 50, 53–4

Yamamoto, Tsunetomo 63
Yang Chu 259–61, 271–2, 305–6
yi (righteousness) 91, 198, 211, 235
yoga 281, 295–6, 299